Dart for Absolute Beginners

David Kopec

Apress®

Dart for Absolute Beginners

ISBN-13 (pbk): 978-1-4302-6481-1

ISBN-13 (electronic): 978-1-4302-6482-8

President and Publisher: Paul Manning
Lead Editor: Ben Renow-Clarke
Development Editor: Chris Nelson and Douglas Pundick
Technical Reviewers: Matthew Butler and David Titarenco
Editorial Board: Steve Anglin, Mark Beckner, Ewan Buckingham, Gary Cornell, Louise Corrigan, Jim DeWolf, Jonathan Gennick, Jonathan Hassell, Robert Hutchinson, Michelle Lowman, James Markham, Matthew Moodie, Jeff Olson, Jeffrey Pepper, Douglas Pundick, Ben Renow-Clarke, Dominic Shakeshaft, Gwenan Spearing, Matt Wade, Steve Weiss
Coordinating Editor: Christine Ricketts
Copy Editor: Michael G. Laraque
Compositor: SPi Global
Indexer: SPi Global
Artist: SPi Global
Cover Designer: Anna Ishchenko

Distributed to the book trade worldwide by Springer Science+Business Media New York, 233 Spring Street, 6th Floor, New York, NY 10013. Phone 1-800-SPRINGER, fax (201) 348-4505, e-mail orders-ny@springer-sbm.com, or visit www.springeronline.com. Apress Media, LLC is a California LLC and the sole member (owner) is Springer Science+Business Media Finance Inc (SSBM Finance Inc). SSBM Finance Inc is a Delaware corporation.

For information on translations, please e-mail rights@apress.com, or visit www.apress.com.

Apress and friends of ED books may be purchased in bulk for academic, corporate, or promotional use. eBook versions and licenses are also available for most titles. For more information, reference our Special Bulk Sales–eBook Licensing web page at www.apress.com/bulk-sales.

Any source code or other supplementary material referenced by the author in this text is available to readers at www.apress.com. For detailed information about how to locate your book's source code, go to www.apress.com/source-code.

To my parents, Danny and Sylvia

Contents at a Glance

Contents

Flash 277

Silverlight 277

Recent Developments 277

Server Side 278

CGI 278

Perl 279

PHP 279

ASP 280

Java 280

Python 280

Ruby 281

JavaScript 281

Trends 282

Where Does Dart Fit In? 283

Evolution of the Web Browser 283

Microsoft and Netscape Duke It Out 283

Firefox Emerges from the Ashes of Netscape 284

Mobile and a Revitalized Browser Ecosystem 284

Importance Today 285

■Appendix C: Dart Timeline 287

■Appendix D: Great Resources 289

Dart 289

Books 289

Web Sites 289

Articles 290

HTML & CSS 292

Books 292

Web Sites 292

About the Author

David Kopec, a veteran of two web startups, is a software developer, entrepreneur, and author from New York. He is passionate about the use of computer technology for improving human welfare. David holds a bachelor's degree in economics and English and a master's degree in computer science, both from Dartmouth College. Get in touch with him on Twitter @davekopec or by e-mail at dartbook@oaksnow.com.

About the Technical Reviewers

Matthew Butler is a software developer and system administrator with Seaside Communications where he uses Dart on a number of inhouse tools. He has over 14 years experience in the industry in various roles. Matthew has contributed source code and documentation directly to Google's Dart programming language and has been active in the Dart community since 2012.

He spends his evenings at home in Nova Scotia, Canada, with his wife Julie Ann and his boys Cody and Jaxon. You can contact him at www.google.com/+MatthewButler

David Titarenco is a twenty-something software engineer from sunny Los Angeles. With more than a decade of experience, he specializes in Java, JavaScript, Go, and C/C++ back end development but he recently held a number of positions that also familiarized him with front end technologies like jQuery, Ext.js, Backbone, CoffeeScript, and Scala.

David is a proponent of open source and has contributed to high-profile projects like Google Go and the Java Kilim microthreading library. A lover of startups, he founded nearly half a dozen in the past six years and shows no signs of letting up. David graduated magna cum laude from UCLA where he studied philosophy and mathematics. He sometimes blogs at http://dvt.name and can be reached at david.titarenco@gmail.com.

Acknowledgments

I would like to thank **Lars Bak** and **Kasper Lund** of Google, the creators of Dart, for taking time out of their busy schedules to sit down for an interview. They provided their time very generously and made themselves available as well for significant follow-up. Thanks must also go to another Googler, **Seth Ladd**, who wrote the foreword to this book. Thanks, Seth!

There is an increasing trend for technical books to be self-published. I knew I wanted a traditional publisher for this book, and Apress was the first (and only) publisher I approached. I want to thank **Ben Renow-Clarke** for believing in *Dart for Absolute Beginners* from the beginning and guiding the project throughout its life.

A lot of people don't realize that when a technical book gets published by a traditional publisher, you're getting not just the author's insight but an entire team, including an acquisition editor (**Ben Renow-Clarke**), copy editor (**Michael G. Laraque**), development editors (**Chris Nelson** and **Douglas Pundick**), and coordinating editors (**Christine Ricketts** and **Anamika Panchoo**). I would like to thank all of them, as well as many unnamed at Apress and its partners who worked on the cover, layout, etc., to deliver the book that you're reading today.

I have to single out **Chris Nelson** for the level of care and consideration he put into *Dart for Absolute Beginners*. He really helped fill in the creases. The technical reviewer, **Matthew Butler**, was detail-oriented and great at catching my errors. Thanks, Matt!

I would like to give a special shout-out to professors **Devin Balkcom, Tom Cormen, Scot Drysdale** (who in addition to teaching me *programming languages*, gave me tips for my interview with Lars and Kasper), and **Gevorg Grigoryan** at Dartmouth College. Some examples I first saw in their classes, years ago, made it into this book.

I'd like to thank my family and friends for being supportive of me writing this book. I come from a long line of teachers/professors, including my dad, brother, aunt, and grandmother. This book is my contribution to that tradition. My dad got me started computer programming when I was eight years old and always made sure I had the resources I needed to be good at it. My mom more than anyone else supported our family during a very difficult time period that coincided with the writing of this book. Thanks, Mom, for making sure everyone was okay!

Finally, although trite and cliché, I'd like to thank you, the reader. A lot of people today choose to follow a hodgepodge of online tutorials to figure out beginners' programming. They miss out on the experience of having one voice, which knows how much they know at every step of the process, teach them clearly and deliberately. Your support of books like this, through your purchase, makes it possible for them to continue to exist in an online tutorial world. I think you'll be a better programmer for it.

—David Kopec

New York
May 2014

Foreword

Now is a great time to learn web development. The modern Web today is feature-rich, works across multiple devices, and delivers high-fidelity experiences that delight and astound. You don't have to ask anyone's permission to build something amazing and publish it for the world. All the tools you need are available for free.

Your journey begins with Dart, a programming language that is approachable, easy-to-learn, and powerful. Inspired by the good parts of many popular languages, and built to get you up and running quickly, Dart provides the tools you need to build web apps, without the dark corners or alleyways you might find in traditional web development. Getting started with Dart means you can avoid the false starts and "old wives tales" of web development, which have built up over years and years of evolution.

Dart for Absolute Beginners accelerates your web development career. Using this book's mix of practical examples and fundamentals, you will learn how to build apps for the modern Web with a modern language and tools. You will also learn how the Web works and gain a better appreciation of the web stack, important context for any new developer.

I wish I had a tool like Dart when I started web development, but I'm glad you do. Have fun—and welcome to the Web!

—Seth Ladd

Introduction

Dart is not just a new language, it's a new platform for modern web development. It's a superb place to start learning to program, with an eye toward the future of the Web. In recent years, the idea that everyone should "learn to code" has become a popular notion. With this book, and Dart, you have everything that you will need to "learn to code" with cutting-edge tools. The goal of this book is to make learning to program as straightforward as possible.

Who Is This Book For?

Creating a web site is not difficult. There are countless tools, both free and commercial, that enable individuals to quickly and easily get their desired content onto the Web. For most people, and most cases, those tools are enough.

This book is not just about creating web sites; it's about taking one's first steps toward being able to understand and use the technologies behind the Web. This book is aimed at those with a very limited knowledge of web technologies who wish to learn them from the ground up. *More than anything else, though, this book is an introduction to programming*.

If you are already an experienced programmer, this book is not for you. If you know a little HTML but want to take your skillset to the next level, this book is probably for you. If you simply have an intense curiosity about computers and the Web but have no knowledge of how they work, this book may be for you. If you want to get started developing your own web-based programs with Dart but have no prior experience, then this book is definitely for you.

No prior knowledge of HTML, CSS, Dart, or even the fundamentals of programming is assumed. Programming is not easy. The reader of this book cannot expect to have mastered programming by its end. She can expect to be capable of writing her own small-to-medium-size programs. She will be able to understand others' source code. She will have a firm grasp on the fundamental knowledge and skills necessary to continue her journey. In short, she will be on her way to being a *programmer*.

Why Should I Learn Dart?

Fundamental to web development is the use of a programming language. Dart is a new, relatively easy-to-learn programming language from Google. The Web has now existed for more than two decades. JavaScript, the main client-side programming language used on the Web, is regarded by many to contain some fundamental flaws that have persisted through several revisions of the language. Dart was developed as a fresh start.

One of the most problematic issues with JavaScript is its tendency toward sloppy, hard-to-maintain code. Many would point out that this is largely the result of the programmers using JavaScript rather than any fundamental issue with the language itself. Yet, because such a wide swath of developers use web languages, differing in background and experience, it makes sense to utilize a language such as Dart, which enforces a structured design for programs from the get-go. Of course, a sloppy program can be written in any language—Dart just makes it a little harder.

JavaScript, although object-oriented, does not take the concept of a class hierarchy and inheritance to heart. These concepts make programming large projects easier and are at the core of Dart. Chapters 10 and 11 fully explore these concepts. As of the writing of this book, the latest statistics show native Dart to be approximately two times faster than JavaScript. Yet, Dart still can be compiled back to JavaScript (think of this for now as "converted to JavaScript"), so that any modern web browser can run programs written in Dart.

Dart has a large built-in library (think of this as a real library: you can borrow code from this virtual library to help you do things with your program, just as you can borrow books from the real library to help you do things in real life) that makes doing many common programming tasks easier. Dart also has a powerful packaging system, so that libraries built by other institutions and programmers can easily be utilized by anyone.

In short, Dart is a modern, convenient, and compatible language designed for productivity. It may very well be the future of the Web.

About This Book

This book is structured in short, easy-to-digest chapters that concentrate on one key concept each. The idea is to make the book pleasant to read and not intimidating for a first-time programmer.

The chapters are designed to be read in order, with each building on the previous. Some of the chapters contain no code, while others are very heavy with code. Both code-heavy and code-light chapters are equally important, if you intend to get the most out of this book.

This book does not include extensive hands-on lessons regarding how to use Dart Editor, a web browser, or any other tools, beyond the language itself. The respective web sites for such pieces of software are better resources for learning about them than any book can be. Terms that are likely new to a beginning programmer are italicized and defined in-text or in footnotes.

The chapters are filled with examples that you are meant to type into your computer line-by-line (no copy-and-pasting, please!). *Dart for Absolute Beginners* takes the philosophy of "learning by doing." While your hand may be held, you will not be babied. The idea is to make the reader accustomed to what real Dart code may look like before she necessarily understands all of its intricacies. Do not be intimidated! Keep following along. Each chapter ends with exercises to give you more practice with the chapter's concepts. The more you do, the more the chapter's concepts will begin to seem clear.

Again, it is recommended that you type the source code from this book into your computer yourself (rather than download it from the Web). It has been speculated in other beginners' programming books that doing so will help you learn. The author of this book agrees.

A Note on Scope

It is not the goal of *Dart for Absolute Beginners* to exhaustively cover every feature of the Dart language. Instead, as an introductory text, it is the goal of this book to make you comfortable with the majority of the language's features. The details are left for further study. With that said, the vast majority of the language is covered. The topics left out are elaborated in Chapter 17.

Conventions Used in This Book

Source code throughout this book is formatted in the same way (in terms of bold and italic) in which it would appear in Dart Editor. The appearance of an ellipsis (…) indicates that some code is left out, so as not to be too verbose. Code is only left out of examples that you are not expected to run. All examples that have been designed to be run are complete.

A Note on Dart Versions

During the writing of this book, Dart evolved from version 1.0 to version 1.5. All of the source code contained within the book should run correctly on any of those Dart releases. The Dart standard library, and certainly the language specification, have largely stabilized. It is likely that the source code within this book will continue to be compatible with Dart releases for the foreseeable future, but Dart is a fluid and evolving platform. Updated source code, should any incompatibilities arise, will be available online through GitHub, as soon as possible.

Online Source Code Repository

All of the book's source code at its time of publication is available online on its Apress product page at www.apress.com/9781430264811. You can also get the latest source code on GitHub at https://github.com/davecom/Dart-for-Absolute-Beginners.

Get in Touch with the Author

Do you have questions or comments? Do you need help working through an example or exercise? Please, do not hesitate to reach out on Twitter to @davekopec or by e-mail at dartbook@oaksnow.com.

CHAPTER 1

■ ■ ■

Getting Set Up

It is sometimes said, "showing up is half the battle." If that phrase were to be applied to learning how to program a computer, then successfully completing this chapter would be analogous to "showing up." Once you have your Dart programming environment set up and are comfortable using its basic functions, you may find the rest of this book as easy as copying text from book to screen. You will then evolve from our first phrase to another apt one—"learning by doing."

Getting the Tools

Dart is a new language, and its tools are still evolving. Currently, the tools developed by the authors of the language (Google Inc.) are ubiquitous among Dart developers. This situation will likely evolve quickly as adoption of the language accelerates. For now, it makes deciding on a virtual work environment relatively easy. Happily, these still-evolving tools are free, easy to use, and multiplatform.

To get started, you will need a fairly modern computer (anything from the last decade should work) running Mac OS X, Windows, or Linux, an Internet connection, and the ability to follow directions. Setting up your computer to develop Dart programs is remarkably simple, thanks to the intuitive and easy-to-navigate home of the language on the Web, `www.dartlang.org`. Head over to the Dart web site in a web browser of your choice and download **Dart Editor**. Instead of duplicating the Dart web site's installation instructions here, you can read the most up-to-date installation instructions for your *operating system*[1] on the official site. Go ahead and install Dart Editor.

The Dart Editor bundles several components you should be aware of.

- *Dart Editor*: This is the program you will be using to organize your Dart projects and write the actual source code. It will automatically update itself and the other components that are bundled with it so that you are always up to date.

- *Dartium*: A version of the Google-sponsored open-source web browser Chromium that is specially tailored to run Dart programs at maximum speed by including a built-in Dart Virtual Machine.

---

[1]The low-level software that forms a layer between application programs and computer hardware. It provides services for applications to interact both with the hardware and with each other. It also provides basic building blocks that make developing new applications easier. Well-known personal computer operating systems include OS X, Windows, and Linux. The most popular mobile operating systems are Android and iOS.

- *Dart Virtual Machine*[2] (VM): This is the environment that runs your Dart program. More information about Dart Virtual Machine is available in Chapter 2.

- *Dart2JS*: A program that can convert your Dart programs into *JavaScript,*[3] so that they will run on any web browser.

You will only interact directly with Dart Editor and Dartium. The Dart Virtual Machine and Dart2JS work behind the scenes to execute your programs. Dart Editor is used to write Dart programs. Dartium is used to run them. When Dart programs are run in web browsers without the Dart Virtual Machine, they first have to be translated into JavaScript. Dartium is the fastest way to test and debug your Dart programs.

■ **Note**   You could write Dart programs in any text editor and use the command line Dart tools to run them. Dart Editor is just easier to use. There are other Dart development environments available, but they are beyond the scope of this book.

Using Dart Editor

Dart Editor is what is known as an *integrated development environment*[4] (IDE). It may be intimidating when you first open it, but in reality it is fairly easy to use. For now, play around with Dart Editor, the help menu, and the instructions on www.dartlang.org to learn how to do the following five things (this will also help you get familiar with using these resources):

- Creating a new project (or "Application" in Dart Editor's lingo)

- Editing files in the project

- Saving files in the project

- Adding new files to the project

- Running programs

Dart Editor is bundled with several example programs. Use them to work on figuring out how to perform all of these actions. You should try running each of the example programs in Dartium by clicking the run button (it looks like a DVD player's play button) in Dart Editor. Check them out; they're fun!

You will quickly find that using an IDE is not unlike using a word processor. The File menu is your starting point for the first four tasks bulleted above, and a colorful icon with a "play" button is used for running your program.

Once again: This book is not a tutorial on how to use Dart Editor. At the time of writing, Dart Editor is still evolving, perhaps even faster than the Dart language itself. Therefore, a written tutorial about it would make this book quickly obsolete. There are superb resources on the Dart web site and within Dart Editor for learning how to use it. But, perhaps the best way to learn a program like Dart Editor is to just explore it on your own.

When you start a new application in Dart Editor (File ➤ New Application from the menu bar), you have a choice of different application types. We will typically be using "Command Line" or "Web Application."

---

[2]A piece of software that emulates (pretends to be) hardware in order to execute programs written for a hardware-independent architecture.
[3]Invented by Netscape in 1995, JavaScript is a standardized programming language available on all modern web browsers. It is the main client-side programming language of the Web. For more information about JavaScript, check out Appendix B.
[4]A type of software used for developing other software. At minimum, it includes a module for editing source code, integration with a compiler, and integration with a debugger.

THE RELATIONSHIP BETWEEN GOOGLE AND DART

Google Inc. is the 800-lb. gorilla behind a lot of the World Wide Web's emerging technologies, including Dart. Google's large investment in research and development has led to the emergence of two widely publicized programming languages over the past few years. The first was Go, a general-purpose systems programming language. Dart, a more uniquely web-focused language, is the second.

As the creator of some of the most widely used web-apps on the planet, Google's quest to improve the state of web programming is, of course, largely self-serving. Google began utilizing Dart on internal, consumer-facing projects long before its 1.0 release. While Dart is presently developed largely by Google-employed developers, Google is in the process of standardizing the language with an international standards body.

JavaScript, the language Dart aims to challenge, was similarly first developed by Netscape Corporation before being standardized as ECMAScript by a standards body (Ecma International, in that case). Google's efforts to shape the future of web programming and challenge JavaScript have occurred in parallel to those of Microsoft Corporation and its TypeScript language. For more information about Dart's history, check out Appendix C.

Choosing a Suitable Work Environment

It's a good idea to put all of your Dart documents in one well-organized folder on your computer. You will find over and over again that being well-organized makes software development an easier task. You should bookmark useful Dart resources in one accessible bookmarks folder in your web browser. Having reference material at your fingertips will save you a lot of time when programming. Be sure to bookmark some of the resources in Appendix D.

Programming is a mentally intense task. It's important to have a quiet, comfortable place from which to work. Being ergonomic (having a comfortable keyboard, mouse, chair, and monitor setup) really is important, despite whatever jokes you may have heard about it. Having an ergonomic work environment is also conducive toward more enjoyment of programming.

Some programmers find music soothing while writing code, but others find it distracting. Generally, the more distracted you are, the worse code you will write, and the more difficult it will be to write. This may seem obvious, but when you struggle with a program, take a minute to step away from your computer. You may find that returning to the problem after a short while away will provide you with some new clarity when you take a second crack at figuring it out.

■ **Tip** Remember to take breaks! You will enjoy programming more if learning it does not become a chore. Try to remind yourself every two hours to spend some time away from the keyboard.

How to Read This Book

The chapters of this book are meant to be approachable in one sitting. They are not especially long, but that does not mean you will necessarily pick up the concepts in each quickly. The chapters are written in an order that builds conceptually from one to the next. For example, it would probably not be a good idea to read Chapter 4 before Chapter 3, because Chapter 4 is composed of several example programs, which demonstrate the concepts from Chapter 3. Therefore, the chapters are meant to be read sequentially.

If you find yourself stuck on a specific concept, it may be worth moving on. There are very few individual concepts that are so essential that you will not understand the rest of the book if you do not understand one prior concept. You will get more out of the learning process by letting the book's material paint a broad stroke in your mind than you will by trying to color in every detail explained.

The example programs are meant to be interesting and fun. If you find one particularly boring, then don't spend much time on it! Not every part of learning to program can be fun, but you should at least enjoy writing some of the programs. Sometimes when you first read a new concept, it will not be clear until you implement it in an example program. That's why doing the examples is important.

The exercises at the end of each chapter are meant to reinforce the chapter's concepts. There is not one right answer for most of the exercises. They are like practice problems. You should not feel compelled to complete every exercise, just the ones that you find helpful.

Utilizing the Web As You Learn

Presumably, you bought this book because you wanted something deeper than the tutorials that turn up in a search engine. Yet search engines and learning resources on the Web in general can be very effective when used carefully. It may be difficult to learn how to program Dart from scratch without a book, but when you have a specific question or problem beyond the scope of *Dart for Absolute Beginners*, nothing beats some of these excellent web resources. Appendix D has even more.

Search Engines

Search engines like Google and Bing will probably be your first stop when you have a question that you can't find the answer to in this book. Make sure to carefully evaluate the source of any information you find through a web search. Some sources are more reputable than others, and with a new language like Dart, this is especially important. Stick to information written by experienced developers and articles from respected digital publications.

Stack Overflow

Stack Overflow is a web site where developers help other developers. If you're a little more desperate to get your question answered, try putting your question on `www.stackoverflow.com`, and don't forget to tag it with "Dart." Users of Stack Overflow are not very tolerant of questions that could have been answered by a simple web search, so check out the search engines before you turn to Stack Overflow. Save it for the nuts that are harder to crack.

Official Dart Sources

The Dart web site has a reference manual that covers every element of the language. More important, `www.dartlang.org` also contains explanations of all of Dart's *APIs*.[5] As a beginner, the Dart Mailing Lists are probably not especially interesting to you at this point, but following them may help you delve deeper into the language, beyond the scope of this book.

---

[5]A well-defined interface (usually in the form of a library) that a piece of software can use to access functions/data provided by the operating system or another piece of software.

Social Media

The Dart blogosphere is increasingly vibrant. Dart has an official community on Google+ where the Dart Team posts announcements regarding new language features and direction. Connecting directly with other Dart developers is one of the best ways to learn, because they can relate to being in the position of first learning Dart. Part of the prosperity of a language depends on its community. Unlike some notorious programming language communities, the Dart community is friendly and inviting to newcomers.

Dart for Absolute Beginners Web Site

All of the source code and projects in this book can be downloaded from the *Dart for Absolute Beginners* book page at www.apress.com.

Do not just go to the web site and download all of the code, though; instead, take the time to type the source code into your computer directly from this book. You will learn significantly more by typing in the code yourself. Think about it like learning to read. A new reader will learn more by reading a book himself than he will by having it read to him. However, it's good to know that all of the source code is there on the web site if you need it.

Summary

The creators of the Dart language provide an easy-to-use integrated development environment called Dart Editor that includes all of the tools you need to get started. Before proceeding with the rest of the book, you should spend some time experimenting with Dart Editor's included example programs and familiarizing yourself with its basic functions. It is important to do programming work in a quiet, comfortable environment. It is also important to stay organized. All of the source code from this book is available online, but you will learn more if you type it into Dart Editor yourself. Selected web resources may be helpful as supplemental material as you learn Dart.

EXERCISES

1. Try modifying some of the example programs that come with Dart Editor, one line at a time, and then run them to see the effect(s) of your change. Don't worry about breaking them; they're examples!

2. Try to run the Dart example programs in a web browser other than Dartium. Can you figure out how? Does one web browser run the examples faster than another?

CHAPTER 2

■ ■ ■

Your First Dart Programs

It is a tradition in programming to introduce a new programmer to a language with a program that produces a message of "Hello, World!" This should be the easiest task you ever do in programming. Here's how you do it in Dart.

Hello, World!

Start a new application of type "Command Line" in Dart Editor called "HelloWorld." You can do this by going to the File menu and selecting "New Application." A dialog will pop up that allows you to select the application type ("Command Line"), a name for the application ("HelloWorld"), and the place on your computer where you want to store the application's files (up to you). You will then see several files created for you by Dart Editor listed in Dart Editor's left pane. This pane is labeled "Files." The .dart extension indicates that a file contains Dart source code. If you open helloworld.dart by double-clicking it, you may see that it is already filled in for you with boilerplate code provided by Dart Editor. Change helloworld.dart so that its code matches Listing 2-1.

■ **Note** Is the word *orange* the same as the word *Orange*? Not in Dart, and maybe not with regard to file names on your computer. Be careful with case.

Listing 2-1. Hello, World!

```dart
void main() {
  print("Hello, World!");
}
```

You can run the program by going to the Run menu in Dart Editor and selecting the menu item labeled "Run." The button in Dart Editor's toolbar with a triangle that looks like an audio program's play button has the same function. Go ahead and run the program. You should see "Hello, World!" printed in the console (Dart Editor's bottom pane). It is not a very exciting program, but you've officially run your first bit of Dart code! Here's how it works.

```dart
void main() {
```

This line declares a *function* called main(). We'll learn more about functions in Chapter 5. In short, they are a block of statements that the computer executes when the function is "called." They are like a page in an instruction manual that can be turned to anytime. main() is always the entry point of a Dart program—the place where the program begins execution. main() is automatically called (executed).

The void indicates that the main() function will not return any value. Again, this will make more sense as we continue. Do not worry too much about it now! The opening curly brace indicates where the function starts. The empty parentheses mean that this function takes no arguments.

```
print("Hello, World!");
```

Our main() function has only one statement (or "instruction," if you want to think about it that way). This statement, on line 2, calls a function built into Dart named "print," which will print out any line of text to the console. A piece of text is known as a *string*, and in its *literal*[1] form is contained within quotes. So, this function, print(), takes one *argument*,[2] a string literal, and prints it out to the console. The semicolon at the end of the line indicates where the statement ends.

```
}
```

The closing curly brace indicates where the main() function ends. Try changing the string literal that print() outputs to the console and see if it works. Okay, we must admit that this program does not do very much.

■ **Note**   Dart's official style guide specifies two spaces for indentations. Indentation is used to make a block of code more readable, but in Dart, it is not technically required (unlike in a language such as Python). For example, in the main() function above, the indentation indicates that the print() statement makes up the body of the main() function. If you removed the two spaces before the print() statement, the program would still run. We will use two spaces throughout this book for all code indentations, whether it be Dart, HTML, or otherwise. However, programs will still run with a different indentation scheme. Dart Editor's default settings will insert indentations correctly for you without you needing to think about it most of the time.

IT GETS MORE EXCITING

One of the reasons that new programmers give up is that they quickly realize how involved programming really is. You can't program Facebook right away. In fact, it takes a while to even be able to program a calculator, and there's a lot of fairly dry material before you get there.

There are many concepts to learn, and if you were not prepared for how "academic" the learning process could get, then you may become overwhelmed. You absolutely can learn to program though! It just takes time and concerted focus on your part. If you thought by the second chapter that you would have a better idea regarding what programming is all about, then you may have to alter your expectations.

Don't be discouraged if you're disappointed by how slowly things move. We are going to rapidly ramp up the pace so that by Chapter 4, you're actually writing programs that do something interesting.

---

[1]A way of representing an exact value in source code.
[2]A piece of data that is provided to a function and represented by a variable (covered in Chapter 4).

A Fancier Example

Let us try doing a more fancy form of Hello World. Once again in Dart Editor, go to the File menu and select "New Application." Create a new application of type "Web Application" and call it "HelloWorldFancy." We are going to create the program that you see in Figure 2-1. It allows the user to enter a name in a text box, and then greets that name. You may be thinking, "This is not much more exciting than our first program!" Don't quit yet. . .we have to start somewhere.

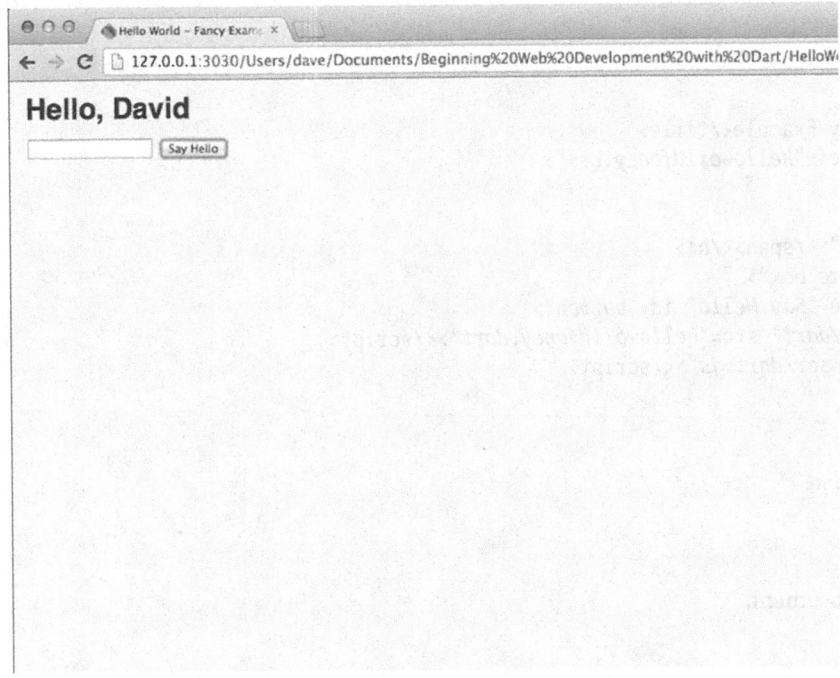

Figure 2-1. *This is what HelloWorldFancy will look like*

You will notice that Dart Editor creates both a `.dart` file and an `.html` file. You will find these files within the "web" folder under your expanded project in the Files pane on the left side of Dart Editor. As you probably know HTML[3] is the *markup language*[4] that defines what a web page looks like. You will have to use HTML any time that you want to create something that will appear on the Web. An HTML document is made up of a set of tags like `<html>` or `<img>`. Most tags have a matching end tag that defines where that part of the document finishes, such as `</html>`. You will see this shortly.

---

[3]Hypertext Markup Language is the main format for documents displayed in a web browser.
[4]A syntax used for annotating a document.

Your First HTML Document

Open the file helloworldfancy.html by double-clicking it in the "Files" pane (it's within the "web" folder within your project). Dart Editor once again may have provided you with a default implementation. Change it to look like Listing 2-2 (if it's blank, enter the following):

Listing 2-2. helloworldfancy.html

```
<!DOCTYPE html>
  <html>
    <head>
      <meta charset="utf-8">
      <title>Hello World - Fancy Example</title>
      <link rel="stylesheet" href="helloworldfancy.css">
    </head>
    <body>
      <h1>Hello, <span id="name"></span></h1>
      <input type="text" id="name_box">
      <input type="submit" value="Say Hello" id="button">
      <script type="application/dart" src="helloworldfancy.dart"></script>
      <script src="packages/browser/dart.js"></script>
    </body>
  </html>
```

Let's go over this HTML line by line.

```
<!DOCTYPE html>
```

Indicates that this is an HTML document.

```
<html>
```

The <html> tag indicates the start of the HTML proper.

```
<head>
```

The <head> tag is the start of the "header" section of the document. This is an area where document setup takes place.

```
<meta charset="utf-8">
```

This line says that this document uses the universal character encoding "UTF-8." Don't worry about it for now!

```
<title>Hello World - Fancy Example</title>
```

<title> defines the title of the document, which will appear in the web browser at the top of the window and as the title of any bookmarks made of the page. </title> is our first closing tag. It is the space between the opening tag and the closing tag that makes up the content of our tag. Therefore, whatever is between <title> and </title> will appear at the top of the browser window.

```
<link rel="stylesheet" href="helloworldfancy.css">
```

This line says that this document uses a *cascading style sheet* called `helloworldfancy.css`. Cascading style sheets are used to organize the "look" of a web page. They define things like fonts, borders, colors, and the size of content areas. You will notice that our link tag has two pieces of information, called `rel` and `href`. These are known as attributes. You do not have to understand these specific attributes at this time. You will learn various attributes and what they are used for as you learn HTML.

```
</head>
<body>
```

These lines represent the end of the header section and the beginning of the body section, respectively. The body is where the majority of content of an HTML document is located.

```
<h1>Hello, <span id="name"></span></h1>
```

`<h1>` is a headline tag. It is the place for a large (as in font size, not area) block of text. `<span>` is a generic tag used to organize a piece of inline content. You will see spans all over modern HTML. Our goal is to fill the span here programmatically from Dart. This `<span>` tag has an attribute called `id`. `id` is a way of labeling a tag. It is especially useful for allowing us to later reference this `<span>` tag from our Dart program when we need to manipulate it.

```
<input type="text" id="name_box">
<input type="submit" value="Say Hello" id="button">
```

The first `<input>` tag creates a text box where you can enter your name. The second `<input>` tag creates a button you can click. It is the `type` attribute that causes one `<input>` tag to represent a text box, while the other represents a button. The `value` attribute of the latter tag specifies what the button should say, as in what text should appear within the button.

```
<script type="application/dart" src="helloworldfancy.dart"></script>
<script src="packages/browser/dart.js"></script>
```

These `<script>` tags tell the web browser to import and execute the Dart program that we are about to write. The second `<script>` tag is for compatibility with browsers that do not have a Dart virtual machine (at the time of writing, this is all browsers except Dartium, which comes with Dart Editor), so that they can execute the JavaScript version of the program.

```
</body>
</html>
```

The last two closing tags indicate the ends of the body and `html` sections, respectively.

Wow, that was a lot of explaining for a little HTML document! In the future, we will not go over every HTML document in such great detail. As long as you start to understand the idea of tags and attributes, you should be able to follow along for the rest of the book. If you ever want to research specific tags or attributes, check out the HTML resources in Appendix D.

Learning HTML will not make you a better programmer, but it will make you capable of producing nice-looking web sites. HTML is used for displaying content—it is not used for manipulating content. There is a clear division between what can be done with HTML and what can be done with a web programming language like Dart. The latter goes far beyond display and into the realm of interactivity, computation, and intelligent responses to input. It was common in the '90s for people to confuse web designers (who knew HTML) with programmers. Don't make that mistake in the 21st century!

Hello World Fancy in Dart

Our Dart program is actually much shorter than our HTML. Change `helloworldfancy.dart` to look like Listing 2-3.

Listing 2-3. helloworldfancy.dart

```
import 'dart:html';

void main() {
  querySelector("#button").onClick.listen(sayHello);
}

void sayHello(MouseEvent event) {
  querySelector("#name").text = (querySelector("#name_box") as InputElement).value;
  (querySelector("#name_box") as InputElement).value = "";
}
```

```
import 'dart:html';
```

We will be using Dart's built-in HTML *library*[5] for interacting with our HTML document from our Dart code. import is used to include a *package*. A package can be thought of as a bundle of code that we want to access.

```
void main() {
  querySelector("#button").onClick.listen(sayHello);
}
```

Our main function is composed of one line, which is one statement. The first part of this line, `querySelector("#button")`, looks for the HTML element with the id attribute of "button." Go back and look at our HTML document. You will find there that the HTML attribute id is being used to define which element is the button. The next part of the line, `.onClick`, says, "from the element with the id of 'button' that we have found, access its property for setting what to do when it is clicked." Notice that a dot is used as an accessor. `.listen(sayHello)` finally says that when a click on this button occurs, the function `sayHello()` should be called. All statements in Dart end with a semicolon. In short, this line says "when the HTML element with the id of 'button' is clicked, call the function `sayHello()`."

```
void sayHello(MouseEvent event) {
```

This line defines the beginning of the `sayHello()` function. void means that this function returns nothing. The function `sayHello()` takes one argument, a MouseEvent named event. This *parameter*[6] is automatically populated by Dart when the user clicks our button. We could access this parameter to find out more about the click that occurred, but that is unnecessary in our little program.

```
querySelector("#name").text = (querySelector("#name_box") as InputElement).value;
```

`querySelector("#name").text` is a way of saying "find the HTML element with the id of 'name' and access its text property." The text property is as you would expect—the actual text that is displayed on the screen for this element. = is an assignment operator. It is used to set values. In this case we are trying to set the text of the HTML

---

[5]A piece of software that does not explicitly interact with the user but rather is accessed via APIs by other developers to add functionality to their programs. In Dart, libraries are provided via "packages."
[6]A variable that represents an argument provided to a function when it is called.

element with the id of "name." The left side of an assignment operator is always what we are assigning to, and the right side is what we are assigning from. (querySelector("#name_box") as InputElement) is a way of saying "find the HTML element with the id of 'name_box' and represent it as an InputElement." An InputElement is a special type of HTML element that receives input from the user. In this case, as defined in our HTML document, our "name_box" receives text input from the user. .value accesses the value of the user's input. This is ultimately what is assigned back to the text of our "name" element. In short, this line says "assign the value of the HTML input element with the id of 'name_box' to the text property of the HTML element with the id of 'name.'"

```
(querySelector("#name_box") as InputElement).value = "";
```

By reading over again the description of the previous line, you should be able to understand this one. In short, "Find the HTML element with the id of 'name_box'. Represent it as an InputElement. Set its value to be blank." Earlier, we learned that double quotes are used to define a string literal. Two double quotes next to each other with nothing between them represent an empty string, a blank if you will. The goal here is to reset the text box to be blank when the user clicks the button.

```
}
```

The last closing bracket is where the function sayHello() ends. It is also the end of our program.

For only three lines of real "meat," our program may seem pretty complicated. This is both a testament to how compact yet expressive the Dart programming language can be and how early we are on our journey of learning Dart.

You should now try running the program. You will notice that it automatically loads in Dartium, the Chrome-based web browser with a built-in virtual machine for the Dart language. Play around with the result. Try entering a name, clicking the button, erasing the name, and then clicking the button again. Why does it erase the name that was previously displayed?

Input and Output

While seemingly obvious concepts, understanding *input* and *output* (sometimes abbreviated to I/O or IO) is fundamental to understanding how to write a good program. In short, input is information that the computer takes in for processing, and output is information that the computer delivers to the user.

An *input device* is a tool that helps the user deliver input to the computer. The input devices we'll be using in this book will primarily be the keyboard and the mouse. Other input devices you may be familiar with include a touch screen, Wacom tablet, microphone, and camera. An *output device* does the opposite. The main output device we will be using is the monitor (or "screen" to be more generic), but another you are surely familiar with is the printer.

When we write command-line applications with Dart, only the keyboard is used as an input device and our only output is textual in nature. Our first HelloWorld program was such a command-line program and didn't even take keyboard input—it took no input at all. As we saw, print() is used in a command-line application to output text to the user. Hello World Fancy was a web-based program with a *graphical user interface*[7] (GUI). It took input via a text box and a button (yes, even a click of the mouse is a type of input) and delivered textual output on a web page. Did you ever think of your headphones as an output device? You should, because they are one.

As our programs get more advanced, it will be important to think about the best ways to take input from the user and the best ways to present output to the user. The makers of operating systems (such as Apple and Microsoft) have guidelines about how to design user interfaces for developers of programs that run on their platforms. On the Web, it is more of a Wild West type of atmosphere. This accounts for why some web companies spend as much on designers as they do on developers. The entire area of input/output with regard to user interface design falls under an academic discipline known as *Human-Computer Interaction*.

---

[7]As opposed to a command-line interface, a graphical user interface utilizes graphical elements, such as pictures, text boxes, buttons, and menus, for human-computer interaction. It is the main interface for interacting with computers running OS X and Windows.

The Learning Curve

It would not be unreasonable for Hello World Fancy to have looked very intimidating to you. The goal in this chapter is to dive into some code that "does something" to get your feet wet, even if that means you do not understand all of it. However, the situation is not supposed to be analogous to throwing a child into a pool and telling him to "sink or swim." A better analogy would be giving a culinary student a piece of cake to taste before he learns all of its ingredients.

Learning how to program is like learning to speak a new language. Luckily, programming languages have much smaller vocabularies (typically, less than 100 keywords) than human spoken languages. Learning the keywords is not the end of the learning process, though. The other side of the coin is learning a new way of thinking.

Programming requires thinking in abstract terms. In programming, values and actions are represented by abstract entities. A common misconception about programming is that it requires mathematical sophistication. When learning basic programming, the ability to think abstractly is much more helpful than any knowledge of advanced mathematics.

Since the number of actual keywords is limited, you do not have to possess a great memory either (plus you can always look something up in this book or online). There is really just not that much to memorize. Let the computer's memory be the only one you worry about. That's why reference materials were invented.

If memorization or math skills will not help you learn, then what will? How can you improve on those abstract thinking skills? The number-one way to become a better programmer is to program. It's the quintessential discipline where "practice makes perfect." You need a resource like this book to have the central concepts explained to you and ease the initially steep learning curve. But more than anything, people who become good programmers do a lot of programming. Don't just do the programs in this book. Come up with some programs to do on your own as you learn Dart. Ultimately, solving problems on your own will be both more rewarding and more educational than reading anyone else's code. The exercises at the end of each chapter should give you some ideas and starting points.

Summary

In this chapter, you saw your first two Dart programs. Although both were relatively simple, Hello World Fancy incorporated HTML, user input, and events. Despite being just eight lines of code, it could seem intimidating to a brand-new programmer. Programming has a relatively steep learning curve. The goal of the rest of this book is to ease the incline of that curve.

EXERCISES

1. Turn our Hello World Fancy program into a Mad Lib. You will have to add more text boxes, buttons, and <span> tags to the HTML file. You will also have to modify the Dart source.

2. Try creating a web site about a topic of your choice in pure HTML. You can find more information on all of the different tags in the resources in Appendix D.

3. Browse the HTML source of some of your favorite web sites. Go to them in your web browser, and then in one of the menus, there should be an option such as "Show Page Source." You might not understand most of it, but see what elements correlate with things you see on the page.

4. The first web site ever is still available! It's straight out of the early 1990s. You can find it at http://info.cern.ch/hypertext/WWW/TheProject.html. Go to that address in your web browser and in the menus, find an option to "Show Page Source," as in Exercise 3. It's a lot simpler, right? That site was created in 1993. It still renders fine in the latest web browser. Do the tags look familiar? HTML hasn't changed that much in two decades.

CHAPTER 3

Some Programming Fundamentals

The goal of this chapter is to present enough information about programming so that you feel comfortable with the next section of the book, where we start to write some longer Dart programs, without becoming overwhelmed.

Code As Instructions

Think about your computer as the best servant that money can buy. A servant that can do anything you can imagine, as long as it does not involve anything in the physical world (unless your computer is a robot, of course). Unfortunately, your servant does not speak English. Rather, your servant speaks binary. Luckily, you have a translator, Dart, to help you get your commands across.

All of programming can be broken down into simple instructions. Store this in there. Move this to here. Tell that to do this. Try to think in the mindset of instructions, as we cover some of the basic concepts involved in programming. The following are by no means the *only* concepts, but they are a good starting point for a new programmer.

Variables

In our Hello World Fancy program in Chapter 2, we did not formally *declare*[1] any of our own variables. However, variables are a basic building block of programming languages. Do you remember high school algebra? Where "x" was a variable that represented a number? Variables in programming are not too different. A variable is used to represent a value and to hold onto it for future use. = is used differently in Dart than it is in algebra. As has been mentioned before, = is used in Dart for assignment (assigning values to variables). In Dart, == is used for equality. We will see that distinction shortly.

```
var x = 5;
```

In Dart, this code assigns the value of 5 to the variable x. Similarly, the next example assigns the string literal "antelope" to the variables animalWord.

```
var animalWord = "antelope";
```

In the next example, the variable coolWord is assigned the value of the string literal "antelope" Variables may also have a *type*. For now, you can think of a type as a way of insisting that a variable only hold a specific kind of value, although this is not completely accurate. coolWord is specified to be of type String.

```
String coolWord = "antelope";
```

---

[1] A statement that gives a variable an identifier (a name) and optionally, in Dart, a type.

Now we can reassign to coolWord another value of type String.

```
coolWord = "dog";
```

But, we cannot assign a non-String to coolWord.

```
coolWord = 5;  //WRONG - This will raise a warning.
```

Types are optional in Dart. However, they are useful when we want to ensure the safety of some of our variables by enforcing a specific type. Types are also helpful when debugging. No, we do not want to do division on the word "antelope"! In this book, we will make extensive use of types, because they can provide a reassuring level of clarity for a new programmer and can arguably be considered to be best practice.

■ **Note** You just saw our first comment in the wild (//WRONG - This will raise a warning.)! However, comments should not be rare beasts. Comments are pieces of text directly placed within code used to document it (in most cases, comments are used to better explain how code works in plain English). Dart supports two types of comments. // is used for a one-line comment. Any text following // is not processed by Dart. However, as soon as the end of the line is reached, Dart reverts to processing all subsequent text. Multiline comments in Dart are between the symbols /* and */. It is very important to vigorously comment your code, even if you will be the only person reading it. Not only will writing about your code help you conceptually wrap your mind around what you're trying to do, but if you or someone else has to look at it again in the future, you are essentially future proofing it by well-documenting how it works.

Technically, all variables in Dart are references to objects. These objects contain values and actions. For example, the variable coolWord refers to a String object, which holds a value of "dog." You will learn more about what an object is in Chapter 10. Until then, it may be helpful to forget about the fact that variables only refer to objects and instead think about them as simply holding values. We will use this simplification until Chapter 10, but you should be aware that it is a simplification.

There are six special types in Dart that are fundamental to the language and can be described with literals. These are integers, floating-point numbers, strings, booleans, lists, and maps. We have already seen some examples of integers and strings. We will learn more in this chapter about both of them. Lists and maps are the primary subject of Chapter 6. Booleans are declared with the keyword bool. Booleans can only hold one of two values, true and false.

■ **Note** Why is String sometimes uppercase and sometimes lowercase? String (uppercase) refers to the formal Dart type, String. However, string (lowercase) refers to the general concept of a string. The same is true of *list* and *map*.

Numbers can be separated into integers (int) and floating-point numbers (double). Integers hold whole numbers. Floating-point numbers, defined with the keyword double, hold numbers that require decimal points to describe them. Table 3-1 summarizes the fundamental types in Dart that can be expressed with literals.

Table 3-1. *Fundamental Dart Types That Can Be Described with Literals*

Type	Description	Example Literals
int	Integers	5, -20, 0
double	Floating-Point Numbers	3.14159, -3.2, 0.00
String	Strings	"hello", "g", "To be or not to be?"
bool	Booleans	true, false
List	Lists (Chapter 6)	[1,2,3], ["hi", "bye"]
Map	Maps (Chapter 6)	{"x": 5, "y":2}

Operators

Operators are used for doing operations. "What's an operator?" you say. Well you already know one! = is the assignment operator. We've been using the = operator to assign the value on the right of an expression to the variable on the left. Dart comes with arithmetic operators that work as you would expect.

```
int something = 2;
int other = 2;
int total = something + other;  //total is 4
total = total / other;  //total is 2 again
something = 2 * 4;  //something is now 8, note total is not changed
```

Basic arithmetic is obviously essential for performing any kind of mathematics. There are also arithmetic operators that are provided just for convenience. The most useful of which may be ++ and --. These operators are known as the increment and decrement operator, respectively. They increment or decrement the integer value pointed to by a variable.

```
int x = 1;
x++;  //x now equals 2
x--;  //x is 1 again
x = x + 1;  //x is 2 yet again... see the similarity to ++?
x = x - 1;  //Do you see where we've been going with this?
```

As in traditional mathematics, operators have an ordered *precedence* in Dart. You may remember the acronym PEMDAS from your elementary-school days (Parentheses, Exponents, Multiplication, Division, Addition, Subtraction) as a way to describe the order in which mathematical operations should be processed. If two operators have the same precedence, then they are simply evaluated from left to right, with the left-most being evaluated first. PEMDAS matches the precedence of arithmetic operators in Dart, and Dart provides parentheses for expressions as well.

```
int x = ((5 + 5) * 5);  //x is 50
int y = (5 + (5 * 5));  //y is 30
int z = 5 + 5 * 5;  //z is 30, like y
```

Operators are used for a lot more than just assignment and arithmetic. They provide a programming language with some built-in functionality that gives the programmer a "base" from which to build. We will see more Dart operators as we progress. Table 3-2 summarizes the arithmetic operators we learned in this section. Appendix A contains a listing of most of Dart's operators.

Table 3-2. Some Basic Arithmetic Operators in Dart, Ordered by Precedence

Operator	Description	Example
++	Increment by 1	x++;
--	Decrement by 1	x--; //same precedence as ++
*	Multiplication	x = y * 5;
/	Division	x = 6 / 3; //same precedence as *
+	Addition	x = y + 2;
-	Subtraction	x = 20 - 4; //same precedence as +

■ **Note**   The assignment operator, =, has a lower precedence than all of the arithmetic operators.

FROM SOURCE CODE TO MACHINE CODE

You want your computer to do something. A programming language is a way of formalizing what you want it to do. The computer cannot natively understand a programming language. It simply understands *binary*[2] (ones and zeroes)—or to be more exact and technical, electrical signals that are either present or not present.

How do we go from a programming language to something the computer can understand? The programming language we write in must be converted. The program that does this conversion is known as a *compiler*, and when a piece of source code is converted to machine code, we say that it is "compiled."

In most traditional languages, the compiler works ahead of time before the program is run, so that the actual executable is already in machine code. Originally, JavaScript was interpreted. An *interpreter* converts source code into machine code at runtime, one line at a time. This is always slower than running machine code, which is compiled ahead of time. Modern JavaScript implementations have a *just-in-time compiler*. Unlike an *ahead-of-time compiler*, a just-in-time compiler converts source code into machine code when it is needed, instead of ahead of time. This also has a performance cost (mostly a startup cost—doing the actual compilation) but is very significantly faster than an interpreter.

Because your Dart code will generally be run as converted JavaScript, your programs will get to take advantage of the latest in JavaScript just-in-time compiler technology. When run under the native Dart Virtual Machine, your programs will run even faster.

---

[2] A system of representing data or computer instructions using only the symbols 1 and 0. In binary, ones and zeroes strung together represent numerical values in base-2 (a number system based on the powers of 2).

Strings

You have already seen strings throughout the first few chapters of this book. Strings are a way of representing text in your programs. Now let's learn a few more concepts that will be useful in your programs.

```
"Hello"
'Hello'
```

Both of these are equivalent string literals in Dart. You are free to use either single or double quotes for string literals, but we will use double quotes throughout this book for consistency.

```
int temp = 75;
String weatherReport = "It is rainy and $temp degrees";
String obviousReport = "If it were 30 degrees cooler it would be ${temp - 30} degrees.";
```

This is called *string interpolation*. We are inserting the value of our variables into our strings. If it is just a single variable, we can use a dollar sign. If it is an expression, we must use the ${} syntax.

```
print("\"I am very tired,\" she said.");
//prints out: "I am very tired," she said.
```

We can escape special characters to use them in our strings. A backslash, \, is used to do the escaping. The character directly following the backslash within a string literal is included in the string as is. If we don't want to worry about special characters in a string, then we can use so-called raw strings. They are preceded with an *r* and represent exactly what falls between their quotes.

```
String myRawString = r"Here are my \ not \special backslashes\";
print(myRawString);   //Prints: Here are my \ not \special backslashes\
```

Dart incorporates a standard for encoding strings known as *Unicode*.[3] This allows Dart strings to represent characters from foreign languages as well as special symbols, without any additional work necessary on the part of the programmer. All of the following are valid strings in Dart:

```
"Hello"
"你好"
"مرحبا"
"☺☃△♡"
```

Control Structures

Often in programming, it is necessary to enable the machine to make a decision.

```
if (temperature > 75) {
  print("It is hot today.");   //print is used to output text to the console
}
```

---

[3]A character encoding standard that accommodates the expression of characters not present in the Latin alphabet, unlike prior computing standards. All popular modern operating systems support Unicode, although that was not the case only a decade ago. Many programming languages still do not have built-in support for Unicode, unlike Dart, which does.

The statements within the curly braces of an if-statement will only be executed if the statement inside of its parentheses is true. In this case, "It is hot today." will only be printed to the console if the variable temperature holds a value greater than 75. > is an operator for comparison that means "greater than." If it's not hot today, maybe we want to print something else out.

```
if (temperature > 75) {
  print("It is hot today.");
} else {
  print("It is not that hot today.");
}
```

That statement within the curly braces after the else will always be executed when the value held by temperature is not greater than 75. It will not be executed when the temperature is above 75.

```
if (temperature > 75) {
  print("It is hot today.");
} else if (temperature > 50) {
  print("It is mild today.");
} else {
  print("It is cold today.");
}
```

Now there are three distinct possibilities. else if enables us to expand the number of branches in our decision tree. If the temperature is greater than 75, then we will say it is hot. If the temperature is less than or equal to 75 but greater than 50, then we will say it is mild. If the temperature is less than or equal to 50, then we will say that it is cold. If you do not follow, go over it again and think about it in the English terms from this paragraph.

More About Booleans

When the boolean type, bool, was first briefly introduced a few pages ago, you may have wondered how a type with only two possible values could really be useful. Booleans are fundamental to an area of mathematics known as boolean algebra, which deals with logic. Computer hardware at its core is a very complicated boolean algebra machine. The ones and zeroes can be thought of as truth-values. To restate the same idea more clearly, true and false can be thought of as the 1 and 0 that the computer understands. Indeed, the programming language C originally did not have a boolean type and instead relied on integers of value 1 or 0 as pseudo booleans. While this could work in a language like Dart, it's more convenient and readable to actually have a separate type for true and false.

Booleans expressions are pieces of code that ultimately evaluate to either true or false. The if-statements that we just worked with were actually evaluating boolean expressions within their parentheses and executing the following statements between the curly braces if and only if the evaluation was true. You understood this intuitively, but by defining it more formally, we now understand what can and cannot be evaluated by an if-statement.

```
bool b = true;
if (b) {
  print("True");  //will print: True
}
```

There are other operators for evaluating equivalency other than > in Dart. They are summarized in Table 3-3.

Table 3-3. Equivalency Operators in Dart, Ordered by Precedence

Operator	Description	if Example
==	Equal To	if (x == 10) {...}
!=	Not Equal To	if (x != 10) {...}
>	Greater Than	if (x > 10) {...}
<	Less Than	if (x < 10) {...}
>=	Greater Than or Equal To	if (x >= 10) {...}
<=	Less Than or Equal To	if (x <= 10) {...}

Another logical operator is ! (sometimes referred to as "bang" or "not"), which is used to negate a value. !true is equivalent to false. Similarly, !false is equivalent to true.

```
bool b = true;
if (!b) {
  print("True");  //will not be executed
} else {
  print("False"); //will print: False
}
```

The not operator can also be applied to a more comprehensive expression. Notice how the expression has to be wrapped in parentheses for the ! operator to be applied to it successfully.

```
if (!(temperature > 75)) {
  print("It is NOT hot today.");  //prints only if temperature is NOT > 75
}
```

Switch Statements

A switch-statement makes it convenient to decide between many different possibilities.

```
switch (favoriteAnimal) {
  case "dog":  // if favoriteAnimal is equal to "dog" do the following
    print("Bark!");
    break;  //we need one of these at the end of every case but default
  case "cow":
    print("Moo!");
    break;
  case "cat":
    print("Meow!");
    break;
  default:
    print("Your animal is a new species to me!");
}
```

The variable we are comparing is the one in parentheses immediately following the switch-statement. In this case, it is favoriteAnimal. break statements appear at the end of every case. Not including one may raise an *exception*.[4] The default option is a catchall if none of the other cases matched the value of the variable in question. It does not require a break statement at its end. It is good practice to always include a default clause. This is mostly for safety reasons—to deal with unexpected values. switch-statements can work with other types as well. They can also have empty cases that "fall-through" to the next case when there is a match. Here is another example:

```
switch (digit) {
  case 0:
    print("Zero");
    break;
  case 1:
  case 3:
  case 5:
  case 7:
  case 9:
    print("Odd");
    break;
  case 2:
  case 4:
  case 6:
  case 8:
    print("Even");
    break;
  default:
    print("Not a Digit");
}
```

Loops

Often in programming, we will have to repeat some lines of code. Rather than type them again and again, we have something known as a loop. Technically, loops are control structures too, but for readability, they are presented in a separate section here. Notice that, like if-statements, loops evaluate boolean expressions.

```
int beersOnTheWall = 99;
while (beersOnTheWall > 0) {
  print("$beersOnTheWall bottles of beers on the wall, $beersOnTheWall
      bottles of beer.  Take one down, pass it around, ${beersOnTheWall - 1}
      bottles of beer on the wall.");
  beersOnTheWall--;
}
```

The while-loop will keep executing the lines between the parentheses until beersOnTheWall is no longer greater than 0. Do you remember the -- operator? Again, it is an operator that subtracts 1 from a number. It is used equivalently to this line of code:

```
beersOnTheWall = beersOnTheWall - 1;
```

---

[4]An action that interrupts a program—usually one that is not intended to occur. In most cases, exceptions are errors. It is safe to think of the two as being synonymous for the most part. Exceptions should be handled by a program, or it may crash.

Try executing the beersOnTheWall program in Dart Editor by creating a new project of the application type "Command Line" and putting the statements above within the main() function.

```
int beersOnTheWall = 99;
do {
  print("$beersOnTheWall bottles of beers on the wall, $beersOnTheWall
      bottles of beer.  Take one down, pass it around, ${beersOnTheWall - 1}
      bottles of beer on the wall.");
  beersOnTheWall--;
} while (beersOnTheWall > 0);
```

This is exactly the same as the last loop, except that in a do-while-loop, the check is at the end of the loop instead of at the beginning. This doesn't make a difference for our program, but it can be useful in situations where you always want the first iteration of the loop to execute, regardless of whether the comparison evaluates to true or false.

```
for (int beersOnTheWall = 99; beersOnTheWall > 0; beersOnTheWall--) {
  print("$beersOnTheWall bottles of beers on the wall, $beersOnTheWall
      bottles of beer.  Take one down, pass it around, ${beersOnTheWall - 1}
      bottles of beer on the wall.");
}
```

Again, this loop is exactly the same as our last two. It looks very different, though, doesn't it? for-loops are compact and extremely useful. Within the parentheses, you have three statements. The first is an opportunity to create a variable and set its value (this variable is only accessible within the for loop, if it is declared here). The second is a comparison that must hold for us to continue the loop. The last is what we want to do at the end of each iteration of the loop. Here is another example:

```
int total = 0;
for (int count = 1; count <= 10; count++) {
  total = total + count;
}
print("The sum of the numbers 1 through 10 is: $total");
```

Variables can also be declared within a loop. If that happens, then the variable is local to the loop and cannot be accessed outside of it. Why could our total variable not be declared inside the loop, as in the following example?

```
for (int count = 1; count <= 10; count++) {
  int total = 0;  //WRONG
  total = total + count;
}
print("The sum of the numbers 1 through 10 is: $total");  //ERROR
```

It's wrong because total would then be reset during every iteration of the loop. It's further wrong because total could then not be accessed outside the loop, as it is in the print() statement.

Another common pattern is to have a loop within a loop. The first loop is called the outer loop, while the second loop is called the inner loop. The variables declared in the outer loop before the start of the inner loop can be accessed in the inner loop. However, no variables in the inner loop can be accessed outside of it. Here is an example that prints the numbers 1 through 10 with the values of their exponents from 1 to 10.

```
for (int x = 1; x <= 10; x++) {  //outer loop
  int powerTotal = 1;
  for (int y = 1; y <= 10; y++) {  //inner loop
    //print the powers of x
    powerTotal = powerTotal * x;
    print("$x^$y is $powerTotal");
  }
}
```

Remember, for every iteration of the outer loop, the entire inner loop runs. So there are 10 different ys for every x.

Summary

That's all for now! To summarize:

- **Variables** are used to refer to information for later use.

- **Strings** are how we represent text.

- **Operators** provide us with the basic built-in functionality of the language.

- **Control Structures** allow us to use the computer for decision making, or "branching."

- **Loops** are a convenient way to do repetitive tasks.

EXERCISES

1. Use loops and string interpolation to print out a multiplication table from 1 to 10.

2. In 1626, Peter Minuit supposedly purchased the island of Manhattan for the equivalent of $1,000 in modern-day currency. Use what you have learned in this chapter to calculate how much money Peter Minuit's estate could have earned had he put the $1,000 in the bank and earned a 2% annual interest rate instead.

3. Can an if-statement coupled with else if and else be used in the same fashion as a switch statement? Why or why not?

4. Search the Web for the concepts we learned today in another programming language. Does the example code look similar?

CHAPTER 4

■ ■ ■

Five Small Programs to Showcase Fundamentals in Dart

In Chapter 3, you learned some programming fundamentals that should have given you a basic understanding of a few of the concepts we will require to write programs. In this chapter, we will demonstrate those fundamentals in action. The following programs will all fit entirely within the main() function.

Number Guessing Game

I'm thinking of a number. Can you guess what it is? It's ten, because that's about the number of minutes that I think it will take you to input the Number Guessing Game into Dart Editor. Create a new command-line application in Dart Editor called "NumberGuessingGame." Open numberguessinggame.dart and replace its contents with Listing 4-1.

Listing 4-1. Number Guessing Game

```dart
import 'dart:math';
import 'dart:io';

void main() {
  int guess;
  Random rand = new Random();  //create a random number generator
  int answer = rand.nextInt(100);  //gets a random integer from 0 to 99
  do {
    print("Enter your guess:");
    String temp = stdin.readLineSync();  //read in from the keyboard
    guess = int.parse(temp); //convert String to integer
    if (guess < answer) {
      print("Too low!");
    } else if (guess > answer) {
      print("Too high!");
    }
  } while (guess != answer);
  print("You got it!");
}
```

NAMING VARIABLES

When choosing the name of a variable in your program, you should feel empowered to choose as descriptive a name as possible, regardless of verbosity. It will make your code more readable by both your future self and others, if you choose a highly descriptive name. By convention, most Dart variables should begin with a lowercase character. The convention of capitalizing the letters that begin the words after the first in a multiword variable title is known as camel case (for example: `thisIsAVariable`, `waterBottle`, `firstName`) and is also a Dart convention. Programmers have a tendency to use short non-descriptive variable names because it saves typing. A few extra keystrokes are worth the clarity that descriptive variable names provide.

Try running the program and entering some integers between 0 and 100 to get a sense of its flow (statistically, you should be able to beat it in about six guesses). We need the `dart:math` package for random number generation. We need the `dart:io` package to get user input from the keyboard. Let's go over some specific lines you may not be familiar with.

```
Random rand = new Random();  //create a random number generator
int answer = rand.nextInt(100);  //gets a random integer from 0 to 99
```

The goal is to get a randomly generated integer between 0 and 99. `new Random()` creates a new Random object. This is the object from the `dart:math` package that is used for random number generation. The `nextInt()` method finds an integer between 0 and one below the integer that it takes as an argument (in this case, 100). So, `nextInt(11)` would find a random integer between 0 and 10.

```
String temp = stdin.readLineSync();  //read in from the keyboard
```

`stdin` is a built-in object of the `dart:io` package used for reading input from standard input. This is our way of getting user input for our command-line Dart programs. `readLineSync()` will pause the program until the user presses the Return (Enter) key. Whatever was entered before the Return key was pressed will be stored in the `String` named `temp`.

```
guess = int.parse(temp);  //convert String to integer
```

`int.parse()` will convert a string into an integer. The result will be stored in the integer named guess. We need an integer, so that we can compare `guess` to `answer`. Have you tried entering a non-integer into the program? This is the line that will crash the program if you do so! If this were a program to be used by others, we would definitely have to catch some errors here! The rest of the program should be pretty self-explanatory. Notice, in particular, that the congratulatory statement, "You got it!" is printed when the loop exits. This is because when the comparison in the `do-while`-loop no longer holds, the player has successfully entered a `guess` that is equivalent to `answer`.

Temperature Converter

Fahrenheit and Celsius are two scales for measuring the same thing—temperature. There is a simple formula for converting from Fahrenheit to Celsius and vice versa. If F represents the value we want to convert in degrees Fahrenheit and C represents the same for Celsius, then the formulas are

- $F = 1.8C + 32$

- $C = (F - 32) / 1.8$

When we create a program to process these formulas for a user, we must know both the direction that the user wants to convert, as well as the number of degrees that have to be converted. The following program takes input from the user's keyboard to get these values. It utilizes the dart:io package to get access to the function readLineSync() for reading keyboard input.

Listing 4-2. Temperature Converter

```dart
import 'dart:io';

void main() {
  print("A:Convert Celsius to Fahrenheit\nB:Convert Fahrenheit to Celsius");
  String selection;

  do {
    selection = stdin.readLineSync().toUpperCase();   //get uppercase input
  } while (selection != "A" && selection != "B");  //think of && like AND

  print("Enter the starting temperature:");
  String inTemp = stdin.readLineSync();
  int temp = int.parse(inTemp);

  switch (selection) {
    case "A":
      print("$temp degrees Celsius is ${temp * 1.8 + 32} degrees Fahrenheit");
      break;
    case "B":
      print("$temp degrees Fahrenheit is ${(temp - 32) / 1.8} degrees Celsius");
      break;
    default:
      break;
  }
}
```

Notice the do-while-loop. It will not stop looping until the user's input is either an "A" or a "B." Let's go over it in more detail.

```dart
selection = stdin.readLineSync().toUpperCase();   //get uppercase input
```

stdin.readLineSync() is a call to a function that gathers input from the user's keyboard until the user hits the Return key. Whatever the user typed is returned as a String. Before we let the variable selection point to that String, we transform it, so that it is all uppercase. The reason for this is to ensure that if the user enters "a," it is equivalent to the user entering "A." We do not want case to matter. The call to toUpperCase() achieves the case conversion. You can think of stdin.readLineSync() as the command-line equivalent of the text box in Hello World Fancy. The following line of code, after selection is assigned, evaluates the validity of selection.

SYNCHRONOUS VS. ASYNCHRONOUS

When `stdin.readLineSync()` is executed, our program waits for input. It stops in its tracks and does not execute any further until it receives the user's input. In computing, we say something is *synchronous* when it waits for an event to happen before continuing. In contrast, something that is *asynchronous* occurs simultaneously with other happenings. For example, most web servers are asynchronous. They accept requests from new users before necessarily completing the requests of previous users.

```
} while (selection != "A" && selection != "B");  //think of && like AND
```

The conditional that decides whether our program can exit the loop utilizes a new operator that we have not seen before, `&&`. `&&` is a logical operator that returns `true` if both the boolean expression on its left is `true` **and** the boolean expression on its right is `true`. `&&` evaluates the two expressions from left to right. If the first expression is `true`, then it evaluates the second. If the second expression is `true`, then it returns `true`. If the first expression is `false`, then it immediately returns `false`. If the first expression is `true`, but the second expression is `false`, then it returns `false`. The way that the `&&` operator works from left to right is known as *short circuit evaluation*. If the first expression is `false`, the second expression will never be evaluated.

The expression to the left of `&&` in our code is `selection != "A"`. We are checking here that the variable `selection` is **not** equivalent to the literal "A". If it is equivalent to the literal "A", then the expression evaluates to `false`, the `&&` expression evaluates to `false`, and we exit the loop. If `selection` is equivalent to "A", then the right side of the `&&` is evaluated `selection != "B"`. The same rules apply again. If `selection` is equivalent to "B", then we exit the loop; otherwise, we evaluate the entire expression to `true` and go back to the beginning of the do-while-loop.

If one were to convert this entire complex statement into English directions, one might write: "Go back to the beginning of the loop, if the variable `selection` is not equivalent to "A" **and** the variable `selection` is not equivalent to "B". Otherwise, exit the loop." `&&` is known as *logical and*. "And" is a good way to think of it—an `&&` expression is true if and only if both of its component boolean expressions are true.

Are you thoroughly confused by this loop yet? Hopefully not, but if you are, take a look at Table 4-1. It illustrates various potential user entries on the keyboard, the evaluation of each boolean expression, and the ultimate outcome of the `&&` statement.

Table 4-1. *Example Evaluation of Do-While Loop Expressions from Temperature Converter*

User Input	selection	selection != "A"	selection != "B"	selection != "A" && selection != "B"
zzzz	ZZZZ	true	true	true
5	5	true	true	true
a	A	false	not evaluated	false
B	B	true	false	false

Hopefully that clears up any remaining confusion. If not, try removing the `&&` as well as the second boolean expression. Then you should try running the program. Now try adding it back in, but change the `String` literals that are used for comparison. Experiment with various values.

```
String inTemp = stdin.readLineSync();
int temp = int.parse(inTemp);
```

Once again, `stdin.readLineSync()` is used to read user input from the keyboard. Unfortunately, this time its default return type, a `String`, is not sufficient for the rest of our program. We cannot use a mathematical formula on a `String`. We need a number. How can the `String`, `inTemp`, become the `int`, `temp`? That is the purpose of the call to `int.parse()`. `int.parse()` takes an argument, a `String`, and returns an `int` that is representative of the value the `String` is conveying. For example, `int.parse("55")` will return an `int` with the value 55. There's one problem: `int.parse()` has no way of knowing whether it is being provided with a valid `String` that can be represented by an integer or whether it is being provided with garbage. If it is being provided with garbage, it will throw an error.

If you try running Temperature Converter and providing garbage such as "cool" instead of a more hospitable `String` such as "70," then you will notice that it will throw an error, and the program will crash. In a real-world scenario, you better have some error-checking in place! It is never a good idea to trust the input of your user. He may be malicious, or may be prone to typos.

```dart
switch (selection) {
    case "A":
      print("$temp degrees Celsius is ${temp * 1.8 + 32} degrees Fahrenheit");
      break;
    case "B":
      print("$temp degrees Fahrenheit is ${(temp - 32) / 1.8} degrees Celsius");
      break;
    default:
      break;
}
```

■ **Note**   Error-handing in Dart revolves around so-called exceptions. Exceptions are one of the topics covered in Chapter 12. More basic error-handling simply involves a lot of `if`-statements, which are not unlike real-life "what if" scenarios, as in "if this unexpected thing happened or value is received, tell the user an error happened and gracefully handle the situation by doing X." We will handle the exception raised by `int.parse()` in the Math Test program in this chapter.

We stored the result of what type of conversion the user wants to achieve via the variable `selection`. With this `switch`-statement, we use that variable to decide which of the two formulas to run. Notice that because of our `do-while`-loop, the `default` case will never apply. Both cases utilize string interpolation to calculate the output.

The first interpolation, `$temp`, places the value of the variable `temp` directly into the `String`. The second interpolation, contained within curly braces preceded by a dollar sign, `${...}`, performs calculations on the `temp` variable using Dart's built-in arithmetic operators and then inserts the results back into the `String` literal. In both cases, the `break` statement is required.

Temperature Converter may be the first program that you've written that does something legitimately useful. Unfortunately, with a command-line interface such as it has, it is unlikely that you would ever use it on a regular basis, especially since Google can do temperature conversion for you. On the other hand, perhaps it got you thinking about how you can solve real-world problems in your personal or professional life with the tools of programming.

The next two programs are rather math-heavy and are included to illustrate more Dart programming concepts, rather than to teach you anything about their underlying mathematics. If you don't understand the math, don't worry about it. Some people find this kind of math fun, while most people rather leave it to textbooks. If you fall into the latter category, feel free to skim some of the explanations, as long as you understand programming concepts such as `for`-loops, `if-else` blocks, and floating-point arithmetic (`doubles`). Pay particular attention to some new concepts introduced: constants, as well as the operators `+=` and `*=`.

The Monty Hall Problem

There was an old TV game show, hosted by a fellow named Monty Hall, that featured a segment during which a contestant was given a choice among three doors. Behind one of the doors lay a fantastic prize, while the other two concealed duds. The contestant was asked to pick a door. Then came a twist! After the contestant had picked a door, the host revealed what was behind one of the remaining two doors that did not conceal a prize. The contestant was finally offered to switch his selection in favor of the remaining door or retain the original choice.

The probability problem based on this scenario asks a simple question: Should a contestant in the same situation switch doors or keep the original choice? For example, if the contestant chose door number 1, and the host revealed that door number 2 does not contain the prize, should the contestant switch his guess to door number 3? Figure 4-1 illustrates the problem in the case of this particular scenario.

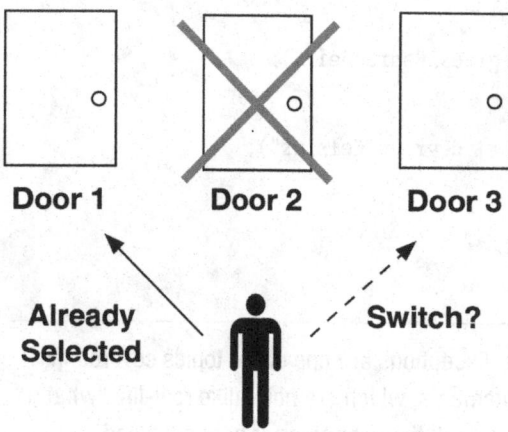

Figure 4-1. *The Monty Hall Problem*

Do you know the answer? Think about it for a minute before reading any further....

You may think that it does not make a difference whether the contestant switches doors or keeps the door that he originally chose, since there are two doors remaining, and, therefore, each has a 50% chance of containing the prize (one out of two). You would be correct if the door that was eliminated had never existed. However, it did exist, and its very existence and elimination changes the probability of one of the remaining doors.

The correct answer, probability-wise, is to switch doors. When the problem begins, there are three possible doors, each representing a one-third (33.3%) chance of concealing the prize. Our contestant chooses door 1, having a one-third chance of being right. In our particular scenario, therefore, it is useful to think of both doors 2 and 3 cumulatively representing two-thirds the chance of leading to the prize. After door 2 is eliminated, and knowing that doors 2 and 3 together represent two-thirds of the chance of yielding the prize, door 3 alone represents that two-thirds chance. Therefore, if the contestant switches to door 3, he has a two-thirds chance of winning the prize, while by staying with door 1, the contestant keeps his one-third chance. It is in the contestant's interest to switch.

Do you believe it is? Perhaps you don't, and you would be in good company. The Monty Hall Problem became notable because of just how many people got it wrong. The problem was featured (although it had already existed for decades) in a 1990 issue of *Parade* magazine. The author of a column titled "Ask Marilyn" received thousands of responses by mail regarding the problem, insisting that the "switch" solution was incorrect. She even claimed to have received about one thousand letters insisting the solution was incorrect from Ph.D.'s, including some in mathematics and statistics (they were incorrect, the switch is the right solution).[1]

---

[1]John Tierney, "Behind Monty Hall's Doors: Puzzle, Debate and Answer?" www.nytimes.com/1991/07/21/us/behind-monty-hall-s-doors-puzzle-debate-and-answer.html, July 21, 1991.

Programming can be used for simulating real-world situations, in order to arrive at a solution to a problem that would be tedious to work through without a computer. We can use Dart to prove to ourselves that switching doors is really the right solution to the Monty Hall Problem. In Listing 4-3, we do just that, by running a simulation of the problem one million times and calculating what percentage of the time switching leads to guessing the right answer. In our simulation, we always initially choose door 1. Door 2 or 3 is eliminated, and we always switch our guess to the remaining door. We then see what percentage of times we correctly guessed. Because we switched doors every time, we would expect this percentage to be approximately 66%, if switching really is better than staying with our initial choice of door 1, as the solution to the Monty Hall Problem implies.

Listing 4-3. The Monty Hall Problem

```dart
import 'dart:math';

void main() {
  const int TRIALS = 1000000;
  int correct = 0;
  Random rand = new Random();
  for (int i = 0; i < TRIALS; i++) {
    int randDoor = rand.nextInt(3) + 1;  //random door 1 to 3
    int guess = 1;  //we guess door 1
    int eliminated;

    if (randDoor == 2) {
      eliminated = 3;  //door 3 eliminated
    } else if (randDoor == 3) {
      eliminated = 2;  //door 2 eliminated
    } else {  //randDoor must be 1
      eliminated = rand.nextInt(2) + 2;  //door 2 or 3 randomly eliminated
    }

    if (eliminated == 2) {
      guess = 3;  //switch our guess to door 3
    } else if (eliminated == 3) {
      guess = 2;  //switch our guess to door 2
    }

    if (guess == randDoor) {
      correct++;
    }
  }
  print("The percentage of correct guesses was ${(correct / TRIALS) * 100}%");
}
```

Once again, as in Number Guessing Game, the dart:math package is used to get access to randomly generated integers. You should try running this program. Notice that the output occurs seemingly instantaneously. Think about what just happened. Your computer executed the code within the for-loop one million times—instantly. The next time that you see the hourglass or beach ball and you are waiting for something on your PC to complete, think about how much work it must be doing!

```dart
const int TRIALS = 1000000;
```

Here is something we have not seen before—a *constant*. Constants are values that cannot be changed. They are permanently set to what they are first initialized with. In this case, it would be illegal to later try to change the value of TRIALS. For example, the following would result in an error:

```
const int TRIALS = 1000000;
TRIALS = 5;   //ERROR: TRIALS cannot be changed
```

Constants are optimized because they can be evaluated before a program is even run. It is convention to name them in Dart with all capital letters. Multi-word Dart constants should be written with underscores (_) between the words. For example: THIS_IS_A_CONSTANT.

```
int randDoor = rand.nextInt(3) + 1;   //random door 1 to 3
```

Why is it necessary to add 1 to the result of rand.nextInt(3)? If you remember from Number Guessing Game, rand.nextInt() returns a number between 0 and the integer passed to it. We are passing 3 to it. Therefore, it will return an integer between 0 and 2. Our doors are labeled 1, 2, and 3. We want a random integer between 1 and 3. By adding 1 to whatever we get back from rand.nextInt(3), we will ensure that we have a number between 1 and 3.

```
if (randDoor == 2) {
  eliminated = 3;   //door 3 eliminated
} else if (randDoor == 3) {
  eliminated = 2;   //door 2 eliminated
} else {   //randDoor must be 1
  eliminated = rand.nextInt(2) + 2;   //door 2 or 3 randomly eliminated
}
```

Now it is time to remove one of the two doors that the contestant did not pick. Because the contestant picked door 1, we have to eliminate either door 2 or door 3. The door that contains the prize, randDoor, cannot be eliminated. Therefore, if the prize-revealing door is door 2, we should eliminate door 3. If the prize-revealing door is door 3, we should eliminate door 2. That is the logic that the first if-statement and the else if-statement implement.

However, if the prize is actually behind door 1 (randDoor is equal to 1), then we randomly choose to eliminate either door 2 or door 3. randDoor is either 1, 2, or 3. Therefore, because we check if it is door 2 or 3 in the if clause and the else if clause, we know it must be door 1, if we get to the else clause. To randomly select between door 2 and 3 for elimination in this case, we use the statement eliminated = rand.nextInt(2) + 2;. This is reminiscent of the addition of 1 to the random-number assignment of randDoor. However, in this case, rand.nextInt(2) will return an integer between 0 and 1 (so literally either 0 or 1). By adding 2, the randomly generated integer is either 2 or 3.

By the end of these three conditional clauses, a final decision has been made about which of doors 2 or 3 to eliminate. What still remains for our simulation is the switch. Since we will be switching every single time, the switch needs to occur based on which door was eliminated. Obviously, the door we switch to as our guess from door 1 must not be the door that was eliminated.

```
if (eliminated == 2) {
  guess = 3;   //switch our guess to door 3
} else {   //eliminated must be 3
  guess = 2;   //switch our guess to door 2
}
```

These five lines of code are very straightforward. We know that we selected eliminated to be either 2 or 3, so if it is not 2 (the else clause), then it is 3, and we should assign the remaining other door, 2, to guess. However, can you think of a shorter way to achieve the same result? Perhaps the same functionality as these five lines of code could be accomplished with just one line, as follows:

```
guess = 5 - eliminated;  //5-3 = 2 and 5-2 = 3
```

You can try removing the original five lines of code and replacing them with this one. You can then try running the program again. Do you notice any difference? You shouldn't. Although this is a more efficient way of writing our code, it is less readable. Except in situations where performance is critical, you should favor readability over efficiency in your programs. The 5 in the preceding example is what is known as a *magic number*. Magic numbers are integer or floating-point literals that appear in programs to help them operate correctly but with little explanation for their purpose. Magic numbers should almost always be avoided!

```
if (guess == randDoor) {
  correct++;
}
```

■ **Tip**   If you find yourself using a magic number in a program, it usually is better represented by a constant.

---

correct maintains a count of how many times switching led to choosing the right door. It is our ultimate indicator for the entire simulation. There is no need to modify it when our switch did not lead to revealing the right door, because we are ultimately implicitly maintaining the number of incorrect guesses with the expression iterations - correct available to us. Further, correct/iterations is the ratio of correct guesses that will allow us to calculate whether we are getting close to the 2/3 ratio that we expect.

```
print("The percentage of correct guesses was ${(correct / trials) * 100}%");
```

After looping one million times, our final result is calculated within a string interpolation and printed neatly to the console. Despite being a calculation based on two integer values, correct/iterations provides us with a floating-point (decimal) result. That result is multiplied by 100 to generate a proper percentage, and a % symbol is added on the end (outside of the calculation—in the actual string).

■ **Note**   Another type of division is integer division, where the result of two integers divided is also an integer. The result is rounded down. For example, 3/2 is equal to 1 in integer division. To perform integer division in Dart, use the ~/ operator. In what context might integer division be useful?

By now, you have probably run the program at least once, right? Are you surprised? It does indeed make more sense to switch doors than it does to stay with one's original choice. All of those Ph.D.'s were wrong! Of course, the result we get is not exactly 2/3. No randomly generated simulation will ever be exact, but it's pretty darn close. So, the next time you are on a game show, perhaps you will remember The Monty Hall Problem and win some money.

Pi Calculator

Pi (represented by the Greek letter π) is a magical number that you probably learned in middle school. It's useful for trigonometry and many other branches of mathematics. It represents the ratio between a circle's diameter and its circumference (circumference = diameter * pi). Pi is an irrational number and therefore cannot be represented exactly by a fraction. It also has an infinitely long decimal expansion that does not repeat. It has become something of a phenomenon for individuals with exceptional memories to memorize its decimal expansion for thousands of digits. Similarly, there has been a competition among computer scientists to calculate its decimal expansion the furthest. As of the writing of this book, the record is a calculation of pi to eight quadrillion digits.[2]

We are not going to attempt a very long calculation. In fact, our calculation will not even be very accurate. Conveniently, Dart includes pi as a constant in its `dart:math` package, so we have something to compare our result to. When we import the `dart:math` package, we can access pi by simply using `PI`. (Remember that thing about constants being all capitalized?) To test this, you can run the very short program in Listing 4-4.

Listing 4-4. Testing PI Constant in `dart:math`

```
import "dart:math";

void main() {
  print(PI);
}
```

You will see that the built-in pi value of 3.141592653589793 is printed. With this available to us, any calculation of pi we do is obviously just an exercise—not something useful. There are many methods for calculating pi. The one that we are going to use is called the Leibniz Formula for Pi and is named after the famous 17th-century mathematician Gottfried Leibniz (who discovered calculus at the same time as, but independently of, Isaac Newton). The formula is expressed as an infinite series that is equivalent to pi/4. Figure 4-2 shows this series.

$$\frac{1}{1} - \frac{1}{3} + \frac{1}{5} - \frac{1}{7} + \frac{1}{9} - \frac{1}{11} + \frac{1}{13} + \cdots = \frac{\pi}{4}$$

Figure 4-2. Leibniz Formula for Pi

Can you see the pattern in the series? The denominator of the added fractions increases continuously by 2, while the numerator remains 1. The fractions alternate between positive and negative. Each of the fractions is an operand in the equation. The further the series is continued, the more accurate it becomes at calculating pi. Listing 4-5 is a Dart version of the Leibniz Formula for Pi. It is simply a direct translation from mathematics to Dart code of the formula. In our program, we expand the series out to one hundred thousand operands via a `for`-loop.

---

[2]Daniel Cooper, "Researcher breaks Pi calculation record with the help of NVIDIA," www.engadget.com/2013/03/15/researcher-breaks-pi-record-with-nvidia/, March 15, 2013.

Listing 4-5. Pi Calculator

```dart
import 'dart:math';

void main() {
  const int ITERATIONS = 100000;   //the higher the more accurate
  double series = 1.0;
  double denominator = 3.0;
  double negate = -1.0;

  for (int i = 0; i < ITERATIONS; i++) {
    series += (negate * (1 / denominator));
    denominator += 2.0;
    negate *= -1.0;
  }

  double pi = 4 * series;
  print("We calculated pi as $pi");
  print("The real pi is $PI");
  print("We were off by ${PI - pi}");
}
```

series represents the total of the addition of all of the fractions in the series at any given time in the process of our computation. We initially set it to `1.0` because that is equivalent to the first fraction in the series, 1/1. denominator is the denominator of the fraction of each operand in the series. Because we already handled 1/1 with series, the first operand will be 1/3, so denominator is initially `3.0`. negate is a value that flips between -1.0 and 1.0. It is multiplied by the operand at each step of addition of the series to switch between addition and subtraction of the respective operand.

```dart
series += (negate * (1 / denominator));
```

This is the meat of the formula, the actual accumulation of a new operand into series during each iteration of the loop. A new operator is present that you have not seen before, +=. += is similar to ++. Instead of adding just 1 to a variable's value though, it adds whatever is on the right side of the operator. For example:

```dart
int total = 20;
total += 3;  //total is now 23
total = total + 3;  //this line is equivalent to the last line, now total is 26
```

In other words, this line of code is adding the result of (negate * (1 / denominator)) to the value referenced by series and storing the result of the addition back into series. (1 / denominator) is a representation of the operand. It can be thought of as one of the fractions in the Leibniz Formula. It is multiplied by negate in order to represent it as one of the positive or negative operands from the formula. The next two lines are actually about preparation for the next iteration of the loop and, therefore, the next operand.

```dart
denominator += 2.0;
negate *= -1.0;
```

denominator increases, as we would expect, by 2, each iteration of the loop. Notice that the type double is used for denominator and negate, even though they will only ever refer to whole numbers. Because they take part in floating-point multiplication and division they will be converted on the fly to floating-point values anyhow—but they could have been declared as integers, and it would not have affected the ultimate output of the program.

*= is another operator that we have not seen before. As you have probably guessed, it is similar to +=. It takes a value, multiplies it by another value, and the variable then references that new value. For example:

```
int total = 3;
total *= 2;  //total now refers to 6
total = total * 2;  //this line is equivalent to the last line, now total is 12
```

Therefore, the statement negate *= -1.0 is a mechanism for alternating the value referred to by negate between 1.0 and -1.0. Each iteration of the loop, it will either be representative of the calculation 1.0 * -1.0 or -1.0 * -1.0.

```
double pi = 4 * series;
print("We calculated pi as $pi");
print("The real pi is $PI");
print("We were off by ${PI - pi}");
```

Finally, to finish our implementation of the Leibniz Formula for Pi, we have to remember that the series from the formula is equal to pi/4. We therefore need to multiply its result by 4 to get an actual value of pi. String interpolation is used to print out both our calculated version of pi as well as the dart:math library's constant version of pi (represented by the completely capitalized PI). The final print() statement outputs the difference between these two versions.

The calculated version is off, but not by much. To get a more accurate (but, of course, more computationally complex and, therefore, longer to compute) value of pi, try increasing ITERATIONS by a couple orders of magnitude. Being able to express mathematical formulas as code is a skill that is incredibly helpful for scientists. Programming is increasingly becoming a must-have skill for researchers in biology, physics, and chemistry, not to mention the social sciences. It is hard to imagine major studies being done in the area of economics without software packages such as Stata and R that combine data manipulation with an internal programming language.

Math Test

Are you tired of all of the math yet? Hopefully not, because we have one more mathy program to go. However, this one does not require any special formulas or specific understanding. In fact, it's okay if you get all the math wrong for this one. It's just an arithmetic test, not unlike one you might have taken in elementary school. Listing 4-6 outlines the program "Math Test." Math Test is a fairly long program compared to the previous ones that we have looked at, but it's not significantly more complicated. Rather, it combines all of the concepts from the other programs into one tidy game. It utilizes dart:math for random number generation, and dart:io for user input from the keyboard.

Listing 4-6. Math Test

```
import 'dart:io';
import 'dart:math';

void main() {
  Random rand = new Random();
  int correctAnswer, userAnswer, operand1, operand2, operation;  //all ints
  int questionsAttempted = 0, numCorrect = 0;  //ints initialized

  while (true) {
    operation = rand.nextInt(3);   //random number 0, 1, or 2
    operand1 = rand.nextInt(11);   //random number 0-10
    operand2 = rand.nextInt(11);   //random number 0-10
```

```dart
    switch (operation) {
      case 0:  //addition question
        print("$operand1 + $operand2 = ");
        correctAnswer = operand1 + operand2;
        break;
      case 1:  //subtraction question
        print("$operand1 - $operand2 = ");
        correctAnswer = operand1 - operand2;
        break;
      case 2:  //multiplication question
        print("$operand1 * $operand2 = ");
        correctAnswer = operand1 * operand2;
        break;
      default:
        break;
    }

    String inTemp = stdin.readLineSync();

    try {
      userAnswer = int.parse(inTemp);
    } on FormatException {  //uh oh, could not be turned into integer
      print("Thanks for playing!");
      print("You got $numCorrect out of $questionsAttempted correct.");
      break;
    }

    if (userAnswer == correctAnswer) {  //right answer?
      numCorrect++;
      print("Correct!");
    } else {
      print("Wrong!");
    }

    questionsAttempted++;
  }
}
```

It is possible to declare more than one variable of the same type at a time. This is convenient simply for formatting and space purposes. It is also possible to initialize more than one variable at a time, again as long as they are of the same type.

```dart
int correctAnswer, userAnswer, operand1, operand2, operation;  //all ints
int questionsAttempted = 0, numCorrect = 0;  //ints initialized
```

The first line declares a large number of variables but does not initialize them. correctAnswer represents the answer that we are looking for from the user, while userAnswer represents the user's actual answer. operand1 and operand2 are the two numbers in the math equations that will be added, multiplied, or subtracted. operation is a random number that will determine which type of mathematical operation is actually performed. The second line initializes two variables that will be used for counting how many questions the user has tried to answer and how many the user has actually successfully answered correctly.

```
while (true) {
```

What does this mean!? A while-loop keeps executing as long as the boolean expression that is checked each iteration is true. In this case, it always will be! This is what is known as an *infinite loop*. An infinite loop is a loop that will never stop executing. Infinite loops can be bugs (indeed, they sometimes are the cause of computer crashes) or, in some instances, they can be useful. This is one of those useful instances.[3] We want our program to keep asking math questions until the user does not want to answer any longer. A break statement will immediately exit a loop.

```
operation = rand.nextInt(3);   //random number 0, 1, or 2
```

operation is not an operator like +, -, and * itself. It is instead a random number that will be used to select between +, -, and *. The switch-statement that follows it creates the math question and the answer based on which random number is represented by operation.

```
try {
  userAnswer = int.parse(inTemp);
} on FormatException {   //uh oh, could not be turned into integer
  print("Thanks for playing!");
  print("You got $numCorrect out of $questionsAttempted correct.");
  break;
}
```

When inTemp cannot be parsed as an integer, it will raise an exception. In Temperature Converter or Number Guessing Game, entering a non-integer would crash the program. By catching the exception here, we are avoiding that fate. Put another way, we are handling the error instead of letting it go unnoticed. Exceptions are one of the subjects covered in Chapter 12. All you need to know here is that when inTemp cannot be parsed (in other words, a FormatException is raised), the statements in the curly braces following on FormatException will be executed. Specifically, we interpret the user entering any text other than a number (therefore, text that cannot be parsed as an integer) as the user wanting to exit the program. The player's statistics are printed, and then the break statement does the actual exiting.

break is a statement that exits a loop. When a break is encountered, execution immediately moves to the next statement following the curly brace that closes the innermost loop. In this case, break will cause our infinite while loop to end. The if else block and the line incrementing questionsAnswered will both be skipped. When execution picks up, the main() function will already be at its end, and the program will naturally exit. Figure 4-3 illustrates the order of execution following the break statement, or if the FormatException is never raised.

---

[3]Technically, our loop is not truly infinite, because we do provide for a way to exit it... By definition, a true infinite loop would simply loop forever. A common place where such pseudo-infinite loops are used is in a so-called event loop. Event loops are pseudo-infinite loops where a program constantly checks for user input and executes an action if some such action has occurred. For example, an event loop may constantly check for mouse clicks. If a mouse click occurs, it sends a notification to some part of an app. Either way, it goes through another iteration checking for another mouse click. And then it goes around again.

```
try {
  userAnswer = int.parse(inTemp);
} on FormatException {  //uh oh, could not be turned into integer
  print("Thanks for playing!");
  print("You got $numCorrect out of $questionsAttempted correct.");
  break;
}

if (userAnswer == correctAnswer) {  //right answer?
  numCorrect++;
  print("Correct!");
} else {
  print("Wrong!");
}

questionsAttempted++;
}
}
```

Figure 4-3. Order of execution from break statement

The rest of Math Test consists of syntax and ideas that you have already seen in other programs. Can you imagine it with a timer and a nice HTML interface? It's not that far away from actually being a useful game for elementary school students. It's not that hard to create something useful with Dart after all. Soon you will have the skills necessary to create games your kids (or friends) will want to play.

Summary

The short programs in this chapter were intended to reinforce the concepts first outlined in Chapter 3. Programming is a discipline that very much embraces the concept of "learning by doing." The new concept of constants, the keyword const, the && operator, and the operators += and *= were also introduced. A value declared with const cannot be changed. It is defined completely at compile time (before the program is run). Constants are preferable to so-called magic numbers, number literals used in a program with little explanation. The && operator is for creating a boolean expression that is true if, and only if, the two sub-expressions surrounding it (one to its left and one to its right) are true. += and *= are operators that take a variable, perform addition or multiplication, respectively, on it and another value, and then store the results back in the variable. The method stdin.readLineSync() can be used to get input from the user's keyboard in a command-line program.

EXERCISES

1. Modify Number Guessing Game so that it allows the user to choose the range of the random number. Further modify it to allow the player to play again when the game is over.

2. Fix Temperature Converter so that it does not accept input temperatures from the user that cannot be translated into integers. You will have to borrow some code from Math Test.

3. Simulate the Monty Hall Problem with more than three doors. Does it still make sense to switch?

4. Turn the Monty Hall Problem into an interactive simulation whereby the user can select the initial door chosen instead of it always being door 1. The user should also be able to decide whether to switch or stay with his initial door choice.

5. Try some other values for ITERATIONS in Pi Calculator. How does it modify the accuracy of the ultimate pi calculation? How many ITERATIONS is too many (at what point does it take too long to compute)?

6. Try implementing a different formula for calculating pi. You should be able to find several more on the Web. The dart:math package includes several trigonometric functions that you might need.

7. Add division to Math Test. How can you handle the decimal numbers that occur when a question like 3/2 has an answer such as 1.5?

# CHAPTER 5

Functions

You may remember the concept of functions from a math course. Or, perhaps they are a completely foreign concept to you. Either way, they are one of the basic units used for organizing source code. In some programming languages, functions go by another name, such as subroutines or procedures. In Dart, functions can stand on their own or be a part of objects. In the latter case, they are known as methods and are covered in Chapter 10.

What Is a Function?

Functions are not strictly necessary to write programs. Indeed, other than using the main() function as an entry point for our programs, we have not actually been actively creating our own functions thus far. Although they are not *strictly* necessary, they certainly are necessary if one wants to keep one's sanity during the writing of a complex application.

Functions allow a program to be broken down into *callable units*. A callable unit is a portion of code that can be executed via an identifier (or "called") from another, not necessarily related, part of a program. For example, you may have a function that causes the computer to beep, logically called beep(). You may want the computer to beep both when the user hits the wrong key and when the user has a new e-mail message. You can call the same beep() function from both places. This saves you having to write the logic for doing the beep twice. It also keeps your code well-organized.

The smaller a function, the easier it is to reason about it. Further, it is easier to reason about an entire program that is logically broken up into many smaller functions than it is to reason about an equivalent program that is made up of just a few huge functions. Indeed, breaking up a large piece of code into several smaller functions can improve readability, ease of maintenance, and the ability to identify specific areas that are performance bottlenecks.

What does a function look like? Well, you have already seen the main() function. It looks like this:

```
main() {
  // main function's code goes here
}
```

The first part is the title of the function. In this case, that is main. After that, the parentheses are empty here, but in the next section, you will see that they can also contain parameters. The code between the curly braces is the meat of our function. That is the actual code that will be executed when our function is called. Here is another example for our hypothetical beep() function:

```
beep() {
  // code here to make the computer make a sound
}
```

You have also already seen function calls. The main() function is called by the system when our program starts executing, so we should never actually see it being called explicitly. However, a call to our beep() function may look something like:

```
beep();
```

You should notice that the only difference between a call of the beep() function and its original definition is that the call does not contain the function's definition (what is placed between the curly braces). If we had to redefine it to call it, there would be no convenience!

Function Parameters

Functions may have no parameters, as in the aforementioned beep() function. Does the beep() function need any information to determine how it works? Perhaps it does not. Actually, the beep() function may need to know how long it should play its sound for. In that case, we would need to provide it with that information. The information would be provided via a function parameter as in the following:

```
beep(int milliseconds) {
  // make a sound play for milliseconds of time
}
```

When beep() is later called with a certain number of milliseconds, it will then be its job to play a sound for that number of milliseconds. For example, we may call beep(500), which would be passing the integer literal 500 to beep() to fill in the parameter milliseconds. milliseconds will then be a local variable accessible within beep() that points to an integer with a value of 500.

Parameters can be any type. For example, we may want to create a function sayHello() that works with a String. Here is what that may look like:

```
sayHello(String name) {
  print("Hello, $name!");
}
```

The Locality of Variables

Function parameters become variables within a function. Variables within a function are a type of *local variables*. Local variables have a *scope* that is limited to the block of code within which they are defined. This means they can only be accessed from within that block. For example, the variables we have been defining in the main() function cannot be accessed in another function. Similarly, in the following code snippet, the variable name cannot be accessed in main():

```
someFunction() {
  String name = "Thomas";
}
main() {
  print(name);  // ERROR, name does not exist in this context
}
```

Variables can also be local to blocks of code that are within functions. A variable may be local to a for-loop, for example, and not accessible outside of it. Or, it could be local to an if-statement, switch-statement, etc. Here is a more complex example that illustrates locality further:

```
main() {
  for (int i = 0; i < 10; i++) {
    bool dog = true;

    if (dog) {
      int howMany = 100;
    }

    if (howMany == 100) {  // ERROR, howMany is only accessible within the if-statement above
      dog = false;
    }

    print("howMany is $howMany");  // ERROR, howMany is not accessible here either
  }

  if (dog) {  // ERROR dog is not accessible here, since it is local to the for-loop
    print("dog is true");
  }

  dog = true;  // ERROR dog is not accessible here either
}
```

Variables can also be declared outside of functions. In the case where they are, they are no longer local variables. A variable declared at the so-called top level of a Dart source file is accessible anywhere within it. For example, the following program is completely legal. You will notice that name2 is used in main(), which is declared before name2.

```
String name1 = "Tom";

sayHello(String name) {
  print("Hello, $name!");
}

main() {
  sayHello(name1);
  sayHello(name2);
}

String name2 = "John";
```

■ **Tip**   While top-level variables can be declared anywhere, it is considered good style to declare them at the beginning of a source code file, just after the imports of any packages.

Multiple Parameters

Functions need not be limited to zero or one parameter. They can contain any number of parameters. Our beep() function, may need to know which sound to play. Another parameter can provide that information.

```
beep(int milliseconds, String soundName) {...}  //... is used here to represent more code
```

Commas separate multiple function parameters. In general, it should be a goal to make a function as self-sufficient as possible. In other words, top-level variables are generally frowned upon when they are used in situations where the design could be better served by function parameters. Take a look at the following program and try to imagine how the top-level variable numberOfPrints could be eliminated in favor of a function parameter.

```
int numberOfPrints = 0;

printMany(String forPrinting) {
  for (int i = 0; i < numberOfPrints; i++) {
    print(forPrinting);
  }
}

main() {
  numberOfPrints = 10;
  printMany("I will not overuse top-level variables.");
}
```

You should take note that the for-loop in printMany() will execute numberOfPrints times. This design may seem simple enough for a small program of a few lines of code. In a more complex program, things will quickly become unwieldy when top-level variables are used inappropriately. What if numberOfPrints is changed by another function when we do not expect it to be? If there were 20 top-level variables, would it not be hard to keep track of which are being used where? Here is a better, cleaner, more compact version of the same program:

```
printMany(String forPrinting, int numberOfPrints) {
  for (int i = 0; i < numberOfPrints; i++) {
    print(forPrinting);
  }
}

main() {
  printMany("I will not overuse top-level variables.", 10);
}
```

Do you see why this is more logical? numberOfPrints is declared as a parameter of printMany(), since it will be accessed exclusively in printMany(). The goal is to associate a variable as closely as possible with the place in the program where it is utilized.

Function Return Values

Not only can functions receive information by way of parameters, they can also return information to their caller by way of a *return value*. The return value is preceded by the keyword return. The type of the return value can be indicated before the name of the function. For example, perhaps a function multiply() returns the product of two numbers.

```
int multiply(int num1, int num2) {
  int product = num1 * num2;
  return product;
}
```

In English, this function can be described as: "The function named multiply takes two integers as parameters and returns their product as an integer." How are return values used? They take the place of the function call in the code block where the function is called. That sounds a bit strange. We better look at an example with multiply().

```
main() {
  int result = multiply(5, 5);  // result will be equal to 25, the product returned by multiply
  print("2 multipled by 2 is ${multiply(2, 2)}");  // 4 is inserted for multiply(2, 2)
}
```

If no return type is specified in the definition of the function, then it can either return anything or return nothing. That sounds very ambiguous. It is good practice to specify a return type when a function will return a value.

```
multiply(int num1, int num2) {  // VALID code, but wouldn't it be less ambiguous to specify int?
  int product = num1 * num2;
  return product;
}
```

As we have seen in our previous examples, however, a function need not have any return type at all. In that case, the function's return type can simply be left blank. Alternatively, it can be specified explicitly that a function does not return a value with the keyword void.

```
void sayHello(String name) {  // void specifies this function does not return a value
  print("Hello, $name!");
}
```

This version of sayHello() is operationally completely equivalent to the previous version that we defined, but void explicitly indicates that it does not return a value. If a void function did return a value, that would be an error. Why is the keyword void useful if it is never required? Perhaps, like types in themselves, it is a helpful sanity check both for the programmer and the compiler. In other words, if we know we don't want a function to return a value, and we declare it void, it is good that we later get an error when we forget it is void and accidentally try to return a value.

■ **Note**   Technically in Dart, all functions have a return value, even if they are declared void. A void function, or a function with no return type specified (and nothing returned), has an implicit "return null;" appended to it by the system.

When a function reaches a return statement, it will immediately exit. No code in the function will be executed after a return statement is executed.

```
int luckyNumber() {
  return 7;  // function exits here
  print("I'm thinking of a number...");  // DEAD CODE, never executed
}
```

This can be useful when a function should exit prior to some large operation taking place. For example, perhaps a function already has enough information to produce its return value, so it does not need to keep executing a long loop. It can also be confusing if a function has too many different possible points of exit, and it cannot easily be determined which one will be followed. In other words, use `return` statements when they make sense, but not excessively.

Single-Line Functions

Dart has *syntactic sugar*[1] that makes it possible to declare short functions more compactly. The syntax => is used for separating the return type, name, and parameters of a single-line function from its implementation. As with regular functions, specifying the return type of a single-line function is optional. Single-line functions do not use `return` statements. Instead, the return value is implied. The evaluated result of the expression on the right of the => is the return value. The following are examples of some functions we saw earlier in the chapter, implemented as single-line functions:

```
sayHello(String name) => print("Hello, $name");  // just as valid as next version
void sayHello(String name) => print("Hello, $name");  // same as previous but with void
int multiply(int num1, int num2) => num1 * num2;  // think of as return num1 * num 2;
int luckyNumber() => 7;  // return is implied
```

Single-line functions are not inherently any more or less useful than their longer counterparts. They are simply another way of defining the same thing. They are supplied by the language for convenience.

Rock-Paper-Scissors

It's time to use our newfound knowledge of functions for a longer example program. Rock-paper-scissors is an old schoolyard game that can be used for quick decision making. In the usual setup, there are two players. After the chant of "Rock, Paper, Scissors, Shoot" both players show a hand gesture that either indicates a rock, a piece of paper, or a pair of scissors. Scissors beats paper, paper beats rock, and rock beats scissors. If the two players come up with the same gesture, then it is a tie. Figure 5-1 illustrates the game of rock-paper-scissors for the uninitiated.

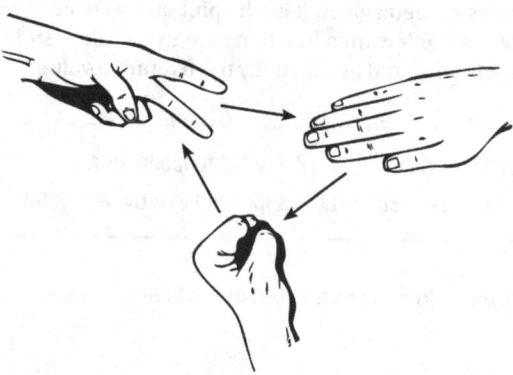

Figure 5-1. *The game of rock-paper-scissors*

---

[1]Syntax that makes it easy to do or express something in a programming language, typically with more compact language. For example, x *= 5 is syntactic sugar for the longer form x = x * 5. The operator *= can be thought of as a kind of syntactic sugar.

Create a new command-line application in Dart Editor. Call it "RockPaperScissors". Fill in rockpaperscissors.dart with the code in Listing 5-1.

Listing 5-1. rockpaperscissors.dart

```dart
import 'dart:io';
import 'dart:math';

/// Get a player move via keyboard input
/// If the player does not enter a valid move
/// return "Quit" so that the main game loop
/// knows to end the game
String getPlayerMove() {
  print("Would you like (R)ock, (P)aper, or (S)cissors?");
  String selection = stdin.readLineSync().toUpperCase();

  switch (selection) {
    case "R":
      return "Rock";
      break;
    case "P":
      return "Paper";
      break;
    case "S":
      return "Scissors";
      break;
    default:   // if anything but R, P, or S
      return "Quit";
      break;
  }
}

/// Return a random move in the form of a string of either
/// "Rock", "Paper", or "Scissors"
String getComputerMove() {
  Random rand = new Random();
  int move = rand.nextInt(3);   //random int from 0 to 2

  switch (move) {
    case 0:
      return "Rock";
      break;
    case 1:
      return "Paper";
      break;
    case 2:
      return "Scissors";
      break;
    default:
      break;
  }
}
```

```
/// Determine if the player or the computer won
/// by comparing [playerMove] to [computerMove]
String whoWon(String playerMove, String computerMove) {
  if (playerMove == computerMove) {  //if the same, it's a tie
    return "Tie";
  } else if (playerMove == "Rock" && computerMove == "Scissors") {
    return "You Win!";
  } else if (playerMove == "Scissors" && computerMove == "Paper") {
    return "You Win!";
  } else if (playerMove == "Paper" && computerMove == "Rock") {
    return "You Win!";
  } else {  // if it's not a tie and you didn't win, computer won
    return "Computer Wins!";
  }
}

void main() {
  while(true) {  // main game loop (quasi infinite loop)
    print("Rock, Paper, Scissors Shoot!");
    String playerMove = getPlayerMove();

    if (playerMove == "Quit") {
      return;  // returning from void function exits it
    }

    print("You played $playerMove");
    String computerMove = getComputerMove();
    print("Computer played $computerMove");
    print(whoWon(playerMove, computerMove));
  }
}
```

There is no syntax in this program that you have not seen before. Instead, spend your time looking at how the program is split into functions and how calling those functions works. main() consists of a quasi-infinite loop that:

- Calls the function getPlayerMove() to get the player's move selection via keyboard input

- Exits the program (with a return statement) if getPlayerMove() returns "Quit"

- Calls getComputerMove() to get a randomly generated computer move

- Calls whoWon() with both moves to determine who won

How does the return statement exit the main() function? return from a void function immediately moves execution from the line of the return back to the caller of the function. Since main() is called by the system, you can think of a return from main() as returning control to the system.

Did you understand the logic behind the giant if-block in whoWon()? If the two players have chosen the same option, then the game is a tie. Then the block checks all of the possible types of wins for the human player. If the game is neither a tie nor a win for the human player, then we know that it must be a win for the computer—hence the purpose of the else-block.

The key to rock-paper-scissors is that, unlike the programs of Chapter 4, the logic of the program is cleanly split between several different functions that interoperate. This is a far superior design in comparison to a giant main() function. Of course rock-paper-scissors could be implemented as a giant main() function. It just would be more of a mess.

■ **Note**   Did you notice the three slashes before some of the comments in rock-paper-scissors (///)? Previously, all comments were preceded by two slashes. Three slashes are used for documentation purposes. Comments before a function with three slashes will be included by the Dart compiler in automatically generated documentation. Further, any identifiers in the code that are included in a three-slash comment with square brackets ([ ]) around them will be linked in documentation automatically. Another special type of comment used for documentation purposes begins with /** and ends with */. It is equivalent to the /// syntax, but the comment can extend multiple lines.

For more information about Dart's special syntax for documentation (known as Dart Doc), check out the article "Guidelines for Dart Doc Comments," by Kathy Walrath, on the `dartlang.org` web site. You can find it at: `https://www.dartlang.org/articles/doc-comment-guidelines/`.

Optional Parameters

Functions in Dart can have optional parameters. Optional parameters are parameters that the function caller can choose not to supply. It can be checked from within a function whether an optional parameter was supplied with a value or not. Optional parameters can also have default values; therefore, if values for them are not supplied, they will still be usable within the function. This is often a more logical way to go vs. having the necessity to check if an optional parameter was supplied with a value. There are two types of optional parameters: positional and named.

Optional parameters are useful in instances when you want to make a function more flexible while at the same time maintaining a simple version for basic-use cases. Optional parameters are not an excuse to write very large functions. While a function with many optional parameters can be very flexible, it can also be intimidating, with all of the options that it provides. If you find yourself writing a function with many parameters, you may want to consider whether it would be better served as two (or more) functions.

Positional Optional Parameters

Positional optional parameters are defined with square brackets within a function definition. For example, the following function repeat() has an optional parameter called repetitions.

```
void repeat(String word, [int repetitions]) {  // repetitions is optional
  if (repetitions != null) {  // check if repetitions was supplied
    for (int i = 0; i < repetitions; i++) {
      print(word);
    }
  } else {  // repetitions was not supplied, so just print once
    print(word);
  }
}
```

The != operator is used here to check whether the optional parameter repetitions was supplied. If an optional parameter is not supplied a value, and it does not have a default value, then it will have the value null. In the case of repeat(), it will print word repetitions times, if repetitions is supplied. If repetitions is not supplied, it will print word just one time. This function can be simplified by using a default value for repetitions.

```
void repeat(String word, [int repetitions = 1]) {
  for (int i = 0; i < repetitions; i++) {
    print(word);
  }
}
```

This version of repeat() is completely equivalent to the previous version, but both the if clause and the else clause have been eliminated. There is no special case when repetitions is not supplied, because we will always have a value for repetitions. The = operator is used within the square brackets to set the default value of an optional positional parameter.

Commas separate multiple optional positional parameters. When a function with optional positional parameters is called, its optional parameters must be supplied in the same order that they are defined.

```
void repeat(String word, [int repetitions = 1, String exclamation = ""]) {
  for (int i = 0; i < repetitions; i++) {
    print(word + exclamation);  // the + operator can concatenate strings
  }
}
void main() {
  repeat("Dog");  // legal
  repeat("Dog", 2, "!");  // legal
  repeat("Dog", 2);  // legal
  repeat("Dog", "!");  // ILLEGAL
  repeat("Dog", "!", 2);  // ILLEGAL
}
```

As can be seen from this example's comments, when it comes to optional positional parameters, order matters. Both optional parameters do not need to be supplied, but whether one or two is supplied, they must be supplied in the right order. exclamation cannot be provided without repetitions being supplied first. There's also a new use of a symbol we have seen before, +. + is used in this example as a *string concatenation* operator. String concatenation is the act of putting two strings together. When + is placed between two strings, the result in Dart will be a new string that combines them from left to right.

Named Optional Parameters

Named optional parameters are very similar to positional optional parameters, but they are defined and called differently. When a function with them is called, the order they are supplied with does not matter. They are defined with curly braces {} and colons to separate their name from their default value. Like positional optional parameters, commas separate them. Also like positional optional parameters, they do not need to have default values. In cases when named optional parameters are not supplied with a value, they will also have a default value of null.

```
void repeat(String word, {int repetitions: 1, String exclamation: ""}) {
  for (int i = 0; i < repetitions; i++) {
    print(word + exclamation);  // the + operator can concatenate strings
  }
}

void main() {
  repeat("Dog");  // legal
  repeat("Dog", repetitions: 2, exclamation: "!");  // legal
  repeat("Dog", repetitions: 2);  // legal
  repeat("Dog", exclamation: "!");  // legal, even without repetitions
  repeat("Dog", exclamation: "!", repetitions: 2);  // legal, even out of order
}
```

Although they are more verbose than positional optional parameters, named optional parameters are also slightly more flexible, because of their indifference toward order. You will also notice that with named optional parameters, we can provide a value for exclamation without providing a value for repetitions. We could not do that with positional optional parameters.

Functions as First-Class Citizens

When it is said that a programming language supports functions as so-called first-class citizens, it means four things.

- Functions can be referred to by their name in the program.

- Functions can be passed as arguments to other functions.

- A function can be returned as the result (return value) of another function.

- Functions can be included in data structures.[2]

This is true in Dart. Functions in Dart need not just be called—they can also be passed to other functions. In such a scenario, one function would have a parameter that it expects to be another function. The caller of said function would supply it with the title of the function that it wants to pass. This sounds more confusing than it really is.

```dart
void talkAbout(String toShout, shoutFunc) {
  print(shoutFunc(toShout));
}

String exclame(String toExclame)  => toExclame + "!";

String manyTalk(String toMany) {
  String allTogether = "";
  for (int i = 0; i < 10; i++) {
    allTogether = allTogether + toMany;  // keep concatenating onto the end of allTogether
  }
  return allTogether;
}

void main() {
  talkAbout("Hello", exclame);
  talkAbout("TicToc", manyTalk);
}
```

exclame() is a simple one-line function that appends an exclamation point onto the end of a String and returns the result. manyTalk() concatenates ten of the same String together and returns the result. Both of them take a String and return a String. They can therefore both be used in talkAbout(). main() can pass either one to talkAbout() by simply using its title.

Generally, one function can be substituted for another when they have the same *signature*. A function's signature is defined by the combination of its parameters' types and its return type.

We're not going to look at returning functions from functions, because, frankly, at this point in your journey with Dart, you would have little use for such functionality, and it would probably confuse you more than help you. We will discuss more about functions being used as parts of data structures when we start looking at the idea of object-oriented programming in Chapter 10.

---

[2]Harold Abelson, Gerald Jay Sussman, and Julie Sussman *Structure and Interpretation of Computer Programs – Second Edition* (Cambridge, MA: MIT, 1996), Section 1.3.

Functions Within Functions

Functions can be defined within other functions. These, too, can be referenced by variables and passed to other functions. Let's put both of the utility functions from our last example within main().

```
void talkAbout(String toShout, shoutFunc) {
  print(shoutFunc(toShout));
}

void main() {
  String exclame(String toExclame)  => toExclame + "!";

  String manyTalk(String toMany) {
    String allTogether = "";
    for (int i = 0; i < 10; i++) {
      allTogether = allTogether + toMany;  // keep concatenating toMany onto the end of itself
    }
    return allTogether;
  }

  talkAbout("Hello", exclame);
  talkAbout("TicToc", manyTalk);
  talkAbout("Wow", (String s) => s.toUpperCase());  // a function with no title!?
}
```

Did you notice the *anonymous function* in the last line of main()? That's right, a function with no title to identify it is known as an *anonymous function*. Dart allows the definition of anonymous functions, even within a function call, as above. Anonymous functions are useful in situations where a function does not need to be called from multiple parts of a program by its identifier, or where they simply make sense stylistically. For example, perhaps a function takes another function as a parameter. If the function that is going to be passed to it is particularly small, it may look more "clean" to implement it as an anonymous function than to create a separate full-fledged function. When talkAbout() runs from this call, the identifier shoutFunc will refer to this anonymous function, and it will be callable through shoutFunc().

Recursive Functions

Recursion is a topic that many new programmers struggle with. You will not need an extensive understanding of recursion to complete this book, so if you don't get it, just keep moving. Simply put, *a recursive function is a function that calls itself*. If you think about it, this is not completely dissimilar (although it's certainly not the same) from the concept of loops that we learned in Chapter 3. A recursive function is used for repeating code. If the state of the function does not change, and it has no preset exit condition that is reached, a recursive call can turn into an infinite loop.

```
void forever() {
  forever();
}
```

forever() is indeed an infinite loop. Here is a recursive function that will repeatedly add one String to another String.

```
String addOn(String original, String additional, int times) {
  if (times <= 0) {  // exit condition to end "recursive loop"
    return original;
  }
  return addOn(original + additional, additional, times - 1);  // recursive call
}
```

Let's work through a call of addOn("Hello", "!", 2).

- The first time addOn() is called original is set to "Hello", additional is set to "!", and times is set to 2.

  - times is not less than or equal to zero.

  - addOn() is called again via a return statement.

- This time around, original is set to "Hello!" (through string concatenation via the + operator), additional is again set to "!", and times is set to 1.

  - Once again, times is not less than or equal to zero.

- Finally, addOn() is called with original set to "Hello!!", additional set to "!", and times set to 0.

  - In this final iteration, times is equal to zero, so the if-statement is true and original, which is set to "Hello!!" is returned.

Table 5-1 illustrates addOn("Hello", "!", 2) through each iteration.

Table 5-1. *The Iterations of addOn("Hello", "!", 2")*

Iteration	original	additional	times	times <= 0
1	"Hello"	"!"	2	false
2	"Hello!"	"!"	1	false
3	"Hello!!"	"!"	0	true

addOn() demonstrates that recursive functions need two things to be effective:

- A base case: this is a clear end-state that is checked for such as with if (times <= 0)

- A recursive case: this ends with a recursive call with a change of state, such as addOn(original + additional, additional, times - 1)

Any situation that is not a base case should be a recursive case.

Anything that can be accomplished with recursion can also be accomplished with iterative code (loops and conditionals). In many cases, the iterative code will also be more performant, since each recursive call of a function requires that new memory be set aside for all of its parameters/local variables. There are instances when recursive code can be more performant. Recursive code can also be more compact and elegant than iterative solutions to the same problems. Compilers for some programming languages are talented at optimizing recursive code. An in-depth study of recursion is beyond the scope of this book, but an introductory book on computer science, such as the classic, *Structure and Interpretation of Computer Programs* by Harold Abelson, Gerald Jay Sussman, and Julie Sussman (MIT, 1996), may be helpful, if you are interested. For a book-length discussion of recursion, check out *Thinking Recursively* by Eric S. Roberts (Wiley, 1986).

Fibonacci Sequence

The Fibonacci sequence is a sequence of numbers where any two adjacent numbers added together are equal to the next number in the sequence. For example, the fourth and fifth numbers in the sequence (if we consider the sequence to be 0 indexed) are 2 and 3, respectively, so the sixth number is 5 (2 + 3). The seventh number is 8, since the fifth and sixth numbers are 3 and 5 (3 + 5). It was made famous by 13th-century Italian mathematician Leonardo Fibonacci. A classical recursive problem for programmers is to write a function fib(n) that will generate the nth number in the Fibonacci sequence. Figure 5-2 shows the sequence itself. Figure 5-3 is a mathematical definition for the formula that generates the sequence for all n >= 2. It simply says that any number in the sequence is equal to the sum of the two numbers before it, as was discussed earlier in this paragraph.

0, 1, 1, 2, 3, 5, 8, 13, 21, 34, 55, 89, 144, 233, 377, …

Figure 5-2. *Fibonacci sequence*

$$fib(n) = fib(n-2) + fib(n-1)$$

Figure 5-3. *Formula for Fibonacci sequence where n >= 2*

Now it's time to code a function that can generate any chosen element of the Fibonacci sequence. Let's first try to understand the base case. We have a formula that is only useful for n >= 2. It is natural, then, to think that n = 0 and n = 1 must be special cases. They are, in fact, our base cases. fib(0) is just 0, and fib(1) is just 1. We need to hard-code them. Listing 5-2 is a Dart implementation of a recursive program to solve fib(n). You will see that the if-statement encodes these base cases. The recursive case is a simple restatement of the formula in Figure 5-3.

Listing 5-2. Fibonacci Sequence

```
import 'dart:io';

/// Find the nth term in the Fibonacci sequence
int fib(int n) {
  if (n < 2) {  // base case
    return n;
  }
  return fib(n - 2) + fib(n - 1);  // recursive case
}

void main() {
  int n;

  print("What n do you want to lookup in the Fibonacci sequence?");
  String inTemp = stdin.readLineSync();

  try {
    n = int.parse(inTemp);
  } on FormatException {  // uh oh, could not be turned into integer
    print("That was not an integer.");
    return;
  }

  print("fib($n) = ${fib(n)}");
}
```

Although this program works, it's highly inefficient. Every call of `fib()` for n >= 2 results in two more calls of `fib()` because of the recursive case. Therefore, the number of calls to `fib()` grows exponentially by a power of 2. Don't try any values of n greater than 50, unless you have a lot of time or a supercomputer at your disposal.

Factorial

Do you remember what a factorial is? It's the multiplication of all the positive integers counting up toward a positive integer. In other words, 5 factorial (denoted 5!) is the product 1 * 2 * 3 * 4 * 5. The short program in Listing 5-3, similar in structure to the Fibonacci Sequence program, showcases both recursive and iterative methods for calculating a factorial, so that you can compare the two.

Listing 5-3. Factorial

```dart
import 'dart:io';

/// Calculate n! recursively.
int factorial(int n) {
  if (n <= 1) {  // base case
    return 1;
  }
  return n * factorial(n - 1);  // recursive case
}

/// Calculate n! with a for-loop
int factorial2(int n) {
  int total = 1;
  for (int i = n; i > 0; i--) {  // working backwards
    total *= i;
  }
  return total;
}

void main() {
  int n;

  print("What factorial do you want to calculate??");
  String inTemp = stdin.readLineSync();

  try {
    n = int.parse(inTemp);
  } on FormatException {  // uh oh, could not be turned into integer
    print("That was not an integer.");
    return;
  }

  if (n <= 0) {  // check for bad input
    print("That's not a positive integer!");
    return;
  }
```

```
    print("n! = ${factorial(n)} calculated recursively.");
    print("n! = ${factorial2(n)} calculated iteratively.");
}
```

Of course factorial() and factorial2() should always return the same result. If they don't, we have a problem! factorial() is not a performance hog like fib(). Feel free to try this program out with a large number.

FUNCTIONAL PROGRAMMING LANGUAGES

There are several different programming paradigms. Perhaps you've come across the terms *object-oriented* or *procedural* in the past. Perhaps not. You can think of a programming paradigm as a style of getting things done. Sherlock Holmes, Adrian Monk, and Hercule Poirot are all great detectives. Perhaps all of them are capable of solving any case. Yet, they each have their own style that will make each of them especially suited for certain cases. Programming paradigms are similar. They all can solve the same set of problems, yet one may be better suited than another for solving a particular problem.

The most popular programming paradigms today are object-oriented, procedural, and functional. Object-oriented programming is the topic of Chapters 10 and 11. Procedural is pretty much how we've been programming thus far—breaking up our programs into logical subunits that contain statements that alter the state of the program. Functional programming is something different.

In a purely functional programming language, there is little or no modification of state. The values that variables refer to cannot be changed; they are *immutable*[3]. Functions have no side effects (they do not change anything outside of themselves). Making the same function call will always result in the same result, if the arguments provided to the function are exactly the same. Functional programming languages tend to eschew loops in favor of recursive functions. It's certainly a different way of thinking.

Popular functional programming languages include Scheme and Haskell. Dart can be programmed in a functional style, if one chooses, but unlike a true functional programming language, it does not enforce the style in any way. Dart is a multi-paradigm language in that it can be used in a procedural, functional, or object-oriented style. As you will see, though, Dart is probably most at home when used with an object-oriented style.

Summary

Functions are some of the fundamental building blocks used to write programs. They take input in the form of parameters and provide output in the form of a return value. They can be called multiple times via their identifier (name). Functions are important not only as a computational tool, but also as a means of organizing source code. Code should be divided as much as possible into small, easily understandable functions. Single-line functions are syntactic sugar for defining small functions. Optional parameters provide function callers with increased flexibility. Recursive functions can be conceptually difficult to understand, but once grasped, can provide cleaner solutions to certain problems. + is not only used for addition; it is also the string concatenation operator. Functions can appear within other functions—Inception!

---

[3]An immutable variable is one whose value cannot be changed after it is created. A *mutable* variable's value can be changed.

EXERCISES

1. Rewrite the Temperature Converter program from Chapter 4 with functions.

2. Change rock-paper-scissors so that it can be played against another human opponent. Each player's selections need to somehow be hidden. Perhaps clearing the screen with a lot of blank lines could work?

3. *Refactor* (a software development term for *rewrite more cleanly*) Math Test from Chapter 4, using the concept of functions as first-class citizens. Each operation, +, -, * should be a separate function.

4. Write a new version of the Fibonacci Sequence program that does not use a recursive function as a solution. Can you think of an iterative solution? If you can't, you can find one quickly on the Web that you can easily translate into Dart code.

5. Write a function for checking if a number is prime. You will need to use the % operator. If x % y == 0, then when x is divided by y (x / y), there is no remainder. Write a second function that calculates the first n prime numbers that uses the first function.

CHAPTER 6

■■■

Data Structures

Data structures are a means of organizing information for storage and retrieval. This chapter's title is a bit of a misnomer, since it's not really about the concept of data structures in general (or how they work), but, rather, three specific data structures built into Dart. Dart's Lists and Maps will likely be sufficient for 95% of your future data structure needs. Dart provides specialized syntax for working with each. Sets are good for data in which all the elements need to be unique. Learning to use these data structures effectively will be key to your success with the Dart language.

Lists

Lists are useful for storing information sequentially. That information may be sorted or unsorted. It can be of any type. It can be of any length. Up to this point in the book, we have been storing single pieces of information via individual variables. With Lists, we can for the first time store multiple pieces of information in one place.

What are some real-world collections of information that can be modeled with a List? Perhaps a shopping list? Perhaps a to-do list? Anything with the word *list* in it, surely. Let's think more abstractly. How about the amino acids in a strand of DNA? How about the landmarks that are passed on the way to the mall? In English, we may think of these latter examples more as "sequences" than as "lists." The difference between these two terms is that in English, a sequence is generally ordered, whereas a list may or may not be. All of these are appropriate for storage in a Dart List.

Even though we may not care about the ordering of a particular Dart List, all Lists are inherently ordered. Every element in a List has an *index*. An element's index is an integer representing its position in the List. Interestingly, the first element in a List is given the index 0. This is known as zero-indexing. After that first element, each of the following elements has an index that increases by one. So, the first element will have index 0; the second element will have index 1; the third element will have index 2; etc. Later in this chapter, we will see why this zero-indexed numbering scheme is useful.

A List can be created with any number of elements (including zero, an empty List). Elements can later be added or removed. Items within a List can also be changed without needing to be taken out and put back in. Enough talking about Lists; let's see them in action.

■ **Note** In several other programming languages, arrays are the basic data type used for organizing information that is organized in Dart using a List. A Dart List, for most intents and purposes, is equivalent.

List Syntax

Dart Lists make extensive use of square brackets, [ ], for both defining List literals and referencing individual elements. An empty List is simply a list that contains no elements. We can create an empty List in many different ways. All of the following are equivalent ways of creating an empty List.

```
List ex1 = [];  // [] is literal syntax for an empty List
var ex2 = [];   // variable declared without a type
List ex3 = new List();  // we've seen the new keyword before, for creating Random objects
var ex4 = new List();
```

Lists can also be created pre-populated with elements. To do this, we use List literals, which again use square brackets. Commas separate individual elements.

```
List ex5 = [12, 15, 26];  // List literal which contains three integer literals
List ex6 = ["hello", "hi", "howdy", "hey"];  // List with 4 elements, all Strings
List ex7 = ["hello", 5, "do it", 23.26];  // notice the mixed types of the various elements
int x = 99;
String s = "ninety nine";
List ex8 = [x, s];  // List literal made from variables
```

The indexes of elements defined with a List literal are numbered from left to right. What's the index of "hello" in the List ex7? Remember that zero-indexing thing? It's 0. What's the index of 23.26 in ex7? It's 3. Indexes are important because they are the easiest way to refer to specific elements within a List. Of course, the square brackets play a role again. ex7[0] refers to the 0th element in the List ex7. Therefore, ex7[0] refers to "hello". ex7[3] refers to 23.26.

The length of a List refers to the number of elements in it. It does not matter what the value of those elements is. The length of ex5 is 3. The length of an empty list, like ex1, is 0. The length of ex7 is 4. The length of a List can be obtained with the length property, such as in the code snippets ex5.length or ex7.length. You will observe that the last element in a List will always have an index that is one less than its length. Combining our newfound knowledge of referring to an element in a List by its index, and determining the length of a List, we can now use for-loops to iterate through a List and do something with each of its elements.

```
List greetings = ["hello", "hi", "howdy", "hey"];
for (int i = 0; i < greetings.length; i++) {  // notice the < operator here...
  print(greetings[i]);
}
```

Let's think carefully about the variable i. It will be used to refer to the index of the element in greetings that we want to pull. It starts at 0, which makes sense, since Lists are zero-indexed. i will be continually increased by 1. Notice that we iterate while i is less than greetings.length. This is important because there is no element in greetings at the index that greetings.length represents. Trying to refer to greetings[greetings.length], or greetings[4], or greetings[i] after i is set to 4 would be an error. With zero-indexing, we know that the index of the last element in a List will always be one less than its length.

Dart also has a convenient type of loop called a for-in-loop (or for-each-loop, in some languages). It can be used for quickly and simply iterating through all of the elements of a List. Here is the last example rewritten with a for-in-loop.

```
List greetings = ["hello", "hi", "howdy", "hey"];
for (String greeting in greetings) {  // greeting will refer to each element of greetings
  print(greeting);
}
```

There are no fine-grained controls with this type of loop—it will always loop through every element of the List in question until the loop ends or we break out of it. greeting will in turn refer to each and every element of greetings. A for-loop that iterates via indexes, as in the previous example, is more useful in situations in which we want only to iterate partially through a List. In such a case, a particular range of indexes can be specified. Or, perhaps we want to go backward through a List. Instead of incrementing the index variable (i in this example), we can simply decrement it.

```
for (int i = greetings.length - 1; i >= 0; i--) {...}  // backwards, notice that we must use >=
```

It is very easy to add elements onto the end of a List after it is created. List objects have a method called add() that will append an element to the end of a List, therefore simultaneously increasing its length by one. Another method, remove(), will remove the first instance of an element occurring in the List (compared by value).

```
List dogsOwned = ["Cocker Spaniel", "Springer Spaniel", "Golden Retriever", "Poodle"];
dogsOwned.add("Black Lab");
//dogsOwned is ["Cocker Spaniel", "Springer Spaniel", "Golden Retriever", "Poodle", "Black Lab"]
dogsOwned.remove("Springer Spaniel");
//dogsOwned is ["Cocker Spaniel", "Golden Retriever", "Poodle", "Black Lab"]
dogsOwned.add("Poodle");
//dogsOwned is ["Cocker Spaniel", "Golden Retriever", "Poodle", "Black Lab", "Poodle"]
dogsOwned.remove("Poodle");
//dogsOwned is ["Cocker Spaniel", "Golden Retriever", "Black Lab", "Poodle"]
```

Finally, Lists utilize a feature of Dart known as *generics* (covered in detail in Chapter 12) to enable the specification of the type of elements that a List will contain. So far, the Lists that we have been working with have been able to hold elements of any type. In fact, they can even hold elements of more than one type (ex7, ex8). Here are some examples of Lists that can only hold a specific type. You will quickly catch on to the syntax.

```
List<int> myNums = [0, 1, 1, 2, 3, 5, 8, 13];  // recognize this sequence?
List<String> myStrings = ["strawberry", "lavender", "aqua", "violet"];
List<String> myBad = ["strawberry", 13, "lavender", 8];  // WRONG can only holds Strings
List<List<int>> myListOfLists = [[1, 2, 3], [4, 5, 6]];  // a List of Lists!
List<int> myNums2 = new List<int>();
myNums2.add(5);  // we can only add ints to myNums2
```

myNums and myStrings should be fairly self-explanatory. myBad is not correct (although it will run; see the following Note) because it declares with <String> that it will only hold Strings, yet it's defined with both Strings and ints. myListOfLists is pretty meta! It's a List that contains other Lists...Ya dig?

■ **Note**   Dart does not enforce generics in production. That's right; in production, Dart will not stop a List<int> from having Strings added to it. What's the point, then? To catch the unexpected behavior before it happens, while still in development (Dart will show a warning).

Birthday Paradox

It's time to simulate another paradox. This one requires quite a bit less explanation than The Monty Hall Problem. There are 365 days in a year. Yet, if we put just 23 random people into a room, there is a 50% chance that two of them will have the same birthday (not year, though, of course). It's called the Birthday Paradox. Do you believe it? Perhaps it will have to be proven to you. Listing 6-1, Birthday Paradox, is the proof.

In the following simulation of the Birthday Paradox, we will be using dates. Dates can be represented in Dart using DateTime objects. We construct DateTimes by providing a year, month, and day to represent the date in question. We will be using the same year for all of the dates, since we don't really care about the year (we're interested in the rest of the date). We will randomly generate integers for the month (1–12) and day of the month (1–28). Our day of the month will be a random number between 1 and 28 for simplicity's sake, since the shortest month has 28 days. We could write more code and generate the right random number for each month of the year, but it would make the example program a little longer than it needs to be. We'll leave that to the exercises at the end of the chapter. Of course, this use of 28 slightly changes the probabilities, but it's close enough.

Our strategy is to generate 23 random birthdays and store them in a List. We then check if the List has any duplicates. If it does, then we increase a counter called matches. We do the whole thing over and over again ITERATIONS times. The Birthday Paradox is true if the number of times there was a duplicate birthday is approximately 50% of the total times that we run the simulation (in other words, we expect matches / ITERATIONS to be about 0.5).

Listing 6-1. Birthday Paradox

```dart
import "dart:math";

/// Returns a List with 23 randomly
/// generated birthdays in it
List<DateTime> generateBirthdays() {
  List<DateTime> birthdays = new List<DateTime>();
  Random r = new Random();
  const int YEAR = 1987;
  const int NUM_MONTHS = 12;
  const int NUM_DAYS = 28;  // For simplicity we limit to 28
  const int BIRTHDAYS_TO_GENERATE = 23;

  for (int i = 0; i < BIRTHDAYS_TO_GENERATE; i++) {
    int randMonth = r.nextInt(NUM_MONTHS) + 1;  // random number 1-12
    int randDay = r.nextInt(NUM_DAYS) + 1;  // random number 1-28
    birthdays.add(new DateTime(YEAR, randMonth, randDay));
  }
  return birthdays;
}

/// Returns true if [l] has duplicate elements
/// Otherwise returns false
bool containsDuplicates(List l) {
  for (int i = 0; i < l.length; i++) {
    if (l.skip(i + 1).contains(l[i])) {  // check if rest of l contains i
      return true;
    }
  }
  return false;
}

void main() {
  const int ITERATIONS = 10000;
  List<DateTime> birthdays;
  int matches = 0;
```

```
for (int i = 0; i < ITERATIONS; i++) {
  birthdays = generateBirthdays();  //new list of birthdays each iteration
  if (containsDuplicates(birthdays)) {
    matches++;
  }
}

print("There were at least two people with the same birthday ${(matches / ITERATIONS) * 100}% of
the time.");
}
```

generateBirthdays() creates a List with 23 elements, all of which are DateTime objects representing randomly generated birthdays within the same year. A lot of constants are used to avoid the placement of magic numbers in the code. The DateTime objects are actually created and added to the List in this line:

```
birthdays.add(new DateTime(YEAR, randMonth, randDay));
```

The inner parentheses are executed first. In this case, a DateTime object is created using the randomly generated month and day as well as the constant year. That new DateTime is then added to the birthdays List (which can only contain DateTime objects). containsDuplicates() is a more generic function. It takes a List of any kind and determines whether that List has any duplicate elements (any elements of the same value). It iterates through the List, as we have seen before. However, you may find this line confusing:

```
if (l.skip(i + 1).contains(l[i])) {
```

What is happening here? A List's skip(int x) method returns a version of the List (l in this case) without the first x elements included. contains() is a method that checks whether there is an element equivalent to the one provided as an argument. In short, this line is checking the rest of the List, beyond the element we are currently indexing to, for another copy of that element. Why is it okay to skip the first i + 1 elements? Once we get to the ith element, we have already checked all of the elements before the ith element for duplicates in the rest of the List. Therefore, it's more efficient not to check them again. Also, we don't want to check an element against itself (that's the 1 added to i). If this confuses you, don't worry. These things can be hard to visualize. Try drawing it out with paper and pencil (or on your tablet, perhaps).

Simple Blackjack

Simple Blackjack is a dumbed-down version of blackjack that features just one suit (13 cards), one player, and the dealer. A deck of 13 cards is shuffled. The dealer first draws a card, which is shown to the player. The player then receives 2 cards. The player can continually draw more cards (hit) or hold his position (stay). If the player's card total exceeds 21, he busts (loses). After the player is done, the dealer draws more cards, until his total is greater than or equal to 17. If the dealer busts, the player wins. If the dealer and the player both do not bust, then whoever has a higher card total wins the game. The king, queen, and jack cards count as 10 points. The ace card counts as either 1 or 11 points.

As you may have guessed, we will be storing the deck of cards in a List. Conveniently, Dart Lists have a method, shuffle(), that will randomly sort whatever is in them. We can use this method as a means of shuffling our deck of cards. The full Simple Blackjack program is in Listing 6-2.

Listing 6-2. Simple Blackjack

```dart
import "dart:io";

/// Calculate the score of the [cards] List
int calculateScore(List cards) {
  int score = 0;
  bool hasAce = false;  // only one ace in Simple Blackjack

  for (var card in cards) {  // use var because card can be int or String
    if (card is int) {  // is operator, check type of card
      score += card;
    } else if (card == "A") {
      hasAce = true;
    } else {  // must be king, queen, or jack
      score += 10;
    }
  }

  if (hasAce) {
    if ((score + 11) > 21) {  // don't let ace cause bust
      score += 1;
    } else {
      score += 11;
    }
  }

  return score;
}

/// Print everyone's scores and decks
void printStatus(playerCards, dealerCards) {
  print("");  // blank line
  print("Player's Total is ${calculateScore(playerCards)}:");
  print(playerCards);  // automatically prints contents of List
  print("Dealer's Total is ${calculateScore(dealerCards)}");
  print(dealerCards);
  print("");  // blank line
}

void main() {
  List deck = [2, 3, 4, 5, 6, 7, 8, 9, 10, "J", "Q", "K", "A"];
  List playerCards = [], dealerCards = [];

  deck.shuffle();

  print("Dealer draws first card.");
  dealerCards.add(deck.removeLast());  // move 1 card from deck to dealerCards
  print("Player receives two cards.");
  playerCards.add(deck.removeLast());  // move 1 card from deck to playerCards
  playerCards.add(deck.removeLast());
  printStatus(playerCards, dealerCards);
```

```
while (true) { // player decision loop
  print("Do you want to (H)it, (S)tay, or (Q)uit?");
  String selection = stdin.readLineSync().toUpperCase();  // get uppercase input

  if (selection == "H") {  // hit
    playerCards.add(deck.removeLast());
    printStatus(playerCards, dealerCards);

    if (calculateScore(playerCards) > 21) {
      print("You busted!  You lose!");
      exit(0);  // quits the program
    }
  } else if (selection == "S") {  // stay
    break;  // stop offering to hit, leave this loop
  } else if (selection == "Q") {  // quit
    exit(0);  // quits the program
  }
}

print("Dealer draws rest of cards.");
while (calculateScore(dealerCards) < 17) {  // keep drawing cards till 17
  dealerCards.add(deck.removeLast());
}
printStatus(playerCards, dealerCards);

if (calculateScore(dealerCards) > 21) {  // dealer bust
  print("Dealer busts!  You win!");
} else if (calculateScore(dealerCards) > calculateScore(playerCards)) {
  print("Dealer wins!");
} else if (calculateScore(dealerCards) < calculateScore(playerCards)) {
  print("You win!");
} else {  // must be a tie by default
  print("It's a tie!");
}
}
```

calculateScores() iterates through cards, a List of cards (either the player's or dealer's), and adds up their point value as follows:

- If card is a number, then it simply adds the number to the score.

  - The List cards can be a mix of ints and Strings. Therefore, to determine whether a particular card is a number, the is operator is used. is checks whether a variable is of a particular type.

- If card is an ace, we mark a boolean. There's some interesting logic, since an ace can count either as 1 or 11 points.

- If card is anything else, then we know it's a face card and worth 10 points.

printStatus() is a simple function that prints out the current scores and each player's current hand. You will notice that using print() on a List outputs a very human readable representation of it, not unlike a List literal.

The main() function is not unlike the main() functions of the other small games we have programmed. We have not seen the exit() function before. exit() immediately exits the program. It takes one argument, an integer that represents whether there was an error. 0 means no error. An interesting line is the one used for removing a card from the deck and adding it to the player's hand.

```
playerCards.add(deck.removeLast());
```

removeLast() is a List method that will remove the last element from a List and return it (in this case, from our shuffled deck). Therefore, after removeLast() is called, a List's length will be one shorter, and it will lose one of its elements. In this line, the result of removeLast(), the removed element, is passed as an argument to the add() method on playerCards. So, in one line, two operations are going on. First, an element is removed from deck, and then that same element is added to playerCards. Just for crystal clarity, here is another example utilizing removeLast(). Look at the comments to see what's going on.

```
List greatFruits = ["Banana", "Apple", "Grape", "Orange"];
List okayFruits = ["Guava", "Cherry"];
greatFruits.removeLast();  // greatFruits is now ["Banana", "Apple", "Grape"]
okayFruits.add(greatFruits.removeLast());  // greatFruits is  now ["Banana", "Apple"];
// okayFruits is now ["Guava", Cherry, "Grape"];
```

Simple Blackjack is pretty fun. This program has a ton of text, so Listing 6-3 shows some sample output, to give you an idea of what you should be seeing on your screen, just in case you made a typo (and to encourage you to actually type it in)!

Listing 6-3. Simple Blackjack Sample Output

```
Dealer draws first card.
Player receives two cards.

Player's Total is 15:
[8, 7]
Dealer's Total is 5
[5]

Do you want to (H)it, (S)tay, or (Q)uit?
H

Player's Total is 16:
[8, 7, A]
Dealer's Total is 5
[5]

Do you want to (H)it, (S)tay, or (Q)uit?
H

Player's Total is 19:
[8, 7, A, 3]
Dealer's Total is 5
[5]
```

```
Do you want to (H)it, (S)tay, or (Q)uit?
S
Dealer draws rest of cards.

Player's Total is 19:
[8, 7, A, 3]
Dealer's Total is 21
[5, 10, 6]

Dealer wins!
```

The house always wins.

Maps

Maps are useful for associating pieces of data with identifiers (pseudo names that point to those pieces of data). In other programming languages, Maps are known as dictionaries or associative arrays. The dictionary analogy may be particularly apt. When getting information from a Map, you will look up your data using a so-called *key*. Then, you will receive a *value* in return. This is like looking up a word in an English-language dictionary. You look up a word (the key) and get back its definition (the value).

Both the keys and the values can be of any Dart type, but it is most common for the keys to be Strings. Maps are unordered. This is where the dictionary analogy falls apart. Whereas an English-language dictionary is sorted alphabetically, a Map is not necessarily sorted at all. English-language dictionaries are sorted alphabetically, so that it is easier for humans to look up words. Since we are not going to be learning about how Maps are implemented, we do not need to worry about how the system goes about looking up a key. We just need to know that it works!

Unlike Lists, Maps are not used for storing sequential information (since they maintain no particular order). With a List, we pull its various elements by their indexes. Maps are indexed by their keys. Keys can be descriptive, whereas List indexes are simply sequential integers. There is no equivalent way to descriptively tag information with Lists. These descriptive keys come with one caveat: they must be unique. A Map may not contain more than one of the same key. It can, however, contain duplicate values. Figure 6-1 illustrates good uses of Lists vs. good uses of Maps.

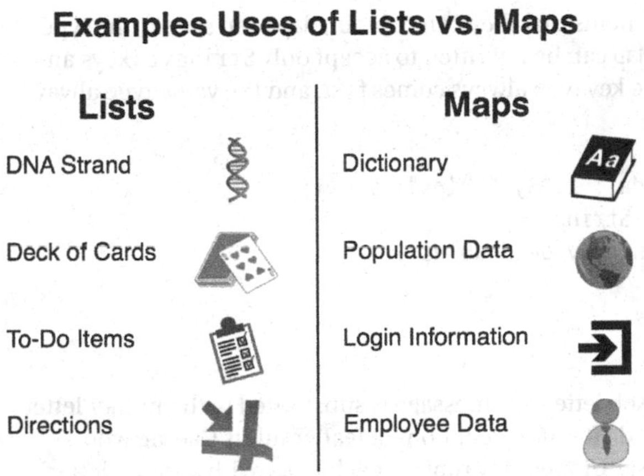

Examples Uses of Lists vs. Maps

Lists	Maps
DNA Strand	Dictionary
Deck of Cards	Population Data
To-Do Items	Login Information
Directions	Employee Data

Figure 6-1. List examples vs. Map examples

Map Syntax

Similarly to Lists, Dart comes with built-in syntax for declaring Map literals. This syntax may seem familiar, since it is the same as the syntax that we used for optional named parameters in Chapter 3. It makes heavy use of curly braces, colons, and commas. Here are a few ways to create an empty Map:

```
Map a = {};  // just two empty curly braces facing one another
var b = {};
Map c = new Map();
var d = new Map();
```

Map literals utilize the syntax "key: value, key: value, etc." Every key must be paired with a value (even if that value is just an empty String). Obviously, the converse is true: every value must also be paired with a key. There is a one-to-one relationship between the number of values stored and the number of keys stored.

```
Map countryCapitals = {"France": "Paris", "USA": "Washington", "Japan": "Tokyo"};
Map nameAge = {"Matt": 27, "John": 18, "Sarah": 17, "Larry": 80};  //String keys, int values
Map employees = {345: {"name": "Donald Smith", "Department": "Accounting", "Salary": 1000},
                 220: {"name": "Mark Anderson", "Department": "Sales", "Salary": 950},
                 572: {"name": "Elizabeth Brahmen", "Department": "Marketing", "Salary": 975}};
```

Let's go over all three of these Maps. countryCapitals has Strings for both its keys and its values. nameAge has Strings for keys and ints for values. employees is the most complex. It features ints for keys (an employee id perhaps?) and other Maps for values. Those inner Maps feature Strings for keys and either Strings or ints for values.

Pulling values out of Maps is not completely unlike pulling values out of Lists. We also use square brackets, but instead of using an index to refer to the element of interest, we use a key to refer to the value of interest. We can use this same syntax for assigning new key/value pairs or changing old key/value pairs.

```
Map productPrice = {"Gum": 0.95, "Soda": 1.05, "Chips": 1.99};
double gumPrice = productPrice["Gum"];  // gumPrice is now 0.95
productPrice["Cookie"] = 0.50;  // a new key/value pair added to productPrice
productPrice["Soda"] = gumPrice;  // the value for the key "Soda" is now 0.95
```

Just as Lists can utilize generics to specify the type of elements that they can contain, Maps can specify the type of keys and values that are valid in them. The productPrice Map can be rewritten to accept only Strings as keys and doubles as values, using the syntax Map<String, double>. The key type always comes first, and the value type always comes second.

```
Map<String, double> productPrice = {"Gum": 0.95, "Soda": 1.05, "Chips": 1.99};
productPrice[34] = 1.34;  // WRONG, keys can only be Strings
productPrice["Bagel"] = "Free";  // WRONG, values can only be doubles
```

Caesar Cipher

A Caesar Cipher is an incredibly simple form of encryption. Each letter in a message is substituted with another letter a certain number of alphabet positions away from it. It is named after the great Roman leader Julius Caesar, who purportedly used it in his correspondence. One example: Caesar Cipher may replace each letter with another letter three places ahead in the alphabet, so that A becomes D, F becomes I, etc. A popular Caesar Cipher is ROT13, which is a movement of 13 letters (one-half the English alphabet).

In Listing 6-4, we implement a Caesar Cipher with ROT13. The function getROT13Map() takes the English alphabet as a List and uses it to form a Map with the original letters as keys and the substitution letters as values. It indexes into the alphabet List and moves 13 letters forward, for the first 13 letters (a–m), and 13 letters backward, for the rest of the alphabet (n–z). It is also careful to add both the lowercase and the uppercase versions of each letter.

You will see a Map method called containsKey() in the main() function. It checks whether a Map has the key specified to it as an argument. This is how we check whether we can encode the character from the user's input. Our program can't encode punctuation or spaces, so we just ignore non-letters. To break the user's input into a List that we can easily iterate, we use the String method split(). split() takes a String and divides it into little pieces that it returns cobbled together as a List. The String is divided at the substrings specified by the argument to split(). If split() is supplied with a blank String, as in our program, then it simply returns a List of all of the characters in the String in question. For example "Hello".split("") will return ["H", "e", "l", "l", "o"].

Listing 6-4. Caesar Cipher

```dart
import "dart:io";

/// returns a Map that maps letters to other letters
/// 13 places away in the English alphabet
Map getROT13Map() {
  const List<String> ALPHABET = const ["a", "b", "c", "d", "e", "f", "g", "h", "i", "j", "k", "l",
"m", "n", "o", "p", "q", "r", "s", "t", "u", "v", "w", "x", "y", "z"];
  const int CHANGE = 13;   // how many places to move letters
  Map<String, String> code = {};

  for (int i = 0; i < ALPHABET.length; i++) {
    if (i < CHANGE){  // move first 13 letters 13 places forward A=N
      code[ALPHABET[i]] = ALPHABET[i + CHANGE];
      code[ALPHABET[i].toUpperCase()] = ALPHABET[i + CHANGE].toUpperCase();
    } else {  // last 13 letters go 13 places back N=A
      code[ALPHABET[i]] = ALPHABET[i - CHANGE];
      code[ALPHABET[i].toUpperCase()] = ALPHABET[i - CHANGE].toUpperCase();
    }
  }
  return code;
}

void main() {
  Map<String, String> secretCode = getROT13Map();
  print("Enter the text you want to encrypt:");
  String original = stdin.readLineSync();  // user input
  String changed = "";
  for (String character in original.split('')) {  // get List of characters
    if (secretCode.containsKey(character)) {  // containsKey() checks if key exists
      changed += secretCode[character];
    } else {
      changed += character;
    }
  }
  print(changed);
}
```

Baseball Statistics Exercise

Do you know anything about baseball? Here's everything that you need to know for this quick exercise:

- A Hit(H) is either a Single(S), a Double(D), a Triple(T), or a Home Run(HR).

- Batting Average(BA) is equal to Hits(H) / At-Bats(AB).

- On-Base-Percentage(OBP) is equal to Hits(H) + Walks(W) / At-Bats(AB).[1]

Write a function, addStats(), that given a Map<String, num> assumed to contain the keys AB, S, D, T, HR, and W adds the key/value pairs for H, BA, and OBP. The function does not return anything. Instead, it modifies the Map that it is provided as an argument. This should be quite easy. If you can do it without looking at the answer (coming up after this paragraph), then you "get" the basics of Maps. If not, reread this entire section on Maps. Maps are important in Dart because they're used very frequently.

■ **Note** The type num can represent either of the types int or double. This will make more sense after you read Chapter 10.

```
void addStats(Map<String, num> statMap) {
  statMap["H"] = statMap["S"] + statMap["D"] + statMap["T"] + statMap["HR"];
  statMap["BA"] = statMap["H"] / statMap["AB"];
  statMap["OBP"] = (statMap["H"] + statMap["W"]) / statMap["AB"];
}
```

Sets

There are more than three data structures provided with Dart, but the two you will see most frequently in code will almost certainly be Lists and Maps. Sets may be a distant third. A Set is operated on similarly to a List (items are added and removed with no identifiers, unlike a Map), but what it represents is quite different. Unlike a List, the default implementation of a Set in Dart does not maintain any particular order. Therefore, its elements do not have indexes. Also, all of the elements in a Set must be unique. Therefore, a Set cannot have the int literal 231 placed in it twice.

Items are added to a Set using the methods add() and addAll(), which add one item or multiple items at once (addAll() takes a List as an argument and adds all of the elements of the List to the Set). Items are removed from a Set using the remove() method. If you try to add an item to a Set that already exists in it (established by comparison with the == operator), then the new item will not be added. A Set can be created empty, or it can be created from a List, using the from() *factory method* (yet another object-oriented concept covered in Chapter 12).

```
Set blankSet = new Set();  // empty set
Set elementals = new Set.from(["wind", "water", "fire", "earth"]);  // Set created from List
elementals.add("fire");  // not an error, but does nothing since "fire" already in elementals
elementals.addAll(["thunder", "lightning"]);  // adds both "thunder" and "lightning" to the Set
elementals.remove("water");  // "water" is gone
```

Surprise, surprise, Sets can also specify at creation what type of elements they will contain. Since elements in Sets do not have indexes, we need to iterate through Sets using a for-in-loop. The Set method intersection() will return a Set of elements that are in both the Set it is applied to and the Set supplied to the method as an argument.

---

[1]This is a simplification of OBP. The real formula is a little more complicated.

```
Set<String> jerryColors = new Set.from(["blue", "red", "green"]);
Set<String> maryColors = new Set.from(["red", "green", "yellow"]);
Set<String> bothColors = jerryColors.intersection(maryColors);  // contains "red" and "green"
for (String color in bothColors) {
  print(color);
}
```

Revised containsDuplicates()

When a List is converted to a Set, the new Set will drop any duplicate elements in the List, because all of the elements in a Set must be unique. (That's its useful property, remember?) Therefore, the containsDuplicates() function from the Birthday Paradox program can be significantly simplified using Sets. Instead of actually comparing all of the elements in the List in question, we can just convert the List to a Set and see if the length of the Set is shorter than the length of the List. If it is, then we know that at least one element of the List was removed during the conversion process because it was a duplicate.

```
/// Returns true if [l] has duplicate elements
/// Otherwise returns false
bool containsDuplicates(List l) {
  Set s = new Set.from(l);  // create a new Set by converting the List
  if (s.length < l.length) {
    return true;
  }
  return false;
}
```

Great Set Use Cases

The defining property of a set is that it only holds unique elements. Dart Sets are therefore useful in any scenario in which duplicate values will be a problem. The overhead of constantly calling a function such as containsDuplicates() on a List can be immense if it needs to be checked constantly. Using a Set as a data structure gives us a built-in check on the exclusion of duplicates. Here are some basic use cases:

- *Voting*: Each individual should only vote once, so we want a Set of voters, not a List of voters.

- *Players in a multiplayer game*: The same player shouldn't be able to connect twice.

- *Students in a class*: A student shouldn't be able to register for a class twice.

THE SCIENCE OF DATA STRUCTURES

In this chapter, there is only discussion regarding how to use data structures, not how they are implemented. That is the topic of a semester-long college course. How is the data actually organized within the computer's memory system? How does Dart's List implementation know where the fifth element of a given List is, as opposed to the fifty-fifth?

There are not just lists, maps, and sets. There are also arrays, graphs, trees, heaps, queues, stacks, etc. And then each of these general categories of structures has several subtypes with differing implementations. For example, a doubly linked list with a sentinel may provide the same operations as a singly linked list, but its implementation differs significantly. They can both be used for most of the same purposes, but one may perform well in circumstances where the other is slow.

In short, different implementations of a data structure will have different performance characteristics. Typically, the operations that a user will be most interested in performance-wise are: retrieving an element from anywhere within the structure, retrieving an element from one of the structure's ends, adding an element to an arbitrary place in the structure, adding an element to one of the structure's ends, searching the structure, and traversing the structure. The time to accomplish these operations can vary very significantly.

Imagine the task of adding a follower to a top celebrity's Twitter feed. Some data structures would need to traverse the entire list of millions of followers to add that latest follower. Other structures would already have a pointer to the exact location where that follower's data should be appended. At this point in your Dart journey, you will not be facing such performance dilemmas, but it's something to keep in mind when you take on larger projects.

Summary

Lists, Maps, and Sets are data structures built into Dart. All three can hold multiple different data types at once, or it can be specified that a particular List, Map, or Set can only hold one data type (via generics). Lists and Maps have their own unique literal syntax.

Lists are useful for storing ordered, sequential information. All elements in a List are assigned integer indexes. The first element is assigned zero, and the indexes of the rest of the elements increment by one as the order is progressed from the beginning of the List to the end.

Maps store unordered pairs of keys and values. Every key must have a value, and vice versa. Keys can be any data type, but they are most often Strings. All of the keys in a Map must be unique. One reason Maps are useful is because the identifier of a piece of information (the key) is much more descriptive than a List index.

The default Dart implementation of a Set is unordered. Sets contain only unique elements. Sets can easily be created with List literals and the from() factory constructor. A quick way to remove the duplicates from a List is to convert it to a Set.

A for-in-loop is a convenient way of iterating through all of the elements in a List or a Set. It does not offer as much fine-grained control as a normal for-loop, but it is a good way to quickly iterate through a Set, since Sets do not have indexes. DateTime objects are used for representing dates and times in Dart. The String method split() can be used for quickly tokenizing a String into a List containing its component parts.

EXERCISES

1. What are some pieces of data in your day-to-day life that could be well represented by some of the Dart data structures that were discussed in this chapter? Why would one data structure be well suited for a particular type of data and another not?

2. Fix our simplification in the Birthday Paradox program. Generate the right random number for the day of the month, based on what month is randomly selected, instead of always generating a number between 1 and 28. In other words, if the month is April, the randomly generated number should be between 1 and 30, 1 and 31 for December, and 1 and 28 for February, etc. How much does this fix change the probabilities?

3. Create a full blackjack game based on Simple Blackjack. It should include multiple suits of cards, implement the full rules of blackjack, including splits (Wikipedia is your friend), and allow for multiple players. Warning: This is a complex, time-consuming exercise.

4. Create a program that implements a different Caesar Cipher (not ROT13). Extend it further to also encode spaces and punctuation. Do some historical digging and see if you can re-create an actual cipher used by Julius Caesar.

5. In what instances does uniqueness of data elements matter enough that Sets would be preferred over Lists? It's not always so obvious. For example, you may say that in a shopping list you don't want duplicate items. But what if the user just added the same item twice because he needed two of it? Try to think of some scenarios where Sets absolutely make sense.

6. Browse the online Dart API documentation to learn about the Queue data structure, which is built into Dart's standard dart:collection library. How does a Queue differ from a List?

7. There is a proposal to add syntax for Set literals to Dart. What do you think this syntax should look like?

CHAPTER 7

■ ■ ■

How Does the Web Work?

We're going to take a break from writing Dart programs (but we hardly got started, you say!) to understand the fundamentals of the World Wide Web, in preparation for working with it more extensively in our Dart programs. Hopefully you will find this detour and the hodge-podge of information about the Web that it features informative and interesting. Given what a large impact the Web has had on everyone's lives, it would probably be good if the public at large knew more about how the Web works.

Retrieving a Web Site

You saw in Chapter 2 that the structure and content of a web site is defined in an HTML document. HTML stands for Hypertext Markup Language. *Hypertext* simply means documents that have links to other documents. In Chapter 2, the HTML document lived locally on your computer. However, as you are probably aware, when you visit a web site, its HTML document typically originates on a remote server that you connect to through the Internet.

On the Web, documents are requested, sent, and received. There is a language for making these requests and for sending documents. It is called Hypertext Transfer *Protocol*[1] (HTTP). That is the "http" that you see at the beginning of a *URL* (Uniform Resource Locator), as in

```
http://www.yahoo.com/
```

When you type this into your web browser's address bar, you are instructing your web browser to send a request to Yahoo's servers for an HTML document. We call the HTML document at the root of a web site an *index*, and it is typically labeled "index.html." Try going to the web site

```
http://www.yahoo.com/index.html
```

It looks familiar, right? It's the same document. For cleanliness, requesting the index document directly is typically not required. URLs can refer to document types other than HTML. For example, the following URL refers to a GIF image:

```
https://www.google.com/images/logo.gif
```

---

[1] A well-defined standard for communication over the Internet. A protocol is a "standard for communication," if you will. Some non-HTTP examples include: SMTP (Simple Mail Transport Protocol), a protocol for sending e-mails; FTP (File Transfer Protocol), a protocol for transferring files; and TCP (Transport Control Protocol), a protocol that underlies relay through the Internet for the other protocols.

Not surprisingly, the remote servers that understand HTTP that you connect to run software called a web server. The most popular web server (as of 2014) is called Apache and is a free, open-source program, managed by a nonprofit foundation. Apache is most commonly used on computers running the free, open-source operating system Linux. The most popular commercial, closed-source web server is IIS from Microsoft, which runs on Windows. There are many other popular web servers.

Typically, computers that serve web sites utilize powerful hardware. The more requests a web server receives, the more simultaneous connections it must maintain. The more bandwidth a server needs to utilize (think online video), the more powerful hardware it will need to be fitted with in order to maintain high throughput. Web services for very popular web sites will run across hundreds, even thousands of different computers, each splitting up the workload.

If the HTML document that you request is the same one that was uploaded to the web server in the first place, then we call it a *static* document. If the document needs to be customized somehow for each user, or according to the circumstance of each request, then we call it *dynamic*. Static documents can be pure HTML, served by a web server. Dynamic documents are typically handled by a server-side programming language. Static documents require less server-side resources to process and usually are returned faster to the requester than dynamic documents.

An example of a dynamic document might be the web mail interface you use to read your e-mail (something like gmail.com). Several actions need to take place on the server behind the scenes to show you the page that displays your inbox, since it won't look the same every time it is accessed. An example of a static document might be a résumé. The résumé is sent over the wires to your web browser exactly as it looks on the web server's hard disk.

Dart, as we will be using it in this book, is a client-side programming language (although it can be used as a server-side programming language too). This means that the programs we write will run in the user's web browser. Languages such as PHP, Python, and Java are among the many that are typically used on the server side. Programs written in them are used in conjunction with the web server to create dynamic content for the user.

The line between server-side and client-side programming languages continues to blur as languages such as JavaScript and Dart are used on both ends. However, the fundamental difference between a program running on the server or on the client remains. A program running on the server, for instance, can access a company's catalog of products directly through a database. A program running on the client side will need to communicate with a program running on the server, in order to get access to the same database. Client-side programs run within a sandboxed environment in the web browser. In this environment, they have restrictions in terms of access to hardware, operating-system services, and the file system. Figure 7-1 illustrates the difference between a client-side and server-side environment.

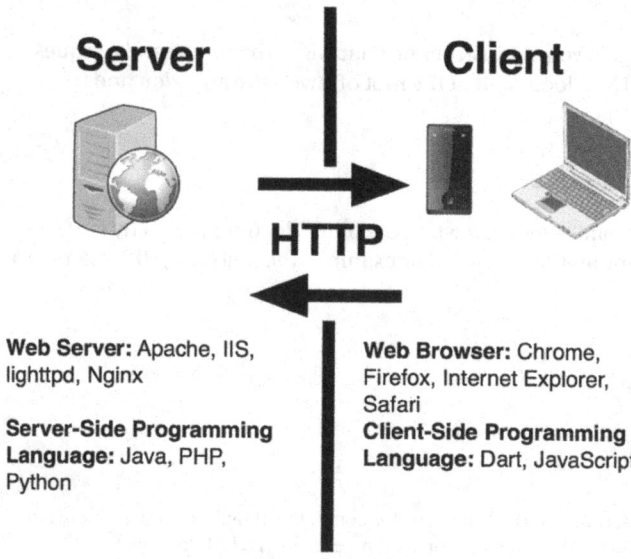

Figure 7-1. Server-side Web vs. client-side Web

A NOTE ON SECURITY

Unfortunately, security has become a paramount issue when programming for the Web. By default, HTTP transfers data in plaintext. In other words, it is possible for anyone listening (a hacker tapping into your Wi-Fi network, for instance) to read the contents of most transmissions over HTTP. For this reason, it is now common, and certainly best practice, for any kind of identifiable data to be transmitted over HTTPS. HTTPS (Hypertext Transfer Protocol Secure) utilizes encryption to ensure that data is seen only by the desired server and client.

If a program you write in Dart stays client-side (it has no interaction with a server and simply runs in the web browser, without communicating to the outside world), then you can be a little less security-conscious. However, anytime your program transmits data to a web server, the proper mentality is caution. There are people who want to do harm to your program, no matter how mundane its subject matter.

Perhaps the most security-intense aspect of web programming is user authentication. Under no circumstance should user passwords be stored in plaintext. Typically, they are stored as secure hashes (which is beyond the scope of this book). An alternative to worrying about user authentication is to off-load it to a third-party provider. Google, Facebook, Twitter, and just about every major web company offers authentication APIs for developers. Using these APIs, a user can "log in through Facebook" to your site. Let Facebook worry about some of the security, so you do not have to. Of course, off-loading security to a third party has its own perils.

The Web's Place on the Internet

In everyday language, the World Wide Web has become somewhat synonymous with the Internet. Yet, the two are not one and the same. The Web is a part of the Internet, but not the whole thing. Just like Earth is part of the solar system, but not the whole thing. It's just one stopping-off point in a much more complex system. It's certainly the most visible, the most accessed, and the liveliest, but it's—one more time—not the whole thing!

TCP (Transport Control Protocol) and IP (Internet Protocol) are the two protocols that underlie most of the information transmitted over the Internet. They determine how information is packaged, routed, and delivered from one computer to another. As we already know, HTTP and HTTPS are the two protocols that are used for the Web. Like other protocols used on the Internet, they run on top of TCP/IP. There are a lot more protocols running across the Internet, though, and you use many of them every day. Do you use e-mail? POP3, IMAP, and SMTP are the most common e-mail protocols. Do you use Spotify, iTunes Radio, or Pandora? They send your music over streaming audio protocols. Have you ever printed to a wireless or networked printer? That's another protocol. How about shared files with a Windows computer? You probably used SMB, and we're not talking about *Super Mario Bros*. DropBox, Skype? Yet more protocols. So, the Web (and HTTP/HTTPS) is just one piece of the Internet of your life.

"Hold on," you say: "I access my e-mail, my streaming music, and my files through a web browser. So, aren't they part of the Web?" Yes and no. The Web provides the interface via which you access these services, but it is not necessarily used for the underlying transport of information. For example, when you access a web-based interface to your e-mail, there may be communication happening both over HTTP (well, actually, HTTPS, hopefully) and POP3 at the same time.

The Web is an incredibly cost-effective user-interface platform for Internet companies to adopt, because it alleviates the need to develop a separate client program for every platform that they support. However, at the same time, a web app does not always offer the performance and capabilities that a native application[2] does. The original iPhone only supported web apps, but its app ecosystem really took off when Apple allowed developers to create native apps. This was in 2008, long before Dart, and the modern Web. Can a purely web-based platform be successful

---

[2]A specific program running outside of the web browser's sandbox.

today? Google's Chrome-based laptops are an attempt at one. Mozilla is trying the same thing with a new line of web-powered smartphones. Perhaps the Web just needs a modern programming language to enable apps to be made that can be native app replacements. Enter Dart.

Just how much of the Internet is the Web? Well, it depends on how we measure the size of the Internet. It also depends on where we decide that the Web ends and the rest of the Internet begins. For example, in 2013, the number-one source of traffic on the Internet, accounting for more than 50% of the total, was streaming video.[3] The largest individual source of traffic was Netflix. Netflix can be accessed from a web browser, but it can also be accessed from a native app. Do we count its use as web traffic or not?

The popularity of various arms of the Internet has varied significantly over time. Although UPI reported that Netflix and YouTube were the biggest sources of traffic in 2013, in 2009, ipoque found in its "Internet Study 2008/2009" that the majority of Internet traffic was through P2P (peer-to-peer) file sharing. See Figure 7-2 for a breakdown across several geographical regions from that study.

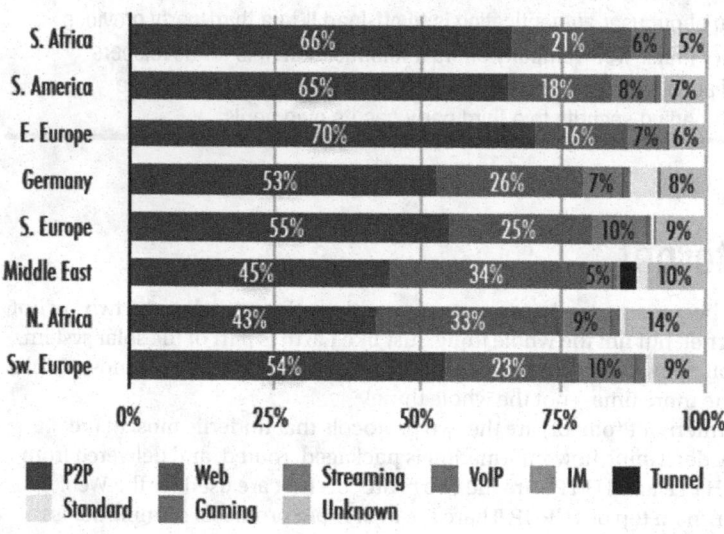

Figure 7-2. *ipoque "Internet Study 2008/2009" breakdown of Internet traffic by type*[4]

In short, the Web is a rich and diverse platform that provides the foundation for applications that access other Internet services. It is not always an end unto itself, but, rather, an interface layer on top of other technology. The Internet is composed of many protocols other than those that power the Web, and you probably use some of them on a daily basis. So, the next time that you hear someone confuse the Web with the entire Internet, feel free to kindly correct him, or just feel a small sense of superiority of knowledge.

---

[3]UPI, "Netflix, YouTube account for half of all Internet traffic,". www.upi.com/Science_News/Technology/2013/11/11/Netflix-YouTube-account-for-half-of-all-Internet-traffic/UPI-83571384206980/, November 11, 2013.
[4]ipoque, "Internet Study 2008/2009," http://www.ipoque.com/sites/default/files/mediafiles/documents/internet-study-2008-2009.pdf, 2009.

Defining a Web Site's Look

We saw in Chapter 2 that HTML is used to define the structure and content of a web site. Cascading style sheets (CSS) are used with HTML documents to define what they look like, or their "style," if you will. This includes such things as fonts, borders, backgrounds, sizes, distances, etc. Listing 7-1 is the CSS document that Dart Editor auto-generated for our Hello World Fancy program (Chapter 2) when we first created it.

Listing 7-1. CSS for Hello World Fancy

```
body {
    background-color: #F8F8F8;
    font-family: 'Open Sans', sans-serif;
    font-size: 14px;
    font-weight: normal;
    line-height: 1.2em;
    margin: 15px;
}

h1, p {
    color: #333;
}

#sample_container_id {
    width: 100%;
    height: 400px;
    position: relative;
    border: 1px solid #ccc;
    background-color: #fff;
}

#sample_text_id {
    font-size: 24pt;
    text-align: center;
    margin-top: 140px;
}
```

The section that begins with body defines a style that all of the content within the <body> tag of an HTML document should follow (unless it is overridden by the style of another tag—for example, a <div> tag within <body> that has a specified style that conflicts with <body> will override it for its content). Most of the style content is pretty self-explanatory. px stands for pixels. em is a unit of measurement for font sizes. #F8F8F8 defines a RGB (a color composed of different values for the strength of the colors red, green, and blue) color in hexadecimal[5] (numbers, base 16).

The next section changes the color of the text in the <h1>, and <p> tags.

The last two sections describe the styles of the HTML elements with the ids sample_container_id and sample_text_id, respectively. The # sign before the CSS definition indicates that it is an id and not a generalized tag such as h1.

_____

[5]Don't be intimidated by hexadecimal-defined RGB colors. Honestly, it's a fairly stupid and cryptic way to define colors in a human readable format such as CSS. You can use online color tables to quickly look up the hexadecimal value of a color you want to use in your CSS. Some great color table resources are provided in Appendix D. Very few people memorize hexadecimal RGB color values (there must be a better way to spend your time). Almost everybody looks them up.

79

When a web site is loaded, the CSS that is used to style it may be dynamically decided, based on the device or web browser that it is running on. In this way, the same HTML can be styled appropriately on both a phone and a laptop. You will not be learning much more CSS than the preceding in this book. For more information about CSS, you should check out the resources in Appendix D.

Non-HTML on the Web

Web servers are good at serving HTML, but they can also be used to serve other kinds of documents. HTTP can be used to request images, PDFs, really any kind of file that you can think of. In fact, almost every web page will contain not only HTML, CSS, and JavaScript but also images, sounds, and videos.

Have you ever right-clicked a picture and asked your web browser to open it in a new window? You may have noticed that its URL explicitly includes the image's file name. In this instance, your web browser is requesting a non-HTML document over HTTP. When an HTML document has images embedded in it via <img> tags, your web browser does the same thing behind the scenes. It puts out an HTTP request to the web server hosting each and every image, one at a time.

Other formerly popular file types on the Web were Java applets and Adobe Flash programs (by the way, Java is a very different language from JavaScript; the two are mostly related via a mid-1990s marketing department). These both operated via web browser plug-ins. Java and Flash are becoming increasingly scarce as the capabilities of JavaScript (which again Dart translates to) have become more extensive and have replaced much of what Java and Flash were used for. Video-streaming clients and some games are the last vestiges of Flash's former importance, but even these are moving toward a JavaScript (and Dart) future.

It is fairly difficult for a Dart program to interoperate with the Flash plug-in or a Java applet. However, the Dart language comes with a library for interoperation with JavaScript. Check out the dart:js library in Dart's online docs for more information. Interaction with images is covered in Chapter 8.

Web Browsers

This is the point in the continuum of web development where things start to get tricky. Each web browser needs to interpret the HTML, CSS, and JavaScript (or Dart in the case of Dartium) that it receives, in order to render it on the screen for the user's viewing pleasure. Unfortunately, different web browsers may render the same content differently.

There are published standards that each web browser is supposed to follow. The World Wide Web Consortium (W3C) establishes most of these standards. You can read them yourself at www.w3.org. Unfortunately, these standards are quite complex and always leave a little bit of room open for interpretation. The situation has improved significantly over the past decade. Once upon a time, it was a necessity to code a site with many workarounds for individual browsers. Today, a single implementation that follows standards is much more likely to work as intended across all major modern browsers.

It is still important to test your work across every major web browser and platform, though. As of 2014, that includes Microsoft Internet Explorer (Windows, Windows Phone), Google Chrome (Mac, Windows, Linux, Android, iOS), Mozilla Firefox (Mac, Windows, Linux, Android), and Apple Safari (Mac, iOS). Other browsers exist (Opera, for example) and have millions of users, but these browsers will still likely make up less than 5% of your user base.

Nothing beats checking out your web site on each browser yourself, but there are tools to help, since checking four different browsers across five different platforms can be rather intimidating. One helpful tool is http://browsershots.org, which will show you a screenshot of what your site looks like on multiple browsers simultaneously. If you are running on a Mac or on Linux and you don't have access to Windows, you can get virtualized or emulated versions of Microsoft Internet Explorer running through free tools such as Virtual Box and Wine.

Sometimes, one web browser will support a technology that another will not. If you decide to use this technology, you should be aware that you may be turning away users that do not use a web browser supporting it. An example is WebGL, a 3D graphics technology accessible from Dart, which is disabled by default in Safari (as of version 7.0). Another example is the video standard WebM, which Safari and Internet Explorer do not support as of the writing of this book. There are many more examples, so be careful! Most of the libraries included with Dart are supported by all current major web browsers.

Often, choosing to use a cutting-edge web technology is a trade-off between user experience and breadth of audience. Let's again think about WebGL. Perhaps you want to create a 3D game that plays in the web browser, and WebGL is the most convenient technology for you to use. Let's pretend you're not worried about the game running on mobile platforms, since you intend its controls to be keyboard-and-mouse-based. Okay, so we have three platforms to worry about: Linux, Windows, and Mac. Across those platforms, there are four major web browsers: Chrome, Firefox, Internet Explorer, and Safari. We know that Safari does not support WebGL by default (and our users may not be sophisticated enough to know how to turn support on). If, hypothetically, Safari has about 10% market share among desktop browsers (a fair estimate[6]), then by the use of WebGL, we are turning away about one-tenth of our potential user base. But wait, there's more! While Firefox and Chrome have supported WebGL for a fairly long time in web terms and auto-update their users to the latest version of the browser, Internet Explorer has only supported WebGL since version 11. Since Internet Explorer does not auto-update, many users are still using earlier versions. In fact, we can safely say, based on the latest stats, that at least another 10% of desktop web browser users are on Internet Explorer versions pre-11. Therefore, choosing WebGL has really limited our target audience by 20% between Safari and pre-11 Internet Explorer users. This is, of course, an approximation, since some users have multiple browsers and are willing to switch to view a specific page.

That was a bit of a tangent, but it really illustrates the necessity of being cognizant of the ever-evolving browser market. Web browsers are incredibly sophisticated pieces of software developed by large organizations handling millions of lines of code. With the use of Dart, HTML, and CSS, the web browser in itself becomes the platform. There's less of a need to code for Mac, Linux, or Windows and more of a need to code for Chrome, Firefox, Internet Explorer, or Safari. Ultimately, a carefully designed web app can treat the Web as a universal platform. A write once, run anywhere ideal.[7]

Domains, IP Addresses, and IP Routing

To get your Dart program exposed to the masses, you will need to get it uploaded onto a publicly facing web server. Acquiring a web site consists of two parts:

- *Hosting*: Obtaining space on a web server to store your files

- *Domain Registration*: Acquiring a name, such as mywebsite.com or specialwebsite.ws, through a central registrar that will uniquely, and human readably, identify your site

Every device connected to the Internet has a unique address. This is called an *IP address* (Internet Protocol address). When you enter a domain in your web browser, it requests the IP address of the web server that you are trying to reach from a Domain Name Server (DNS). Domain Name Servers keep central lists that map all domains to their respective IP addresses. When you register a domain, through a site such as GoDaddy or Register.com, you are paying to have that central list updated with a key representing your domain name and a value representing the IP address of the server where your content is hosted.

---

[6]Wikipedia, "Usage Share of Web Browsers," http://en.wikipedia.org/wiki/Usage_share_of_web_browsers, November 23, 2013.
[7]The folks behind Dart test each release version of it against all modern web browsers. As of Dart 1.4, that definition of *modern* includes only Internet Explorer versions 9.0 and above.

Finally, once your web browser knows the IP address it is trying to contact, your request for a particular piece of content goes through several routers, hopping from one to another, until it reaches the destination web server. Each of these routers uses simple routing algorithms to infer the path of least resistance to the ultimate destination. Yet, they must also take traffic and other hard-to-predict factors into consideration when routing your request. Therefore, the path is not always perfect—in fact, it is often not perfect. A request from your home to a web server in the city next door may first be routed through another country! In 2013, it was reported that hackers briefly redirected a large amount of web traffic through Belarus (Figure 7-3).[8]

Figure 7-3. *A cartoon about web traffic redirection*

A BRIEF HISTORY OF THE WEB

The Internet's history can be traced all the way back to the 1960s and a US Department of Defense project known as ARPANET. Tim Berners-Lee, a British computer scientist, first conceived of the World Wide Web in 1989, while he was working at the CERN (European Organization for Nuclear Research) European Particle Physics Laboratory.[9] His motivation was to better connect information stored on disparate computer systems. Berners-Lee implemented the first web browser and web server in 1990 on NeXTStep, an operating system that is a direct ancestor of iOS and OS X. He created the original specifications for HTML and HTTP. Berners-Lee continues to work on the Web as the director of the W3C.

In the early 1990s, CERN made the Web an open platform, and the first widely used web browser, named Mosaic, was developed at the National Center for Supercomputing Applications (NCSA) at the University of Illinois at Urbana-Champaign. It was soon followed by Microsoft Internet Explorer and Netscape Navigator (created by a

---

[8]RT, "Internet's new biggest threat? How web traffic can be secretly redirected," http://rt.com/usa/mtm-renesys-redirect-internet-775/, December 5, 2013.
[9]W3C, "Tim Berners-Lee," www.w3.org/People/Berners-Lee/, November 23, 2013.

team led by former Mosaic developers), which dueled for market share supremacy. Eventually, Internet Explorer won, and Microsoft was sued by the governments of the United States and European Union for its monopoly of the web browser space, thought to have come about by the bundling of Internet Explorer with Windows. Microsoft's web browser monopoly eventually succumbed to competition from Mozilla (a nonprofit created from the ashes of Netscape), Apple, and Google. NCSA also developed one of the first popular web servers, but since the 1990s, Apache has dominated the server space.

In the 1990s, the Web experienced exponential growth, eventually leading to the dot-com bubble. Excessive speculation in technology startups, centered on the delivery of services over the Web, led to an economic recession in the year 2000. Since the end of the dot-com bubble, web innovation has focused on user-created content. This phase has come to be known as "Web 2.0" and has included the rise of the user-edited encyclopedia Wikipedia, social networks such as Facebook and Twitter, and the video-sharing site YouTube.

The Web became so large that finding content within it eventually evolved into a domain of its own. Search engines such as AltaVista and Excite battled until Google emerged in 1999 and achieved dominance and near-monopoly status, thanks partially to a superior algorithm for indexing the ever-expanding Web. One of the first original Web directories, Yahoo!, founded in 1994, is still one of the most visited sites on the planet. *E-commerce* is a buzzword that simply refers to selling goods on the Web. Large e-commerce sites include eBay and Amazon. Notably, many of today's largest web companies (aside from social networking) were founded in the 1990s (including Google, Yahoo, eBay, and Amazon) and managed to navigate the dot-com bubble. They are highly influential in the direction of the Web and the technologies that underlie it.

The World Wide Web was not the first hypertext system, nor even the first to be widely available on personal computers. The proprietary HyperCard, created by Apple, was released in the 1980s for free on Macintosh computers. However, Apple failed to capitalize on its early lead by realizing the full potential of HyperCard with a networked product. The Web also quickly superseded previous Internet systems used for browsing documents such as Gopher. For more information about the history of the Web, you should check out Appendix B, which focuses on the history of programming the Web.

A Little More HTTP

How does HTTP actually work? It's a pretty simple protocol. First, the client (in other words, the web browser) sends a request to the server that includes the resource it wants to access (specified by a URL) and a "verb" describing what it wants to do to that resource. HTTP 1.1 (the current version) specifies eight possible verbs. However, in practice there are two verbs that are used very frequently: GET and POST. The header of a GET or POST request, among other things, may include the name of the web browser being used, the so-called User Agent, and the Referer, the place from which the requester is coming.

GET is used for requesting a resource that will not have any side effects. In other words, it is for requesting resources that are largely a retrieval operation. When you type a web site's address into the address bar in your web browser and go to it, you are executing a GET request. When you follow an HTML link, you are executing a GET request. Both GET and POST requests can include parameters (not unlike function parameters). For example, if we want to perform a search on Google, we need to specify what we want to search. GET parameters can be specified within the URL using a combination of the symbols ?, &, and =. Not all characters can be put within a URL; for example, spaces turn into %20. A search on Google using a GET request for the term "the best dog breed" could potentially be (although this isn't Google's exact format)

```
http://www.google.com/?q=the%20best%20dog%20breed
```

In this example, q is a GET parameter, and "the best dog breed" encoded in a URL-safe format is the value sent with the request to fill in that parameter. ? specifies the beginning of a list of parameters. = divides the name of a parameter from its value. Multiple parameters are strung together using &. Perhaps a web site named davesawesomeweatherservice.com takes both a zip code and whether the user wants the weather in Fahrenheit or Celsius as a parameter. The URL for a GET request might look like this:

```
http://www.davesawesomeweatherservice.com/get_weather?zip=11566&scale=Fahrenheit
```

get_weather is the name of the resource we are trying to access. zip and scale are parameters. 11566 and Fahrenheit are values for those parameters. Although GET requests are not supposed to have side effects, in reality, a server-side program can do whatever it wants with the requests it receives. For example, maybe davesawesomeweatherservice.com records in a database whether Celsius is more popular than Fahrenheit.

POST requests, unlike GET requests, do not append their parameters/values to the end of the URL. POST requests can be used for larger sets of data, including files. POST requests are typically generated using HTML forms (although GET requests can be too, and POST requests do not have to be). We saw part of an HTML form in Chapter 2. Listing 7-2 is a complete HTML form that may be used for submission of information to the get_weather resource on davesawesomeweatherservice.com's home page.

Listing 7-2. get_weather Form

```html
<form action="/get_weather" method="POST">
  <input id="zip" name="zip" type="text">
  <select id="scale" name="scale">
    <option>Fahrenheit</option>
    <option>Celsius</option>
  </select>
  <input type="submit" value="Submit">
</form>
```

The action attribute of the <form> tag points to the resource that the form will be submitted to. The method attribute could be "GET" in another scenario. The <input> tag can represent multiple different types of input elements. The type that it is representing is specified by the type attribute. The first <input> tag is a text box, while the second is a button that when clicked will cause the form's content to be changed into a POST request and sent to the get_weather resource. <select> is a drop-down menu that has two options: Fahrenheit and Celsius. The name of the parameters that the form elements represent is specified by the id and name attributes. Figure 7-4 shows this form rendered in Safari 7.0.

Figure 7-4. get_weather rorm rendered

After a GET or POST request is received, the server will generate its response. The beginning of that response will also be a header, and it begins with a status code. Table 7-1, shows some common HTTP status codes. You've probably at least seen the 404 status code before when following a *dead link*. A dead link is a link that points to a resource that no longer exists. There are many more status codes than those listed in the table, but you won't ever come in contact with the vast majority of them.

Table 7-1. *Common HTTP Status Codes*

Status Code	Name	Description
200	OK	The request was completed successfully.
307	Temporary Redirect	The resource has temporarily moved; here's the new URL.
308	Permanent Redirect	The resource has permanently moved to a new location.
401	Unauthorized	The user is not authorized to access this resource.
403	Forbidden	The resource that is trying to be accessed is restricted.
404	Not Found	The resource that was sought does not exist.
408	Request Timeout	The server could not process the request in a timely manner.
500	Internal Server Error	A generic error message, usually a programmer error.

On top of the status code, the header of the HTTP response will also include the length of the data being sent, the name of the server software, the type of data being sent, and more. The body of the response will be the data itself—an HTML document, an image, etc. The command-line tool cURL comes preinstalled on most OS X and Linux systems. When run with the –v option, it shows a complete HTTP request and response, including headers. Listing 7-3 shows this. We cut off the HTML document beyond its start tag (the ellipsis is where the document is cut off).

Listing 7-3. Examining HTTP with cURL

```
Davids-MacBook-Air:~ dave$ curl -v http://www.example.com/
* Adding handle: conn: 0x7fdf71003a00
* Adding handle: send: 0
* Adding handle: recv: 0
* Curl_addHandleToPipeline: length: 1
* - Conn 0 (0x7fdf71003a00) send_pipe: 1, recv_pipe: 0
* About to connect() to www.example.com port 80 (#0)
*   Trying 93.184.216.119...
* Connected to www.example.com (93.184.216.119) port 80 (#0)
> GET / HTTP/1.1
> User-Agent: curl/7.30.0
> Host: www.example.com
> Accept: */*
>
< HTTP/1.1 200 OK
< Accept-Ranges: bytes
< Cache-Control: max-age=604800
< Content-Type: text/html
< Date: Mon, 25 Nov 2013 01:45:42 GMT
< Etag: "359670651"
```

```
< Expires: Mon, 02 Dec 2013 01:45:42 GMT
< Last-Modified: Fri, 09 Aug 2013 23:54:35 GMT
* Server ECS (ewr/1590) is not blacklisted
< Server: ECS (ewr/1590)
< X-Cache: HIT
< x-ec-custom-error: 1
< Content-Length: 1270
<
<!doctype html>
<html>
...
```

Can you identify the HTTP request header? Here it is:

```
> GET / HTTP/1.1
> User-Agent: curl/7.30.0
> Host: www.example.com
> Accept: */*
```

And here's the HTTP response header:

```
< HTTP/1.1 200 OK
< Accept-Ranges: bytes
< Cache-Control: max-age=604800
< Content-Type: text/html
< Date: Mon, 25 Nov 2013 01:45:42 GMT
< Etag: "359670651"
< Expires: Mon, 02 Dec 2013 01:45:42 GMT
< Last-Modified: Fri, 09 Aug 2013 23:54:35 GMT
* Server ECS (ewr/1590) is not blacklisted
< Server: ECS (ewr/1590)
< X-Cache: HIT
< x-ec-custom-error: 1
< Content-Length: 1270
```

By the way, the < symbol is inserted by cURL.

A Full Web Transaction

Okay, at this point you know enough about the Web to understand what happens when you enter an address in your web browser and ask it to display a page. Let's walk through an entire scenario step by step for our imaginary site davesawesomeweatherservice.com. Here's what it might look like, broadly speaking:

1. The user enters the URL http://www.davesawesomeweatherservice.com/ in his web browser. Let's say the browser is Firefox.

2. A DNS server is contacted and returns the IP address that the domain davesawesomeweatherservice.com points to.

3. Firefox sends a GET request to the web server.

4. The web server, let's say Apache, handles the request and pulls the index document.

5. The index document is generated dynamically by the programming language PHP on the server.

6. The PHP program that generates the index document pulls information about the latest record temperatures from a MySQL database (MySQL is the name of a database program) and generates an HTML document that it passes back to Apache.

7. Apache creates an HTTP response header with the status code 200. It returns `index.html` to the client.

8. Firefox starts rendering the HTML page. It includes a reference to a CSS document that defines the style in which the HTML elements should be rendered. It also includes several images, the HTML form from the previous section, and some JavaScript code.

9. Firefox sends GET requests for the CSS file and images.

10. Apache sends the CSS file and the images back directly (they don't go through PHP). These responses are also status 200.

11. Firefox finishes rendering the page and displays it.

12. Firefox executes the JavaScript code on the page.

13. The user fills out the form and clicks Submit.

14. Firefox sends a POST request to the server with the parameters/values entered.

15. Apache calls a different PHP program (different from the one that creates the index page) that crafts the response, and steps 6–12 basically repeat.

16. The user gets his weather forecast.

It's not rocket science, but doing something that seems trivial on the Web, like getting a weather forecast, actually involves a lot of moving parts. Considering how much happens between the user's web browser and the web server (and we didn't even talk about what's happening on at the TCP/IP level) for every page visited, it's surprising that the Web is not more fragile. Actually, maybe you've witnessed its fragility firsthand—with some of those HTTP error status codes.

Summary

There's an alphabet soup of technologies that goes into powering the modern Web. You do not need to be an expert on all of them to get by. To be successful creating web apps with Dart, you should spend most of your time on HTML and CSS. You should maintain a broad understanding of the rest.

EXERCISES

1. Create a personal web site as a way to play around with HTML and CSS. Use the resources in Appendix D to become more familiar with it. If you don't feel comfortable, don't upload it to the Web!

2. Download a lesser known web browser, such as Opera. Can you find a web site that looks different in this web browser than in a more mainstream one? Can you identify what HTML element is being rendered differently? Can you find web sites that look different in the major web browsers?

3. Right-click an image on your favorite web site and select "Open Image in New Window" (or the equivalent in your browser). Check out the URL. No HTML involved!

4. Create another CSS file to stylize the site you created in Exercise 1. Have an option on the site to switch between the two different looks.

5. Set up your own web server. Most desktop operating systems come with built-in web servers. Search the Web to find out how to turn on yours.

6. Follow up Exercise 5 by serving a page containing a Dart program through your web server. Load the page in Dartium.

■■■

# CHAPTER 8

Using Dart to Interact with HTML

Dart was originally designed primarily for client-side web development. In this chapter, we take Dart to the Web in a big way. You will learn how to use Dart to interact with every part of a web page. There are multiple popular libraries for doing client-side web development with Dart, including two popular Google-sponsored projects: `Polymer.dart` and `Angular.dart`. In this book, we will be using the more primitive `dart:html` library, which is included in the base Dart SDK. It provides a good jumping-off point for the study of other libraries. Take note that when you create a new project in Dart Editor, you should be selecting the project type "Web application" and not "Web application (using the Polymer library)," as you work through this chapter and the rest of the book.

The DOM

The so-called Document Object Model (DOM) is the basis for interaction with HTML documents from JavaScript or Dart. In the DOM, every element of an HTML document is organized in a *tree* structure and is referenceable by attributes, including its `id`, `class`, and `type`. The DOM tree can also be traversed blindly. Through the DOM, we can access all of an HTML element's attributes and children. The tree always starts with a root node that represents the entire HTML document.

WHAT IS A TREE?

A tree is a common hierarchical data structure in computer science in which data is organized in nodes connected by branches. Each node contains a value and may or may not be connected to other nodes by branches. Each node in a directed tree is either the parent or the child of each node that it is connected to. In this way, a directed tree can only reach nodes through one route. A directed tree with a simple data structure is depicted in the following illustration.

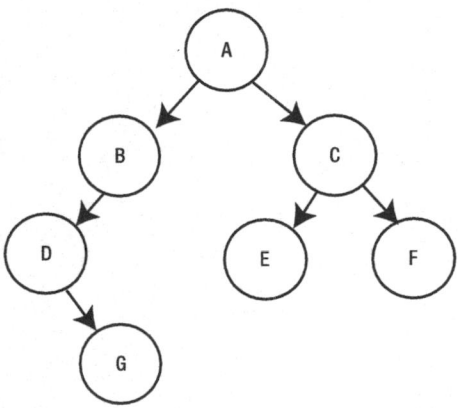

In this tree, the node with the value "A" is the root node. It has two children, "B" and "C." The beginning of an arrow is the parent node, and the end of an arrow is the child node. In other words, the arrow denotes the parent-child relationship between nodes. "D" is the child of "B," and "D" is the parent of "G." As in genealogical trees, nodes can be ancestors or descendants of one another. "E" is a descendent of "A." "B" is an ancestor of "G." Two nodes with the same parent are said to be siblings. "E" is a sibling of "F."

Certain types of trees specify the number of children a node may have, or the order of nodes, organized by their values. For example, in a binary tree, a type of directed tree, each node can have a maximum of two children and one parent. The tree in the illustration is a binary tree.

Listing 8-1 is a simple HTML document called mustard.html. Figure 8-1 is a rendering in Firefox of that document, and Figure 8-2 is a DOM tree that could represent that document. You will notice that the tree represents not only the relationship between nodes but also the values of those nodes, including the attributes of the HTML elements. What is unfortunate about DOM trees is that finding an individual node generally requires starting from the root node and traversing several branches before finding the particular node of interest. This can be slow.

Listing 8-1. mustard.html

```html
<!DOCTYPE html>
  <html>
    <head>
      <meta charset="utf-8">
      <title>Great Mustard Flavors</title>
    </head>
    <body>
      <h1>Great Mustard Flavors</h1>
      <h2>Yellow</h2>
      <p>Yellow mustard is the most common type of mustard. It is good on hot dogs.</p>
      <h2>Dijon</h2>
      <p>Dijon mustard is a traditional, more strongly flavored variety.
        <a href="http://en.wikipedia.org/wiki/Dijon_mustard">Read more about it.</a>
      </p>
    </body>
  </html>
```

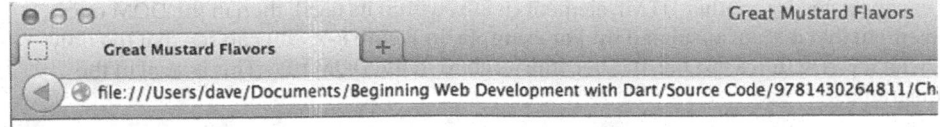

Great Mustard Flavors

Yellow

Yellow mustard is the most common type of mustard. It is good on hot dogs.

Dijon

Dijon mustard is a traditional, more strongly flavored variety. Read more about it.

Figure 8-1. mustard.html rendered in Firefox

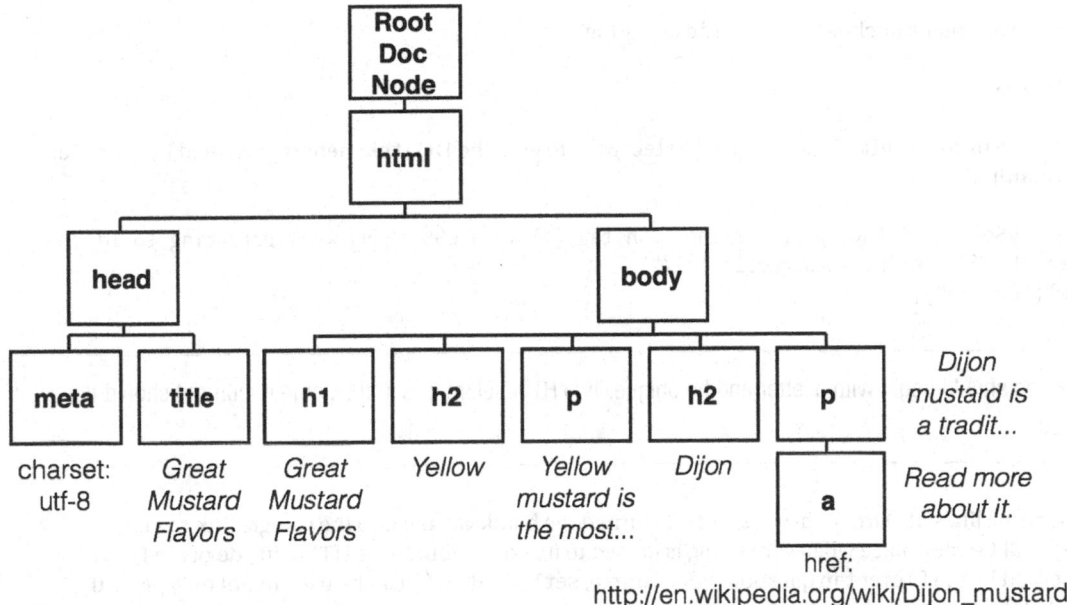

Figure 8-2. mustard.html DOM tree

If an HTML element is encapsulated by another HTML element (it falls within its tags), then in the DOM tree, it becomes the child of the element that it is encapsulated by. For example, in Figure 8-2, you can see that the only <a> tag from our document, which was within a <p> tag, has become its child in the DOM tree. This is seen in the bottom-right corner of the diagram.

Tagging the Tags

Web browsers are responsible for converting raw HTML documents into DOM trees accessible from Dart. dart:html provides functions that allow us to traverse those DOM trees to get objects that represent individual DOM elements. We can blindly traverse the DOM tree to find the elements that we are interested in, but it is much more convenient to tag them.

The mainstay of our tagging will be to utilize the id attribute of HTML elements and then refer to them in our Dart code by their id. Any HTML element can have an id attribute. The dart:html function querySelector() will grab an HTML element by its id. querySelector() returns an object of type Element. Although we have not yet covered object-oriented programming (Chapter 10), you have already worked with several other complex Dart object classes, such as String and Map. Element provides methods for getting HTML attributes, setting HTML attributes, manipulating text within DOM nodes, and more.

In HTML, anchor tags, <a>, are used for creating links from one document to another. Their href attribute is the URL that the link points to. Anything between the opening and closing tag will be what can actually be clicked/tapped to follow the link. For example, if we have an HTML anchor tag that goes to Google's home page, it may look like this:

```
<a href="http://www.google.com/">Google</a>
```

Suppose we have a blank anchor tag with an id of "myTag".

```
<a id="myTag"></a>
```

We can then use the dart:html function querySelector() to grab the DOM element represented by the myTag anchor tag and manipulate it.

```
Element a = querySelector("#myTag");  // the hash tag (#) is a CSS thing when referring to id
a.setAttribute("href", "http://www.google.com/");
a.setInnerHtml("Google");
```

■ **Note** id names should begin with a letter and be unique. Two HTML elements in the same document should not have the same id.

Using these three lines of Dart, we have essentially turned the blank <a> tag into the Google link <a> tag. setInnerHtml() will literally place whatever String is passed to it as an argument as HTML inside of the DOM element represented by the Element in question. For example, setInnerHtml() can be used to not only place the word *Google* but also place it as a large header with opening and close <h1> tags.

```
a.setInnerHtml("<h1>Google</h1>");
```

It is also possible to get the HTML within an Element as a String.

```
String theHTML = a.innerHtml;
print(theHTML);  // prints <h1>Google</h1>
```

If we just want the text within an Element, and not all its HTML, we can use the text property.

```
String justTheText = a.text;  // text is a property, not a method so no parentheses
print(justTheText);  // prints Google
```

There are multiple different subtypes of Element that can be specifically referenced. In Chapter 2, we used the as operator to *cast*[1] an Element to a specific subtype. For example, a <div> HTML tag can be represented by a DivElement.

The children property of an Element returns a List<Element> of all of its child nodes. This List, or the append() method, can be used to add Elements to the DOM tree.

```
DivElement d = new DivElement();
d.text = "Hello";
Element myElement = querySelector("#myElement");  // hypothetical Element
myElement.children.add(d);  // adds d as a child of myElement
myElement.append(d);  // equivalent to the last line
```

Responding to Events from the DOM

Any visible DOM element can be clicked (or tapped, on a touch screen), and those clicks can be captured by Dart. Some DOM elements can also take keyboard input. Keyboard events can be captured through the dart:html library. Form elements are commonly used for taking user input. In this section, you will learn, by example, how to capture and respond to events in your web-based programs.

ElementStream is a special type of object that keeps track of events directed at a particular Element. Each Element has multiple ElementStream objects keeping track of all of the different kinds of events that can be affecting it. Each ElementStream begins with the word on. Clicks are handled by the onClick ElementStream. Key presses are handled by the onKeyPress ElementStream. The listen() method of an ElementStream can be used to set a function that responds to the generated events. Do you remember the following line from Chapter 2's Hello World Fancy program that specifies that the sayHello() function should be called when the HTML element tagged with the id of button is clicked?

```
querySelector("#button").onClick.listen(sayHello);
```

The function that is specified with the listen() method must have the correct *signature*.[2] For instance, functions that respond to a click event must have one parameter, a MouseEvent. That MouseEvent object can tell us more about the event that happened. MouseEvent has properties that can tell us such things as whether the Shift key was held down during the click, or where exactly on the screen the click occurred.

BMI Calculator

Body Mass Index (BMI) is a way of screening for health problems based on a person's weight and height. It is not a definitive diagnostic tool. For example, a person with a high BMI can still be healthy (please do not refer to this book for medical advice). The formulas for calculating BMI in imperial and metric units, as stated by the CDC,[3] are

- BMI = Weight in Pounds / (Height in Inches)^2 * 703

- BMI = Weight in Kilograms / (Height in Meters)^2

---

[1]This is a way of changing one data type to another data type. In Dart, the as operator tells the DartVM to specifically treat one type as another compatible type.
[2]A combination of return type and parameter types in the specification of a function.
[3]Centers for Disease Control and Prevention, "About BMI for Adults,"
www.cdc.gov/healthyweight/assessing/bmi/adult_bmi/index.html, 2011.

You can see that the only difference between the two formulas is that when dealing with imperial units, we must multiply the result by the constant 703. The formula returns a number that works on a unique scale. A reproduction of the CDC's scale is in Table 8-1.

Table 8-1. *BMI Scale*

BMI	Weight Status
< 18.5	Underweight
>= 18.5 and < 25.0	Normal
>= 25.0 and < 30.0	Overweight
>= 30.0	Obese

We are going to create a program that allows the user to enter his height and weight in either imperial or metric units and obtain his BMI as well as its implication from Table 8-1. In Dart Editor, start a new project of type "Web application" and name it "BMICalculator." If you don't see bmicalculator.html initially, you may need to expand the folder called web in Dart Editor's file pane. Change bmicalculator.html to look like Listing 8-2.

Listing 8-2. bmicalculator.html

```html
<!DOCTYPE html>

<html>
  <head>
    <meta charset="utf-8">
    <title>BMI Calculator</title>
    <link rel="stylesheet" href="bmicalculator.css">
  </head>
  <body>
    <h2>BMI Calculator</h2>
    <input type="number" id="weight_input"><span id="weight_units">pounds</span>
    <br>
    <input type="number" id="height_input"><span id="height_units">inches</span>
    <br>
    <input type="radio" id="unit_type1" name="unit_type" value="imperial" checked>imperial
    <input type="radio" id="unit_type2" name="unit_type" value="metric">metric
    <br>
    <input type="submit" id="submit" value="Calculate">
    <h3 id="result1"></h3>
    <h3 id="result2"></h3>
    <script type="application/dart" src="bmicalculator.dart"></script>
    <script src="packages/browser/dart.js"></script>
  </body>
</html>
```

We have seen most of this HTML before in Chapter 2 and Chapter 7. When an <input> tag's type attribute is set to "number", it appears as a text box with specialized numerical controls (increment and decrement buttons) attached. You have surely seen radio buttons before on the Web. You should notice two interesting things about the <input> tags of type radio here. One is that the first ends in checked. This indicates that the imperial radio button is initially selected. The second is that both radio <input> tags have the same name attribute. This is because they are associated—only one can be selected at a time.

 tags are used for line breaks. The words *imperial* and *metric* are simply placed after their respective radio buttons, in order for the word to appear next to the button. There are also special HTML tags, called <label>, that can be used for this purpose. The Dart code that you will need to put into bmicalculator.dart is in Listing 8-3.

Listing 8-3. bmicalculator.dart

```dart
import 'dart:html';

bool imperial = true;
const int IMPERIAL_MULTIPLIER = 703;

void main() {
  querySelector("#unit_type1").onChange.listen(changeUnits);
  querySelector("#unit_type2").onChange.listen(changeUnits);
  querySelector("#submit").onClick.listen(calculate);
}

/// Change the units displayed by the inputs
/// and update [imperial]
void changeUnits(Event e) {
  // if imperial is checked
  if ((querySelector("#unit_type1") as RadioButtonInputElement).checked) {
    imperial = true;
    querySelector("#weight_units").text = "pounds";
    querySelector("#height_units").text = "inches";
  } else { // metric is checked
    imperial = false;
    querySelector("#weight_units").text = "kilograms";
    querySelector("#height_units").text = "meters";
  }
}

/// Check the height and weight inputs are valid
/// Calculate the bmi and display the results
void calculate(MouseEvent event) {
  double height, weight;
  // get the height and weight
  try {
    weight = double.parse((querySelector("#weight_input") as InputElement).value);
    height = double.parse((querySelector("#height_input") as InputElement).value);
  } on FormatException {  // uh oh, could not be turned into double
    window.alert("Only numbers are valid input.");  // popup alert
    return;
  }
  // do the actual calculations
  double bmi = weight / (height * height);
  if (imperial) {
    bmi = bmi * IMPERIAL_MULTIPLIER;
  }
  // update the display with a BMI rounded to 1 decimal digit
  querySelector("#result1").text = "Your BMI is " + bmi.toStringAsFixed(1);
  String comment;
```

```
if (bmi < 18.5) {
  comment = "Underweight";
} else if (bmi >= 18.5 && bmi < 25.0) {
  comment = "Normal";
} else if (bmi >= 25.0 && bmi < 30.0) {
  comment = "Overweight";
} else {
  comment = "Obese";
}
querySelector("#result2").text = comment;
}
```

main() sets up our event listeners. You should notice that the function changeUnits() is the onChange listener for both of the two radio buttons. Within changeUnits(), which radio button is selected is determined using the checked property.

calculate() uses the old tricks from our command-line input programs regarding checking if text input is actually numerical. If the inputted text can't be parsed as doubles, then calculate() shows a pop-up via window.alert() and returns before doing anything else. The actual BMI calculation is the same for metric or imperial units, except for a single multiplication. The method toStringAsFixed() rounds the variable bmi to a single decimal place and returns it as a String.

You can now try running the program. You should see a result similar to that in Figure 8-3. Try some nonnumerical inputs and check out the alert pop-ups.

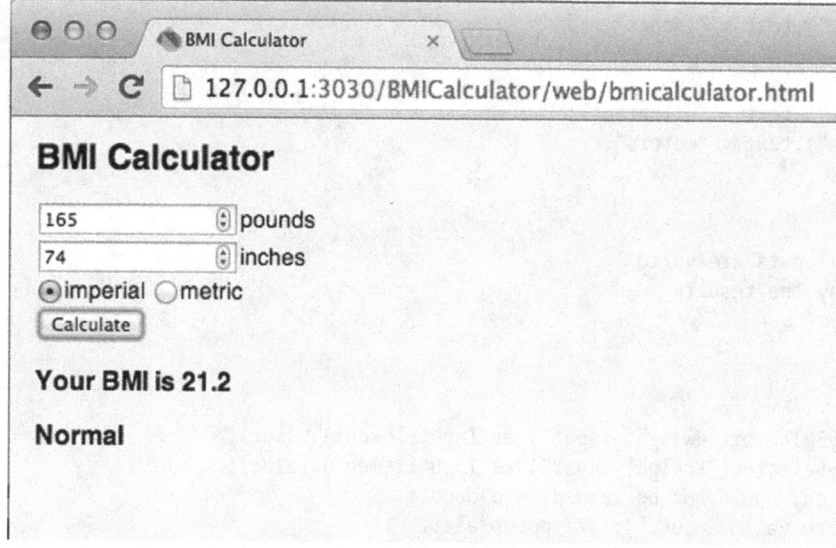

Figure 8-3. *BMI Calculator running in Dartium*

Images

The mainstay of displaying images with HTML is the `<img>` tag. Its `src` attribute is a URL that points to an image file that is then displayed on the page. For instance, to show the Google logo, we could have an `<img>` tag similar to the following:

```
<img id="google_logo" src="http://www.google.com/images/logo_sm.gif">
```

By manipulating the `src` attribute of an `<img>` tag, we can show or hide an image using Dart.

```
querySelector("#google_logo").setAttribute("src", "");  // make the image disappear
```

What if we want to include an image in our project? What if the project is not yet published to the Web, and we therefore do not yet know the URL that the image will appear at? URLs can be relative. If we have an image with the file name dog.png and we put it in a folder called "images" that is in the same folder in which our .dart and .html files reside, then we can refer to its URL as simply `"images/dog.png"`.

```
querySelector("#google_logo").setAttribute("src", "images/dog.png");  // show dog picture
```

■ **Note** When displaying images on the Web, you need to be cognizant that web browsers only support certain file formats. The most common are GIF, JPEG, and PNG. If you create an image in Adobe Photoshop, it first needs to be exported to one of these formats before you include it in your Dart project. Recently, all of the major browsers have come to support an open standard for vector graphics known as SVG. Exporting to SVG is a good alternative for pictures created in a vector graphics program like Adobe Illustrator.

Memory Game

This is a simple game of memory. Sixteen cards with four different images (four cards of each image) are facedown on a table. The player can flip any two cards at a time. If the two cards have the same image, then those cards remain flipped. If the two cards have a different image, they return to being facedown, and the player earns a strike. If the player earns three strikes, he loses. The game we aim to create appears in Figure 8-4.

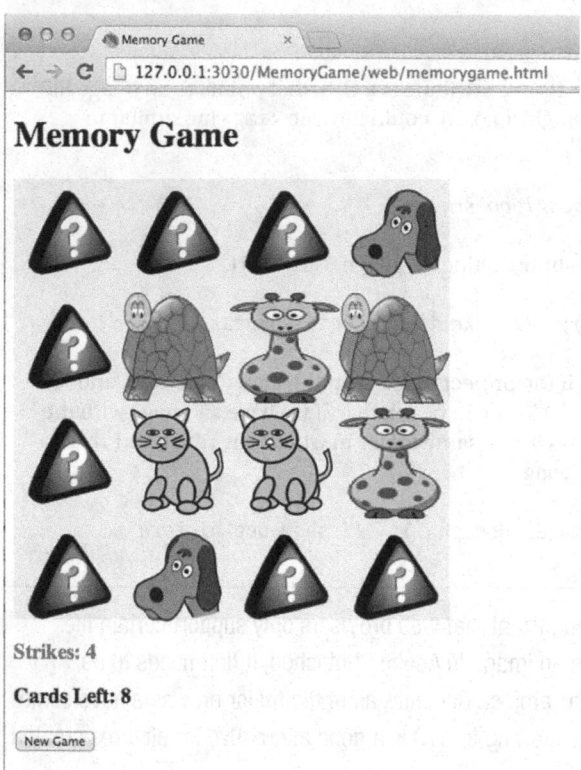

Figure 8-4. *Memory Game running in Dartium*

This project uses several PNG images for the cards. You can create your own images or use images included with the source code available from the Source Code/Downloads tab on the book's Apress product page (www.apress.com/9781430264811). Either way, ensure that they are placed in the right folder (images) relative to your source code. This folder will not previously exist. You will need to create an images folder within the web directory. Also, ensure that they have the same file names that are used to refer to them from the code.

■ **Tip**   File paths are annoying things. Often what you think is a programming error will really be an incorrect file path. File paths on Windows follow a different format than file paths on OS X and Linux. The Dart SDK will automatically convert file paths between operating systems.

Start a new web application project in Dart Editor called "MemoryGame." To create the interface for this game, and to ensure it looks right, we are going to use some simple CSS. As you have probably noticed, every new project of type "Web application" that is created in Dart Editor automatically has a .css file created for it. Change memorygame.css to look like Listing 8-4.

Listing 8-4. memorygame.css

```
#strike_text {
  color: red;
}
```

```css
#left_text {
  color: black;
}

#card_box {
  width: 400px;
  height: 400px;
  background-color:beige;
}
```

Could the CSS be any more self-explanatory? Each section refers to a different element in the HTML file that is tagged with the respective id. card_box is the area in which the 16 100-pixel-by-100-pixel cards will reside; hence, it is 400 pixels wide and 400 pixels tall. Speaking of the HTML, Listing 8-5 contains memorygame.html.

Listing 8-5. memorygame.html

```html
<!DOCTYPE html>

<html>
  <head>
    <meta charset="utf-8">
    <title>Memory Game</title>
    <link rel="stylesheet" href="memorygame.css">
  </head>
  <body>
    <h1>Memory Game</h1>
    <div id="card_box"></div>
    <h3 id="strike_text">Strikes: <span id="num_strikes"></span></h3>
    <h3 id="left_text">Cards Left: <span id="num_left"></span></h3>
    <button id="new_game_button">New Game</button>

    <script type="application/dart" src="memorygame.dart"></script>
    <script src="packages/browser/dart.js"></script>
  </body>
</html>
```

The only thing of note here is that we did not include any <img> tags. The image elements are created on the fly in our Dart code. It would be quite annoying to type out 16 <img> tags with id attributes! Okay, so the CSS and HTML are pretty simple…here comes the Dart. Replace memorygame.dart with Listing 8-6.

Listing 8-6. memorygame.dart

```dart
import 'dart:html';
import 'dart:async';  // for Timer

// A lot of constants makes for maintainable code as opposed
// to using magic numbers (or magic Strings for that matter)
const int NUM_CARDS = 16;
const int NUM_OF_EACH = 4;
const String CARD_BACK = "images/card_back.png";
const List<String> CARD_FILE_NAMES = const ["images/dog.png", "images/cat.png",
                                            "images/giraffe.png", "images/turtle.png"];
```

```dart
int strikes, cardsLeft;
List<String> cards;  // the actual deck
ImageElement lastClicked; // last card clicked if not two clicked

/// Resets the game board for a new game
void reset() {
  strikes = 0;
  cardsLeft = NUM_CARDS;
  querySelector("#num_strikes").text = strikes.toString();
  querySelector("#num_left").text = cardsLeft.toString();
  // find all <img> Elements in the DOM and change their src
  // attribute to be that of the facedown card
  for (ImageElement img in querySelectorAll("img")) {
    img.src = CARD_BACK;
  }
  //create the randomly ordered deck of cards
  cards = new List();
  for (String cardFileName in CARD_FILE_NAMES) {
    for (int i = 0; i < NUM_OF_EACH; i++) {
      cards.add(cardFileName);
    }
  }
  cards.shuffle();
}


/// Main game logic, checks if two cards have been matched
/// or not; also flips cards when clicked
void cardClicked(MouseEvent event) {
  ImageElement clickedCard = event.target; // which card was clicked
  // if the card's already turned over, ignore
  if (!clickedCard.src.endsWith(CARD_BACK)) {
    return;
  }
  // otherwise flip it over
  int clickedNumber = int.parse(clickedCard.alt); // thing we stored
  clickedCard.src = cards[clickedNumber];

  if (lastClicked == null) {
    lastClicked = clickedCard;
  } else {

    if (clickedCard.src == lastClicked.src) { // we have a match!
      cardsLeft -= 2;
      querySelector("#num_left").text = cardsLeft.toString();

    } else { //we have a strike!
      strikes++;
      querySelector("#num_strikes").text = strikes.toString();

      //flip them back after 2 seconds
      ImageElement tempClicked = lastClicked;
      Timer t = new Timer(const Duration(seconds: 2), () {
```

```
          clickedCard.src = CARD_BACK;
          tempClicked.src = CARD_BACK;
       });
    }
    lastClicked = null;
  }
}

void newGame(MouseEvent event) => reset();

void main() {
  // add the img elements, you didn't think we were going to type
  // <img...> 16 times, did you? Computers are better at repetitive tasks.
  for (int i = 0; i < NUM_CARDS; i++) {
    ImageElement ie = new ImageElement(height: 100, width: 100);
    ie.onClick.listen(cardClicked);
    ie.alt = i.toString(); // a way of tagging the cards
    querySelector("#card_box").append(ie);
  }
  querySelector("#new_game_button").onClick.listen(newGame);
  reset();
}
```

You may notice a library you haven't seen before, dart:async. dart:async has a class called Timer that can be used for triggering an asynchronous event (a non-blocking event, or one that does not interrupt the program) in the future. In Memory Game, a Timer is used for flipping a pair of cards back over after a two-second delay, if they were not a match.

main() is responsible for setting up the ImageElements and attaching event listeners to both the ImageElements and the new game button. It leaves most of the heavy lifting of setting up the game to reset(), which also, incidentally, is what is called when the new game button is clicked. That call happens indirectly. The function newGame() is actually called. This is because onClick event listeners need to have a MouseEvent as a parameter in their signature. reset() does not have a MouseEvent parameter. By abstracting game setup into reset(), we are able to save duplicative code that would otherwise need to appear in both main() and newGame().

There's a little trick in main(), with regard to the created ImageElements. We do not keep references to the ImageElements in any data structure. Instead, we tag each ImageElement with a number in its alt attribute. alt is an HTML <img> tag attribute that displays alternative text in a *tooltip*[4] when the mouse pointer hovers on top of an image. Later, we will pull this number in cardClicked(), to check which card was actually clicked. The number corresponds to an index into the cards List, which can then provide the image's file name that should appear for that card. In essence, it's a bit of a hack. We're using the alt attribute for something other than its originally intended purpose.

■ **Note**   While this hack is sort of neat, it's not the proper use of the alt attribute. The alt attribute is meant to provide a textual description of an image. This attribute is useful if the image does not load (we still understand what was supposed to be there) and for the blind who can't see the image. It's important to try to make your web pages accessible to as wide an audience as possible.

---

[4]This is a small pop-up, usually only containing text, that appears when the mouse pointer hovers over something to better explain what it does.

reset() resets the scoring variables as well as their displays (strikes, cardsLeft). It flips all of the cards back over. And finally, reset() creates a new randomly sorted deck of card names that represents which cards are where. Let's look in particular at the for-loop that flips all of the cards over.

```dart
for (ImageElement img in querySelectorAll("img")) {
  img.src = CARD_BACK;
}
```

querySelectorAll() is similar to querySelector(), except that instead of always returning one Element, it returns a List of Elements that match the query. Up to this point, we have only been querying by the id attribute. That is why we have used the # sign, which in CSS selector language precedes the id that we are looking for. Now, we want to retrieve every <img> in the document. To query by tag type, you simply use the name of the tag. In this instance, that is "img". querySelectorAll("img") returns a List of every ImageElement in the DOM tree. The loop's body simply sets those ImageElements' src attributes to be CARD_BACK, effectively flipping the cards over.

cardClicked() is a complex function that we'll go over in great detail. It is triggered any time an ImageElement is clicked. It starts by pulling which element was clicked through MouseEvent's target property. That ImageElement is saved in the variable clickedCard.

```dart
ImageElement clickedCard = event.target; // which card was clicked
```

If a card was already flipped over by being clicked, we do not have any business with it if it's clicked again. Therefore, we ignore the click and return:

```dart
if (!clickedCard.src.endsWith(CARD_BACK)) {
  return;
}
```

The if-statement is true when the card that was clicked does not have an src attribute that refers to the CARD_BACK image. You will notice that we are using the method endsWith(), and you might wonder why we are not just comparing CARD_BACK to clickedCard.src with the == operator? The answer is a little clunky. When Dart sets the src attribute with a relative path URL, it appends the full URL prefix (such as http:// or file://, which is used for local files) to the beginning of src. In other words, we may be comparing a String such as http://www.example.com/images/card_back.png to the String images/card_back.png. In such a case, the two Strings still end the same way—namely with images/card_back.png. Hence, the use of endsWith() is justified.

If we have not returned by this point, then we know the user clicked a card that is still showing its back. It's time to flip it over. We use that trick with the alt attribute to grab which card has been clicked, index into the cards List, and pull the correct file name for flipping the card over. The alt attribute is stored as a String, so it needs to be parsed into an int.

```dart
int clickedNumber = int.parse(clickedCard.alt); // thing we stored
clickedCard.src = cards[clickedNumber];
```

These lines are immediately followed by a seemingly simple if-statement, with some complex intentions.

```dart
if (lastClicked == null) {
  lastClicked = clickedCard;
} else {
```

lastClicked is a variable that is used for keeping track of the card/ImageElement that was clicked in the situation when two cards are clicked, one after the other. null is a special Dart keyword that means a variable references nothing. Only when no valid cards have yet been clicked is lastClicked set to a particular ImageElement. In every other instance, we do not need to know the last card clicked, and therefore set lastClicked to null. In other words, if lastClicked is equal to null, then all that the rest of cardClicked() needs to do is set it to the ImageElement that was just clicked, since this is possibly the beginning of a two-card click sequence. If lastClicked already refers to an ImageElement, then we know this is the end of a two-card click sequence, and we need to check whether the user got a match or receives a strike. We are then in the else-block.

```
if (clickedCard.src == lastClicked.src) { // we have a match!
  cardsLeft -= 2;
  querySelector("#num_left").text = cardsLeft.toString();

} else { //we have a strike!
```

If the two cards that have been clicked have the same src attribute, then the player has a good memory, and the cards are permanently left flipped over and cardsLeft is decremented and redisplayed. Otherwise, the player made an error, and we have a strike.

```
    strikes++;
    querySelector("#num_strikes").text = strikes.toString();

    //flip them back after 2 seconds
    ImageElement tempClicked = lastClicked;
    Timer t = new Timer(const Duration(seconds: 2), () {
      clickedCard.src = CARD_BACK;
      tempClicked.src = CARD_BACK;
    });
  }
  lastClicked = null;
 }
}
```

strikes is incremented and redisplayed. We create a temporary variable, tempClicked, that will hold a reference to the card that was clicked before clickedCard, because lastClicked will soon be set to null. A Timer is created. This is the object we mentioned earlier that will allow for an event to occur in the future asynchronously. In this case, we set it to occur in two seconds. When that event occurs, an anonymous function is run that flips over both of the cards from this two-card click sequence. Two seconds in the future, the local variable tempClicked will not have changed, but the global variable lastClicked will have already been set to null. Why do we do this? Because we want to let the user see for two seconds the cards that he wrongly chose before they are flipped back over. Finally, lastClicked is set to null, because our two-card click sequence is over.

Go ahead and run Memory Game. It's actually pretty fun!

Drawing with an HTML Canvas

The latest version of the HTML specification, HTML5, introduced a new element, known as a *canvas*, that can be used for interactive drawing by client-side scripting languages such as JavaScript and Dart. In reality, before HTML5, several browsers had supported the canvas control for many years. Now that it's standardized and supported by all major browsers, it's safe to use with your Dart programs.

■ **Note**   Generally, you don't have to worry about different versions of HTML anymore. All current browsers support the majority of the HTML5 specification. In the past, especially during the days of HTML 3 and HTML 4, there was a large discrepancy regarding the parts of the specification implemented by each browser. For more information about the history of the HTML specification, you can check out appendix B.

HTML Canvas Basics

Canvas is useful when you want to draw without a gluttony of DOM elements getting between you and the ultimate image on the user's screen. Good examples of this would be a game or animation. Messing around with <img> tags might be okay for a simple card game, but as soon as characters need to be jumping and running, as in, say, a platform game, it would be much more efficient to be able to draw to the screen directly. The canvas is inserted into an HTML document with a tag not unlike any other HTML tag, <canvas>. Its attributes can specify a height and width. It's not a bad idea to give it an id too, of course.

```
<canvas id="myCanvas" width="500" height="500"></canvas>
```

Then the canvas element can be grabbed with the querySelector() function of dart:html as a CanvasElement, so that we can draw to it.

```
CanvasElement myCanvas = querySelector("#myCanvas");
```

The CanvasElement property context2d is what we actually use for doing the drawing operations. It can do things like draw rectangles, lines, circles, arcs, images, text, and more. The following three lines draw a red rectangle in the middle of the screen:

```
CanvasRenderingContext2D myCanvasContext = myCanvas.context2D;
myCanvasContext.setFillColorRgb(255,0,0);  // RGB is Red, Green, Blue levels from 0-255 each
myCanvasContext.fillRect(myCanvas.width/2, myCanvas.height/2, 100, 200);  // x, y width, height
```

Were you confused by the RGB thing? RGB is an acronym that stands for "red, green, blue." It is common in computing to see colors defined as these three component colors, since almost any color can be made as a combination of them. The RGB scale goes from 0 to 255 for each component color. In our example, red is set to 255, green to 0, and blue to 0. This is in essence a pure red. There are pretty color swatches on the Internet that show colors and their respective RGB values. Check out Appendix D for some specific resources.

■ **Tip**   RGB black is 0, 0, 0. RGB white is 255, 255, 255.

The x coordinate of what is being drawn to the screen increases from left to right. Interestingly, and unlike what you might expect, the y coordinate increases from the top of the canvas to the bottom of the canvas. For example, the following line draws a 50-pixel-by-50-pixel rectangle 100 pixels to the right of the left edge of the canvas and 200 pixels below the top of the canvas.

```
myCanvasContext.fillRect(100, 200, 50, 50);  // rectangle A
```

The next line draws a 50-pixel-by-50-pixel rectangle 400 pixels to the right of the left edge of the canvas and 400 pixels below the top of the canvas.

```
myCanvasContext.fillRect(400, 400, 50, 50);  // rectangle B
```

In these fillRect() calls, the x and y coordinates refer to the top-left corner of the rectangle being drawn. Figure 8-5 illustrates the relative locations of the two rectangles, with the first being labeled "A," and the second being labeled "B." It also shows the general direction that x and y increase in.

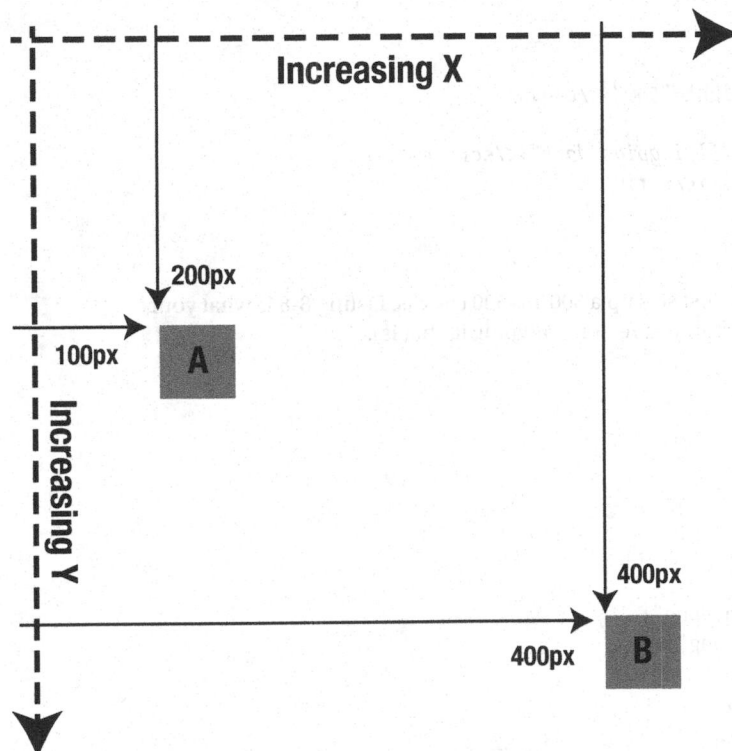

Figure 8-5. *Canvas rectangle example*

Flying Pigs

In this simple example, one pig after another pig flies across an HTML canvas. If the user can click a pig before it reaches the other side, he gets a point. As in Memory Game, if you don't want to create your own images, you can get images from the source code bundle on the *Dart for Absolute Beginners* product page on the Apress web site. Make sure to put your images in an images folder within the same folder as your Dart and HTML source code.

Create a new web application in Dart Editor called "FlyingPigs." Modify flyingpigs.html to look like Listing 8-7.

Listing 8-7. flyingpigs.html

```
<!DOCTYPE html>

<html>
  <head>
    <meta charset="utf-8">
    <title>Flying Pigs</title>
    <link rel="stylesheet" href="flyingpigs.css">
  </head>
  <body>
    <h1>Flying Pigs</h1>
    <canvas id="myCanvas" width="500" height="500"></canvas>

    <script type="application/dart" src="flyingpigs.dart"></script>
    <script src="packages/browser/dart.js"></script>
  </body>
</html>
```

There's nothing special about this HTML; it just sets up a 500-by-500 canvas. Listing 8-8 is what your flyingpigs.dart source file should look like (when you're done retyping it, that is).

Listing 8-8. flyingpigs.dart

```
import 'dart:html';
import 'dart:async';  // for Timer
import 'dart:math';  // for Random

const int PIG_WIDTH = 100;
const int PIG_HEIGHT = 50;
const String PIG_RIGHT = "images/pig_right.png";
const String PIG_LEFT = "images/pig_left.png";

int pigX, pigY, score = 0, speed;
CanvasElement myCanvas;
ImageElement pigImage;

/// Called by a Timer 60 times per second
void update(Timer t) {
  pigX += speed;  //update pig's location
  // get a new pig when the last one has gone off screen
  if (pigX < (-PIG_WIDTH) || pigX > myCanvas.width){
    newRandomPig();
  }
  draw();
}

/// Draw a background, the pig, and the score
void draw() {
  CanvasRenderingContext2D myCanvasContext = myCanvas.context2D;
  //draw the background
  myCanvasContext.setFillColorRgb(0, 0, 255);  // Blue
  myCanvasContext.fillRect(0, 0, 500, 500);  // 0x, 0y, 500 width, 500 height
```

```dart
    //draw the score in black at the top right of the screen
    String scoreText = "Score: $score";
    myCanvasContext.setFillColorRgb(0, 0, 0);   // Black
    myCanvasContext.fillText(scoreText, myCanvas.width-100, 30); // string, x, y
    //draw the pig
    myCanvasContext.drawImageScaled(pigImage, pigX, pigY, PIG_WIDTH, PIG_HEIGHT);
}

/// Sets up a new pig at a random location
void newRandomPig() {
  // if it's 1 it will go right, otherwise left
  Random rand = new Random();
  speed = rand.nextInt(10) + 5;  // random speed 5 to 14 pixels/frame
  pigY = rand.nextInt(myCanvas.height - PIG_HEIGHT);  // random y
  int leftOrRight = rand.nextInt(2);
  if (leftOrRight == 1) {  // going from left to right
    pigX = 0;
    pigImage.src = PIG_RIGHT;
  } else {   //going from right to left
    pigX = myCanvas.width - PIG_WIDTH;
    pigImage.src = PIG_LEFT;
    speed = -speed;  // move left not right
  }
}

/// When the canvas is clicked, we need to check if the user hit a pig
void clickHappened(MouseEvent me) {
  //check if click was within the pig's space
  int clickX = me.offset.x;
  int clickY = me.offset.y;
  if (clickX > pigX && clickX < pigX + PIG_WIDTH
      && clickY > pigY && clickY < pigY + PIG_HEIGHT) {  // we have a hit
    score++;
    newRandomPig();
  }
}

void main() {
  myCanvas = querySelector("#myCanvas");
  myCanvas.onClick.listen(clickHappened);
  pigImage = new ImageElement();
  newRandomPig();
  // This Timer will call update() approximately 60 times a second
  Timer t = new Timer.periodic(const Duration(milliseconds:17), update);
}
```

main() pulls the canvas for the global variable myCanvas and adds clickHappened() as a click listener, creates the ImageElement that will hold the pig's image, calls newRandomPig() to initially set up the pig, and creates a Timer that will fire every 17 milliseconds repeatedly (a millisecond is 1/1000th of a second). This is effectively 60 frames per second. Every time the Timer fires, it will call the update() function. Timers created using the periodic() constructor (which means they repeat) must have callback functions that take the Timer as a parameter. Hence, the update() function has one parameter, a Timer.

update() itself is quite simple. It moves the pig by incrementing pigX by speed. Then it checks if the pig has moved all the way off the screen, in which case it calls newRandomPig(). Finally, it calls draw().

draw() fills a big blue rectangle over the entire canvas as a kind of background. score is drawn as part of a black String. The actual pig is drawn by scaling pigImage to PIG_WIDTH and PIG_HEIGHT and placing it at pigX and pigY.

newRandomPig() randomly generates speed and pigY. If speed is positive, then the pig will move from left to right. If speed is negative, then the pig will move from right to left. It then generates a random variable, leftOrRight, that is either 0 or 1. If leftOrRight is 1, then the pig will be going from left to right, and so its starting x coordinate, pigX, is 0. Otherwise, if leftOrRight is 0, then pigX is all the way to the right—PIG_WIDTH subtracted from myCanvas.width. In this case, speed is also negated, so that the pig will move from right to left. In either case, the pig has a different image if it is going left than if it is going right and pigImage is set appropriately.

clickHappened() gets the location that the click occurred within the canvas by pulling its x coordinate and y coordinate from the mouse event's offset property. offset represents the point that was clicked with coordinates relative to the canvas. clickHappened() checks whether these coordinates are within the rectangle occupied by the pig's image. If they are, it increments score and calls newRandomPig().

Flying Pigs is a shell that could, with a little bit of polish, become a fun game. With the combined power of the HTML canvas and Dart, it's easy to get cross-platform games built. There are game libraries for Dart, such as StageXL (www.stagexl.org), that make it even easier. If you're interested in 3D games, Dart includes support for WebGL, an emerging standard based on the industry-wide specification OpenGL. Be warned, though, working with WebGL is significantly more complicated than doing 2D graphics with canvas. WebGL is also not yet supported by all web browsers. Figure 8-6 shows Flying Pigs running in Dartium.

Figure 8-6. *Flying Pigs running in Dartium*

Summary

Web browsers convert HTML into a DOM tree. This is a hierarchy of elements that represent each and every tag in the document. The dart:html library provides functions and objects for interacting with the DOM tree. One useful pattern is to set the id attribute of HTML tags and pull their respective DOM objects using the querySelector() function.

HTML form elements are useful for bringing user input to your Dart program. Almost any element in the DOM tree can be set up to generate events (mouse clicks, keyboard input, etc.) that your Dart program can respond to. Images can be displayed using HTML <img> tags and can be manipulated from Dart using the ImageElement class. URLs of images can be relative paths, and they will be automatically expanded by Dart. More complex drawing can be done with an HTML canvas element. The dart:async library provides a Timer class, which can be used for scheduling asynchronous events in the future, including repeating events.

EXERCISES

1. Create a Dart web app that draws a binary tree using the HTML canvas element. There should be a way for the user to input the structure of the tree. Perhaps an HTML form fits the bill.

2. Enhance the interface of BMI Calculator. Remove the submit button. Create an interface that calculates the BMI live as heights and weights are entered into the text boxes. It should also auto-update when units are changed from imperial to metric.

3. Create an improved version of Memory Game that allows the user to configure the difficulty level using HTML form elements (radio buttons, selection boxes, etc.). A greater difficulty level may include more cards and more images to be displayed. As an extra bonus, add winning and losing conditions. For example, perhaps it's three strikes and you're out.

4. Limit the amount of time that Flying Pigs can be played, and limit the amount of missed clicks that can occur before a game is over.

5. Write a simple *Space Invaders* clone using Dart and an HTML canvas. It's quite an involved project, but at this point, you actually have all the skills necessary to complete it. The one part of the traditional game that may be beyond your current knowledge is the barriers. Perhaps, skip those! You could combine the List of ImageElements from MemoryGame with the collision-detection algorithm from Flying Pigs to have a significant portion of the game already built (aliens and bullets hitting aliens, respectively). It will be interesting to compare your effort to Alien Invaders of Chapter 11, once you get to it.

CHAPTER 9

Hangman

You are halfway through this book. It's the end of your sophomore year, and your classes are starting to get serious. Soon you're going to be taking object-oriented programming, advanced Dart, and something funky called isolates. Take a deep breath, apply for some good internships, and take it all in. You've made it far enough that your accomplishments deserve a mini-culminating experience. Hangman is your thesis. It will encompass all of the knowledge you've acquired in the first eight chapters. We will ease into Hangman with a warm-up problem first: Word Scramble. Word Scramble encompasses a lot of the knowledge from Chapter 8 and is useful for review.

Word Scramble

In Word Scramble, a randomly selected word has its letters changed into a random order and then displayed to the user. The user is then tasked with figuring out what the original word was. Create a new web application in Dart Editor called "WordScramble."

The HTML

Listing 9-1 has the simple HTML for this program, which should go in wordscramble.html.

Listing 9-1. wordscramble.html

```
<!DOCTYPE html>

<html>
  <head>
    <meta charset="utf-8">
    <title>Word Scramble</title>
    <link rel="stylesheet" href="wordscramble.css">
  </head>
  <body>
    <h1>Word Scramble</h1>
    <h3>You have <span id="seconds_left"></span> seconds remaining.</h3>
    <h2 id="scrambled_word"></h2>
    <input type="text" id="guess">
    <h2><span id="num_correct">0</span> Correct</h2>
    <h2><span id="num_missed">0</span> Missed</h2>
```

```
      <script type="application/dart" src="wordscramble.dart"></script>
      <script src="packages/browser/dart.js"></script>
   </body>
</html>
```

The Dart

Listing 9-2 has the Dart code for this warm-up program. It belongs in wordscramble.dart. We once again use the dart:async library for the Timer class.

Listing 9-2. wordscramble.dart

```dart
import 'dart:html';
import 'dart:async';

String secretWord;
int numCorrect = 0;
int numMissed = 0;
int secondsLeft = 60;
List wordList = ["ANTELOPE", "ARKANSAS", "AWESOME", "PICKLE", "CEILING",
                 "SUPREME", "CAREFUL", "WRITING", "FUNHOUSE", "FOREVER"];

/// Check if the user has entered the de-scrambled word
void checkGuess(Event e) {
  String guess = (querySelector("#guess") as InputElement).value.toUpperCase();
  if (guess == secretWord) {  // player got it right
    numCorrect++;
    querySelector("#num_correct").text = numCorrect.toString();
    newWord();
  }
}

/// Once a second update the time display and check if
/// the player has run out of time
void tick(Timer t) {
  secondsLeft--;
  querySelector("#seconds_left").text = secondsLeft.toString();
  if (secondsLeft <= 0) {  // player missed one
    numMissed++;
    querySelector("#num_missed").text = numMissed.toString();
    newWord();
  }
}

/// Randomly pick a new word and scramble it for display
void newWord() {
  secondsLeft = 60;
  wordList.shuffle();
  secretWord = wordList[0];
  List<String> tempList = secretWord.split("");  // divide word into letter strings
  tempList.shuffle();  // scramble the word for display
```

```
querySelector("#scrambled_word").text = tempList.join();  // put it back together
(querySelector("#guess") as InputElement).value = "";  // clear input text
}

void main() {
  querySelector("#guess").onKeyUp.listen(checkGuess);
  Timer t = new Timer.periodic(const Duration(seconds: 1), tick);
  newWord();  // get us started the first time the program is run
}
```

main() sets up checkGuess() as a listener for everything typed into the input box with id guess. It creates a Timer that calls tick() every second and initializes the program with a call to newWord(). newWord()randomly selects a word from wordList, turns that word into a List of letters that can be scrambled (with shuffle()), and displays the List joined back into a String. Oh, and it also clears the input box. checkGuess() finds correct user guesses when the text in the guess input box is the same as secretWord. tick() has the job of decrementing the seconds left display and checking if the user ran out of time. If the user did run out of time, then numMissed is incremented and newWord() is called.

Wow, as you get more advanced with Dart, our descriptions can become a lot less long-winded! Our program is a little bit limited as it stands now, because the word list is hard-coded into the program. It would be much more flexible to hold the words in some kind of external resource. Figure 9-1 shows Word Scramble running in Dartium.

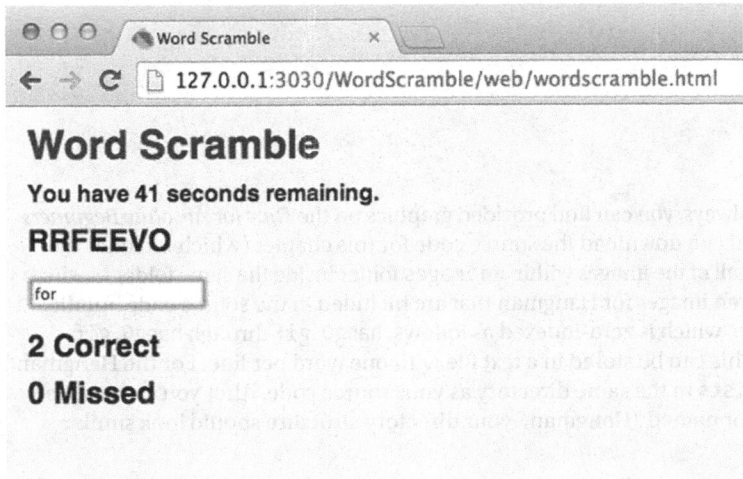

Figure 9-1. *Word Scramble running in Dartium*

Hangman

Hangman is a classic word guessing game. A word is hidden, with underscores replacing its letters. You guess what it is, one letter at a time. If you guess a letter that is in the word, its location in the word is revealed. If the letter appears multiple times, then all of its locations are revealed. Therefore, you can only guess each letter once. You have a limited number of guesses. As the number of wrong guesses increases, a picture of a person being hung is increasingly completed, until it shows the person fully executed. The game we aim to create appears in Figure 9-2.

Figure 9-2. *Hangman running in Dartium*

The Game Resources

You will need some graphics for Hangman. As always, you can find provided graphics on the *Dart for Absolute Beginners* product page on the Apress web site, where you can download the source code for this chapter (which includes the images and a sample word list). You should put all of the images within an images folder inside the same folder in which your Dart source code is located. There are seven images for Hangman that are included in the source code bundle. They are labeled with numbers in the file name, which is zero-indexed as follows: hang0.gif through hang6.gif.

For Hangman, we also need a word list. This can be stored in a text file with one word per line. For the Hangman program, you will need a folder called word_lists in the same directory as your source code. After you create a new project of type "Web application" in Dart Editor named "Hangman," your directory structure should look similar to Figure 9-3.

Figure 9-3. *Directory structure for Hangman, as it appears in Dart Editor's files pane*

The HTML and CSS

Listing 9-3 has the source HTML that should go in hangman.html. There's nothing new here for you to discover.

Listing 9-3. hangman.html

```
<!DOCTYPE html>

<html>
  <head>
    <meta charset="utf-8">
    <title>Hangman</title>
    <link rel="stylesheet" href="hangman.css">
  </head>
  <body>
    <h1>Hangman</h1>
    <p>Hit any key to guess a letter.</p>
    <img id="hang_image">
    <div id="letter_list"></div>
    <div id="secret"></div>
    <br>
    <input id="new_game_button" type="submit" value="New Game">

    <script type="application/dart" src="hangman.dart"></script>
    <script src="packages/browser/dart.js"></script>
  </body>
</html>
```

Perhaps the only thing you have not seen before in the CSS is the use of margin-top to provide some spacing between two elements. Listing 9-4 contains the source for hangman.css.

Listing 9-4. hangman.css

```css
body {
  background-color: #F8F8F8;
  font-family: 'Open Sans', sans-serif;
  font-size: 14px;
  font-weight: normal;
  line-height: 1.2em;
  margin: 15px;
}

#secret {
  font-size: 24pt;
  margin-top: 20px;
}

#hang_image {
  width: 256px;
  height: 256px;
}
```

The Dart

Our Dart program needs to model both the secret word (showcasing part of it at a time) and the letters remaining. It also needs to process user keyboard input, change hangman images, and grab a randomly selected word when a new game is started. Listing 9-5 is the Dart source code for Hangman that goes in hangman.dart.

Listing 9-5. hangman.dart

```dart
import 'dart:html';
import 'dart:math';

int wrongGuesses;
const int GUESS_LIMIT = 5;
const String WORD_LIST_FILE = "word_lists/hanglist.txt";
const String CAPITAL_ALPHABET = "ABCDEFGHIJKLMNOPQRSTUVWXYZ";
const List<String> HANG_IMAGES = const ["images/hang0.gif", "images/hang1.gif",
                                        "images/hang2.gif", "images/hang3.gif",
                                        "images/hang4.gif", "images/hang5.gif",
                                        "images/hang6.gif"];
String lettersLeft, secretWord;
bool gameOver;

void main() {
  // listen for keyboard input, also listen for clicks to the new game button
  window.onKeyPress.listen((KeyboardEvent e) {
    String lastPressed = new String.fromCharCodes([e.charCode]);
    lastPressed = lastPressed.toUpperCase();
```

```
    playLetter(lastPressed);
  });
  querySelector("#new_game_button").onClick.listen((MouseEvent me) => restart());
  restart();
}

/// The user has tried to play [letter] - see if it's in the secret word
/// if it is uncover it. If it's not, process a miss.
void playLetter(String letter) {
  if (lettersLeft.contains(letter) && !gameOver) {
    lettersLeft = lettersLeft.replaceFirst(new RegExp(letter), '');
    querySelector("#letter_list").text = lettersLeft;

    //put the letter into the secret word
    if (secretWord.contains(letter)) {
      String oldDisplay = querySelector("#secret").text;  // what the user sees
      String newDisplay = "";  // what we will soon show the user
      for (int i = 0; i < secretWord.length; i++) {
        if (secretWord[i] == letter) {  // put the new
          newDisplay = newDisplay + letter;
        }
        else {  // put the old back in
          newDisplay = newDisplay + oldDisplay[i];
        }
      }
      querySelector("#secret").text = newDisplay;

      if (newDisplay == secretWord) {  // if we won
        gameOver = true;
        querySelector("#letter_list").text = "YOU WIN";
      }
    }
    else {  // secretWord does not contain letter
      wrongGuesses++;
      (querySelector("#hang_image") as ImageElement).src = HANG_IMAGES[wrongGuesses];
      if (wrongGuesses > GUESS_LIMIT) {
        gameOver = true;
        querySelector("#letter_list").text = "GAME OVER";
        querySelector("#secret").text = secretWord;
      }
    }
  }
}

/// Grab a random word from the hanglist.txt file for [secretWord]
void chooseSecretWord() {
  String url = WORD_LIST_FILE;
  HttpRequest request = new HttpRequest();
  request.open("GET", url, async: false);
  request.send();
  String wordList = request.responseText;
  List<String> words = wordList.split('\n');  // convert text file into List of words
```

117

```dart
  // randomly choose a word from the List
  Random rnd = new Random();
  secretWord = words[rnd.nextInt(words.length)];
  secretWord = secretWord.toUpperCase();

  // hide what we display to the user - all underscores for letters
  querySelector("#secret").text = secretWord.replaceAll(new RegExp(r'[a-zA-Z]'), "_");
}

/// Put everything in the starting position
void clearBoard() {
  wrongGuesses = 0;
  (querySelector("#hang_image") as ImageElement).src = HANG_IMAGES[wrongGuesses];
  lettersLeft = CAPITAL_ALPHABET;
  querySelector("#letter_list").text = lettersLeft;
}

/// Reset everything for a new game
void restart() {
  gameOver = false;
  chooseSecretWord();
  clearBoard();
}
```

main()

Unlike in previous programs, in this main() function, we use anonymous functions (remember those from Chapter 5?) as listeners for events. This puts the actual code for the listeners in the same place that they are set up. It makes sense for small listeners, but for larger ones, it may make the function where the listeners are added messy. One anonymous function handles key presses. It capitalizes the letter pressed and calls playLetter(). Another anonymous function calls restart() when the new game button is pressed.

The key pressed listener is added to the global window object. No text box or other control is needed for user input. The listener will capture any text typed while the page is in focus. However, if the web browser's address bar is in focus and not the page itself, keystrokes will not be captured. Therefore, it is necessary to click the page to give it focus to start entering input for a game of Hangman. You may be confused by the call to fromCharCodes() in the key pressed listener. KeyboardEvent does not provide a method that returns a String representing what was entered on the keyboard. Instead, we need to convert a character code into a String.

restart()

restart() is called both from main() when the game first starts and anytime the new game button is clicked. It resets the board by setting gameOver to false, calling chooseSecretWord() and clearBoard(). gameOver is a boolean that ensures keyboard input will not be processed (within playLetter()) after the game ends (the player has won or lost). It is set to false, because we do want to process all keyboard input until the game ends.

chooseSecretWord()

This function reads a text file with terms for Hangman on each line. The file is converted into a List of terms (Strings). Then a term is randomly chosen from the List. The term is made all uppercase, because we work in uppercase throughout the program, so that we're always comparing apples to apples. The display of the word in the <div> tag with id secret is done with all underscores when the word is first selected. The real word is stored in the global variable secretWord. To convert the term's letters into underscores while keeping its spaces (and apostrophes, if it has them or any other non-letter characters), we use a *regular expression*. See the sidebar on regular expressions to better understand what they are and how they work.

Reading a file from a Dart web application is a little bit tricky. Because of security constraints, standard APIs for file reading from the dart:io package are not available in web applications. Instead, in chooseSecretWord(), we actually create an HTTP request for the text file containing the list of Hangman terms. That's the use of the HttpRequest object request. When request is used to retrieve the text file, it is specified that the operation not be asynchronous (async: false)—we want to wait for the text file to be retrieved before we try to manipulate it. In other words, our program will block (wait) until the text file is retrieved. This is the desired behavior, because the rest of the function assumes that the text file was successfully retrieved.

The retrieved list of Hangman terms is converted from a String into a List by using the String split() method (first introduced in Chapter 6). It will use the passed argument (a String) as a delimiter for creating the List of String objects out of the initial String. For example, "dog,cat,apple,orange".split(",") will return a List like ["dog", "cat", "apple", "orange"].

REGULAR EXPRESSIONS

Regular expressions are patterns used for searching within strings (finding places in a string that match a pattern). Almost every popular modern programming language includes a regular expressions API in its standard library. Dart's regular expressions API is based on JavaScript's. In fact, Dart's creators purposefully copied JavaScript's regular expressions specification in order to provide developers with a familiar experience.

To learn more about how to write regular expression patterns, you should check out the regular expression resources in Appendix D. You can use regular expressions with any Dart String. It is a particularly powerful tool to learn well.

In chooseSecretWord(), the pattern searched on for replacing text in secretWord will match any uppercase or lowercase English letter. In this way, non-letters, such as apostrophes and exclamation marks, will be ignored and not replaced by underscores. So, if we have the term *Smuggler's Notch* in our term list, the user will see it as "_____'_ _____."

---

clearBoard()

wrongGuesses is reset. hang_image is set to the first Hangman image. Initially, the entire alphabet has not been played by the player, so lettersLeft is set to that (the constant CAPITAL_ALPHABET). lettersLeft is displayed in the <div> letter_list.

playLetter()

playLetter() is really the heart of Hangman. An uppercase letter from the user's keyboard input is passed to it from the listener in main(). playLetter() checks if the letter is in secretWord and that the game is not over.

```
void playLetter(String letter) {
  if (lettersLeft.contains(letter) && !gameOver) {
    lettersLeft = lettersLeft.replaceFirst(new RegExp(letter), '');
    querySelector("#letter_list").text = lettersLeft;
```

If letter is in lettersLeft and gameOver is false, the String regular expression method replaceFirst() is immediately called so that letter cannot be played again. The regular expression is simply letter itself—we want to match just the actual appearance of the letter. We replace letter with an empty String. In other words, we make the letter disappear from lettersLeft. Then we update the display of lettersLeft.

```
if (secretWord.contains(letter)) {
  String oldDisplay = querySelector("#secret").text;  // what the user sees
  String newDisplay = "";  // what we will soon show the user
  for (int i = 0; i < secretWord.length; i++) {
    if (secretWord[i] == letter) {  // put the new
      newDisplay = newDisplay + letter;
    }
    else {  // put the old back in
      newDisplay = newDisplay + oldDisplay[i];
    }
  }
  querySelector("#secret").text = newDisplay;

  if (newDisplay == secretWord) {  // if we won
    gameOver = true;
    querySelector("#letter_list").text = "YOU WIN";
  }
}
```

If we have a hit—letter is in secretWord—then we have to replace the underscores being displayed where the letter should now appear with the letter itself. oldDisplay represents the current hidden word, underscores and all. newDisplay will be what is shown to the user after the letter that was played is revealed. newDisplay is built up through a for-loop that checks each iteration for whether we are at the location of the letter played within secretWord. If we are, we add it. If we are not, we just add back what was previously displayed to the user (so it could be an underscore, or it could be a letter that was revealed on a previous turn).

Finally, the display is changed to show newDisplay instead of oldDisplay, and we check if the user has now won the game by checking if newDisplay is equivalent to secretWord. If the user has won, gameOver is set to true, so that no further input will be processed, and we notify the user that he's won (replacing the remaining letter list to do so).

```
else {  // secretWord does not contain letter
  wrongGuesses++;
  (querySelector("#hang_image") as ImageElement).src = HANG_IMAGES[wrongGuesses];
  if (wrongGuesses > GUESS_LIMIT) {
    gameOver = true;
    querySelector("#letter_list").text = "GAME OVER";
    querySelector("#secret").text = secretWord;
  }
}
```

In the alternative case (secretWord does not contain letter), we need to increment wrongGuesses, update the Hangman image to reflect we're one step closer to losing, and check if the player lost (too many wrong guesses). If the player lost, gameOver is set to true; the remaining letter list displays "Game Over" instead; and the secret term is revealed.

Halftime Review

In the first eight chapters, you became proficient at writing programs in a procedural style with Dart. Let's review how you did it and what you should know before beginning the second half of *Dart for Absolute Beginners*. If anything looks fuzzy, now may be the time to go back and refresh your memory.

Chapter 1: "Getting Set Up"

You learned about setting up a virtual work environment and a comfortable physical work environment. Most important, you set up Dart Editor—the integrated development environment that we use throughout this book. By now, you should be quite familiar with Dart Editor. You should know how to create new projects, open files, save files, and run programs. If you've made it this far through the book and you've been doing any of the exercises, then you also know how frustrating programming can be. It's important to not give up but instead take breaks when you're frustrated.

Chapter 2: "Your First Dart Programs"

You learned that the function titled main() will always be the entry point to your program. That's true in both command-line and web-based Dart programs. main() will be the first code executed that you write. You also learned that the print() function can be used for outputting text to the console. You had some exposure to the basics of HTML, but you would have to wait for Chapter 7 to further explore HTML.

Chapter 3: "Some Programming Fundamentals"

You learned about variables, operators, strings, control structures, and loops. Specifically, you should be comfortable with the Dart constructs of ints, doubles, Strings, bools, if-statements, switch-statements, while-loops, do-while-loops, and for-loops. You learned the arithmetic (+, -, *, /, ++, --), assignment (=), and comparison operators (==, <, >, !=, <=, >=).

Chapter 4: "Five Small Programs to Showcase Fundamentals in Dart"

You implemented your first sizable Dart programs and learned that computers are good simulators. You learned several new operators, including &&, +=, and *=. The concept of constants was introduced (keyword const), and their suitability in place of so-called magic numbers discussed. You also learned how to read keyboard input from a command-line Dart program.

Chapter 5: "Functions"

Functions have parameters that receive input by way of arguments when they are called. They also have return values. Dart supports first-class, anonymous, and single-line functions. Dart also has special syntax for named and positional optional parameters. Recursive function calls can be mind-bending but a useful abstraction. You learned that the + operator can be used for concatenating strings.

Chapter 6: "Data Structures"

Lists, Maps, and Sets are the most fundamental data structures in Dart. Lists and Maps have built-in literal syntax. In Dart, it can be specified what type of data a List, Map, or Set will hold when it is created. Lists store ordered, sequential information. Maps store pairs of keys and values. Sets store unique, unordered elements. You learned how to loop through these data structures using for-in-loops. Finally, the DateTime class was introduced, as well as the String class's split() method.

Chapter 7: "How Does the Web Work?"

You learned more about HTML, CSS, and HTML forms. You learned a little bit about communication between web browsers and web servers over HTTP. Overall, you got a very brief introduction to the technologies behind the Web—just enough so that you're semi-prepared for Chapter 8.

Chapter 8: "Using Dart to Interact with HTML"

We discussed the DOM tree and how you can manipulate the DOM using the dart:html library. We extensively made use of a pattern in which we used the id attribute of HTML tags to refer to them from our Dart code, using the function querySelector(). You also learned about how the dart:async library's Timer class can be used for scheduling an event in the future.

Looking Forward

Up to this point, we've been programming in a so-called procedural style (using functions as our main organizational structure—the way we've been using them is not to be confused with functional programming [see the side bar in Chapter 5]). The next two chapters concentrate on an alternative style with object-oriented programming. The rest of the book will focus on mastering object-oriented programming and more advanced Dart concepts. As in the first half, the chapters of the second half of the book build on each other, one after the other. All of the same rules apply: take your time; type the example programs yourself into Dart Editor (don't copy and paste); and try some exercises to reinforce your understanding.

Getting to the point where you could write programs that do something useful was a milestone (Chapter 4). Getting to the point where you could write basic web apps was another milestone (Chapter 8). The milestones get murkier from here on out.

The goal is no longer just to get the computer to do something—the goal from now on is to get the computer to do something sophisticated. That also means that the level of sophistication inherent in the techniques necessary for the next few chapters is higher. We're upping the ante!

You may already have all the tools you need to program something that you had in mind when you started this book. If you do, that's great, mission accomplished. However, you won't be able to move on to more advanced books and write larger programs successfully (and *successfully* implies cleanly and efficiently) if you don't take the time to understand most of the rest of the book. That doesn't mean you should get *stuck* on the rest of the book. If a particular more advanced topic confuses you, by all means move on and come back to it later. It just means that you should take the rest of the book seriously, if you want to be a "real" programmer (whatever that means).

Summary

Hangman is an engaging classic game, and you've gained enough experience to implement it in Dart. You learned about reading text files, handling keyboard input, and searching Strings. Give yourself a pat on the back, because you are no longer an *absolute beginner* at Dart.

EXERCISES

1. Add "themes" to Hangman that the user can select. Perhaps one user wants to play in the Old West, while another user wants to play atop Mount McKinley. Each theme has different graphics and word lists.

2. Upgrade Word Scramble. Let the word be randomly chosen from a list of words stored in a text file. Make the program look more attractive using some CSS styling. Have multiple different word lists that the user can choose from.

3. In Word Scramble, event listeners are in separate functions. In Hangman, they are implemented with anonymous functions. When should each technique be used? Does it matter? Do you prefer one over the other stylistically?

4. What concept in the first half of the book did you most struggle with? Write a program that makes extensive use of that concept.

5. Write a program that uses an HttpRequest object for pulling something other than text files.

6. What are some uses of regular expressions that you can think of in programs you use on a daily basis?

CHAPTER 10

∎∎∎

Object-Oriented Programming Fundamentals

Object-oriented programming is a method of representing programmatic ideas that allows for improved abstraction, increased productivity, and better code reuse. Dart is a fully object-oriented programming language, in that it has no concept of *primitive* data types (*primitive* meaning "non-object").[1] In Dart, everything is an object. You've been using objects since the beginning of this book without even knowing it.

What Is an Object?

An object is an abstraction meant to represent a component of a program. Objects can be created, destroyed, given attributes, and made to perform actions. The metaphors that they can represent are really limited only by your imagination. Objects have *instance variables*, which represent their attributes, and *methods*, which represent the actions they can perform.

Object Basics

Every object belongs to a *class*. The class of an object is its type. In other words, objects of the same class are the same type. Objects of the same class have the same instance variables and methods available to them (although the value of those instance variables may differ).

∎ **Note**   In Dart, stylistically, class names are written in CamelCase, like variable and function names. Unlike variable and function names, the first letter of a class name should be capitalized. Instance variable names and method names should also be camelCase, but begin with a lowercase letter.

Perhaps we want to model a game of checkers using classes. We can have one class of objects represent each of the pieces, named `Piece`. The instance variables of this `Piece` class will determine their color, king status, and location on the board. The `Piece` class may have a method for moving pieces and another for drawing them on the screen.

We can have another class that models the `Board`. The `Board` has a method for drawing itself and an instance variable, a `List`, that keeps track of all the `Piece` objects. The `Board` may also have constant instance variables that determine the number of squares and dimensions of the board.

---

[1] In Java, a fairly similar language in many ways to Dart, not everything is an object. An `int` or `double`, for example, is actually a primitive data type that has no methods or instance variables associated with it. (To be clear, in Dart, `int`s and `double`s are objects.)

Finally, our imagined checkers program may have a class, Game, that takes care of all of the user interaction within the game. It has an instance variable to keep track of whose turn it is, another to hold the Board, and methods to handle played moves, checking for wins, and checking for draws. This is just one (incomplete) way of modeling a game of checkers. The classes we've described are shown in Figure 10-1.

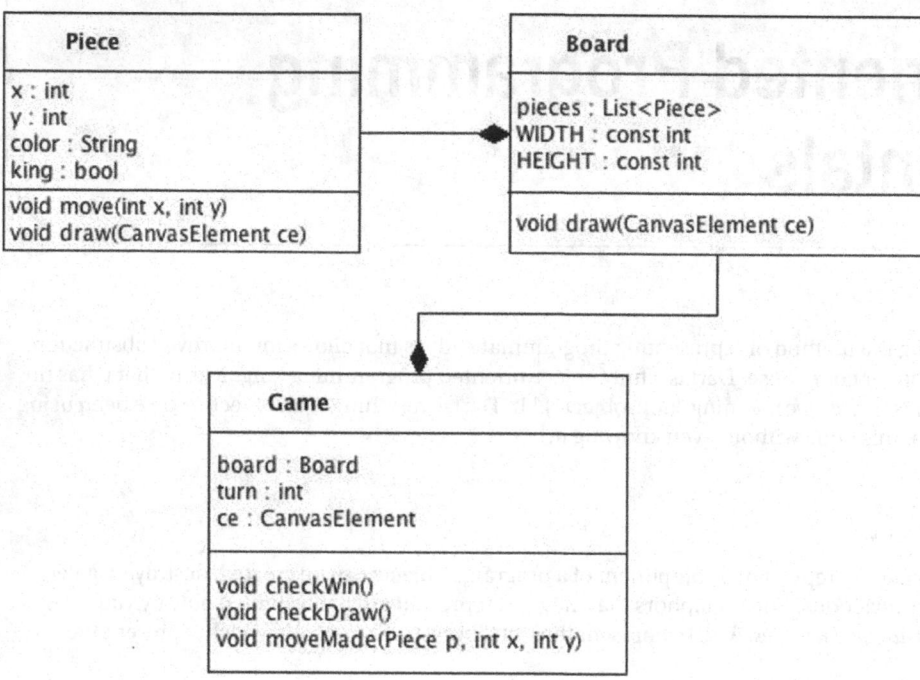

Figure 10-1. *A class model for a checkers program*

References to Objects and Instances

In Chapter 3, you were told that variables in Dart are actually references to objects. We then said, for simplicity's sake, to forget that information until Chapter 10. It's now Chapter 10. Variables are references to objects.

The new operator is used for instantiating new objects. An *instance* of a class is a unique object created of that class type. When an object is created (using the new operator, or literal syntax), a region of memory is allocated large enough to fit all of the instance variables and other data associated with that object. The variable that refers to the object in itself does not use very much memory. It's just a pointer to the address in memory where the object resides.

It is, therefore, easy for multiple variables to refer to the same object. Consider the following List object, animalList1, created with List literal syntax. Think about how it changes throughout the next few lines.

```
List animalList1, animalList2;
animalList1 = ["antelope", "cat", "dog"];
animalList2 = animalList1;
animalList2.add("rabbit");
print(animalList1);  // prints [antelope, cat, dog, rabbit]
```

After the assignment in the third line (animalList2 = animalList1), animalList1 and animalList2 refer to the same object in memory. Therefore, when "rabbit" is added to the object referenced by animalList2, it is also added to the object referenced by animalList1, because they are referencing the same object. That is why "rabbit" is printed as part of animalList1.

The important insight here is that when one variable is assigned to another variable, the object that they refer to is not copied. The reference is copied (because, again, all variables are just references to objects). Figure 10-2 shows this arrangement explicitly. You can see that animalList1 and animalList2 refer to the same object in memory.

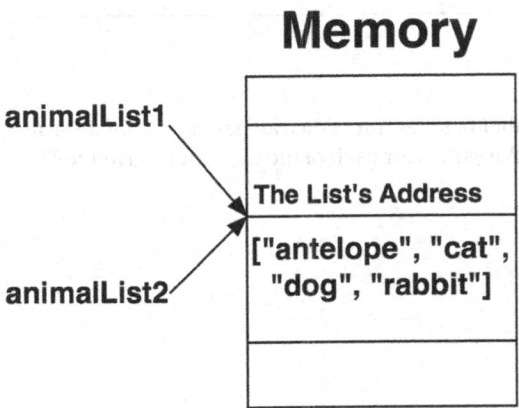

Figure 10-2. *Two references to the same object*

The same is true of objects passed to functions as arguments. They are passed *by-reference*. A reference to the original object is copied into the local variable representing the function's parameter. For instance, in the following dumb example, both animalList and list1 refer to the same List object—and addRabbit() modifies it—not a copy of it.

```
void addAnimal(List animalList) {
  animalList.add("mouse");
}

void main() {
  List list1 = ["watermelon"];
  addAnimal(list1);
  print(list1);  // prints [watermelon, mouse]
}
```

Again, the key insight is that addAnimal() ends up modifying the original object referenced by list1, not a copy of it. A common error that new programmers make is to think that operations on animalList would have no effect on list1. As you can see, the opposite is true. It is simply a copied reference to the same object.

Defining Classes

The keyword class is used for defining a class of your own type. Curly braces encompass the content of the class. This is how a blank class can be defined:

```
class Dice {
}
```

Once the class is defined, we can instantiate new objects based on it. However, we can't really do anything with them yet.

```dart
Dice d = new Dice();
```

■ **Note** Classes cannot be defined within functions or other classes. Dart does not have a concept of *inner classes* like Java does.

Instance Variables

What attributes does a set of dice need to possess? How about a number of sides (most dice are six-sided, but there are other types of dice as well)? How many dice are in the set? What are the values for each of the dice after a given roll? Let's add instance variables for all of these attributes to Dice.

```dart
class Dice {
  int sides;
  int numberOfDice;
  List<int> values;
}
```

Now that our Dice class has instance variables, we can manipulate them.

```dart
void main() {
  Dice d = new Dice();
  d.sides = 6;
  d.numberOfDice = 2;
  d.values = [4, 6];
}
```

The . operator is used for referring to the instance variable of an object. But you probably already figured that out, because we've been using it since Chapter 2! We can also give our instance variables default values when they are first declared as part of a class definition. For example, perhaps the preceding should be the defaults for Dice objects.

```dart
class Dice {
  int sides = 6;
  int numberOfDice = 2;
  List<int> values = [4, 6];
}
```

If no default value is provided, then before an instance variable is assigned a value, it will default to null. Every instance of a class has its own copy of the class's instance variables. So, if we have two Dice objects, changing the sides variable of one will not affect the other.

```dart
void main() {
  Dice d1 = new Dice();
  Dice d2 = new Dice();
  d1.sides = 6;
  d2.sides = 4;
  print(d1.sides);  // prints 6, not 4
}
```

WHAT IS NULL?

The term/keyword `null` has come up throughout this book several times without a clear explanation for a reason: you didn't previously know enough about Dart's object system to appreciate its meaning. `null` is the absence of value. It's a reference to nothing.

When a variable refers to `null`, it means that it refers to no object. It is "empty," in a sense. The default value of all uninitialized Dart variables is `null`. It is common practice to use `null` as a kind of signal value for when an error has occurred. For example, the `Set` method `lookup()` searches for an object in the `Set`. If it can't find it, it returns `null`.

It is also common to check if a variable has been initialized, by checking if it is equal to `null`. Although this is common and practical for safety reasons, in actuality it is even safer to always provide a default value. However, when interacting with other people's code, we can never be sure what they have or have not provided for particular scenarios.

Getters and Setters

Getters and setters are specialized functions (really methods—to be discussed shortly) used for getting and setting so-called *properties*. These properties are really just accessor names. They are not instance variables; rather, they are yet another abstraction between you and data. In practice, properties are used just like instance variables. Trying to explain the concept is much more complicated than the concept itself, so let's just look at some getters and setters.

```
class Dice {
  int _sides = 6;
  int numberOfDice = 2;
  List<int> _values = [4, 6];

  int get maximumValue => sides * numberOfDice;

  int get sides => _sides;
  set sides (int s) {
    if (s < 2) {
      _sides = 2;
    } else {
      _sides = s;
    }
  }
}
```

We have replaced our `sides` instance variable with a combination of a `sides` property (with a getter and setter) and a new instance variable, `_sides`. Instance variables that begin with an underscore are treated as *private* by Dart. What do we mean by private?[2] We mean that only your program (any files within your *library*, a term you'll learn more about later in this chapter) can access them. Other programs don't know they exist.

---

[2]Don't confuse our use of the word *private* here with the keyword `private` in other languages such as C++ and Java. In those languages, it means specifically that an instance variable is only accessible from the instance of the class that it belongs to. In this sense, we are using the term *private* in the same way as Java uses the keyword `protected`.

The instance variable values has also been transformed into _values. There is no need for users of the Dice class to directly manipulate _values. In fact, leaving it open to manipulation would endanger the validity of the entire class. What if the user rolls a number that wins a game, and a malicious program, realizing money is at stake, simply changes the value of values (no underscore)?

The maximumValue property only has a getter. There is no way to set maximumValue. If we attempt to assign a value to maximumValue, Dart will raise an exception, which is a good thing.

Separating how a variable is accessed by outsiders from its actual implementation is known as *data encapsulation*. It's a good idea, because it allows us to later change how our code works, without having to change the interface that other coders use to interact with it. The get and set keywords precede the name of the property and the functions that define it. Getters cannot take any parameters. On the other hand, setters cannot return any values. Getters are purely for getting information, and setters are purely for setting attributes.

We can use properties in exactly the same way that we'd use instance variables.

```
void main() {
  Dice d = new Dice();
  d.sides = 4;
  print(d.maximumValue);
}
```

Internally, Dart actually creates getters and setters for our instance variables, if we don't define them ourselves. By making it easy to switch between implementing an instance variable and a property, Dart allows us to radically change how our code works, without changing how it's accessed. Perhaps when prototyping, you create a bunch of instance variables. Then you realize these variables need a lot of sanity checks when they're set. You change the instance variables over to properties and add validity checks into the setters. Abstraction comes to the rescue.

Data encapsulation is a fundamental tenet of object-oriented programming. We're separating interface (properties and instance variables are accessed the same way) from implementation (properties and instance variables are defined differently). The insight is that it's not wise to expose your data to the whole world. Only trusted manipulators should be tolerated. As the programmer of the class, you are a trusted manipulator. However, your fellow programmers, or even other classes that you are writing, may not be as trusted.

Methods

Okay, so Dice objects are now mildly interesting data structures, but they don't really do very much. That's why we need to provide them with actions in the form of methods. Methods are functions that are attached to an object. What's special about them, as opposed to regular functions, is that they have access to the instance variables of the class they are a part of.

Let's add methods to Dice for rolling the dice and printing the dice.

```
import "dart:math";  // for Random

class Dice {
  int _sides = 6;
  int numberOfDice = 2;
  List<int> _values = [4, 6];

  int get maximumValue => sides * numberOfDice;

  int get sides => _sides;
  set sides (int s) {
    if (s < 2) {
      _sides = 2;
```

```
    } else {
      _sides = s;
    }
  }

  /// generate random values for [_values]
  void roll() {
    List newValues = [];
    Random rand = new Random();  // need to import dart:math
    for (int i = 0; i < numberOfDice; i++) {
      newValues.add(rand.nextInt(sides) + 1);  // number from 1 to sides
    }
    _values = newValues;
  }

  /// print the values of the dice
  void printDice() => print(_values);
}
```

As you already know, methods are accessed using the . operator like instance variables.

```
void main() {
  Dice d = new Dice();
  d.sides = 4;
  d.numberOfDice = 3;
  d.roll();
  d.printDice();  // 3 randomly generated numbers from 1-4 are printed in a List
  d.roll();
  d.printDice();  // 3 randomly generated numbers from 1-4 are printed in a List
}
```

Constructors

Constructors are special methods used for setting up an object when it is first instantiated. A basic constructor is a method with the same name as the class. It can take parameters and is most often used for assigning an object's instance variables.

■ **Note** Dart offers a myriad of options for constructors related to inheritance, a concept covered in the next chapter. The material covered here is just the most basic use of constructors.

Constructor Basics

Let's add a simple constructor to Dice that can be used for initializing all of its instance variables when a new Dice object is created. You will notice that a constructor has no return type.

```
/// ns is for number of sides, nd is for number of dice
Dice(int ns, int nd) {
  sides = ns;
  numberOfDice = nd;
}
```

And here's how this new constructor can be called at instantiation time.

```
Dice d = new Dice(6, 4);  // d has 6 sides and 4 dies
```

Constructors need not be limited to instantiating variables. Any code that could go in a regular method can go in a constructor. However, instantiating variables is such a common use of constructors that Dart has specialized syntactic sugar for just that purpose. The keyword this is used for referring to the instance of a class currently operated on. By using this, we can distinguish between instance variables and local variables. If there is a local variable named numberOfDice, then within the block where it is declared, numberOfDice refers to that local variable, while this.numberOfDice refers to the instance variable. We can write a verbose constructor using the same names as our variables, as follows:

```
Dice(int sides, int numberOfDice) {
  _sides = sides;
  this.numberOfDice = numberOfDice;
}
```

The syntactic sugar that Dart provides, shortens the above constructor to

```
Dice(this._sides, this.numberOfDice);
```

▪ **Note**   If no constructor is specified for a class, Dart implicitly creates a constructor with no parameters that calls the superclass's parameterless constructor (see Chapter 11 on inheritance for more).

Let's think about the Dice class a little bit, now that we've come to this point. After a Dice object is created, one really should not be able to change its number of sides or number of dice. That would be weird in the middle of a game. From now on, we'll only allow those values to be set when a new Dice object is created. Therefore, we should use underscores to make all of those instance variables private. What if someone tries to call printDice() before roll() is ever called? _values will not be properly initialized. We can have _values default value be the empty list, [ ], until roll() is called, which is cleaner than giving it some arbitrary numbers. Another idea is to let _values remain null by default and check in printDice() if it is null and raise some kind of error in that case.

There's also an important value that we cannot ascertain from our Dice objects right now—the sum of the numbers shown in a roll. There should be a property, total, that returns the sum of the numbers in the List _values. The List method fold() takes a starting value and a function that will operate on every two subsequent elements in the List and returns the result. First it applies the function to the starting value and the first element of the List. Then it applies the function on the result of that first operation and the next element of the List. It continues in this pattern through all of the elements of the List. Our specific implementation sums the numbers in _values.

Listing 10-1 shows what our revised Dice class looks like. Since we will use the Dice class in the example game Pig shortly, we also have a new keyword statement, part of, which will be explained soon.

Listing 10-1. dice.dart

```
part of pig;

class Dice {
  int _sides = 6;
  int _numberOfDice = 2;
  List<int> _values = [];
```

```
  int get maximumValue => sides * numberOfDice;
  int get numberOfDice => _numberOfDice;
  int get sides => _sides;
  /// total is the sum of [_values]
  int get total => _values.fold(0, (first, second) => first + second);

  /// constructs a new Dice object
  Dice(this._sides, this._numberOfDice);

  /// generate random values for [_values]
  void roll() {
    List newValues = [];
    Random rand = new Random();
    for (int i = 0; i < numberOfDice; i++) {
      newValues.add(rand.nextInt(sides) + 1);  // number from 1 to sides
    }
    _values = newValues;
  }

  /// print the values of the dice
  void printDice() => print(_values);
}
```

Named Constructors

In Dart, two methods cannot have the same name, even if they have different parameters. Two constructors cannot have the same name either. If we would like more than one way to construct an object at initialization time, we need to use named constructors. Named constructors are regular constructors that also have an identifier associated with them. Perhaps we have a class Temperature that maintains a temperature in Kelvin degrees. It has three constructors. One is for creating a Temperature with a number already in degrees Kelvin. The other two are for converting from Celsius or Fahrenheit.

```
class Temperature {
  double degreesKelvin;

  Temperature(this.degreesKelvin);

  Temperature.fromCelsius(double degreesCelsius) {
    degreesKelvin = degreesCelsius + 273.15;
  }

  Temperature.fromFahrenheit(double degreesFahrenheit) {
    degreesKelvin = 5 / 9 * (degreesFahrenheit - 32) + 273.15;
  }
}
```

Pig

Pig is a simple dice game in which the goal is to score 100 points. During each turn, the player rolls a six-sided die continuously until he either rolls a one or says "stay." If the player rolls a one, the turn is over. If the player says "stay," he accumulates as points all of the numbers that he has rolled during that turn.

To create Pig, we will, of course, be using our `Dice` class. This will be our first program to span multiple source-code files. Create a new command-line application in Dart Editor called "Pig." Let's start by adding the `Dice` class to Pig. Dart has a concept of *libraries*. Libraries can span multiple files, and the code in each can access the code in the others. The keyword `library` is used for declaring a library. It is followed by the name of the library, any `import` statements that the library needs, and a listing of the files that constitute the library, each preceded by the keyword `part`. Those files then have a `part of` statement at the top of their source. All of the files in a library have access to the packages imported. This is why we could remove the `import` of `dart:math` from the file containing the `Dice` class. We're instead putting it where the library is declared. In fact, files that begin with `part of` cannot have any `import` statements within them. All `import` statements must be placed in the file that declares the library.

To create a new file for `Dice` to live in, go to the File menu in Dart Editor and select "New File...". You will want to place a new file called `dice.dart` in the same folder that contains the autogenerated `pig.dart`. This will be a folder called `bin` within the folder `Pig`. Figure 10-3 shows `dice.dart` being placed using the "New File" dialog.

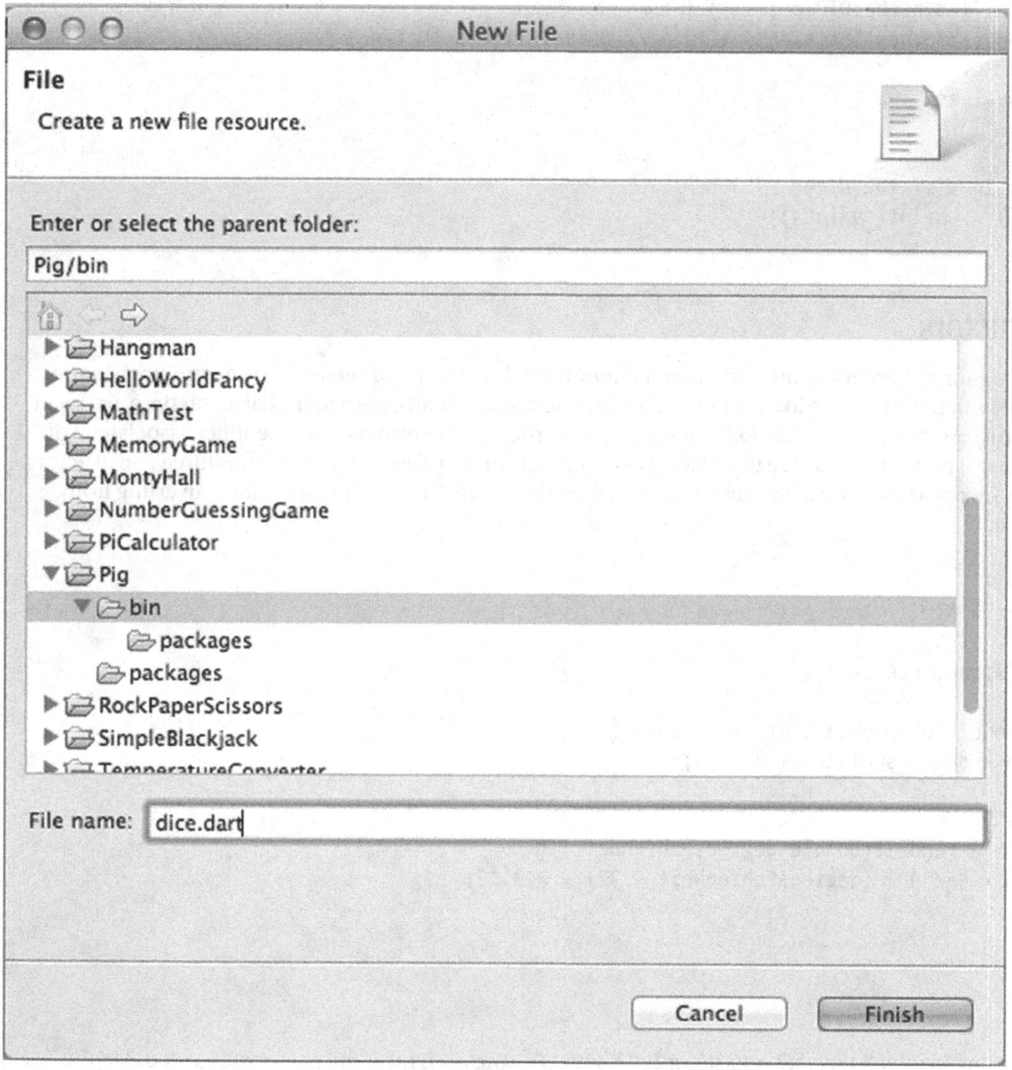

Figure 10-3. `dice.dart` *being created using Dart Editor*

Open up dice.dart and copy the code from Listing 10-1 into it. For Pig, we will also need a simple Player class. In Dart Editor, create another new file, called player.dart, in the same folder. Copy the code from Listing 10-2 into player.dart. Player is a simple class that keeps track of each player's score and name and has a method for getting the player's turn.

Listing 10-2. player.dart

```dart
part of pig;

class Player {
  String name;
  int score = 0;

  Player(this.name);

  /// What does the player want to do?
  String getMove() {
    print("Do you want to (R)oll, (S)tay, or (Q)uit?");
    while (true) {  // exits if proper response, otherwise keeps taking input
      String selection = stdin.readLineSync().toUpperCase();  // get uppercase input

      if (selection == "R") {  // roll
        return "Roll";
      } else if (selection == "S") {  // stay
        return "Stay";
      } else if (selection == "Q") {  // quit
        exit(0);  // quits the program
      }
    }
  }
}
```

■ **Tip**   It is generally a good idea, for organizational purposes, to limit your files to one major class each. It is also a convention to give the file the same name as the class.

The Player class and Dice class are both orchestrated from pig.dart. pig.dart consists of a createPlayers() function, which sets up a List of Player objects that tracks everyone's vital statistics, and a main() function with the game loop inside it. It is no more complicated than the games we saw in Chapter 4. It's only set apart from them because it manages our custom defined objects. pig.dart is listed in Listing 10-3.

Listing 10-3. pig.dart

```dart
library pig;

import "dart:math";  // for Random
import "dart:io";  // for stdin

part "dice.dart";
part "player.dart";
```

```
List<Player> players = [];
Dice d = new Dice(6,1);  // 6 sides, 1 die;

/// initialize [players]
void createPlayers() {
  int numPlayers;

  do {
    print("How many players will be playing?");
    String inTemp = stdin.readLineSync();
    try {
      numPlayers = int.parse(inTemp);
    } on FormatException {  // uh oh, could not be turned into integer
      print("Not a valid selection");
      exit(0);  // exit
    }
  } while (numPlayers < 1);  // can't have <1 players

  // create the Player objects responsible for tracking
  for (int i = 1; i <= numPlayers; i++) {
    print("What is Player $i's name?");
    String name = stdin.readLineSync();
    Player player = new Player(name);
    players.add(player);
  }
}

void main() {
  createPlayers();

  // main game loop
  while (true) {
    for (Player player in players) {
      int turnTotal = 0;
      print("");  // blank line for spacing
      print("It's ${player.name}'s turn with a score of ${player.score}.");

      String move;
      do {
        move = player.getMove();

        if (move == "Roll") {
          d.roll();
          print("${player.name} rolled a ${d.total}.");

          if (d.total == 1) {
            print("${player.name} loses a turn.");
            break;
          } else {
            turnTotal += d.total;
          }
        } else { // Player can only select Roll or Stay, so this is Stay
```

```
      player.score += turnTotal;
      print("${player.name}'s turn ends with a score of ${player.score}.");

      if (player.score >= 100) {   // check for win
        print("${player.name} won!");
        exit(0);
      }
    }
  } while (move == "Roll");
  }
 }
}
```

What you haven't seen before is the library declaration at the top of the file, along with its part declarations. This is the glue that allows the pieces of the program to talk together. All of the packages imported in pig.dart will be available in the other parts of the library—dice.dart and player.dart. Pig is not a complicated program nor a particularly compelling game. Its aim was to serve as a gentle introduction to using custom-made classes and spreading your Dart source code across multiple files.

Class Variables and Class Methods

Every instance of a class has its own copy of that class's instance variables. A single copy of a *class variable* exists for all instances of a class. It is referred to directly through the class's name and the . operator. *Class methods* cannot access instance variables. They can only work with class variables or local variables. They are also accessed through the class name and the . operator. The keyword static is used for declaring a class variable or class method.

```
class SodaCan {
  static double price = 1.00;
  static double capacity = 350.0;
  bool dented = false;

  void drink() => print("Mmm refreshing.");

  static double calculateCostPerMilliliter() {
    return price / capacity;
  }
}

void main() {
  SodaCan.price = 2.00;  // all soda cans cost 2.00
  SodaCan myCola = new SodaCan();
  print(SodaCan.calculateCostPerMilliliter());  // prints 2.00 / 350
  myCola.calculateCostPerMilliliter();  // illegal, method can't be accessed by instances
  myCola.price = 1.50;  // illegal, price can only be accessed through the class name
  SodaCan.drink();  // illegal, instance method can't be used statically
}
```

If you need one value to be the same for all instances of a class, then class variables can be very useful. On the other hand, class methods are often easily replaced by functions. A common pattern is to use class variables for constants (declared with const).

137

A MOVEMENT COMES TO FRUITION

Object-oriented programming seems like a very natural way to create software, yet it was not always accepted in the computer industry. The first programming language to incorporate object-oriented concepts as we know them today was probably Simula 67, which debuted in 1967. However, throughout the 1970s and 1980s, procedural style languages such as BASIC, C, Cobol, Fortran, and Pascal continued to dominate the industry. It was not until the 1990s that the rise of C++ and Java brought object-oriented concepts to the mainstream (although innovation continued on the sidelines with such commercialized but relatively minor languages as Smalltalk, Ada, and Objective-C [the latter of which later hit it big with the Mac/iOS]).

Programmers have gleaned advantages from the code reuse, abstraction, and modeling that the object-oriented paradigm provides to the point where it is rare for a new language to appear that is not object-oriented. Today, all of the top five programming languages (as of 2013), as indicated by LangPop.com, except for C, incorporate object-oriented concepts.[3] C continues to be popular because it is "close to the hardware" and therefore provides speed. It also has a large codebase of existing software written in it. A more recent trend is for languages to incorporate concepts from both the object-oriented and functional paradigms. Examples include Python, Scala, and Dart. C# and Java are also adopting some functional features in their latest specifications.

JavaScript is object-oriented, although it does not provide simple syntax for classes and, therefore, inheritance, an important topic covered in the next chapter (this is coming in the next JavaScript specification, ECMAScript 6). By incorporating some of the common object-oriented features missing from JavaScript, Dart aims to be a more convenient object-oriented language than JavaScript. Although all of your variables in Dart will necessarily be references to objects, Dart does not force you to program in an object-oriented style. In Java, even your `main()` function has to reside as a method within a class. In Dart, you do not need to define any classes to write your program. You could write all of your programs as groups of functions calling one another, as we did in the prior nine chapters.

Doing so would probably be a mistake. It is the goal of this chapter and the following to not only teach you how to program with object-oriented concepts but also to convince you that they are worthwhile. You don't need to become a materialist to embrace objects.

The Game of Life

The Game of Life[4] is a cell-simulation game invented by John Conway in 1970. A grid of square cells is presented. Each cell has eight neighbors. Each cell can be in one of two states—alive or dead. The cells experience generations. Each generation, a living cell with two or three living neighbors stays alive. A cell with any other number of neighbors (less or more) dies. A dead cell with three living neighbors comes to life.

In our version, we will be letting the user initially set the living cells by clicking them on the screen. We will have a Cell class that knows its location, whether it is alive or dead (as a boolean), whether it will be alive or dead in the next generation, and how to draw itself. A Grid class will store all of the cells, update cells based on how many neighbors each has in each generation, and tell all of the cells to redraw. Figure 10-4 is a diagram of these two vital classes.

---

[3]LangPop.com, "*Programming Language Popularity*," http://langpop.com, 2013.
[4]Also known as Conway's Game of Life, Life, or just Game of Life.

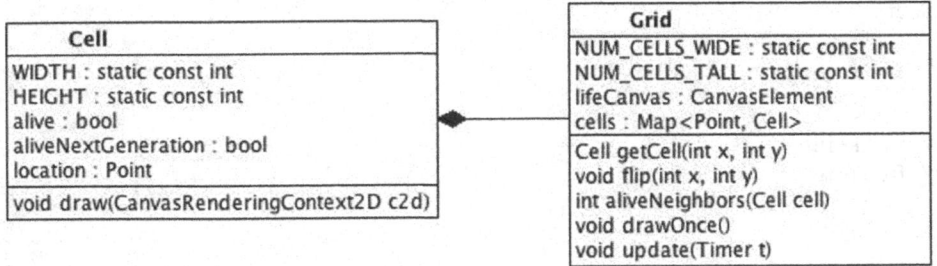

Figure 10-4. Diagrams of the classes Cell and Grid

Create a new web application in Dart Editor called "GameOfLife." Let's get the HTML out of the way. We just need a canvas and a button. Modify gameoflife.html to look like Listing 10-4.

Listing 10-4. gameoflife.html

```
<!DOCTYPE html>

<html>
  <head>
    <meta charset="utf-8">
    <title>The Game of Life</title>
    <link rel="stylesheet" href="gameoflife.css">
  </head>
  <body>
    <h1>The Game of Life</h1>
    <canvas id="lifeCanvas" width="500" height="500"></canvas>
    <br>
    <button id="startStop">Start</button>

    <script type="application/dart" src="gameoflife.dart"></script>
    <script src="packages/browser/dart.js"></script>
  </body>
</html>
```

This time we'll start with the control code that goes in gameoflife.dart instead of our custom classes. We need to

- Define a library that all of our source code files will belong to

- Create a new Grid object when the program starts

- Handle clicks that happen in the canvas and pass them on to the Grid object

- Start and stop a Timer that calls Grid's update() method once a second when the startStop button is clicked

The code in listing 10-5 does all of these things.

Listing 10-5. gameoflife.dart

```dart
library life;

import 'dart:html';
import 'dart:math';   // for Point
import 'dart:async';  // for Timer

part "cell.dart";
part "grid.dart";

Timer timer;
Grid grid;

/// When the canvas is clicked, we need to flip a cell
void clickHappened(MouseEvent me) {
  int clickX = me.offset.x;
  int clickY = me.offset.y;
  grid.flip(clickX, clickY);
}

/// Start or stop the Timer from calling update on grid
void startStopTimer(MouseEvent me) {
  if (timer == null) {
    timer = new Timer.periodic(const Duration(seconds:1), grid.update);
    querySelector("#startStop").text = "Stop";
  } else {
    timer.cancel();
    timer = null;
    querySelector("#startStop").text = "Start";
  }
}

void main() {
  CanvasElement lifeCanvas = querySelector("#lifeCanvas");
  // setup grid
  grid = new Grid(lifeCanvas);
  grid.drawOnce();
  lifeCanvas.onClick.listen(clickHappened);
  querySelector("#startStop").onClick.listen(startStopTimer);
}
```

We imported dart:math to make use of a class called Point, which is useful for storing two-dimensional locations such as the points on our grid. It has an x property and a y property. The Cell class is quite simple really. It keeps track of some fairly obviously named instance variables and has a single method, draw(), which draws alive cells blue and dead cells white. It puts a black box around all cells, so that the grid looks clear. Add a file to your "GameOfLife" project called cell.dart and fill it in with Listing 10-6.

Listing 10-6. `cell.dart`

```dart
part of life;  // gotta love this opening

class Cell {
  bool alive = false;
  bool aliveNextGeneration = false;
  Point location;

  static const int WIDTH = 20;
  static const int HEIGHT = 20;

  Cell(this.location);

  /// Each Cell can draws itself
  void draw(CanvasRenderingContext2D c2d) {
    if (alive) {  // fill living cells blue
      c2d.setFillColorRgb(0, 0, 255);  // blue
    } else {  // fill dead cells white
      c2d.setFillColorRgb(255, 255, 255);  // white
    }
    c2d.fillRect(location.x * WIDTH, location.y * HEIGHT, WIDTH, HEIGHT);

    //have a black outline
    c2d.setStrokeColorRgb(0, 0, 0);  // black
    c2d.strokeRect(location.x * WIDTH, location.y * HEIGHT, WIDTH, HEIGHT);
  }
}
```

The real meat of this program is in the long Grid class. You will need to create a new file, called `grid.dart`, in your project and then fill it with Listing 10-7.

Listing 10-7. `grid.dart`

```dart
part of life;

class Grid {
  static const int NUM_CELLS_WIDE = 25;
  static const int NUM_CELLS_TALL = 25;
  CanvasElement lifeCanvas;
  Map<Point, Cell> cells = new Map();

  Grid(this.lifeCanvas) {
    // initialize  all the cells
    for (int x = 0; x < NUM_CELLS_WIDE; x++) {
      for (int y = 0; y < NUM_CELLS_TALL; y++) {
        Point location = new Point(x, y);
        cells[location] = new Cell(location);
      }
    }
  }
```

```
/// Get a cell at a given location by looking it up
/// in the cells Map. If its coordinates are off the end of the
/// grid, we wrap around to the other side of the grid.
Cell getCell(int x, int y) {
  // wrap around in x direction
  if (x < 0) {
    x = NUM_CELLS_WIDE - 1;
  } else if (x >= NUM_CELLS_WIDE) {
    x = 0;
  }
  // wrap around in y direction
  if (y < 0) {
    y = NUM_CELLS_TALL - 1;
  } else if (y >= NUM_CELLS_TALL) {
    y = 0;
  }

  return cells[new Point(x, y)];
}

/// Switch the status of the cell at the location x, y
void flip(int x, int y) {
  Cell cell = cells[new Point(x ~/ Cell.WIDTH, y ~/ Cell.HEIGHT)];
  cell.alive = !cell.alive;
  cell.draw(lifeCanvas.context2D);
}

/// Check the eight cells around [cell] to see if they're alive
/// count how many of them are
int aliveNeighbors(Cell cell) {
  int x = cell.location.x, y = cell.location.y;
  int newX, newY;
  int numAlive = 0;
  // top left cell
  newX = x - 1;
  newY = y - 1;
  if (getCell(newX, newY).alive) {
    numAlive++;
  }
  // top cell
  newX = x;
  newY = y - 1;
  if (getCell(newX, newY).alive) {
    numAlive++;
  }
  // top right cell
  newX = x + 1;
  newY = y - 1;
  if (getCell(newX, newY).alive) {
    numAlive++;
  }
```

```
  // left cell
  newX = x - 1;
  newY = y;
  if (getCell(newX, newY).alive) {
    numAlive++;
  }
  // right cell
  newX = x + 1;
  newY = y;
  if (getCell(newX, newY).alive) {
    numAlive++;
  }
  // bottom left cell
  newX = x - 1;
  newY = y + 1;
  if (getCell(newX, newY).alive) {
    numAlive++;
  }
  // bottom cell
  newX = x;
  newY = y + 1;
  if (getCell(newX, newY).alive) {
    numAlive++;
  }
  // bottom right cell
  newX = x + 1;
  newY = y + 1;
  if (getCell(newX, newY).alive) {
    numAlive++;
  }
  return numAlive;
}

/// draw the whole grid once - useful before any play takes place
void drawOnce() {
  CanvasRenderingContext2D c2d = lifeCanvas.context2D;
  for (Cell cell in cells.values) {
    cell.draw(c2d);
  }
}

/// figure out what the next generation should look like
/// then flip everyone over into the next generation and redraw
void update(Timer t) {
  // loop through all cells and calculate who's alive next generation
  for (Cell cell in cells.values) {
    int livingNeighbors = aliveNeighbors(cell);
    cell.aliveNextGeneration = false;  // our default stance
```

```
    if (cell.alive) {
      if (livingNeighbors == 3 || livingNeighbors == 2) {
        cell.aliveNextGeneration = true;
      }
    } else {
      if (livingNeighbors == 3) {
        cell.aliveNextGeneration = true;
      }
    }
  }

  // flip the values for the next generation into the current values
  // effectively moving into the next generation and draw everyone
  CanvasRenderingContext2D c2d = lifeCanvas.context2D;
  for (Cell cell in cells.values) {
    cell.alive = cell.aliveNextGeneration;
    cell.draw(c2d);
  }
  }
}
```

Grid keeps track of cells with a Map that maps a cell's location to a Cell object (keys are Points, and values are Cells). In other words, using this Map, we can look up a Cell object by a Point representing its location on the grid. This is very convenient for a program in which we need to constantly find cells by their location.

The length of Grid makes it look more complicated than it really is. In particular, the method aliveNeighbors() is quite long but really quite mechanical in nature. It simply takes the location of the cell in question and looks at the eight cells surrounding it, one after the other, to see if they're alive and adds up how many of them are.

We want the Grid class to maintain a grid that wraps around its edges. A cell at the right edge of the grid should have neighbors on the left edge. Likewise, a cell on the bottom edge should have neighbors on the top edge. The method getCell() uses a little trick to ensure that the grid wraps around. It pulls cells by their x and y location on the grid, but not before it converts any requests beyond the bounds of the grid for the opposing edge.

The flip() method receives coordinates of clicks and needs to switch the alive status of a cell at those coordinates. To figure out which cell belongs to which coordinates, it divides the coordinates by the dimensions of the cells with the ~/ operator. This operator performs truncated division (no decimals). This ensures the resulting Point formed from the division will exist within the Points in cells (our points are all composed of integers).

update(), called by the Timer in gameoflife.dart, is the heart of The Game of Life. It figures out which cells should live in the next generation, based on their number of current living neighbors. After calculating this for every cell (by looping through all of them and utilizing the aliveNeighbors() method), it then loops through all of the cells a second time to actually flip over their alive status to aliveNextGeneration, where it stored what should happen. It's important to do the update() in a two-step process such as this, because otherwise, a cell may be updated while it can still affect its neighbors for the next generation. Figure 10-5 shows The Game of Life in action. If you search the Web, you will find various interesting patterns you can try clicking into the grid that will animate interesting visuals.

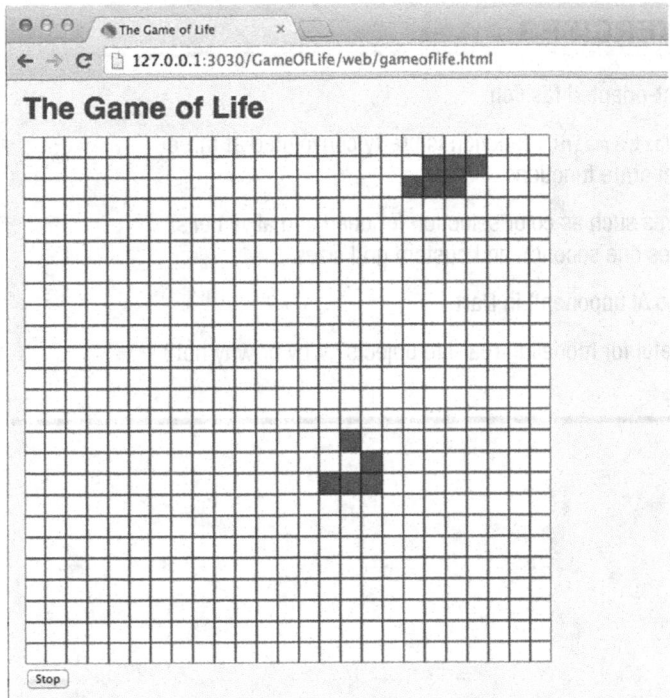

Figure 10-5. *The Game of Life running in Dartium*

Summary

All variables in Dart are actually references to objects. Objects are programmatic structures that represent abstracted components of a program. Object-oriented programming in Dart relies on the ideas of classes, instance variables, and methods. Classes define the structure of objects. Instance variables store an object's attributes. Methods are actions that objects can perform and can be thought of as functions belonging to an object. Properties are specialized object attributes that are convenient for implementing data encapsulation. Constructors are used for initializing objects. Class methods and class variables do not belong to individual instances of an object, but instead, there is a single copy of them for the entire class. Dart provides syntactic sugar for the most common type of constructors—those that set instance variables. It also provides named constructors as a means to have multiple different types of constructors, since two methods in Dart (as well as two constructors) cannot have the same name.

EXERCISES

1. Rewrite Temperature Converter in an object-oriented fashion.

2. Refactor the main game loop of Pig. `pig.dart`'s `main()` function is pretty convoluted at three loops deep. Move some of the code into separate functions.

3. Improve The Game of Life by adding features such as color selection for dead and alive cells, user-set generation lengths (options besides one second), and custom grid sizes.

4. Implement a two-player checkers game (no AI opponent) in Dart.

5. Do you think programmatic objects are useful for modeling real-life objects? Why or why not?

6. How do you think an AI could work for Pig?

■ ■ ■

# CHAPTER 11

Object-Oriented Design

Classes are not just ways of defining solitary objects. They can also be used to define complex relationships between objects that underlie the connections between various aspects of a program. Objects need not be of the same class for us to know at compile time that they share certain attributes. Inheritance, abstract classes, interfaces, and mixins are Dart techniques used for specifying relationships between objects and interfaces for object access.

Inheritance

In real life, some things are like other things but are not exactly the same. We say, then, that they are *related* to one another. For example, pens and pencils are very similar in that they both are writing instruments. They both can be used to write on paper, and they both have a finite lifetime (one is limited by how much ink remains, the other by how much graphite). If we wanted to represent the use of these two writing instruments in code, would it make sense to have one class, WritingInstrument, with many instance variables to accommodate both pens and pencils? It probably would not. Would it make sense, then, to use two classes to represent these entities: Pen and Pencil. In that scenario, there would be much duplicative effort.

There is an alternative. Using inheritance, we can put the common traits of pens and pencils into a *superclass* called WritingInstrument and what differentiates them in *subclasses* called Pen and Pencil. Instances of Pen and Pencil will have all of the instance variables and methods defined in WritingInstrument available to them, as well as any new ones defined by Pen or Pencil, respectively. Have you ever heard the saying "a square is a rectangle but a rectangle is not necessarily a square"? Well, a Pen is a WritingInstrument, but a WritingInstrument is not necessarily a Pen.

The extends keyword is used for defining a subclass/superclass relationship. If a class named B, extends a class named A, then B is a subclass of A, and A is a superclass of B. B inherits all of the instance variables and methods of B. A B is an A. An A is not necessarily a B. Let's see how the extends keyword may be used to define the relationship between Pen, Pencil, and WritingInstrument.

```dart
class WritingInstrument {
  int lifeRemaining = 100;
  String color = "black";

  void write(String what) {
    if (lifeRemaining <= 0) {
      return;
    }

    print(what);
    lifeRemaining--;
  }
}
```

```
class Pen extends WritingInstrument {
  void explode() {
    print("Ink everywhere!");
    lifeRemaining = 0;
  }
}

class Pencil extends WritingInstrument {
  int eraserLife = 100;

  void erase(String toErase) {
    if (eraserLife <= 0) {
      return;
    }

    print("Removed $toErase");
    eraserLife--;
  }
}
```

The is operator can be used to determine the type of a variable. We can use the is operator to prove that a Pen is a type of WritingInstrument but a WritingInstrument is not necessarily a Pen. If you've been following along thus far, then you know that Pen and Pencil both have an instance variable called lifeRemaining because they are both subclasses of WritingInstrument. Therefore, you will notice that lifeRemaining can be manipulated from Pen's explode() method. A Pen object created with the new operator can have its color instance variable manipulated, even though it's only defined in its superclass. Let's look at an example.

```
void main() {
  Pen pen = new Pen();
  pen.color = "blue";
  pen.write("Hey!");
  Pencil pencil = new Pencil();
  pencil.write("Yo!");
  pen.explode();
  print(pen is WritingInstrument);     // prints true
  print(pencil is WritingInstrument);  // prints true
  //pencil.explode();  // illegal, pencil has no explode() method

  WritingInstrument wi = new WritingInstrument();
  print(wi is Pen);     // prints false
  print(wi is Pencil);  // prints false
  print(wi is WritingInstrument);  // prints true
}
```

Let's think about what's going on with all of these is tests combined with print() calls. The is operator returns a bool. print(), as we saw with Lists, is a great way of debugging anything that can be converted to a human readable String. When print() is called on a non-String object, a method named toString() is called on that object. toString() is defined in a class named Object.

Wait a second. How is that relevant to a bool? Well, it turns out that all Dart classes are subclasses of a *base class* named Object. That's right, WritingInstrument is a subclass of Object. bool is a subclass of Object. List is a subclass of Object. Cell from the last chapter's program The Game of Life is a subclass of Object. Then how come we have never seen extends Object? Subclassing Object is done automatically by the system for all classes that don't subclass anything else. All classes are subclasses of Object.

Since Pen and Pencil are subclasses of WritingInstrument, they are also subclasses of Object. They are Object's grandchildren, if you will. Check out the diagram for our class hierarchy in Figure 11-1. Please note that for the sake of brevity, Figure 11-1 does not show the instance variables and methods that are built into Object. If you are interested, you can check them out in Dart's API documentation at: http://api.dartlang.org/dart_core/Object.html.

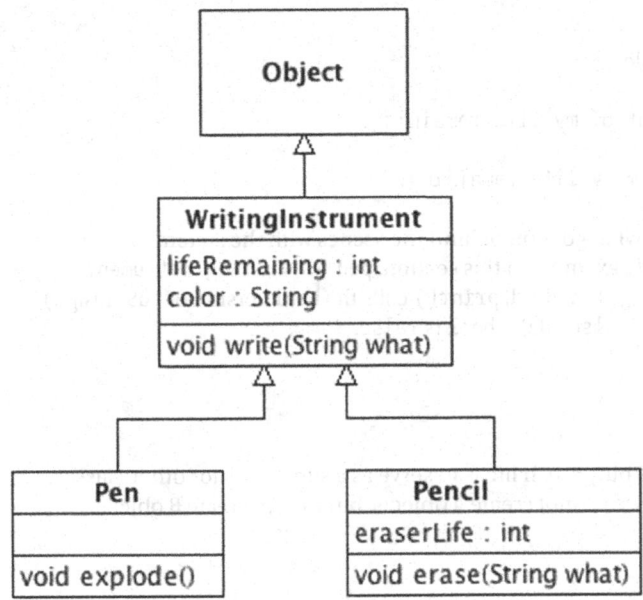

Figure 11-1. *WritingInstrument, Pen, and Pencil class hierarchy*

How is this related to our discussion about toString() and bool? The key is that a subclass can override a superclass's method. Then when that method is called on the subclass, its implementation of the method, rather than the superclass's implementation, will be executed. All objects, because they are subclasses of Object, automatically inherit a toString() method. Let's prove it. Taking our current Pencil class, what will the following lines output?

```
Pencil myPencil = new Pencil();
String temp = myPencil.toString();
print(myPencil);
print(temp);
```

If you're a keen reader, you'll notice that the two lines are printing the same thing, because print() is calling myPencil's toString() method. We end up with Instance of 'Pencil' printed twice to the console. It's a default implementation of toString() in the Object class that simply prints what class an object is an instance of. Let's override toString() in WritingInstrument by adding the following method to WritingInstrument's class definition.

```
String toString() {
  return "I am a $color writing instrument with $lifeRemaining percent of my life remaining.";
}
```

Now, anytime that toString() is called (including by print()) on WritingInstrument, Pen, or Pencil, this new implementation will be called. Let's try it out.

```
Pencil myPencil2 = new Pencil();
myPencil2.color = "orange";
print(myPencil2);
Pen myPen2 = new Pen();
myPen2.explode();
print(myPen2);
```

And this code will output the following to the console:

```
I am a orange writing instrument with 100 percent of my life remaining.
Ink everywhere!
I am a black writing instrument with 0 percent of my life remaining.
```

Now we finally understand enough to comprehend what goes on behind the scenes with the statement print(pen is WritingInstrument) from the earlier code example in this section. pen is WritingInstrument returns a bool. The bool class overrides Object's toString() method. print() calls the bool version of toString(), which returns the String "true" if the bool is true and "false" if the bool is false.

Abstract Classes

An abstract class is a class that cannot be instantiated. Its purpose in life is to serve as a superclass for other classes. For example, if A is an abstract class that B inherits from, we cannot create A objects, but we can create B objects. Abstract classes are declared with the abstract keyword.

```
abstract class A {...}
```

Unlike regular classes, abstract classes do not need to define all of their methods or properties. Instead of a definition between curly braces, abstract classes can choose to use a semicolon to indicate that a method or property definition is left blank. For example, the following is a completely valid abstract class:

```
abstract class A {
  int get myProperty1;
  int get myProperty2;
  int myMethod1();
  void myMethod2();
}
```

You will notice that myProperty1, myProperty2, myMethod1(), and myMethod2() are declared but not defined. Non-abstract subclasses of an abstract class must define the properties and methods that the abstract class leaves blank. If they do not define them, an error will be raised.

Geometry Test

Let's look at another inheritance toy example. Geometry Test is a program that tests one's ability to find perimeters and areas of simple shapes. It uses a base abstract class called Shape and concrete subclasses Rectangle, Square, and Circle. Create a new command-line application in Dart Editor and call it "GeometryTest." Fill in geometrytest.dart with Listing 11-1.

Listing 11-1. geometrytest.dart

```dart
import "dart:math";
import "dart:io";

abstract class Shape {
  double get perimeter;
  double get area;
  String get description;
}

class Circle extends Shape {
  double radius;
  Circle(this.radius);

  double get perimeter => radius * 2 * PI;
  double get area => PI * (radius * radius);
  String get description => "I am a circle with radius $radius";
}

class Rectangle extends Shape {
  double length;
  double width;
  Rectangle(this.length, this.width);

  double get perimeter => length * 2 + width * 2;
  double get area => length * width;
  String get description => "I am a rectangle with length $length and width $width.";
}

class Square extends Rectangle {
  Square(double side) : super(side, side);
  String get description => "I am a square with sides of length $length.";
}

void main() {
  Shape randomShape;
  Random rand = new Random();
  int choice = rand.nextInt(3);

  switch(choice) {
    case 0:
      randomShape = new Circle(rand.nextInt(10) + 1.0);  // adding 1.0 converts to double
      break;
    case 1:
      randomShape = new Rectangle(rand.nextInt(10) + 1.0, rand.nextInt(10) + 1.0);
      break;
    case 2:
      randomShape = new Square(rand.nextInt(10) + 1.0);
      break;
  }
```

```
String inTemp;
double userAnswer;
print(randomShape.description);

print("What is the area of the shape?");
inTemp = stdin.readLineSync();
try {
  userAnswer = double.parse(inTemp);
} on FormatException {   // uh oh, could not be turned into double
  print("Could not interpret input.");
  return;
}
if (userAnswer.roundToDouble() == randomShape.area.roundToDouble()) {
  print("Good job!");
} else {
  print("Wrong, it's ${randomShape.area}!");
}

print("What is the perimeter of the shape?");
inTemp = stdin.readLineSync();
try {
  userAnswer = double.parse(inTemp);
} on FormatException {   // uh oh, could not be turned into double
  print("Could not interpret input.");
  return;
}
if (userAnswer.roundToDouble() == randomShape.perimeter.roundToDouble()) {
  print("Good job!");
} else {
  print("Wrong, it's ${randomShape.perimeter}!");
}
}
```

First, a few notes on style. This program is guilty of the long main() function that we spurned in Chapter 5. It's a toy program, and the emphasis is on the use of inheritance and an abstract class. The main() function is just proof that the class hierarchy works. You will notice a lot fewer comments in this program than we're used to. It's an example of what's called *self-documenting code*. The code is so clearly written, and the classes/variables/methods are so well named, that it documents itself without any comments. At least it's supposed to! Figure 11-2 is a class diagram for Geometry Test.

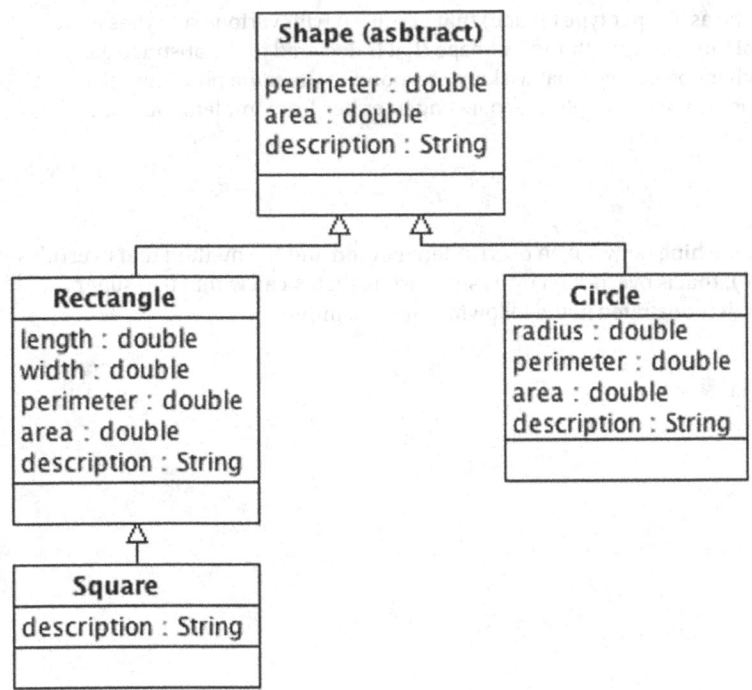

Figure 11-2. *Geometry Test class diagram*

You will notice in main() that randomShape is declared to be of type Shape, yet as we know, abstract classes cannot be instantiated. Instead, depending on a random outcome, randomShape is instantiated as a Rectangle, Square, or Circle object. This is legal because all of these classes are subclasses of Shape. A variable declared to be of a superclass's type can be instantiated as any of its subclasses. However, it only knows about methods/instance variables/properties in its declared type. For example, even if we knew randomShape was instantiated as a Circle, trying to access randomShape.radius would raise a warning. randomShape is a Shape; it is not necessarily a Circle. Even if we (as the programmers) know that randomShape is in actuality a Circle, its declaration was simply as a Shape.

When getting random values for instantiating the various shapes, we add 1.0 to the randomly generated integers. The purpose of the addition of 1.0 is twofold. First, it will ensure that we will have no zero values. A circle with a 0 radius doesn't really make much sense. Second, by adding the literal 1.0, which Dart interprets as a floating-point number, instead of 1, which Dart interprets as an integer, the resulting value will be a double instead of an int. That's right, if a numeric literal is written with a decimal point, Dart automatically considers it to be a double. If you couple that with the fact that the result of adding an int with a double will always be converted into a double (known as *widening*), you have all of the facts necessary to see why adding 1.0 makes sense.

The keyword super is used for referring to the methods or instance variables of a superclass from within a subclass. When used in a constructor, super can be used to refer to the superclass's constructor. In Square's lone constructor, super() is cleverly called to initialize the length and width of a Square via Rectangle's default constructor. Square's constructor simply sets the length and width variables to be the same as the constructor parameter side that it is provided with. Square does not re-implement the properties area or perimeter. It relies on Rectangle's implementations.

The declaration of the variable randomShape as a super type (Shape) that gets used with various subtypes is an example of *polymorphism*.[1] There is one way of interacting with randomShape that is declared in the abstract class Shape. Yet we use randomShape with various other object types that we know respond to the same property calls but actually have different implementations. This is another example of separating interface from implementation.

Super

Beyond constructors, super is useful for distinguishing between an overridden method and the method that overrides it. For example, if class A has a method, silly(), that is overridden by its subclass, B, then a call within B to super.silly() will call A's version of silly(). This is demonstrated in the following short example:

```
class A {
  void silly() {
    print("A's Silly");
  }
}

class B extends A{
  void silly() {
    print("B's Silly");
  }

  void callASilly() {
    super.silly();
  }
}

void main() {
  B b = new B();
  b.callASilly();  // prints A's Silly
}
```

Interfaces

Dart's inheritance model is known as *single inheritance* (as opposed to *multiple inheritance*). In short, this means that you can only include one other class after the extends keyword. However, Dart provides several ways to include attributes from multiple other classes in a new class. One of them is with the keyword implements. The keyword implements is used to indicate that a class implements the interface of another class. What is the interface of a class? It is the combination of accessor names along with their signature (a method that returns an int is different from the same named method that returns a String), including methods, instance variables, and properties, that defines how one can interact with an instance of a class.

---

[1] The use of one interface for multiple different types of objects.

Interfaces Exposed

Every Dart class automatically exposes its interface for reuse. This includes abstract classes. Therefore, any class can implement any other class's interface. A class can implement multiple interfaces. The only requirement is that a class that implements another class's interface must implement it completely. Every method, property, and instance variable declared in the original class must be implemented in the class that implements its interface.

```dart
class A {
  void silly() {
    print("A's Silly");
  }
}

class B {
  void awesome() {
    print("B's Awesome");
  }
}

class C implements A, B {
  void silly() {
    print("C's Silly");
  }

  void awesome() {
    print("C's Awesome");
  }
}

class D extends B implements A {
  void silly() {
    print("D's Silly");
  }
}

void main() {
  A c = new C();
  c.silly();  // prints C's Silly
  c.awesome();  // runs, but generates warning; prints C's Awesome
  D d = new D();
  d.awesome();  // prints B's Awesome
  d.silly();  // prints D's Silly
}
```

Let's talk about c. c is declared as type A, but it's actually an instantiated C. Class C implements both A and B. Therefore, it needs to provide implementations for all of the methods, instance variables, and properties of classes A and B. In this small sample, that just means that it needs to have a version of silly() and a version of awesome().

The line c.awesome() executes but generates a warning. Why does it generate a warning? The class C certainly has a method called awesome(). However, c is declared to be of type A. The class A does not have an awesome() method. c.awesome() runs successfully because we know that internally c is instantiated as a C, and it does have an awesome() method. At runtime, the warning is ignored and c.awesome() is executed. This is a symptom of types being optional in Dart. In a language that strictly enforces its type system, such as Java, c.awesome() would not execute.

155

d is a pure D. By extending B, it inherits B's awesome(). By implementing A, it has to implement a version of silly(). D has no awesome() of its own, so when d.awesome() is executed, the awesome() that is inherited from B is executed.

Casting

Casting is a way of indicating to Dart that we want to treat an object of one type like an object of another type with a compatible interface. In the last example, c.awesome() generates a warning (visible in Dart Editor), because c is actually declared to be of type A, and A does not have an awesome() method. However, c is instantiated as a C object, which does have an awesome() method.

```
A c = new C();
```

There is a way to tell Dart that we want to treat c as a C, even after it was originally declared as an A. We can do it with a *cast*. In Dart, the as operator is used for casting. Using a cast, we can stop the call of awesome() from generating a warning.

```
(c as C).awesome();  // no warning generated; prints C's Awesome
```

We are specifying that c is to be thought of as a C, regardless of the fact that it was originally declared as an A. This is only safe because we know that c was initialized as a C. You may recall that we used the as operator quite extensively in Chapter 2 and Chapter 8 to cast dart:html Elements as Element subclasses. As the developer of both the HTML and the Dart source, we had the foreknowledge of the types of the specific Elements that querySelector() returned.

Mixins

Mixins are another way of appending the attributes of one class onto another without using inheritance. Unlike classes that implement interfaces, classes that use mixins do not need to redefine the behavior in the original class that they are mixing in. The keyword with is used to indicate that a class uses a mixin. A class that is providing a mixin must

- Have no declared constructors

- Not be a subclass of anything other than Object (no extends)

- Make no calls using super[2]

To see how mixins work, first let's declare a class that follows these three rules. This will be the class that we mix into other classes. It will be our *mixin*.

```
class TimeStamp {
  DateTime creationTime = new DateTime.now();
  void printTimeStamp() {
    print(creationTime);
  }
}
```

A class that mixes in TimeStamp will have an automatic TimeStamp created when it is instantiated. Here's a silly use case. Perhaps, in a hospital, NewBorns have a time stamp (indicating when they were born), but Mothers don't.

---

[2]Gilad Bracha, "Mixins in Dart," www.dartlang.org/articles/mixins, November 2013.

```dart
abstract class Patient {
  String name;
  Patient(this.name);
}

class NewBorn extends Patient with TimeStamp {
  NewBorn(String name) : super(name);
}

class Mother extends Patient {
  Mother(String name) : super(name);
}

void main() {
  NewBorn nb = new NewBorn("John Doe");
  Mother m = new Mother("Jane Doe");
  nb.printTimeStamp();
}
```

■ **Note**   As of Dart 1.1, the with keyword can only be used with a class that also uses the extends keyword in its definition. To use a mixin with a class that has no custom superclass, you should explicitly write extends Object with...

One of the great conveniences of object-oriented programming, and mixins in particular, is the ease of code reuse. Perhaps we have a banking application that needs to keep track of transactions. Every transaction should have a time stamp, should it not? We can imagine a Transaction class that uses the same exact mixin as the NewBorn class.

```dart
class Transaction extends Object with TimeStamp {...}
```

When you do enough object-oriented programming, eventually you build up your own reserves of modularized objects that you've written, such as TimeStamp. If they are well abstracted, they can be reused in quite disparate programs. A class can mix in multiple mixins. We can imagine a class in a hierarchy of classes for performing operations on a database using many mixins...

```dart
class DatabaseInsert extends DatabaseOperation with TimeStamp, Ownership, Logging {...}
```

The Cascade Operator

The cascade operator, .., is not really specific to the topic of this chapter, other than that it is used in the upcoming Alien Invaders example. If we want to perform multiple operations on the same object, without having to retype the name of variable that refers to it multiple times, then the cascade operator is our ticket. Take the following lines of code for defining a List called fruits.

```dart
List fruits = new List();
fruits.length = 0;
fruits.add("lime");
fruits.add("orange");
fruits.shuffle();
```

These lines can be rewritten into functionally equivalent code, using the cascade operator.

```
List fruits = new List()
  ..length = 0
  ..add("lime")
  ..add("orange")
  ..shuffle();
```

All of the operations take place on the same List object. The operations are separated by the `..` operator, and their end is marked by a semicolon. The cascade operator is just syntactic sugar. It doesn't save that much typing, but some would argue that it looks cleaner. The cascade operator dismisses the return values of any method calls.

Alien Invaders

Alien UFOs march in columns down the screen toward the player's spaceship, which resides on the bottom of the screen. Both the UFOs and the player can shoot at each other. The player can move left or right on the screen. The goal of the player is to destroy all of the UFOs by shooting them. In our game, the "z" key will move the player left, the "x" key will move the player right, and the space bar will fire. Our goal is to create the demo in Figure 11-3.

Figure 11-3. Alien Invaders running in Dartium

Create a new web application in Dart Editor called "AlienInvaders." Modify `alieninvaders.html` to look like Listing 11-2. There's nothing special to see here, except a 500 by 500 canvas. For this demo, you will also need image files named `background.png`, `bullet.png`, `ship.png`, and `ufo.png` within an images folder in the web folder of Alien Invaders. You can create your own or find these image files within the book's source code bundle at the Apress web site.

Listing 11-2. `alieninvaders.html`

```
<!DOCTYPE html>

<html>
  <head>
    <meta charset="utf-8">
    <title>Alien Invaders</title>
    <link rel="stylesheet" href="alieninvaders.css">
  </head>
  <body>
    <h1>Alien Invaders</h1>
    <canvas id="myCanvas" width="500" height="500"></canvas>
    <p>Use 'z' to move left, 'x' to move right, and the space bar to fire.</p>
    <script type="application/dart" src="alieninvaders.dart"></script>
    <script src="packages/browser/dart.js"></script>
  </body>
</html>
```

We're going to be working with an abstract class called Sprite[3] that classes Player, Alien, and Bullet inherit from. A Sprite knows its location, size, and what it looks like. It also has methods for drawing itself and moving itself. The Sprite class has an abstract method called update() that subclasses can use to update their location or other attributes.

The most interesting aspect of Sprite is its boundingBox instance variable. boundingBox is a Rectangle from the dart:math package that represents a box made up of the edges surrounding the Sprite. The Rectangle class has a method called intersection() that tells us where one Rectangle intersects another. It returns null if the Rectangles do not intersect. We can use this method to tell when Bullets hit other Sprites by checking whether the Bullet's boundingBox intersects the other Sprite's boundingBox. Create a file sprite.dart within the web folder and fill it with Listing 11-3.

Listing 11-3. `sprite.dart`

```
part of alieninvaders;

abstract class Sprite {
  int width, height, x, y;
  ImageElement myImage;
  Rectangle boundingBox;  // for collisions

  Sprite(this.width, this.height, this.x, this.y, String imageName) {
    myImage = new ImageElement()
      ..src = imageName;
    boundingBox = new Rectangle(x, y, width, height);
  }
```

---

[3]A common term used in video game programming to refer to a 2D image that can move around the screen.

```
/// just draws [myImage] in the canvas
void draw(CanvasRenderingContext2D c2D) {
  c2D.drawImageScaled(myImage, x, y, width, height);
}

/// move [dx] in the x direction, [dy] in the y direction
void move(int dx, int dy) {
  x += dx;
  y += dy;
  boundingBox = new Rectangle(x, y, width, height);
}

/// left to subclasses
void update();
}
```

Create files bullet.dart, player.dart, and alien.dart, also within the web folder. Listing 11-4 shows bullet.dart containing the Bullet class, which implements a checkCollision() method such as that described previously. Bullet also has a bool named down, which is set to indicate whether the Bullet is traveling toward the top of the screen or the bottom of the screen.

Listing 11-4. bullet.dart

```
part of alieninvaders;

class Bullet extends Sprite {
  static const int WIDTH = 15, HEIGHT = 15;
  static const String IMAGE_NAME = "images/bullet.png";
  bool down;

  Bullet(int x, int y, this.down) : super(WIDTH, HEIGHT, x, y, IMAGE_NAME);

  /// Move down or up 1 every frame
  void update() {
    if (down) {
      move(0, 1);
    } else {
      move(0, -1);
    }
  }

  /// is the bullet within the space of [s]?
  bool checkCollision(Sprite s) {
    if (boundingBox.intersection(s.boundingBox) != null) {
      return true;
    }
    return false;
  }
}
```

Listing 11-5 shows alien.dart, which contains the Alien class. Listing 11-6 is for player.dart, which contains the Player class. Both of these are fairly straightforward subclasses of Sprite that hard-code their widths, heights, and image names. The update() method of Alien moves each Alien instance 1 pixel toward the bottom of the screen every 60 times that update() is called (the instance variable frameCount keeps track of how many times update() has been called). The Timer that calls update() will run 60 times per second, so this means that Aliens move 1 pixel per second toward the bottom of the screen.

Listing 11-5. alien.dart

```
part of alieninvaders;

class Alien extends Sprite {
  static const int WIDTH = 80, HEIGHT = 40;
  static const String IMAGE_NAME = "images/ufo.png";
  int frameCount = 0;

  Alien(int x, int y) : super(WIDTH, HEIGHT, x, y, IMAGE_NAME);

  /// Move every second or so (assuming 60 frames per second)
  void update() {
    frameCount++;
    if (frameCount % 60 == 0) {
      move(0, 1);  // move one down
    }
  }
}
```

Listing 11-6. player.dart

```
part of alieninvaders;

class Player extends Sprite {
  static const int WIDTH = 73, HEIGHT = 80;
  static const String IMAGE_NAME = "images/ship.png";

  Player(int x, int y) : super(WIDTH, HEIGHT, x, y, IMAGE_NAME);

  void update() {  // doesn't do anything, player updates from keyboard events
    return;
  }
}
```

Figure 11-4 shows the class hierarchy of Alien Invaders. It's pretty flat. All three of the subclasses of Sprite have to implement the update() method because it is not concretely implemented in Sprite itself. However, Player just provides a blank implementation.

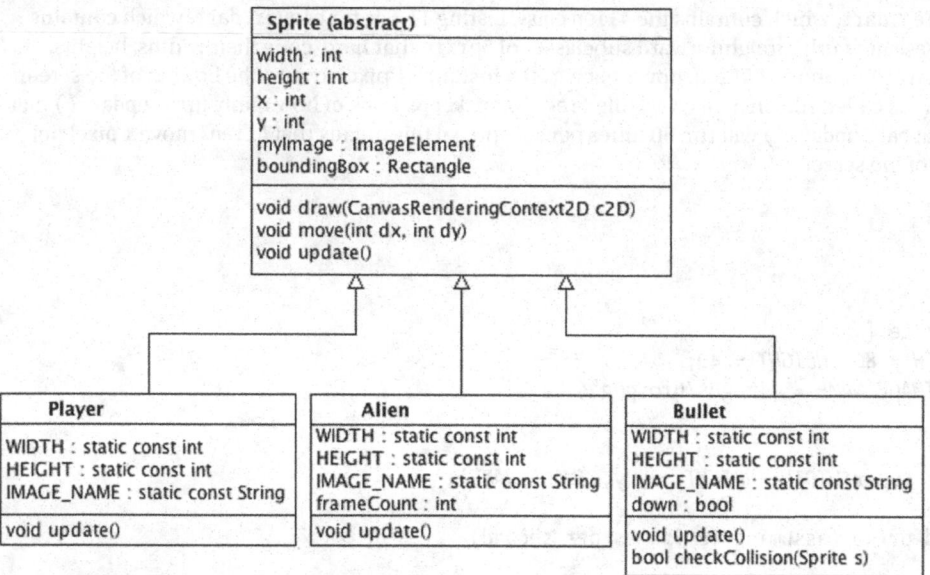

Figure 11-4. *Alien Invaders class hierarchy*

The file that glues everything together, alieninvaders.dart, is not unlike the Chapter 8 example Flying Pigs. It similarly involves a main() function that sets everything up (along with the restart() function), a Timer that calls an update() function 60 times a second, and a connection with a 500 by 500 canvas defined in an HTML file. main() also sets up listeners for keyboard events not unlike the listeners in Hangman of Chapter 9. These keyboard events are used for manipulating player and firing bullets. Listing 11-7 contains alieninvaders.dart.

Listing 11-7. alieninvaders.dart

```
library alieninvaders;

import "dart:html";
import "dart:math";  // for Random and Rectangle
import "dart:async"; // for Timer

part "sprite.dart";
part "player.dart";
part "alien.dart";
part "bullet.dart";

CanvasElement myCanvas;
Player player;
List<Alien> aliens;
List<Bullet> alienBullets;
List<Bullet> playerBullets;
ImageElement background;
Timer t;
```

```
const int CANVAS_WIDTH = 500;
const int CANVAS_HEIGHT = 500;
const String BACKGROUND_FILE = "images/background.png";

/// Called by a Timer 60 times per second
/// Calls update() on all sprites, calls draw()
/// Creates alien bullets and checks for collisions
void update(Timer t) {
  // update everything
  player.update();
  for (Alien alien in aliens) {
    alien.update();
    // randomly fire a bullet
    Random rand = new Random();
    int randomNumber = rand.nextInt(2000);
    if (randomNumber == 100) {
      alienBullets.add(new Bullet(alien.x + Alien.WIDTH ~/ 2 - Bullet.WIDTH ~/ 2, alien.y +
Alien.HEIGHT, true));
    }
  }

  List deleteBullets = new List();
  for (Bullet bullet in alienBullets) {
    bullet.update();
    if (bullet.y > CANVAS_HEIGHT) {  // is bullet off screen?
      deleteBullets.add(bullet);
      continue;
    }
    // check if bullets hit player
    if (bullet.checkCollision(player)) {
      t.cancel();  // stop the game, player is hit
      window.alert("Game Over!");
      deleteBullets.add(bullet);
    }
  }

  for (Bullet bullet in deleteBullets) {
    alienBullets.remove(bullet);
  }

  deleteBullets.clear();
  List deleteAliens = new List();
  for (Bullet bullet in playerBullets) {
    bullet.update();
    if (bullet.y < 0) {  // is bullet off screen
      deleteBullets.add(bullet);
      continue;
    }
    // check if bullet hits alien
    for (Alien alien in aliens) {
      if (bullet.checkCollision(alien)) {
```

```
        deleteBullets.add(bullet);
        deleteAliens.add(alien);
      }
    }
  }

  for (Bullet bullet in deleteBullets) {
    playerBullets.remove(bullet);
  }

  for (Alien alien in deleteAliens) {
    aliens.remove(alien);
    if (aliens.isEmpty) {
      t.cancel();  // stop the game, all aliens dead
      window.alert("You Win!");
    }
  }

  // draw everything
  draw();
}

/// Draw the background and all of the sprites
void draw() {
  CanvasRenderingContext2D c2D = myCanvas.context2D;
  // draw the background
  c2D.drawImage(background, 0, 0);
  // draw all the sprites
  player.draw(c2D);
  for (Alien alien in aliens) {
    alien.draw(c2D);
  }
  for (Bullet bullet in alienBullets) {
    bullet.draw(c2D);
  }
  for (Bullet bullet in playerBullets) {
    bullet.draw(c2D);
  }
}

/// Initialize all of the sprites
/// place the player and the aliens on the screen
void restart() {
  player = new Player(CANVAS_WIDTH ~/ 2, CANVAS_HEIGHT - Player.HEIGHT);
  aliens = new List();
  alienBullets = new List();
  playerBullets = new List();
  // probably don't want to hardcode this for Exercise 3; create the aliens
  const int NUM_ROWS = 3;
  const int NUM_COLUMNS = 5;
```

```
  for (int i = 0; i < NUM_ROWS; i++) {
    int y = i * (Alien.HEIGHT + 10);   // 10 is for spacing
    for (int j = 0; j < NUM_COLUMNS; j++) {
      int x = (CANVAS_WIDTH ~/ NUM_COLUMNS) * j + 10;  // ~/ is integer division
      aliens.add(new Alien(x,y));
    }
  }

  background = new ImageElement()
    ..src = BACKGROUND_FILE;
}

void main() {
  myCanvas = querySelector("#myCanvas");
  window.onKeyPress.listen((KeyboardEvent e) {  // manipulate player with key presses
    String lastPressed = new String.fromCharCodes([e.charCode]);
    switch (lastPressed) {
      case 'z':  // move player left
        if (player.x > 0) {
          player.move(-5, 0);
        }
        break;
      case 'x':  // move player right
        if (player.x < CANVAS_WIDTH - Player.WIDTH) {
          player.move(5, 0);
        }
        break;
      case ' ':  // player fires
        playerBullets.add(new Bullet(player.x + Player.WIDTH ~/ 2 - Bullet.WIDTH ~/ 2,
player.y - Bullet.HEIGHT, false));
        break;
    }
  });
  restart();
  // this Timer will call update() approximately 60 times a second
  t = new Timer.periodic(const Duration(milliseconds:17), update);
}
```

There's a lot there, but the only function with any interesting logic is update(). update() is tasked with

- Calling update() on every Sprite

- Randomly generating bullets from aliens

- Checking if bullets go off screen and deleting them if they do

- Checking if bullets fired by the player hit the alien ships and deleting them if they are hit

- Checking if bullets fired by the aliens hit the player

Look carefully at the code that checks for collisions and removes collided bullets. You may be wondering why the bullets aren't just removed where they are detected as having collided? Why are they put into local Lists and removed from the top-level Lists later? It is illegal to remove elements from a List that is currently being iterated through. For example, the following code is illegal. It is not safe to remove something from a List while it is being iterated through in a loop. This program will crash.

```
List fruits = ["apple", "orange", "banana"];
for (String fruit in fruits) {
  fruits.remove(fruit);  // illegal
}
```

Instead, we need to keep track of the fruits we want to delete and then remove them from the original List after.

```
List fruits = ["apple", "orange", "banana"];
List toDelete = new List();
for (String fruit in fruits) {
  toDelete.add(fruit);
}
for (String fruit in toDelete) {
  fruits.remove(fruit);
}
```

What happens with Bullets and Aliens in need of deletion in update() is parallel to this. Adding Bullets to the screen, both in main() for player-fired bullets and update() for alien-fired bullets, looks pretty complex. Let's break down the line that adds alien-fired bullets to the screen.

```
alienBullets.add(new Bullet(alien.x + Alien.WIDTH ~/ 2 - Bullet.WIDTH ~/ 2, alien.y +
Alien.HEIGHT, true));
```

Okay, so the line starts by declaring that we'll be adding a new Bullet to the List<Bullet> alienBullets. That x coordinate argument looks pretty complex, though. We start with the alien's left edge (alien.x). We add the alien's width divided by 2, using integer division (Alien.WIDTH ~/ 2). This will give us the middle of the alien on the screen. Then we subtract half of the width of the bullet (Bullet.WIDTH ~/ 2). This is so that the bullet is centered in relation to the alien. The second property is the new Bullet's y coordinate. This is set to the front of the alien by adding the alien's height to alien.y, which refers to its top-left corner. Finally, the last argument is true, because we want the bullet to be moving toward the bottom of the screen (the Bullet class's down property). Figure 11-5 explains the placement of the new Bullet's x and y coordinates graphically.

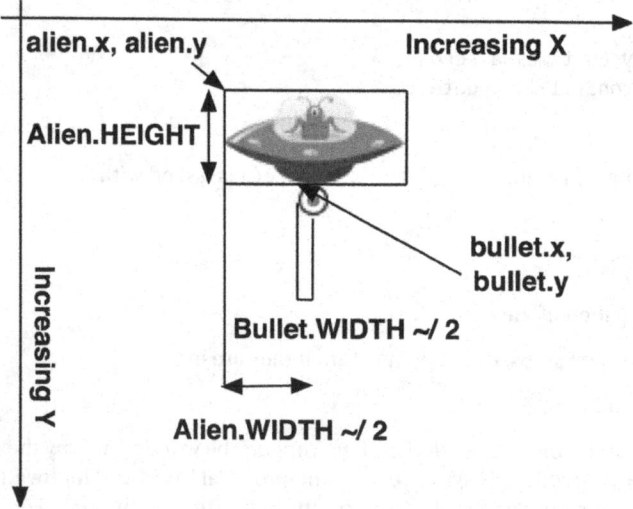

Figure 11-5. *Finding a new bullet's x and y coordinates*

One nice bit of abstraction in Alien Invaders is the idea that each Sprite draws itself. We simply pass the CanvasElement's drawing context to each Sprite object's draw() method and let it do the dirty work. This is much cleaner than drawing everything in the centralized draw() function.

Alien Invaders is the skeleton of a fairly complex game. It introduced several topics prevalent in 2D game programming, such as sprites and collision detection. The small class hierarchy of three subclasses of Sprite showcased a real-world practical use of inheritance. Ultimately, there are often many ways to implement the same program. Even within the realm of object-oriented programming, who is to say that Alien Invaders is implemented the *right* way. Perhaps collision detection is better handled by a mixin. Or perhaps Sprite should've been an interface implemented by the other classes. It's about doing things cleanly and logically in a way that makes sense to you. It's not about utilizing every bit of technology available.

Summary

Inheritance is used for forming class hierarchies with superclass and subclass relationships. Subclasses inherit the methods, instance variables, and properties of their superclasses. Subclasses can also override these. A class is declared to be the subclass of another class with the keyword extends. The superclass version can be referred to explicitly, using the keyword super. Abstract classes cannot be instantiated. They can declare methods and properties with no definition. Concrete subclasses of abstract superclasses must define their undefined methods and properties. All classes in Dart implicitly expose their interface for reuse, using the implements keyword. If a class implements another class's interface, it must implement all of it. A mixin is a special type of class that can have its functionality appended to another class, using the with keyword. The cascade operator (..) is used for doing multiple operations on the same object without having to retype its name. There are many ways to implement the same program in an object-oriented style. It's most important to do things in a clean way that makes sense logically to *you*.

EXERCISES

1. Write a class hierarchy for bank accounts. SavingsAccount and CheckingAccount are subclasses of the abstract class BankAccount. BankAccount has instance variables interestRate and balance. It has methods deposit() and withdraw(). Create a virtual ATM interface for working with bank accounts.

2. In what situations does it make sense to use an abstract base class at the root of a class hierarchy, as opposed to a concrete (non-abstract) base class?

3. Can you think of situations in which interfaces or mixins make more sense than a traditional class hierarchy (using extends)?

4. Turn Alien Invaders into a real game. Add levels of increasing difficulty, different kinds of aliens, lives, scoring, and barriers between the player and the aliens.

5. Add mouse or touch controls to Alien Invaders.

CHAPTER 12

■ ■ ■

Advanced Dart Concepts

This chapter is a bit of a hodgepodge of advanced language features that didn't fit in any other chapter. Since this is a beginner's book, the goal is to give you a taste of each feature, rather than to delve into it deeply. With the possible exception of exceptions, you probably will not find most of these language features useful until you are at the point where you are writing quite sophisticated programs. At the same time, knowing about them is helpful at this stage, because this allows you to read others' code that utilizes them. There's nothing more frustrating than reading someone else's source code that's filled with a language feature that you don't understand.

Operator Overloading

Operator overloading is a way of repurposing Dart's built-in operators to perform operations on your custom defined classes. Dart's built-in classes use operator overloading. As you know from Chapter 5 (although you didn't know the term *operator overloading* at the time), the + operator is overridden by the String class to concatenate two String objects. In this section, we'll take a look at Dart's use of operator overloading in its built-in Point class, and then we'll see how you can use operator overloading in your own classes.

The Point Class

A great example of operator overloading is the dart:math library's Point class. It overrides the operators +, -, *, and ==. A Point represents an x, y location on a two-dimensional plane. How are two Points added together? If Point a represents the location x1, y1, and Point b represents the location x2, y2, then the addition of Point a to Point b (a + b) will yield a new Point with the location x1 + x2, y1 + y2. The use of the – operator is similar.

   * is interesting, because it is overridden to work not with another Point but, instead, with a plain scalar number. The result of a Point, a, * an int, n, is a new Point with location x1 * n, y1 * n. By default, the == operator checks if two variables refer to the same object. In the case of Points, it checks if two Points represent the same location. Let's see the Point class in action.

```
import "dart:math";

void main() {
  Point a = new Point(2, 2);
  Point b = new Point(4, 4);
  b = b - a;
  print(b);  // prints Point(2, 2)
  a = a * 2;
```

```
print(a);  // prints Point(4, 4)
a = b + a;
print(a);  // prints Point(6, 6);
if ((b + b) == (a - b)) {  // this is true
  print("Both sides of the equation hold equivalent values.");
}
}
```

The overridden operators of the Point class work exactly as we would expect. In some ways, operator overloading is a way of extending a programming language. Overridden operators provide new symbolic transformers. The heavy use of overloaded operators can fundamentally change what source code looks like both syntactically and aesthetically.

Overloading Operators in Your Own Classes

Overloading an operator involves adding a special method to your class using the operator keyword. Suppose we have a class called Population that defines the population of a city. It has two variables, name, representing the city's name, and pop, representing the city's population. It overrides the & and + operators. When we want to get a new Population representing the combined populations of two cities, we can use &. The + operator is used for adding people to the population of a city.

```
class Population {
  String name;
  int pop;

  Population(this.name, this.pop);

  operator &(Population other) => new Population(name + " & " + other.name, pop + other.pop);

  operator +(int newPeople) => pop += newPeople;

  String toString() {
    return "$name has a population of $pop";
  }
}
```

The & operator works on operations between two Population objects. However, the + operator operates on a Population object and an int object. Again, they work as you would expect.

```
void main() {
  Population springfield = new Population("Springfield", 2343);
  Population hanover = new Population("Hanover", 4000);
  Population both = springfield & hanover;
  print(both);  // Prints: Springfield & Hanover has a population of 6343
  hanover + 1000;
  print(hanover);  // Prints: Hanover has a population of 5000
}
```

An important caveat is that the order in which an operator is used does matter. Overloading the + operator on Population allowed us to put a Population object on the left side of + and an int on the right side of +. However, the statement 1000 + hanover (as opposed to hanover + 1000) would be illegal, causing a warning in Dart Editor and raising an exception at runtime. For that scenario, we would need to override the + operator on int (which is already used up for actually adding two ints..., so, in other words, it would not be possible).

The way that overriding + on Population looks when applied is a little awkward. We wouldn't write a statement of 5 + 5; in Dart by itself. Yet, the statement hanover + 1000; is legal, but jarring to a programmer unaccustomed to our Population class. The danger of harm to the syntax and aesthetics of a programming language that can be afflicted by operator overloading is clear.

Getting Back to the Point

As you should know, Dart is an open-source language. This means that the source code for all of its libraries, including dart:math, is available for perusing by anyone. Let's take a look at how the creators of Dart actually implement overriding the +, -, *, and == operators in the Point class. Listing 12-1 represents code from the Dart bleeding edge repository on GitHub on January 23, 2014.[1] Please note that comments have been removed from the original source code.

Listing 12-1. Snippets of Code from the Point class of dart:math

```dart
bool operator ==(other) {
  if (other is !Point) return false;
  return x == other.x && y == other.y;
}

Point<T> operator +(Point<T> other) {
  return new Point<T>(x + other.x, y + other.y);
}

Point<T> operator -(Point<T> other) {
  return new Point<T>(x - other.x, y - other.y);
}

Point<T> operator *(num factor) {
  return new Point<T>(x * factor, y * factor);
}
```

There's no magic! Even the wizards behind Dart program like the rest of us. These overloaded operators are not unlike those in our Population class. Two confusing differences are the declaration of a type before the declaration of the operator method (bool operator, Point<T> operator) and the use of <T>. Regarding the first discrepancy, as you know from Chapter 5, declaring the return type of a function/method is optional in Dart. The same is true of operator methods. The latter is the subject of the next section of this chapter, "Generics."

Generics

Please take a moment to think back to Chapter 6. We learned that when declaring a List or Map, we have the option of declaring what type of objects the List or Map will hold. For example, both of the following are legal Dart Lists with equivalent values:

```dart
List fruits1 = ["apple", "banana", "orange"];
List<String> fruits2 = ["apple", "banana", "orange"];
```

---

[1]GitHub, "Dart Bleeding Edge," https://github.com/dart-lang/bleeding_edge, January 23, 2014.

The difference is that it is specified with `fruits2` that the `List` will only hold `Strings`. Let's talk about types. In reality, since types are optional in Dart, we can get around our declaration. However, once again, the point of using types is not to limit ourselves but, rather, to inform and self-document our code. Using types helps prevent errors, both via programmer inspection and via the aid of developer tools.

Generics are a way of enabling code to work with an arbitrary type. Instead of specifying the type that a method, property, or instance variable is or returns, we declare that the code works with a user-specified type. Users then specify the exact type that will be filling in that role at the time that they create an instance.

We can use generics in our own classes by specifying in the class definition that it can take a generic type. We do this with the same `<TypeName>` syntax that we use to define what specific type we're using with a new instance of a class that supports generics. Let's imagine a class keeping track of a product in a store's inventory.

```dart
class InventoryItem <ProductClass> {
  int quantity;
  double price;
  List<ProductClass> productsInInventory;
  List<ProductClass> productsArrivingSoon;
}
```

Since this class can potentially be used with any type of product, it is very flexible. To be perfectly honest with you, it is unlikely you will find a good use for generics (or, should we say, rather unlikely that you will use them properly) until you have been programming for quite a while. Of course, that excludes using the generics built into Dart's collection classes, which is quite a useful mechanism. However, let's look at another example, just for the sake of completeness.

```dart
class Shouter <T> {
  int numberOfTimes;
  T thingToShout;

  Shouter(this.numberOfTimes, this.thingToShout);

  void shout() {
    for (int i = 0; i < numberOfTimes; i++) {
      print(thingToShout);
    }
  }
}

void main() {
  Shouter<int> myShouter1 = new Shouter(23, 34);
  myShouter1.shout();
  Shouter<String> myShouter2 = new Shouter(12, "hello");
  myShouter2.shout();
}
```

This example is not unlike the function `printMany()` from Chapter 5, except it works with any type. That's the power of generics. `printMany()` was not as flexible a mechanism as the `Shouter` class provides. One application where generics are definitely useful is logging (printing error messages to the console). A logging system may need to be able to log any arbitrary type.

Exceptions

Exceptions can simply be thought of as *unexpected happenings that occur while a program is running*. Although that may be a valid formal definition, for practical purposes, most users who run into an exception while a program is executing simply experience them as errors. If they're not *handled*, a program may crash due to unexpected behavior. Exceptions are said to be *raised* when the function where the unexpected behavior occurs *throws* an exception to the piece of code that called it. It is then the responsibility of the code that called the function from which the exception is thrown to either *catch* it and handle it, or throw it yet again further up the chain of callable units. So, exceptions are raised by being thrown and then handled by being caught. Let's first look at Dart's built-in exceptions and then try developing our own.

Working with Dart's Built-in Exceptions

Dart has many built-in exception classes that will be raised by its standard libraries when unexpected behavior occurs. Exceptions are caught using `try-catch-blocks`. The code that may raise an exception is run within the `try-block`, and if an exception occurs, the `catch-block` is executed to handle the exception. Dart also has the keyword on, which, we will see, operates similarly to a catch-block. In Chapter 4's Math Test, we caught our first exception when trying to parse `int` objects from `String` objects using the `int` class's `parse()` method. Let's look at that code (`userAnswer` is declared earlier in the program as an `int`).

```
String inTemp = stdin.readLineSync();

try {
  userAnswer = int.parse(inTemp);
} on FormatException {  // uh oh, could not be turned into integer
  print("Thanks for playing!");
  print("You got $numCorrect out of $questionsAttempted correct.");
  break;
}
```

The `parse()` method throws a `FormatException` if it cannot figure out what sort of integer the `String` passed to it is supposed to represent. Knowing that `parse()` may throw an exception, we placed it within a try-block. The potential `FormatException` will be caught by the on `FormatException` expression and handled by the code within the following block. In this case, we handle a `FormatException` by printing to the console and issuing a `break` statement (to break from the enclosing loop, not shown here).

The difference between using a `catch` expression and an on expression to catch an exception is that `catch-block` gives us access to the underlying object that represents the exception, while on does not. For instance, if we want to know more about the `FormatException` in the previous code, we could use a `catch-block`.

```
String inTemp = stdin.readLineSync();

try {
  userAnswer = int.parse(inTemp);
} catch(fe) {  // uh oh, could not be turned into integer
  print(fe);
  print("Thanks for playing!");
  print("You got $numCorrect out of $questionsAttempted correct.");
  break;
}
```

If a FormatException occurred, fe would be a variable that refers to the object that represents the FormatException. print() would, like with any other object, call that FormatException's toString() method, which ultimately would present useful information on the console. catch-blocks can also optionally contain a stack trace, which explains how the caught exception occurred. The variable that holds the stack trace appears as a second parameter in the catch expression.

```
} catch(fe, stacktrace) {  // uh oh, could not be turned into integer
  print(fe);
  print(stacktrace);
}
```

A try-catch-block can branch, depending on the type of exception that is generated by the code in the try section. Consider the following example program. If the user inputs a number out of the range of indexes possible in the names List (below 0 or above 3), then Dart will throw a RangeError, a type of exception. It will be caught separately from an exception thrown by parse().

```
import "dart:io";

void main() {
  int userAnswer;
  List<String> names = ["Karl", "Mark", "Adam", "Seth"];
  String which;

  print("What index in the names List do you want to look at?");
  which = stdin.readLineSync();
  try {
    userAnswer = int.parse(which);
    print(names[userAnswer]);
  } on FormatException {
    print("Could not understand the input.");
  } on RangeError {
    print("No name for index chosen.");
  } finally {
    print("You selected $which out of ${names.length}");
  }
}
```

Code within a finally expression will execute no matter what. If no exception is raised, it will execute. If a FormatException is raised, it will execute. If a RangeError is raised, it will execute.

Defining Your Own Exceptions

Like everything else in Dart, exceptions are just objects. You can define your own exceptions by creating a class that implements the Exception interface. Interestingly, the Exception interface defines no methods that you need to implement. A blank class can implement the Exception interface (and implicitly does). You throw an exception to calling code using the throw keyword. Listing 12-2 shows a sample program that utilizes custom defined exceptions. You should take particular notice of how the Bar class's checkId() method throws exceptions and how they are handled in main().

Listing 12-2. Custom Defined Exceptions Example

```dart
class UnderageException implements Exception {
  String message;  // for the programmer's reference
  UnderageException(this.message);

  String toString() {
    return message;
  }
}

class TommyException implements Exception {  // look how simple it is!
  String toString() {
    return "TommyException: Tommy is not allowed in here ever!";
  }
}

class Person {
  String name;
  int age;
  Person(this.name, this.age);
}

class Bar {
  List<Person> currentPatrons = new List();

  void checkId(Person p) {
    if (p.name == "Tommy") {
      throw new TommyException();
    } else if (p.age < 21) {
      throw new UnderageException("UnderageException: ${p.name} is not old enough.");
    } else {
      currentPatrons.add(p);
    }
  }
}

void main() {
  Bar bar = new Bar();
  try {
    bar.checkId(new Person("Tommy", 25));
    bar.checkId(new Person("Jimmy", 22));
    bar.checkId(new Person("Sandra", 17));
  } catch (e) {
    print(e);
  }
  print(bar.currentPatrons);
}
```

You should not run the program yet! Now is a good time for you to think carefully about main(). What will be printed to the console at its conclusion? If an exception occurs midway through a try-block, the rest of the block will not be executed. The program moves directly to the catch-block and never returns to the try-block. Okay, you can run the program now. Was what was printed to the console what you expected?

WHEN TO USE EXCEPTIONS

The List class built into Dart has a method called indexOf(). It takes one required parameter, an object that we're looking for within the List. It returns the index of that object within the List as an integer. If the indexOf() method can't find the provided object within the List in question, then it returns -1. Why does it return -1 instead of raising an exception?

Exceptions are for unexpected behavior. It's not unexpected that a method that is used for searching will sometimes receive a search parameter that is not found. To think otherwise would be like saying that if a Web search engine doesn't find a search term, it should show the user an error page instead of stating that zero results were found.

How do you decide when to use an exception and when to indicate an error or problem with a return value? Sometimes, as in the above example, it's obvious. A lot of the time, however, it's a toss-up left up to the programmer to decide. In these circumstances, one needs to consider convenience. It's frankly annoying to wrap a lot of your code in try-catch-blocks.

On the other hand, using exceptions is a good way of organizing your code and allowing callers of your code to gracefully handle errors. It's pretty easy to raise an exception that's built into Dart. However, to truly make your use of exceptions exceptional, defining your own exceptions does not take too much more effort.

Factory Constructors

Factory constructors are specialized constructors that are used in situations where you don't necessarily want to simply create a new instance of the class where the factory constructor is defined. Instead, there may be situations in which you want to do something different, depending on the information passed to the constructor. In the next example, a factory constructor within a class called Ticket creates an instance of one of its subclasses depending on the age parameter.

```dart
class Ticket {
  int age;

  factory Ticket(int age) {
    if (age >= 18) {
      return new AdultTicket(age);
    } else {
      return new ChildTicket(age);
    }
  }

  Ticket._withAge(this.age);
}

class AdultTicket extends Ticket {
  AdultTicket(int age) : super._withAge(age);
}
```

```
class ChildTicket extends Ticket {
  ChildTicket(int age) : super._withAge(age);
}

void main() {
  Ticket t = new Ticket(17);
  print(t is ChildTicket);  // prints true
}
```

In this design pattern, making decisions about what subclass of Ticket to create is moved from being the responsibility of the user of the classes to the classes themselves, via the factory constructor in Ticket. Factory constructors cannot reference this. Figure 12-1 shows abstractly how you can think of this factory constructor.

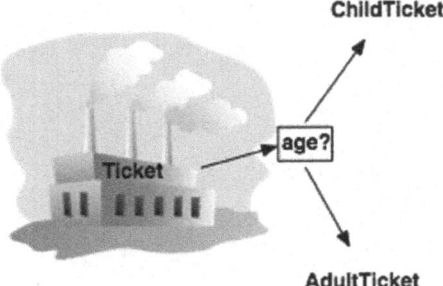

ChildTicket

age?

Ticket

AdultTicket

Figure 12-1. *The ticket factory*

Another design pattern using factory constructors is known as a *singleton*. What if we only ever want one instance of a class to exist? A factory constructor, combined with a class (static) variable, can help. SimpleLogger is an incredibly simple logging solution class (its log() method just prints to the console). Its factory constructor ensures there is never more than one instance of SimpleLogger.

```
class SimpleLogger {
  static SimpleLogger logger;  // our single instance's representation

  factory SimpleLogger() {
    if (SimpleLogger.logger == null) {
      SimpleLogger.logger = new SimpleLogger._internal();
    }
    return SimpleLogger.logger;
  }

  SimpleLogger._internal();  // a private constructor

  void log(Object o) {
    print(o);
  }
}

void main() {
  SimpleLogger myLogger = new SimpleLogger();
  SimpleLogger myLogger2 = new SimpleLogger();
  print(myLogger == myLogger2);  // prints true
}
```

By default the == operator checks if two variables point to the same instance of an object. The fact that myLogger == myLogger2 returns true is proof that we have successfully implemented the singleton pattern. Singletons are useful in two circumstances. The first is memory constrained environments. Since they ensure only one instance of a class exists, they ensure memory is not filled with instances of a particular class. The second is when you want to ensure that state is being maintained through a single instance. For example, you may use a singleton to keep track of all of the high scores in a game. You don't want scores being scattered across several different instances that are hard to keep track of. Figure 12-2 shows the singleton design pattern, with reference to the example.

Figure 12-2. Singleton design pattern

Assert

assert statements are used for testing the validity of a boolean expression in development. They are ignored in production (or in Dart speak, in non-checked mode[2]). Suppose we have a bool called userLoggedIn. There's code that shouldn't run unless userLoggedIn is true.

```
assert(userLoggedIn);  // code following this assert will not run unless userLoggedIn is true
// do something that depends on the user being logged in
```

If userLoggedIn is not true, then an exception of type AssertionError will be raised at runtime as a result of the assert statement. Inserting a lot of assert statements in your code can be a helpful debugging mechanism to ensure that your assumptions about the state of your variables are true. There really is not much downside, except for all of the code litter.

```
assert(person.age < 200);  // nobody lives to 200, this must not be a real age
assert(isRaining && !clearDay);  // it can't be a clear day if it's raining
```

---

[2]In Dart Editor, to run your program in non-checked mode, go to the Run menu, select Manage Launches, and clear the "Run in checked mode" check box.

Typedef

There has been sporadic discussion throughout this book about the concept of a function or method signature. For the purpose of typedef, we are going to consider methods as just another type of function and, therefore, method signatures as simply function signatures. A function signature is defined by a function's parameters (including their types) and return type. We can use typedef to specify a function signature that we want specific functions to match. We're specifying a type of function, or what you can think of as a function interface.

```dart
typedef String uniter(String s1, String s2);

String concatenater(String s1, String s2) => s1 + s2;  // same signature as uniter

String spacer(String s1, String s2) => s1 + " " + s2;  // same signature

String shouter(String s1, String s2) {  // same signature
  String shout1 = s1.toUpperCase() + "!";
  String shout2 = s2.toUpperCase() + "!";
  return shout1 + " " + shout2;
}

void repeatPrint(String s1, String s2, int numberOfRepeats, uniter myUniter) {
  for (int i = 0; i < numberOfRepeats; i++) {
    print(myUniter(s1, s2));
  }
}

void main() {
  uniter u1, u2;
  u1 = concatenater;  // legal because concatenater is a uniter
  u2 = spacer;  // spacer is a uniter
  print(u1("Hello", "Goodbye"));
  print(u2("Hello", "Goodbye"));
  repeatPrint("Hi", "Bye", 3, shouter);  // shouter is a uniter
}
```

Do you understand the function signature of uniter? A uniter is any function that has exactly two parameters, both of which are Strings, and a return type of String. The above little example has some uniter functions that work, as you would expect, by the name uniter—they put Strings together. However, any function that has the same function signature as uniter is a valid uniter. Even one that ignores the String parameters passed to it.

```dart
String blank(String s1, String s2) => "";
```

blank is a valid uniter. The name of a parameter is not part of a function signature. However, for simplicity, we used the same parameter names throughout these examples. Therefore, the following version of blank is also a valid uniter:

```dart
String blank(String first, String second) => "";
```

Metadata

Surely you've heard the term *metadata* used before in the context of current events, but what does it actually mean? Metadata is *data about data*. In the context of Dart, metadata provides a mechanism by which you can annotate the purpose or status of some of your code. Annotations always begin with the @ symbol. Using annotations is a bit like tagging a piece of your code, as shown a bit fancifully in Figure 12-3.

Figure 12-3. *Annotations are like tags for your code*

Dart's Built-in Annotations

Dart has a few built-in annotations, the most common of which are @deprecated and @override. @deprecated is used for specifying that a function/method/etc. may be removed in the future and should no longer be used. If @deprecated is put into your source code, then Dart Editor will sprout a warning when the @deprecated portion is accessed.

```
@deprecated  // marks that tradeMoneyForGold() is going away and shouldn't be used
void tradeMoneyForGold(double amount, String currency) {...}
```

■ **Note**   Annotations do not end with a semicolon.

Why mark something as deprecated instead of just removing it? There may be old code around that still relies on a deprecated function. Using @deprecated enables a transition period that alerts other pieces of code still using a deprecated function to get with the program (no pun intended). Indeed, if you are using an API from Dart's standard libraries that you are warned by Dart Editor is deprecated, you should definitely switch to using something else. In most cases, an equivalent, possibly better, API will already exist.

If in a subclass you specify that a method/instance variable/property is supposed to @override its counterpart in the superclass, then Dart Editor will help you with such things as typos. Annotations like @deprecated and @override are not required, by any means. Like many things in Dart, they are simply there to make the programmer's life easier. If you work alone, then annotations are likely to be a lot less useful for you than they are for programmers in a team environment.

Defining Your Own Annotations

You can create your own annotations by creating classes that have a `const` constructor. Imagine in a team environment different team members are assigned different functions to work on. We want to mark who owns which function. We therefore want to define a convenient annotation @owner.

```dart
class owner {
  final String name;

  const owner(this.name);
}

@owner("John")
void importantFunc1() {
  return;
}

@owner("David")
void main() {
  importantFunc1();
}
```

Although classes are usually defined starting with an uppercase letter, since owner will serve as an annotation, it is defined starting with a lowercase letter. The intention with this annotation is to mark importantFunc1() as John's responsibility and main() as David's responsibility. Does this have any implication for the code itself? No, it does not. It doesn't stop John from working on main() either. It's just a nicety.

Metadata will appear in Dart's automatically generated documentation. In addition, Dart includes reflection classes that allow a program to inspect a class's metadata at runtime. If you're interested in using code to inspect code, then check out the documentation for the Dart library dart:mirrors.

WITH GREAT POWER COMES GREAT RESPONSIBILITY

The powerful features touched on in this chapter are counterproductive when used in excess. Littering a program with annotations makes for ugly, hard-to-read code. When used sparingly, annotations make code easier to read. Likewise, overusing operator overloading can be very confusing when users of your codebase are surprised to find an operator doesn't work as they expected. For this reason, operator overloading is a controversial feature, even in languages that support it (and many modern languages don't include it as a feature).

It has been said that most C++ programmers are not experts on C++ but, rather, on a subset of C++, because it is such a large, complex language. Dart is also a very feature-rich language. You do not need to master its advanced features to be a good Dart programmer. In fact, if you find yourself trying to incorporate a Dart feature in your program and you can't figure out a good way to do so, step back and ask yourself if it really makes the program better or if it just adds complexity.

In short, use advanced language features sparingly, and only when they absolutely make sense. There's no scorecard where the more you include in your program, the better you do.

Summary

Dart has a full complement of advanced features that rivals the completeness of most other modern programming languages. At this stage in your Dart career, it's not important to master these features, but it is useful to know about them. Operator overloading can be used to make working with programmer-defined classes more natural. Generics are useful for doing type-neutral programming. Exceptions are an important mechanism for handling unexpected behavior during the runtime of a program. Factory constructors are a convenience that can be used to ease the creation of new instances of a complex class. assert is used to ensure boolean expressions are true during development but doesn't work in un-checked mode. typedef can be used to clearly define what certain function signatures should look like. Metadata is a good way of documenting your code.

EXERCISES

1. Use operator overloading to create a class that can represent operations on complex numbers. (If you don't know what complex numbers are, this exercise may not be for you—no hard feelings, though.)

2. Create subclasses of the Shape classes from Chapter 11 that override the * operator to allow for the scaling of the various shapes.

3. Utilize generics to implement a class hierarchy for a warehouse. The warehouse should be able to store any kind of physical object—which can be represented by any class.

4. Why are generics used with Dart's built-in collection classes like List and Map?

5. Go back to the simple programs of Chapter 4 and add intelligent custom defined exceptions for incorrect user input. Gracefully handle them occurring.

6. Add a factory constructor to Chapter 11's Rectangle class, which creates Square objects or Rectangle objects, depending on the parameters passed to it.

7. Can you think of any downside about using a lot of assert statements in your code?

8. Modify the classes in the Shape hierarchy of Chapter 11 to include @override annotations.

CHAPTER 13

∎∎∎

Testing Your Work

Software development is an incredibly error-prone process. The best way to identify bugs is to thoroughly test your work. Remember: Computer hardware, in general, doesn't make mistakes. Yes, there have been rare microprocessor bugs.[1] However, usually when computer hardware fails, it's more catastrophic than an everyday error. The vast majority of computer errors are caused by software—be it firmware, BIOS, operating system, or most commonly, application-level software. Your software is bound to have bugs. You are only human; you're not computer hardware. Hence, as a programmer, discovering and preventing bugs may take up as much of your time as creating original code. There are frameworks to help you. The creators of Dart have provided one called `unittest`, which you will learn about in this chapter.

Including External Packages in Your Program

pub is the packaging system for the Dart language.[2] If you want to include libraries in your program that do not come with the Dart language's core, you use pub. You can browse what packages are available on the pub web site at `http://pub.dartlang.org`.

　　You may have noticed that every Dart program that you create with Dart Editor comes with a file called `pubspec.yaml` in its root directory. This file specifies attributes about your project that will be visible to others, should you want to publish it as a package on the pub web site. Important for our purposes, it also specifies which pub packages your project depends on. After specifying said packages, you can run the `pub get` command (accessible with a simple click in Dart Editor) to automatically download all the packages that your program depends on. `pub get` is also available in the Tools menu.

　　`pubspec.yaml` is really just a text file. It can be edited in any text editor, but Dart Editor provides a simple graphical interface for manipulating it. If you double-click `pubspec.yaml`, Dart Editor will open an interface that looks similar to the one in Figure 13-1. You can add dependencies by clicking the button labeled "Add..." in the section titled "Dependencies." A dialog will pop up with many available pub packages listed. You can select the package you want from the list, or enter it by name. After you enter it, you will have the option of specifying a version. This is a good idea (and, in fact, if you don't, Dart Editor will issue a warning), because it ensures that if a new version comes out that breaks your code, your project will not be associated with it when `pub get` is next run.

---

[1]The original Intel Pentium microprocessor had a bug that caused it to incorrectly divide some floating-point numbers. Intel, "Statistical Analysis of Floating Point Flaw: Intel White Paper," `www.intel.com/support/processors/pentium/sb/CS-013007.htm`, 2009.

[2]pub is analogous to Ruby's gem system, Objective-C/Cocoa's pod system, and Python's PyPI.

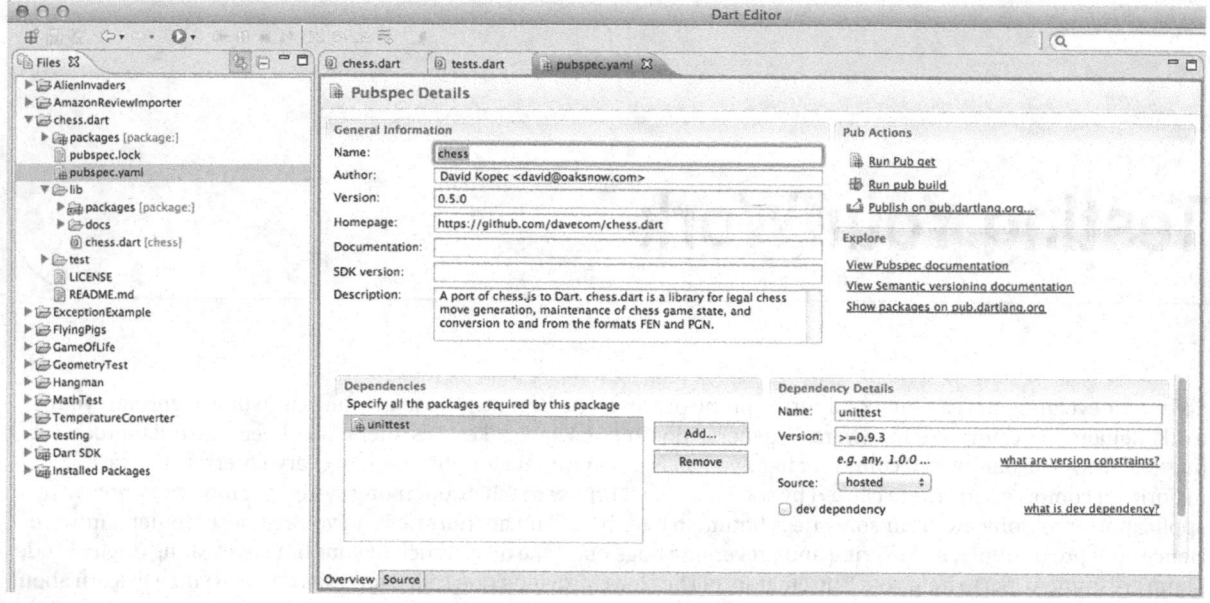

Figure 13-1. *pubspec.yaml editing in Dart Editor*

Unit Testing

Unit testing is one of those terms that sounds fancy but really doesn't mean anything particularly sophisticated. It simply means testing code, one piece at a time. How large or small that piece is, is left up to you. However, it makes sense to test small pieces, because otherwise, when an error occurs, it's hard to determine where exactly that error was. The theory goes that if your program is composed of many small, well-tested pieces of code, then it is more likely to be a robust whole. Often, an individual function or method is a good candidate for a unit test.

Taking a `unittest`

Dart's `unittest` unit-testing framework is straightforward and easy to learn. You define *tests*, which include *expectations* defined by you about the results of the code that you are testing. If the expectations are met, a test passes. If they are not, you are shown the values that caused the expectation(s) to fail. You can put several tests together into a *group*. However, groups have no effect on the tests. They are simply provided for organizational purposes.

The core of using `unittest` is defining tests with a call to the `test()` function. The first parameter that `test()` takes is the name of the test as a `String`. The second parameter is a function that actually performs the test (usually an anonymous function). The test will contain calls to the `expect()` function to define one or more expectations. `expect()` takes a variable being tested as its first parameter and a *matcher* as its second parameter. The matcher defines what the correct value for the variable being tested is, in order for the expectation to be met (and therefore the test to pass).

Consider the following toy example. A function called `exclaim()` is defined that adds an exclamation point to the end of a `String` and returns it (we have seen this before). We want to test that it actually adds the exclamation point successfully.

```dart
import 'package:unittest/unittest.dart';

exclaim(String what) => what + "!";

void main() {
  test("exclaim() test", (){
    String original = "I'm testing";
    expect(exclaim(original), equals("I'm testing!"));
  });
}
```

We expect that after exclaim() adds an exclamation point to "I'm testing", it will be equivalent to "I'm testing!" Therefore, we use the equals() matcher in the expect() call. equals() checks if two values are equivalent. What happens when we run the program?

```
unittest-suite-wait-for-done
PASS: exclaim() test

All 1 tests passed.
unittest-suite-success
```

Let's modify main() to run more than one test on exclaim(). A common pattern is to provide a List of test cases and to loop through them, generating a new test for each. We'll do that for exclaim().

```dart
void main() {
  List testCases = [["Dog", "Dog!"], ["", "!"], ["H e l l o ", "H e l l o !"], ["dog", "dog?"]];
  for (List testCase in testCases) {
    test("exclaim() test" + testCase[0], (){
      expect(exclaim(testCase[0]), equals(testCase[1]));
    });
  }
}
```

The last of these tests won't pass. The unittest library, based on our use of the equals() matcher, will provide us with some very useful output. It will tell us exactly why the test failed, including pinpointing the exact character of difference between the expected value and the actual value. Please note that some of the output from the test run has been replaced with an ellipsis (…) in the following.

```
unittest-suite-wait-for-done
PASS: exclaim() testDog
PASS: exclaim() test
PASS: exclaim() testH e l l o
FAIL: exclaim() testdog
  Expected: 'dog?'
    Actual: 'dog!'
     Which: is different.
  Expected: dog?
    Actual: dog!
            ^
  Differ at offset 3
```

...

```
3 PASSED, 1 FAILED, 0 ERRORS
Unhandled exception:
Exception: Some tests failed.
```
...

There are matchers other than equals(). Many matchers don't take any parameters, and almost all matchers have rather self-explanatory names. Table 13-1 lists some of the most common matchers that come with the unittest library. You can find more in unittest's API documentation. The API documentation also explains how to implement your own matchers.[3]

Table 13-1. *Selected Common Matchers in the unittest Library*

Matcher	Parameter Type
isTrue	None
isFalse	None
isNull	None
isNotNull	None
isEmpty	None
equals()	Object
greaterThan()	num
lessThan()	num
closeTo()	num, num (the latter is the delta allowed)
equalsIgnoringCase()	String
equalsIgnoringWhitespace()	String
matches()	RegExp
orderedEquals()	Iterable
unorderedEquals()	Iterable
containsValue() (used with a Map)	Object

Grouping Unit Tests

As was mentioned before, using the grouping mechanism provided by unittest is purely an organizational maneuver. Groups are created using a call to the group() function. The first parameter that group() takes is a String representing the name of the group. The second is a function, usually anonymous, that contains the tests that the group is composed of. Calls to group() are very similarly structured to calls to test().

Suppose we are testing two functions, exclaim() and another toy function, negate(), that negates a number. We can logically combine the tests for each function into a group. Below is our revised main() function, along with the new negate() function.

---

[3]https://api.dartlang.org/unittest/unittest

```
negate(num n) => -n;

void main() {
  group("exclaim tests", () {
    List testCases = [["Dog", "Dog!"], ["", "!"], ["H e l l o ", "H e l l o !"]];
    for (List testCase in testCases) {
      test(testCase[0], (){
        expect(exclaim(testCase[0]), equals(testCase[1]));
      });
    }
  });
  group("negate tests", () {
    List testCases = [[4, -4], [3,-3], [0, 0]];
    for (List testCase in testCases) {
      test(testCase[0].toString(), (){
        expect(negate(testCase[0]), equals(testCase[1]));
      });
    }
  });
}
```

This only changes the formatting of our output, not the substance of our tests. By default, unittest prints out the group name directly before the test name and does not provide a breakdown of total passes/fails by group.

```
unittest-suite-wait-for-done
PASS: exclaim tests Dog
PASS: exclaim tests
PASS: exclaim tests H e l l o
PASS: negate tests 4
PASS: negate tests 3
PASS: negate tests 0

All 6 tests passed.
unittest-suite-success
```

───

■ **Note** Advanced users can further configure their testing environment using unittest's APIs. For more information, check out the section "Configuring the test environment" of the article "Unit Testing with Dart," by Graham Wheeler, at www.dartlang.org/articles/dart-unit-tests/.

───

Tic-Tac-Toe

Tic-Tac-Toe, also known as Noughts and Crosses, is a simple game played on a three-by-three grid of boxes. One player, represented by the letter X, and another player, represented by the letter O, alternate marking their respective letters on the board, one box at a time. Each player can choose to mark any single box that is available during a turn but may not mark a box that already contains a letter. If a player manages to mark three boxes in a row (whether horizontally, vertically, or diagonally) with her letter, she wins the game. If all the boxes are filled but neither player manages to mark three in a row, the game is a draw. Figure 13-2 shows a game of Tic-Tac-Toe halfway through.

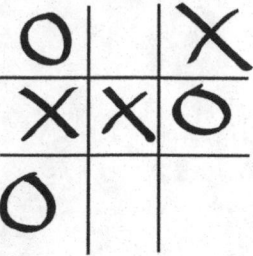

Figure 13-2. *Tic-Tac-Toe mid-game*

Defining the Game

Don't get too excited, we're going to leave writing a Tic-Tac-Toe AI (artificial intelligence) to the exercises, because unfortunately, it's beyond the scope of this chapter, and the chapter already has a lot of code. We will be implementing a two-human-player version of Tic-Tac-Toe that is unit-tested. Create a new web application in Dart Editor called "TicTacToe." In pubspec.yaml, add unittest as a dependency. tictactoe.html should look like Listing 13-1.

Listing 13-1. tictactoe.html

```
<!DOCTYPE html>

<html>
  <head>
    <meta charset="utf-8">
    <title>Tic-Tac-Toe</title>
    <link rel="stylesheet" href="tictactoe.css">
  </head>
  <body>
    <h1>Tic-Tac-Toe</h1>

    <canvas id="myCanvas" width="300" height="300"></canvas>

    <script type="application/dart" src="tictactoe.dart"></script>
    <script src="packages/browser/dart.js"></script>
  </body>
</html>
```

The structure for Tic-Tac-Toe is very simple. The class Board handles game state and drawing, whereas setup and clicks are handled in the file tictactoe.dart. Most processing needs to occur at the time of a click (make a move, check if the game is over, redraw), so clickHappened() in tictactoe.dart calls the appropriate methods in Board. Listing 13-2 includes the code that should go into tictactoe.dart.

Listing 13-2. tictactoe.dart

```
import 'dart:html';
import 'board.dart';

CanvasElement myCanvas;
Board board = new Board();
```

```
/// When the canvas is clicked, we make a move at the appropriate box
/// check if the game is over and redraw the canvas
void clickHappened(MouseEvent me) {
  int clickX = me.offset.x;
  int clickY = me.offset.y;
  num col = clickX ~/ (myCanvas.width / 3);   // calculate box column
  num row = clickY ~/ (myCanvas.height / 3);  // calculate box row
  if (row == 1) {  // reuse col as exact box number
    col += 3;
  } else if (row == 2) {
    col += 6;
  }
  if (board.makeMove(col) == true) {  // returns true if legal move
    board.draw(myCanvas);
    String winner = board.winner;  // check if the game is over
    if (winner != null) {
      window.alert(winner + "  wins!");
    } else if (board.isDraw) {  // can only be a draw if it's not a win
      window.alert("Draw!");
    }
  }
}

void main() {
  myCanvas = querySelector("#myCanvas");
  myCanvas.onClick.listen(clickHappened);
  board.draw(myCanvas);
}
```

The Board class is the heart of Tic-Tac-Toe. The instance variable _boxes is a List<String> that keeps track of the status of each box on the board. We're keeping track of the boxes simply with an index integer for referring to each. The top-left box is 0; the top center box is 1; etc., until we get to the bottom-right box, which is 8. Board's only other instance variable is _turn, which keeps track of whether an X or an O is being played. Both variables have default values that are initialized where they are declared. _boxes is filled with null—which we use to represent an empty box. _turn is set to "X", because X always goes first. Create a new file in the web directory called board.dart and fill it with Listing 13-3.

Listing 13-3. board.dart

```
import "dart:html";

class Board {
  List<String> _boxes = new List.filled(9, null);  // List of length 9 filled with null
  String _turn = "X";  // X always starts

  /// Returns the winning letter if there is one, or null if not
  String get winner {  // check all 3-in-a-rows
    if ((_boxes[0] != null) && ((_boxes[0] == _boxes[1]) && (_boxes[1] == _boxes[2]))) {
      return _boxes[0];
    } else if ((_boxes[0] != null) && ((_boxes[0] == _boxes[3]) && (_boxes[3] == _boxes[6]))) {
      return _boxes[0];
```

```dart
  } else if ((_boxes[1] != null) && ((_boxes[1] == _boxes[4]) && (_boxes[4] == _boxes[7]))) {
    return _boxes[1];
  } else if ((_boxes[2] != null) && ((_boxes[2] == _boxes[5]) && (_boxes[5] == _boxes[8]))) {
    return _boxes[2];
  } else if ((_boxes[3] != null) && ((_boxes[3] == _boxes[4]) && (_boxes[4] == _boxes[5]))) {
    return _boxes[3];
  } else if ((_boxes[6] != null) && ((_boxes[6] == _boxes[7]) && (_boxes[7] == _boxes[8]))) {
    return _boxes[6];
  } else if ((_boxes[0] != null) && ((_boxes[0] == _boxes[4]) && (_boxes[4] == _boxes[8]))) {
    return _boxes[0];
  } else if ((_boxes[2] != null) && ((_boxes[2] == _boxes[4]) && (_boxes[4] == _boxes[6]))) {
    return _boxes[2];
  } else {
    return null;
  }
}

/// Returns true if position is a draw, false otherwise
bool get isDraw => !_boxes.contains(null) && winner == null;

/// Returns a List<int> containing open squares
List<int> get legalMoves {
  List<int> legalMoves = new List();
  for (int i = 0; i < _boxes.length; i++) {
    if (_boxes[i] == null) {
      legalMoves.add(i);
    }
  }
  return legalMoves;
}

/// Attempts to make [move], returns if could be made or not as bool
bool makeMove(int move) {
  if (move < 0 || move > _boxes.length) {  // only 0-8 are legal
    throw new RangeError.range(move, 0, _boxes.length);
  }
  if (_boxes[move] == null) {  // can only play where no prior move
    _boxes[move] = _turn;
    _turn = _turn == "O" ? "X" : "O";  // flip _turn
    return true;
  } else {
    return false;
  }
}

/// Draws current position on myCanvas, respecting width/height
void draw(CanvasElement myCanvas) {
  CanvasRenderingContext2D myCanvasContext = myCanvas.context2D;
  //draw the background
  myCanvasContext.setFillColorRgb(0, 0, 0);  // Black
  myCanvasContext.moveTo(myCanvas.width / 3, 0);
```

```
myCanvasContext.lineTo(myCanvas.width / 3, myCanvas.height);
myCanvasContext.moveTo((myCanvas.width / 3) * 2, 0);
myCanvasContext.lineTo((myCanvas.width / 3) * 2, myCanvas.height);
myCanvasContext.moveTo(0, myCanvas.height / 3);
myCanvasContext.lineTo(myCanvas.width, myCanvas.height / 3);
myCanvasContext.moveTo(0, (myCanvas.height / 3) * 2);
myCanvasContext.lineTo(myCanvas.width, (myCanvas.height / 3) * 2);
myCanvasContext.stroke();
// draw the letter for each box, if one exists
for (int i = 0; i < _boxes.length; i++) {
  if (_boxes[i] != null) {
    num letterX = myCanvas.width / 6;
    if (i % 3 == 1) {
      letterX = myCanvas.width / 2;
    } else if (i % 3 == 2) {
      letterX = myCanvas.width / 6 * 5;
    }
    num letterY = myCanvas.height / 6;
    if (i > 5) {
      letterY = myCanvas.height / 6 * 5;
    } else if (i > 2) {
      letterY = myCanvas.height / 2;
    }
    myCanvasContext.fillText(_boxes[i], letterX, letterY);  // string, x, y
  }
 }
 }
}
```

The winner property checks every possible winning combination and returns the letter that won, if there is one, and null, if there is none. The isDraw property depends on winner and if the board has no null boxes to determine whether the game is a draw. legalMoves returns all the empty boxes still available. makeMove() attempts to place a piece of String _turn at the box move and returns true if the move is made and false if the box is already filled. Finally, draw() draws the Tic-Tac-Toe board along with all of the X's and O's onto a CanvasElement myCanvas.

An operator you haven't seen before is in makeMove(). ? is the conditional operator. A boolean expression is placed before ?. If the expression is true, the conditional operator returns the value before the colon. If the expression is false, the operator returns the value after the colon. For instance, in the following statement, x would be 5, and z would be 23.

```
bool j = true;
int x = j ? 5 : 10;
int z = (0 > 1) ? 45 : 23;
```

Testing Tic-Tac-Toe

If you run the file tictactoe.dart now, you can play a game of Tic-Tac-Toe as in Figure 13-3. How do we know it really works? Well, we can play a ton of games and see if anything goes wrong, or we can introduce some unit tests. Create a new file called test.dart. Fill it with the code in Listing 13-4.

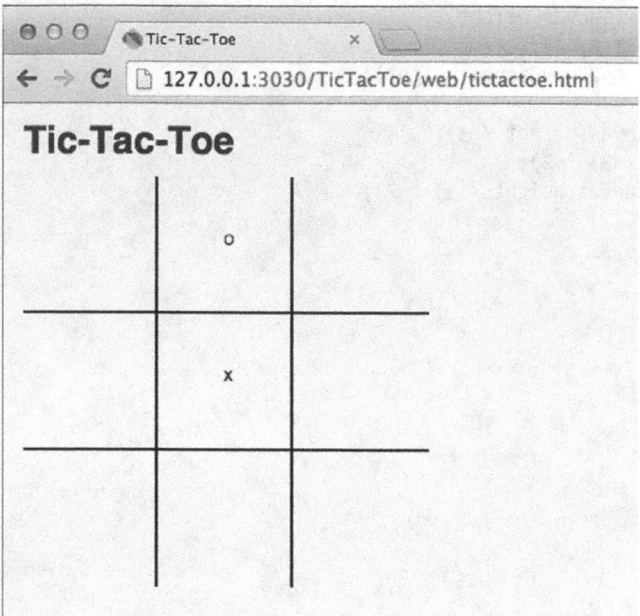

Figure 13-3. Tic-Tac-Toe

Listing 13-4. test.dart

```dart
import "package:unittest/unittest.dart";
import "board.dart";

void main() {
  group("makeMove() Tests", (){  // no duplicate moves allowed!
    List moves = [[5, true], [5, false], [4, true], [3, true], [4, false]];
    Board board = new Board();
    int moveNum = 1;
    for (List move in moves) {
        test("Move " + moveNum.toString(), (){
          expect(board.makeMove(move[0]), equals(move[1]));
        });
        moveNum++;
    }
  });

  // every time we make 9 random moves, the game should end in a win or draw
  group("Random Moves Tests", (){
    const int MAX_MOVES = 9;
    for (int j = 0; j < 10; j++) {  // play 10 random games
      Board board = new Board();
      test("Random Game " + j.toString(), (){
        bool gameWon = false;
        for (int i = 0; i < MAX_MOVES; i++) {
          List legalMoves = board.legalMoves;
          legalMoves.shuffle();
```

```
      board.makeMove(legalMoves[0]);
      if (board.winner != null) {
        gameWon = true;
        break;
      }
    }
    expect(gameWon || board.isDraw, isTrue);
  });
}
});

group("winner Tests", (){  // winner should be the end of the List
  List games = [[[0, 6, 1, 3, 2], "X"], [[3, 0, 7, 4, 2, 8], "O"]];
  int gameNum = 1;
  for (List game in games) {
    Board board = new Board();
    for (int move in game[0]) {
      board.makeMove(move);
    }
    test("Game " + gameNum.toString(), (){
      expect(board.winner, equals(game[1]));
    });
    gameNum++;
  }
});
}
```

If you try running test.dart directly, you will find that an error occurs and you are scolded for not including an HTML file with a program that imports dart:html. This is because board.dart, which we're using, imports dart:html. Create a dummy HTML file that just loads test.dart, such as the one in Listing 13-5. You can then launch the unit tests by running this file from Dart Editor. Dartium will superfluously load to a blank screen when you do.

Listing 13-5. test.html

```
<!DOCTYPE html>

<html>
  <head>
    <script type="application/dart" src="test.dart"></script>
  </head>
</html>
```

These unit tests are not definitive, but they are a good start at cracking the problem space. The first, the group "makeMove() Tests", checks that when duplicate moves are attempted, makeMove() returns false. The next, "Random Moves Tests", plays ten random games and makes sure that every one ends in a win or a draw. The last checks that particular winning positions are indeed counted as wins for the right player.

TEST-DRIVEN DEVELOPMENT

Test-driven development is a fairly new software development methodology that emphasizes unit testing first. If software is being developed in a test-driven way, its unit tests are defined before anything else. For example, if Tic-Tac-Toe were to be developed using test-driven methodology, unit tests for the Board class would be written before the Board class itself is written.

Test-driven development is interesting because it allows the programmer to define the requirements of a program (what tests it must pass) before she actually writes the code that makes it work. Hence, all tests initially fail. Test-driven development advocates believe that test-driven development delivers higher programmer productivity and higher quality code.

Software that needs to meet a preordained specification is particularly well-suited for test-driven development. For example, web browsers need to render HTML files in a very specific way. Web browsers may be a category of software that can benefit from test-driven development, since how elements of a web browser need to work can be defined before one is actually written.

Beta Testing

Not everyone agrees that unit testing is the best way to test all kinds of software. Wil Shipley, a well-known software developer, once wrote "Unit testing is a great way to pay a bunch of engineers to be bored out of their minds and find not much of anything."[4] His views garnered a great amount of debate. Ultimately, unit testing is a very good way of testing infrastructure pieces of software (such as the logic behind a Tic-Tac-Toe game) but may not be well-suited for the user-facing parts of software (such as the user interface presented in a Tic-Tac-Toe game). It's difficult to write unit tests that account for all the different ways that a user may interact with a graphical user interface. Also, how do you account for something "looking right" in a unit test? Even when it comes to infrastructure, unit tests may not be able to cover as much ground as many beta testers pulling software in many different directions.

You've surely heard of *beta* versions of popular applications. What are they? Beta versions are builds of a program that are not yet ready for prime time. When developers release a beta version, they know the software still contains bugs or believe it is likely to contain bugs (just about all software has bugs, we mean *major* bugs or *many minor* bugs).

Software developers release beta versions so that *beta testers* (people using the beta versions) can catch more bugs that the developers can fix before a general release is made. A beta version of a piece of software is only as helpful as the beta testers who use it. Public betas are beta releases that anyone can download. Private betas are restricted to specific testers. The advantage of a public beta is that the software gets more beta testers. However, the advantages of a private beta are many.

- In the case of commercial software, a near–fully functional version of the software doesn't get into the wild "for free."

- Poorly functioning beta software is less likely to hurt the reputation of the developers (people are quick to forget the beta moniker of public betas).

- Private beta testers feel "special." They are more likely to report bugs and thoroughly test a piece of software, thanks to their privileged status.

---

[4]Wil Shipley, "Unit testing is teh suck, Urr," http://blog.wilshipley.com/2005/09/unit-testing-is-teh-suck-urr.html, 2005.

At a minimum, any important piece of software should be beta-tested internally. In many ways, the easy bugs are the ones that show up at compile time. The hard bugs are the ones that take some effort to track down. A combination of unit testing and beta testing is a sound strategy for most complex projects.

Web development adds a new wrinkle to the beta-testing puzzle, because web apps by default are accessible to anyone. If you would like to release a private beta of your Dart web app, you can host it at a password-protected URL. A very common practice is to simply not tell anyone about the URL that a private beta is hosted at. This is, of course, very dangerous if the app has a good reason to remain secret (such as security bugs) and the URL leaks.

You may have also heard of an *alpha* version of some software. An alpha version is a beta of a beta. It's software that's still at a very early phase of development and usually is not ready for any public consumption, not even by beta testers.

VERSION NUMBERING

Traditionally, software has been versioned using one or two decimal places. For instance, 1.0 will be the initial public release of a non-beta version of a piece of software. 1.0.1 might be a minor revision, while 1.1 will be a major update. Alpha and beta releases are sometimes given pre-1.0 numbers, such as 0.5.1 or 0.9.8. However, another naming strategy is to simply add the letters *a* or *b* to the end of the number, such as 1.0b or 1.0b4 (fourth beta of version 1.0).

Web apps can be version-numbered, but since they are always live, their releases tend be more fluid. Are you using the 3.0 version of the Twitter web site or Twitter 10.1? You can't go back in time and use a previous version of Twitter's web site, so its current version number is largely irrelevant to its users. Internally, however, it may be useful to keep track of different releases of your web app, so that you can revert to an earlier version if something goes wrong. With that in mind, it's also a good idea to use a revision control system (touched on in Chapter 15).

Usability Testing

Unit testing and beta testing may help you ensure that your software doesn't crash, but what about finding out whether it's pleasant to use? That's where usability testing comes in.

Usability testing is not concerned so much with bugs but, instead, with how software works. Is it easy to use? Is it intuitive? Does it help its users get their jobs done more quickly? Wealthy companies can afford focus groups. For the rest of us, beta testers may very well also serve as usability testers. We can survey them or, better yet, watch them!

One way to watch how users react to software is to video-record them. This is a time-consuming process. An alternative is to record their screens (with their consent, of course). Many tools exist to enable this, but unfortunately, the setup involved means that it's hard to do on a large scale.

Luckily, for web apps, there's an easier way to record user actions and capture how they're using your software. Tools such as Google Analytics can tell you what buttons users click, how long they spend on a particular web page, and the order in which they complete actions. By installing them site-wide, you can get a wealth of data on every user who utilizes your app.

There is software for usability testing that combines these two approaches—software that records what actions users are taking and records a video of them (through their webcam) at the same time. Of course, due to the elaborate nature of these tests, and privacy concerns, they require a lot of setup with potential beta testers. The problem with all of these video-recording solutions, though, is who wants to watch hours and hours of users staring at a screen? How can useful data be filtered from that? Ultimately, tools such as Google Analytics and surveys are probably more useful on a day-to-day basis.

You should be the ultimate usability tester of your software. You should not put out software that you do not enjoy using yourself. Every time you make a change, run your program. Try to break it, but also try to use the new feature. Make software with a human touch—your own.

Summary

Testing your work is essential in software development. Unit tests are a convenient way to automate testing. Dart's unittest framework is easy to use and easy to integrate with your work. A unit test is an evaluation of a piece of your code based on certain expectations. Expectations are comparisons of variables vs. expected values that need to be correct for their enclosing test to pass. A group is a combination of tests that have a theme in common. Beta testing is the process of refining software through the evaluation of prerelease versions by beta testers. Usability testing is a means of looking at software from the perspective of its users.

EXERCISES

1. Add unit tests to Chapter 9's Word Scramble program.

2. Add a restart button to Tic-Tac-Toe, so that the user doesn't have to refresh the page to restart.

3. Write more robust unit tests for Tic-Tac-Toe. Consider adding a constructor to Board that will enable the loading of a position. This will allow you to check known won positions and drawn positions directly.

4. Tic-Tac-Toe has a bug! After the game is over, the player can still make moves. Add a unit test to detect this bug. Then fix it.

5. Develop an AI for Tic-Tac-Toe. There are a lot of ways to do this, but the most common is perhaps using the minimax[5] algorithm. Create unit tests to ensure the AI makes legal moves and that the AI never loses (a perfect game of Tic-Tac-Toe is a draw). Add the option for the computer to be either X or O (X always goes first). This is a difficult exercise. It may be easier to start by first implementing a dumb AI that just makes random legal moves.

6. Become a beta tester for an unreleased piece of software and report at least one bug. The experience will help you understand the process of releasing beta software to the public. An easy place to start might be with popular open-source projects. For instance, you could download the latest beta of the Firefox web browser and report any issues that you find it has rendering web sites.

---

[5]Wikipedia has a decent article on minimax that includes pseudocode (at least, at the time of this writing…Wikipedia is a living text, after all).

CHAPTER 14

■ ■ ■

Concurrency

Concurrency, which roughly means doing more than one thing at the same time, is among the most difficult topics in software development. In this chapter, we first discuss the importance of parallelism. Then we look into a basic mechanism for asynchronous code in Dart—Futures. Finally, the majority of the chapter will be spent on Dart's Isolates, a tool for doing work in parallel. The aim is to present simple, practical means of incorporating concurrency into your code, rather than delving into the nitty-gritty of this complex topic.

The Hardware Impetus for Parallelism

As recently as a decade ago, most microprocessors could only perform one computation at a time. Moore's Law is an informal belief in the chip industry that the number of transistors that can fit on the same size chip doubles approximately every two years, as technological advancement allows for smaller components. Moore's Law has largely been true over the past 40 years and has led to an exponential growth in the speed of microprocessors.

For many years, one of the main mechanisms through which microprocessors got faster was an increase in the speed at which electrons move through the chip (clock frequency—measured in units such as megahertz and gigahertz). In the realm of PCs, this eventually led in the mid-2000s to desktop microprocessors that ran at almost 5 GHz. And then clock speeds dropped, and some consumers were confused. The high-clock-speed chips that were being designed at the time were also huge energy hogs. The consumer hardware industry was rapidly becoming dominated by laptops and other mobile devices. The high-energy requirements of these chips were incongruous with devices that ran on batteries.

Microprocessor manufacturers found an innovative way to increase performance at lower clock speeds—increased *parallelism*. This meant making microprocessors that could perform more than one task at the same time. The insight is that two buses traveling at 45 MPH can transport more people on a bus route each day than one bus going at 55 MPH. They increased parallelism at all levels of chip design, but the one most obvious to consumers has been the inclusion of more central processing units (CPUs) on the same microprocessor. Each CPU on a microprocessor is known as a *core*. It is not uncommon for a modern high-end server microprocessor to have as many as 16 cores, while most modern smartphone microprocessors have 2–4 cores. That nearly 5 GHz desktop microprocessor of a decade ago had just one core.

Unfortunately, simply adding more cores does not lead to increased performance without software that can take advantage of it. Your average program from a decade ago was only designed to run on one core. It did not break up its work in any kind of parallelizable way, nor call system libraries that split work up among multiple cores. So, when the multicore microprocessors first launched with lower clock speeds than the generation of microprocessors that preceded them, for everyday use, they seemed slower, because software was only taking advantage of one core.

Figuring out how to utilize hardware to execute code concurrently is the purview of the operating system. Modern programming languages provide constructs, such as threads, mutexes, multiprocessing libraries, and in Dart's case, Isolates, that abstract away some of the difficulties of crafting parallelizable code. Dart programs that utilize Isolates are able to split computations among multiple cores.

If modern languages and libraries provide built-in support for parallel programming, then why is it considered so hard? Perhaps the most difficult problem is the safety of memory during parallel operations. Suppose a variable representing a critical integer is accessed by two pieces of code running in parallel. What if one decrements it at the same time that another is accessing it? Will the accessor receive the decremented value or the original? What if other pieces of critical data infrastructure depend on the value being accurate (such as the length of a list)?

There are non-hardware reasons for designing software tasks to run in parallel. In Chapter 4, we briefly touched on the idea of asynchronous vs. synchronous execution. A synchronous task must fully complete before a program continues. An asynchronous task is one that can occur in parallel (in the "background" is often how it is thought about) with other tasks. It is poor design for operations that will take a long time (such as downloading a file from the Internet or running a complex calculation) to block the user from interacting with other parts of a program. These long tasks should be run asynchronously. Even on a microprocessor with only one core, an asynchronous task will not block user interaction. The operating system will smartly divide the microprocessor's time between working on synchronous tasks and working on asynchronous tasks. In other words, even programs that don't need to parallelize for performance reasons may want to use Futures and Isolates, the topics of this chapter.

Futures

The Future class, part of dart:async, is used for getting the result of a computation after an asynchronous task has completed. The class is flexible enough to be used more generally than that, but that shall be its main wheelhouse for our purposes. Several of Dart's built-in classes return a Future when an asynchronous method is called. That Future is then used to do something after the computation finishes. We'll examine Futures in the context of using the Future objects returned by Dart's built-in APIs. You can also define your own Future objects, but doing so entails dealing with some rather complicated "gotchas" that go beyond the scope of this book.

Using Futures with HttpRequest

The HttpRequest class, part of dart:html,[1] is used for grabbing data over the HTTP protocol (i.e., downloading a web page, for example). We used it in Chapter 9 to read the contents of a text file in the Hangman example. HttpRequest has a convenient class method, getString(), which returns a Future<String> representing a resource specified as a URL passed to it as a String. As you must notice, Future objects have a generic type that represents the type of result the asynchronous operation returns. In the case of getString(), it is a String. Let's try grabbing another text file with it—this time, a very large one.

■ **Note** When trying to use the dart:html library in your programs, you will have to create a new application in Dart Editor of type web application. You will receive a warning if you try to access dart:html and any of its classes (including HttpRequest) from a command-line application. This is despite the fact that your program may not need to display anything in Dartium.

The public domain text of Jane Austen's *Pride and Prejudice* is approximately 700 kilobytes in size. That's large enough that it will take a second or two to load. You can find a copy of it labeled pandp.txt in the Chapter 14 folder of the source code bundle for *Dart for Absolute Beginners*. If you want to try the following sample lines of code, you will need to put the file in the web directory of your test program.

```
Future<String> f = HttpRequest.getString("pandp.txt");
```

---

[1]Not to be confused with the HttpRequest class of dart:io, which is a different class.

f is a Future<String> object representing the result of getString(). To access the results of a Future object, we use the then() method. then() takes a function (usually anonymous), which has a parameter, the result of the operation. Let's print the resulting text.

```
f.then((String s) => print(s));
```

Eventually, the full text of *Pride and Prejudice* will be printed to the console. Let's walk through what just happened. The getString() method initiated the asynchronous reading of pandp.txt. It returned a Future that represents the completion of this asynchronous task. The Future was provided with an anonymous function, via the then() method, that will be run when the reading of the file is complete. It has a String parameter, s, that represents the text of pandp.txt fully read from disk.

Do you really believe that pandp.txt will be read asynchronously? What if there were another print() statement after the last line we discussed—something that printed out a test message? Shouldn't it likely be printed before the text of *Pride and Prejudice* because *Pride and Prejudice* is so large and being read asynchronously?

```
print("This should come out before Pride and Prejudice.");
```

It will be! Let's take a look at the whole program, including the dependencies that are needed. The amount of text printed by the program is so great that not all of it will fit inside the console in Dart Editor. If this is the case, you can still see that *Pride and Prejudice* was loaded asynchronously, because the last line will not be the test line that we printed out, even though that print() call was the last line of code in the main() function of our program.

```
import 'dart:html';
import 'dart:async';

void main() {
  Future<String> f = HttpRequest.getString("pandp.txt");
  f.then((String s) => print(s));
  print("This should come out before Pride and Prejudice.");
}
```

Future also has a mechanism for catching errors that occur during an asynchronous task. It is as simple as stringing a catchError() method call with its own anonymous function as a parameter to the end of the then() call. The singular parameter of catchError()'s anonymous function is the error that occurred. Let's change our sample code to catch errors, using catchError().

```
f.then((String s) => print(s)).catchError((Error e) => print(e.toString()));
```

Using Futures with File

For command-line applications, the File class of dart:io can be used for reading text files in much the same way that we used HttpRequest. It, too, provides a Future-based API. The following examples assume a project of type command-line created in Dart Editor with pandp.txt in the same folder as your source code. To read pandp.txt asynchronously and write it to the console when the reading is done, we could use the following (remember to import dart:io):

```
File file = new File("pandp.txt");
file.readAsString().then((String fileContent) => print(fileContent));
```

Stringing Futures Together

If the result of one Future is another Future, then the two Future objects can be strung together using multiple then() calls. In the following example, after pandp.text is read and printed, another Future is returned, which reads and prints it again. It's not the most exciting example. . . but it helps you get the picture.

```
import "dart:io";

void main() {
  File file = new File("pandp.txt");
  file.readAsString().then((String fileContent) {
    print(fileContent);
    return new File("pandp.txt").readAsString();
  }).then((String fileContent) => print(fileContent));
}
```

After *Pride and Prejudice* is printed the first time, the anonymous function from the Future's then() call returns a new Future created by the call readAsString() being made again. then() is then executed on this second Future. Finally, the anonymous function of the second Future's then() call prints *Pride and Prejudice* again.

Isolates

It's great that some of Dart's standard libraries come with methods that run asynchronously and return a Future so that they are convenient to use, but what if we want to define our own asynchronous code? We can define our own Future objects, but they will not be able to take advantage of multicore microprocessors out of the box. We're going to need to use Isolates, part of the dart:isolate package, for that. First we will look at the basics of working with Isolates, step by step, and then we'll conclude with a longer example summing up the previous subsections.

Starting Up an Isolate

If we have a function, funk(), with no return value that we want to run asynchronously, we can use the class method spawn() of the Isolate class to start it running in parallel with the rest of our code. Methods that are spawned from Isolate should have one parameter. spawn() takes two parameters: the function to be spawned and an object that will be passed to the spawned function. If we have no object we need to pass to the spawned function, we can simply pass null.

```
import "dart:isolate";

void funk(var message) {
  print("from funk");
}

void main() {
  Isolate.spawn(funk, null);
  print("from main");
}
```

When running this short program, "from main" may print to the console before "from funk". That weakly proves that funk() is running in parallel, but the two functions might not necessarily run in the same order each time. There are no guarantees as to when funk() will be executing vs. when main() will be executing.

Communicating Between Isolates

There is one and only one way for parallel code running through `Isolates` to communicate in Dart: the classes `SendPort` and `ReceivePort`. `ReceivePort` objects receive messages sent to them through the `SendPort` attached to them (identifiable by the `sendPort` property). Remember that object that can be passed as a parameter to the function that is spawned by an `Isolate`? It is typically used for passing a `ReceivePort`'s `sendPort`, so that messages can be sent back to it.

Calculate Pi Using an Isolate

In Chapter 4, we calculated an approximation of pi using the Leibniz Formula.[2] The more iterations that the main loop of our program ran, the more accurate the calculation, but the more time that it would take to make. Let's try performing the calculation with an `Isolate`. Create a new command-line application in Dart Editor called "IsolatePi." Edit `isolatepi.dart` to look like Listing 14-1. You will notice that `ITERATIONS` has been upped since its appearance in Chapter 4, to 1,000,000,000. One million iterations is not cool. Do you know what's cool? One billion iterations.

Listing 14-1. isolatepi.dart

```dart
import "dart:isolate";

void calcPi(SendPort sp) {
  const int ITERATIONS = 1000000000; // the higher the more accurate
  double series = 1.0;
  double denominator = 3.0;
  double negate = -1.0;

  for (int i = 0; i < ITERATIONS; i++) {
    series += (negate * (1 / denominator));
    denominator += 2.0;
    negate *= -1.0;
  }

  double pi = 4 * series;
  sp.send(pi);  // send the result back
}

void main() {
  ReceivePort rp = new ReceivePort();
  rp.listen((data){  // data is what we receive from sp.send()
    print("Pi is $data");
    rp.close();  // we're done, close up shop
  });
  Isolate.spawn(calcPi, rp.sendPort);  // start the Isolate
}
```

How is a `ReceivePort` and a `SendPort` used to communicate? The `SendPort` method `send()` sends any kind of object across the port. The `ReceivePort` method `listen()` sets up a function to receive the object and do with it as it will. If you want to further prove to yourself that `calculatePi()` is running simultaneously, try adding some other computations and `print()` statements to `main()` that will run while `calculatePi()` is running.

---

[2]It might be a good time to turn back to Chapter 4 and refresh your memory about the original program and the reasoning behind it.

Communication in this example only goes in one direction. The Isolate spawned at calcPi() sends data to the ReceivePort declared in main(). There is no data going back from the code running in main() to calcPi(). If we wanted to do this, we would need to have a ReceivePort set up for the Isolate. The SendPort of this ReceivePort could then be sent back over the other SendPort, and the anonymous function in the listen() call of the original ReceivePort could figure out that this is a SendPort to be used for communication, rather than a String message based on an if-statement and a comparison using the is operator.

Progressive Pi

Before we move on, let's look at another example of one-way communication from a function spawned with an Isolate and a main() function running in parallel. In this example, we have a very practical concern—reporting progress of a complex operation. It's our pi calculation again (sorry, you're probably sick of pi [get it?]), but this time it tells main() as it progresses through the calculation. main() determines whether it is receiving a progress report or the final answer based on the type of object received in the ReceivePort. Create a new command-line project in Dart Editor and call it "ProgressivePi." Fill progressivepi.dart with Listing 14-2.

Listing 14-2. progressivepi.dart

```dart
import "dart:isolate";

void calcPi(SendPort sp) {
  const int ITERATIONS = 1000000000;  // the higher the more accurate
  double series = 1.0;
  double denominator = 3.0;
  double negate = -1.0;

  for (int i = 0; i < ITERATIONS; i++) {
    series += (negate * (1 / denominator));
    denominator += 2.0;
    negate *= -1.0;
    if (i / ITERATIONS == 0.25 || i / ITERATIONS == 0.50 || i / ITERATIONS == 0.75) {
      sp.send("${(i / ITERATIONS * 100)}% Complete");
    }
  }

  double pi = 4 * series;
  sp.send(pi);  // send the result back
}

void main() {
  ReceivePort rp = new ReceivePort();
  rp.listen((data) {  // data is what we receive from sp.send()
    if (data is String) {  // it's a progress report, not the result
      print(data);
    } else {
      print("Pi is $data");
      rp.close();  // we're done, close up shop
    }
  });
  Isolate.spawn(calcPi, rp.sendPort);  // start the Isolate
}
```

If you run Progressive Pi, you will notice that it takes significantly longer to execute than Isolate Pi. Somewhat ironically, the code added to the main for-loop to report back the progress of the pi calculation does almost as much calculation as the pi calculation itself. You will, however, get some high-quality updates as the pi calculation progresses. You should see output similar to the following:

```
25.0% Complete
50.0% Complete
75.0% Complete
Pi is 3.1415926545880506
```

BROWSER LIMITATIONS

A *thread* is the smallest representation of a sequence of code that can run in parallel that an operating system supports. It may surprise you to know that Dart is single-threaded. A so-called single-threaded language needs to spawn a separate *process*, as Dart Isolate objects do, in order to accomplish any kind of parallel processing.

Dart is not alone in being single-threaded. The most popular implementations of Ruby, Python, and importantly, JavaScript, are also single-threaded.

When your Dart code is converted to JavaScript to be deployed to web browsers, Isolate objects will be converted to a JavaScript API known as Web Workers. Most modern browsers support Web Workers, but on browsers that do not, your code will not be able to run in parallel.

■ **Note**   As of Dart 1.4, the Isolate function spawn() cannot be used easily in a Dart browser-based application. Instead, you need to use the alternative function spawnUri(), which operates significantly differently. It is likely that this situation will change in future versions of Dart. Check the Dart API documentation for the dart:isolate package, to get the latest information on using spawn() or spawnUri() in your app.

The Dining Philosophers[3]

Five philosophers are sitting at a circular table. They all want to eat spaghetti, and between them there are five forks. Each philosopher has one fork to his right and one fork to his left. Unfortunately, every fork that is to the left of one philosopher is to the right of another, and vice versa. Each philosopher needs two forks to eat his spaghetti (don't ask). There is an unlimited supply of spaghetti. Figure 14-1 illustrates the problem.

---

[3]This is a classic computer science problem. However, we're not giving it its due in this example, since we're leaving out some of the details and making the problem a lot simpler, through some central direction. Try to solve the problem without any central coordination between the philosophers. It's a lot trickier that way.

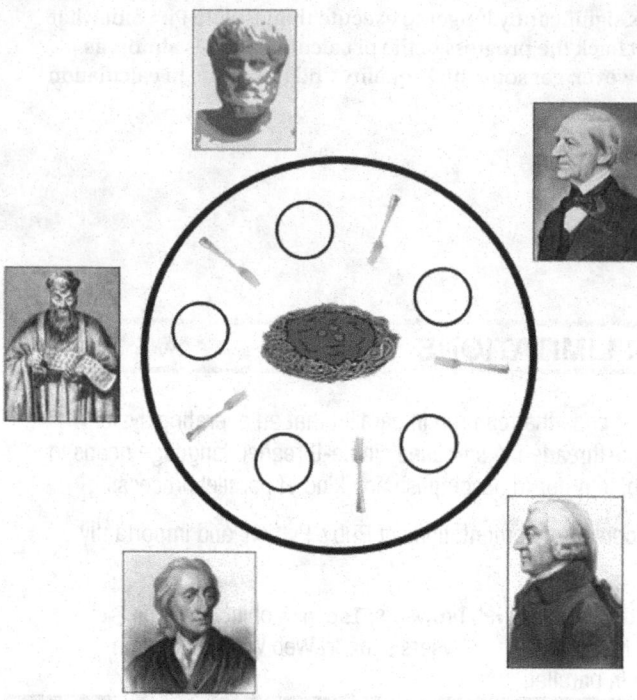

Figure 14-1. The dining philosophers

Normally, the context of this problem is an exploration of shared memory—memory being accessed by multiple threads at the same time. Since this is not the case with Dart Isolate objects (each Isolate has a full copy of the program's memory, and there is no shared memory), our version of the problem is much simpler. We simply are going to try to find a way to centrally coordinate all of the philosophers eating the spaghetti. The only wrench will be that each philosopher will need a variable amount of time to complete his meal.

Create a new command-line application in Dart Editor and call it "DiningPhilosophers." Change diningphilosophers.dart to look like Listing 14-3.

Listing 14-3. diningphilosophers.dart

```dart
import "dart:isolate";
import "dart:async";
import "dart:math";

const int NUM_PHILOSOPHERS = 5;

/// Represents one of our philosopher Isolates
void philosopher(SendPort backToMain) {
  Timer askTimer;
  ReceivePort incoming = new ReceivePort();

  incoming.listen((var data) {  // coming from main
    if (data == "Eat!") {
      askTimer.cancel();  // stop asking to eat
      Random r = new Random();
```

```
      int secondsToEat = r.nextInt(10);  // takes 0-9 seconds to eat
      Timer t = new Timer(new Duration(seconds: secondsToEat), () {
        backToMain.send("Finished!");  // announce done
        incoming.close();
      });
    }
  });

  backToMain.send(incoming.sendPort); // provide a means of communication here
  askTimer = new Timer.periodic(new Duration(seconds: 1), (Timer t){
    backToMain.send("I want to eat!"); // continuously request to eat
  });
}

void main() {
  List<ReceivePort> philosopherReceives = new List(NUM_PHILOSOPHERS);
  List<SendPort> philosopherSends = new List(NUM_PHILOSOPHERS);
  List<bool> forksInUse = new List(NUM_PHILOSOPHERS);

  for (int i = 0; i < NUM_PHILOSOPHERS; i++) {
    forksInUse[i] = false;
    philosopherReceives[i] = new ReceivePort();

    philosopherReceives[i].listen((var data) {
      if (data is SendPort) {
        philosopherSends[i] = data;
      } else if (data == "I want to eat!") {
        print("Philosopher $i wants to eat.");
        if (i == (NUM_PHILOSOPHERS - 1)) {
          if (forksInUse[0] == false && forksInUse[i] == false) {
            print("Telling philosopher $i to eat.");
            forksInUse[0] = true;
            forksInUse[i] = true;
            philosopherSends[i].send("Eat!");
          }
        } else {
          if (forksInUse[i] == false && forksInUse[i + 1] == false) {
            print("Telling philosopher $i to eat.");
            forksInUse[i] = true;
            forksInUse[i + 1] = true;
            philosopherSends[i].send("Eat!");
          }
        }
      } else if (data == "Finished!") {
        forksInUse[i] = false;
        if (i == (NUM_PHILOSOPHERS - 1)) {
          forksInUse[0] = false;
        } else {
          forksInUse[i + 1] = false;
        }
```

```
            print("Philosopher $i finished eating.");
            philosopherReceives[i].close();
        }
    });

    Isolate.spawn(philosopher, philosopherReceives[i].sendPort);
  }
}
```

Despite its relatively short length, this is probably the most complicated program we have attempted in *Dart for Absolute Beginners*. Let's talk about the philosopher() function/Isolate in high-level terms. philosopher() receives a SendPort, backToMain, for sending messages back to main(), as a parameter when it is spawned. It creates its own ReceivePort, incoming, which listens for that wondrous moment when the philosopher is instructed to eat. It sends back incoming's accompanying SendPort, so that the glorious eat message can be passed back. When philosopher() is not listening for the eat message, it is sending requests to eat over backToMain once per second, via a Timer.

Three important List data structures are maintained by main(). One holds ReceivePort objects representing messages coming in from each of the philosophers. Another holds SendPort objects for communicating to the philosophers. Finally, forksInUse is a List<bool> that tracks whether a fork is currently in use by a philosopher or available for others.

The positions of the elements in each array are significant. We're pretending that the philosopher's position (i in the giant for-loop that sets everything up in main()) represents his left fork in the forksInUse data structure, and i + 1 represents his right fork (wrapping around, if we reach the end of the List). Whenever a philosopher asks to eat, and the fork to his left and the fork to his right (i and i + 1) are available, we let him. When he cannot eat, we just don't do anything. When a philosopher is done eating, the bool objects at position i and i + 1 in forksInUse are set to false, allowing the next philosopher who asks to eat and needs the forks to use them.

The philosophers eat for variable amounts of time. Because there are five forks, and each philosopher needs two forks to eat, only two philosophers can eat at a time. If you run the program, eventually all of the philosophers will get to eat, and main() will successfully coordinate that happening. Your output should look something like the following (but will be different each time, due to the random amounts of time each philosopher takes to eat his food).

```
Philosopher 0 wants to eat.
Telling philosopher 0 to eat.
Philosopher 1 wants to eat.
Philosopher 2 wants to eat.
Telling philosopher 2 to eat.
Philosopher 3 wants to eat.
Philosopher 4 wants to eat.
Philosopher 1 wants to eat.
Philosopher 3 wants to eat.
Philosopher 4 wants to eat.
Philosopher 1 wants to eat.
Philosopher 3 wants to eat.
Philosopher 4 wants to eat.
Philosopher 1 wants to eat.
Philosopher 3 wants to eat.
Philosopher 4 wants to eat.
Philosopher 1 wants to eat.
Philosopher 3 wants to eat.
Philosopher 4 wants to eat.
Philosopher 1 wants to eat.
```

```
Philosopher 3 wants to eat.
Philosopher 4 wants to eat.
Philosopher 1 wants to eat.
Philosopher 2 finished eating.
Philosopher 3 wants to eat.
Telling philosopher 3 to eat.
Philosopher 4 wants to eat.
Philosopher 0 finished eating.
Philosopher 1 wants to eat.
Telling philosopher 1 to eat.
Philosopher 4 wants to eat.
Philosopher 3 finished eating.
Philosopher 4 wants to eat.
Telling philosopher 4 to eat.
Philosopher 1 finished eating.
Philosopher 4 finished eating.
```

In this particular run, philosopher 2 took a long time to eat. This problem is a thinker. It's the type of short program that you may need to carefully read over a few times before "getting it." The question is not if you got it specifically, but rather, if you got the concept behind it (managing multiple concurrent actors), so that you can apply it in your own programs.

TACKLE THE LOW-HANGING FRUIT

An ideal program may be programmed from the beginning with concurrency in mind. It may be able to run efficiently on a 32-core microprocessor and take full advantage of every core. Usually, you won't have the time (or inclination) to program the ideal—you have to work with the practical. Practically speaking, you can get immediate gains by taking the longest computations in your program and making them asynchronous.

We naturally think synchronously. That's just how humans process information. We see causes and events everywhere. One thing leads to another. It's much easier to design your programs synchronously, so as a new programmer, you can't be blamed for doing so. The modern wisdom may be to design for concurrency from the start. The modern practicality for a beginning programmer is to write a synchronous program, figure out the most computationally complex parts, and then separate those into asynchronous pieces.

Using Dart's built-in APIs, it's easy to do such things as network access and file reading asynchronously. Take advantage of them. For most programs, that will be the low-hanging fruit, and you won't even begin a conversation about Isolates.

IMPROVEMENTS TO COME?

Concurrency is difficult in every programming language. Dart is not unique in that regard. The APIs covered in this chapter were present in the latest version of the Dart SDK at the time of writing, but there is hope that future versions of the language/SDK will be able to further simplify things. Other languages, such as Go, C#, and Erlang, have developed compelling concurrency innovations at the language level that may find their way into future versions of Dart.

One of the top requests on the Dart Project's issue tracker is to include an `await` statement, not unlike that included with C#. The `await` statement specifies to the compiler that a specific function/method call should be run asynchronously, and the compiler takes care of the rest. Incidentally, the original version of C# did not include `await` either; it was bolted on in a revision.

Summary

Most modern microprocessors can do multiple tasks concurrently, which allows for a speedup in applications that can take advantage of it. Doing complex computational work asynchronously is also important for the responsiveness of applications, regardless of the microprocessor that they are running on. Futures are a mechanism for retrieving the value of an asynchronous task after it has completed. Isolates are a tool for abstracting parallelism and implementing it on a practical high-level basis. Concurrency is hard, but with these Dart tools, it's easy to get started with the low-hanging fruit in your projects.

EXERCISES

1. Use `HttpRequest` to write a program that asynchronously grabs all of your favorite web sites and then loads them in separate windows.

2. Modify our simulations of The Monty Hall Problem (Chapter 4) and the Birthday Paradox (Chapter 6) to run asynchronously.

3. How much more accurate does our pi calculator get with every increase in magnitude of the number of iterations run of the Leibniz Formula?

4. Try The Dining Philosophers with different numbers of philosophers and forks. How does changing the constant `NUM_PHILOSOPHERS` affect the program?

5. Can you think of computational operations that need to be done synchronously (cannot be done in asynchronously)?

CHAPTER 15

■ ■ ■

Tools of the Trade

The tools of software development go beyond a language (Dart), an IDE (Dart Editor), and a runtime environment (Dartium). They generally include an entire toolchain sourced from a myriad of vendors to support each step in the development process. This includes managing versioning, debugging, and additional API support. In this chapter, you will learn about some of the most important nonlanguage tools used by modern developers. The software developers of just a couple decades ago lacked much of this now mission-critical infrastructure, which goes to show that software development is a constantly evolving field.

Git

More than just the pronunciation of *get* with a southern drawl, Git is also the de facto standard *distributed version control system* in the software industry today. Sometimes you hear one of these terms, such as *distributed version control system* (remember *unit test*?), and it sounds a lot more complicated than it really is. This isn't one of those times. Git is complicated. Many believe it is too complicated, but due to its power and sophistication, it has become nearly ubiquitous. It's practically impossible to navigate the modern software development world without at least knowing the basics of Git, which is all we aim to teach you in this section, since you can buy several books wholly devoted to the subject.[1] Git was originally created by Linus Torvalds, the software maestro behind Linux, in 2005. This section assumes the use of Git version 1.8.x or 1.9.x.

Git in a Nutshell

What is a distributed version control system? In short, it's a way to keep track of revisions made to a set of files. Why is this relevant to software development? Perhaps you've used the Track Changes feature in Microsoft Word, or you've seen a revision history in Google Docs. These are useful features because they allow you to both see who is doing what on a document edited by multiple people and to revert to an earlier version of the document if you don't like the most recent changes. Git is a tool you can use to a similar end for your source code. What makes Git much more sophisticated than the Track Changes feature in Microsoft Word (among many, many other things[2]) is that it allows changes to be made to the same files independently on multiple nonconnected computers and then merged back together without one disrupting another.

---

[1]*Pro Git* (Apress, 2009), by Scott Chacon, although a bit dated, is a good Git book for users of all abilities. You can find the print version on Amazon or via the Apress web site. An HTML version is available for free at http://git-scm.com/book.

[2]This comment is in no way meant as an affront to Microsoft Word. Microsoft Word's Track Changes is a fantastic tool; Git's just a much more sophisticated version control system than that included with Microsoft Word.

A directory of files that Git is tracking the changes to is known as a *repository*. Typically, you will have one repository for each software project that you work on. Git does not store every revision of a file ever made. Instead, it stores the changes between each revision at the time that a revision is *checked in*. For example, if the first revision of a text file that listed favorite fruits had one line

grape

and then the next checked-in revision had two lines

grape
orange

Git would store the new revision as a one-line addition of orange to the text file in question. This is an oversimplification (and more analogous to how traditional version control systems work than to Git), but it will suit us for our understanding. By only storing changes, Git uses a lot less disk space than a revision system that stores entire file versions. This model works very well for text files, which generally have quite well-delimitated changes between revisions, but can be tricky for binary files such as images, which are messier. Git may end up simply storing an entirely new version of an entire binary file, even for a small edit to an image. The most recent versions of Git have improved in this regard.

Setting Up a Remote Repository

For the next few sections of this chapter, you will need to use a *terminal* (an application that grants you a command-line interface to your computer's operating system). There are several GUI programs for managing Git listed on Git's web site at git-scm.com. It seems to be the general consensus among introductory books that it is still useful to learn Git's command-line interface. No GUI interface to Git has become the de facto standard yet, although many of them are quite good. Learning the command-line Git interface may also help you understand what the commands available to you in the GUI programs mean. However, if you're very uncomfortable with using the terminal, feel free to try to follow along with one of the GUI programs recommended on Git's official web site (http://git-scm.com/downloads/guis). You will likely find that every command we go over has an analogous button or menu item in the GUI program that you choose.

If you use Linux, you probably know where to find a terminal. If you use OS X, you will find it at /Applications/Utilities/Terminal. On Windows, you will want to look in the Start menu or Start screen for an application called Command Prompt. You may already have Git installed, especially if you're running Linux or OS X. Try typing git --version and pressing enter. If something like git version 1.8.3.4 is printed to the console, you're in luck.

USING THE TERMINAL

Some programmers find using a command-line interface to their computer a useful tool in and of itself. The *shell* (as the command-line interface is called) is scriptable using a specialized language that differs on Windows (batch file scripting) vs. OS X and Linux (Bash scripting). Proponents of the shell argue that it can be faster to type commands than to click the mouse and that the command-line interface is more distraction-free.

You can install a command-line version of the Dart VM that will allow you to run Dart programs from the terminal. At the time of writing, there was no easy way to do this from Dart Editor, but it is a planned future feature for the IDE. To get instructions for your operating system, it's still best to search on Google.

There are two essential system commands you will need to know to work with the terminal. On Windows, dir will list the contents of the current directory. On OS X and Linux, ls will do the same thing. On all three operating systems, cd can be used to move to a directory. For example, if you're in the directory home and there is a directory within home called documents, cd documents will move you to be within the documents directory. cd .. moves you up one directory. So, once within documents, cd .. will move you back to home.

The difficulty of installing Git really depends on your operating system of choice.

- On Ubuntu Linux (only mentioned specifically because it's the most popular distribution; no angry e-mails please) and other Debian-based distributions, you can install Git with the command `sudo apt-get install git`. You'll be prompted for your administrative password. For other Linux distributions, check out the directions on `git-scm.com`.

- On OS X, a slightly outdated version of Git comes bundled with Xcode, Apple's IDE that is available for free on the Mac App Store. It's quite a large download, if you don't already have it installed, and you may instead prefer to get Git by following the directions on `git-scm.com`, its official home on the Web.

- Windows users should get the latest binaries and installation directions from `git-scm.com`.

Once again, you can test that your installation of Git has been successful by typing `git --version` in the terminal.

Before we create a repository, let's try *cloning* somebody else's. To clone a repository is to make an exact duplicate of it in a new location, with links back to the remote location that it was cloned from, for any future revisions added to it. Cloning a repository not only allows you to get a copy of the source code that you can browse on your local machine, it also allows you to submit contributions (changes that you make) back to the original repository that you cloned from. Repositories can be cloned using the `git clone` command. You can find many interesting repositories to clone on GitHub. The command is followed by the address of the repository being cloned. On GitHub, you will find the address of the repository in the box that looks like Figure 15-1. You can find *Dart for Absolute Beginners* on GitHub at `https://github.com/davecom/Dart-for-Absolute-Beginners`. Go there in the web browser of your choice. Through the GitHub web interface, you can view the source code of the repository that you are browsing right from your web browser. You can also see who has contributed to the repository, when it was last updated, and its documentation.

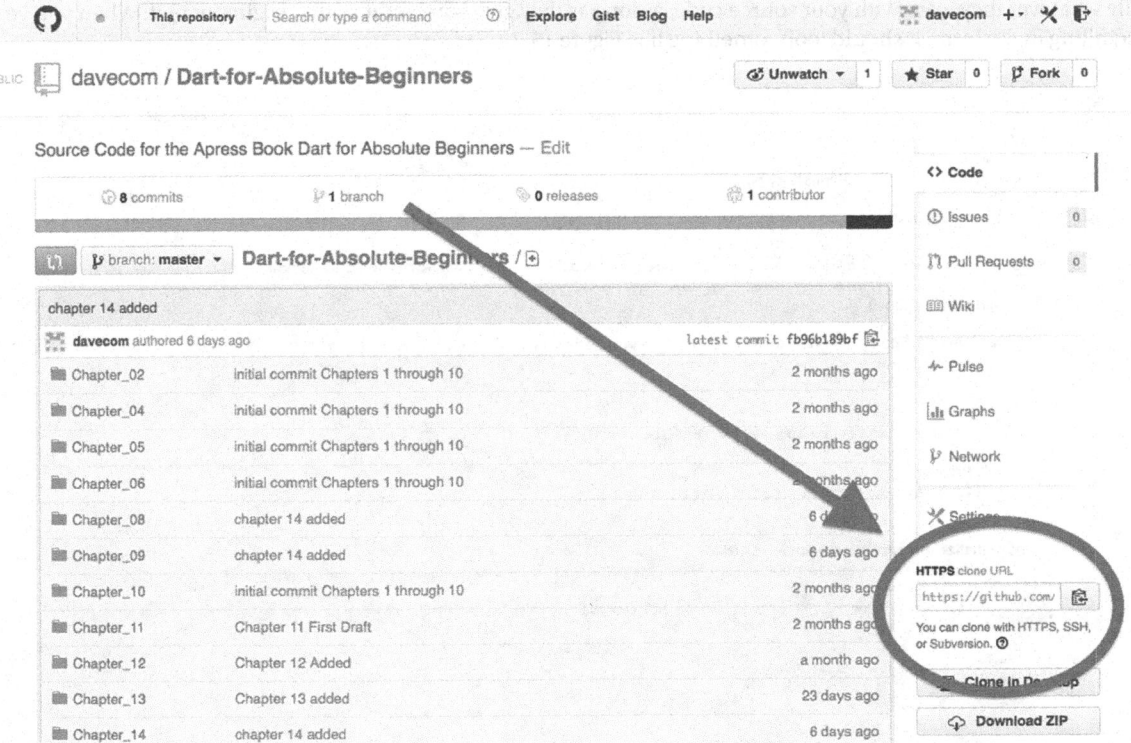

Figure 15-1. *Address box for cloning repository on GitHub*

To clone the `Dart-for-Absolute-Beginners` repository to your computer, try the following in the terminal:

```
git clone https://github.com/davecom/Dart-for-Absolute-Beginners.git
```

This command will create a copy of the *Dart for Absolute Beginners* source code repository in the current directory. Very good, you've cloned your first repository. Now let's try creating a repository on GitHub. Go to github.com and register for an account. Use the + sign at the top right of the GitHub home page to create a new repository (see Figure 15-2).

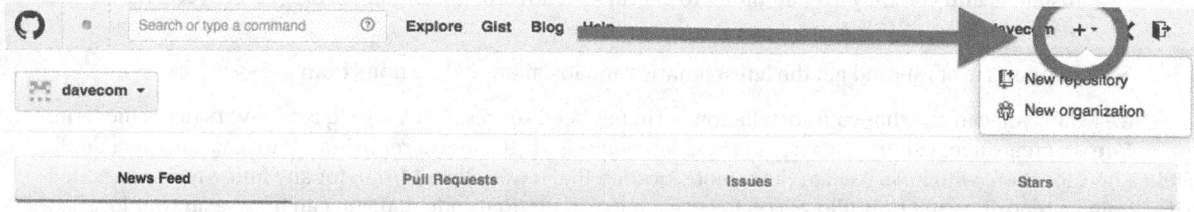

Figure 15-2. + *sign to create new repository on GitHub*

You will be presented with a page that asks you for the name of the repository, a description, whether it should be public or private, whether it should include a README, a `.gitignore` file, and a license. Call the repository "chapter15." For the description, put "Part of the Git Tutorial from Chapter 15 of Dart for Absolute Beginners." We'll be making a public repository (anybody can see it), since creating private repositories requires paying money to GitHub. It's a good idea for all of our repositories to have a README, so check the box for that. Select *Dart* for the `.gitignore` file. Select "MIT License" for the license. The MIT License is a permissive license that allows other people to do basically whatever they want with your source code, as long as they give you credit as the originator of it. When you've finished filling in the form, it should look something like Figure 15-3.

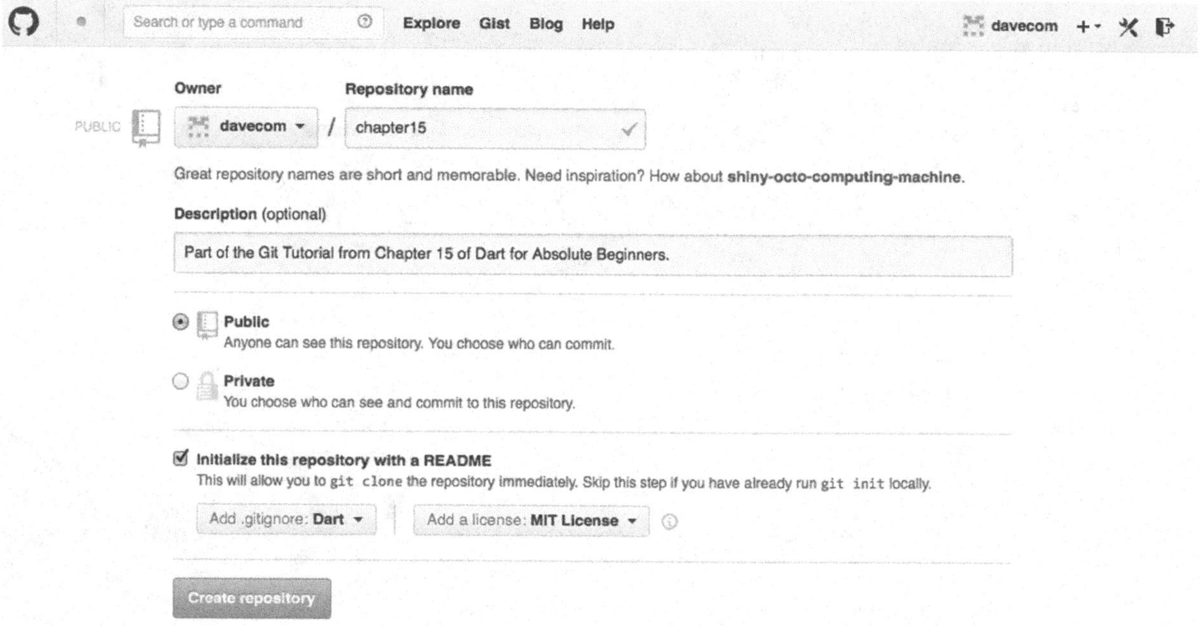

Figure 15-3. *Creating a new repository on GitHub*

Go ahead and create the repository. You'll be taken to a repository page not unlike the one we saw before. Go ahead and copy the address that you'll need for cloning and issue a `git clone` command to get a copy of the repository on your computer. Voilà, you've created your first Git repository on GitHub and cloned it to your computer.

■ **Note**   The .gitignore file specifies file types that will not be added to your repository when you use the `git add *` command. By selecting Dart in GitHub's page for creating a new repository, you will get good defaults set up for you automatically.

CHOOSING AN OPEN-SOURCE LICENSE

The MIT License is a great permissive open-source license. It lets other programmers who come across your source code do just about whatever they want with it, as long as they attribute you as the original author. An even more permissive option is to put your source code into the public domain. Declaring your source code as public domain lets others literally do whatever they want with it.

The two-clause BSD License is essentially equivalent to the MIT License. The three-clause BSD License insists that derivative works cannot use the original author as an endorsee of the derivative without prior written permission. The BSD License and the MIT License are the most popular permissive open-source licenses. Another interesting option is the Artistic License, which comes with a few more restrictions and is similar in spirit to the three-clause BSD License.

The GPL (GNU Public License) is a much more complex legal document than the BSD License or MIT License, which both are essentially two paragraphs. Licensing software with the GPL ensures that all derivative works must also be open-source. In other words, if you create a board class and license it under the GPL and another developer uses that board class to create a chess game, she has to release the source code of her chess game. For this reason, the GPL is sometimes referred to as "copyleft." Others, more derisively, call it viral. The Linux kernel is licensed under the GPL, as are several popular open-source programs. The GPL is a good option if you want to defensively protect your work from being co-opted by others, without contributions back to the open-source community. Naturally, the GPL is generally seen as being less corporate-friendly than the more permissive licenses.

There are many open-source licenses to choose from. It's important that you pick one and include it with any source code that you release publicly, so that other developers know their rights (and yours) when using your work. GitHub makes it easy to include a license when you first start your repository, so take advantage of it.

Committing Changes to the Repository

Okay, so you've successfully cloned the chapter15 repository to your computer now, right? Just in case you haven't, we'll repeat the command, and then we'll dive into the directory and inspect it to see that we really have all of the files. Files that begin with a . character (like .gitignore) do not appear with the ls command, unless you append –all to it. The following commands are from a run on OS X and include the output. Remember: On Windows, you'll be using the dir command instead of ls. The commands (as opposed to the output and command prompt) are written in bold. Of course, based on your operating system, date, and username, your output will look a little bit different. Also, your repository address should match the one that GitHub provides you (it should not include "davecom").

```
davids-air:desktop dave$ git clone https://github.com/davecom/chapter15.git
Cloning into 'chapter15'...
remote: Counting objects: 5, done.
remote: Compressing objects: 100% (4/4), done.
remote: Total 5 (delta 0), reused 0 (delta 0)
Unpacking objects: 100% (5/5), done.
Checking connectivity... done
davids-air:desktop dave$ cd chapter15
davids-air:chapter15 dave$ ls -all
total 24
drwxr-xr-x   6 dave   staff    204 Mar  6 17:09 .
drwx------@ 13 dave   staff    442 Mar  6 17:09 ..
drwxr-xr-x  13 dave   staff    442 Mar  6 17:09 .git
-rw-r--r--   1 dave   staff     41 Mar  6 17:09 .gitignore
-rw-r--r--   1 dave   staff   1073 Mar  6 17:09 LICENSE
-rw-r--r--   1 dave   staff     94 Mar  6 17:09 README.md
```

Great, you've cloned another repository. The .git directory (which is a *hidden* directory[3]) contains configuration files for the Git repository. Leave the terminal open but also open Dart Editor. Create a new command-line project in Dart Editor called "chapter15test." Make sure to place the new project within the chapter15 directory that was created when you cloned the chapter15 repository. Make sure to leave "Generate sample content" checked. Now you can check to make sure this new content was created as we expect.

```
davids-air:chapter15 dave$ ls
LICENSE         README.md         chapter15test
```

Great, so the directory chapter15test is now within the chapter15 directory, but it has not yet been added to our repository. The command git status will show us what's not been added to the Git repository. Try it.

```
davids-air:chapter15 dave$ git status
# On branch master
# Untracked files:
#   (use "git add <file>..." to include in what will be committed)
#
#       chapter15test/
nothing added to commit but untracked files present (use "git add" to track)
```

We use the command git add to add files to a Git repository. We can add individual files (for example, git add filename.txt), but we can also add all of the new files at once using the command git add *.

```
davids-air:chapter15 dave$ git add *
davids-air:chapter15 dave$ git status
# On branch master
# Changes to be committed:
#   (use "git reset HEAD <file>..." to unstage)
#
#       new file:   chapter15test/bin/chapter15test.dart
#       new file:   chapter15test/pubspec.yaml
#
```

---

[3]By default, you won't see hidden directories when browsing your files using the OS X Finder, Windows Explorer, or most file browsers on Linux.

■ **Note** The command git rm is for removing files from a Git repository.

You will notice that the git status command shows our additions as "Changes to be committed." When working with Git, the git add and git rm commands don't actually change anything until the changes made are committed. The git commit command is used for making a commit. It is typically used with the –m option to specify what changes have been made, with a short message (the message looks like a Dart String literal), as in the following:

```
davids-air:chapter15 dave$ git commit -m "Added chapter15test project"
[master bdd5607] Added chapter15test project
 2 files changed, 7 insertions(+)
 create mode 100644 chapter15test/bin/chapter15test.dart
 create mode 100644 chapter15test/pubspec.yaml
```

Great, so now our changes (adding the new files) have been committed to the repository. If you visit the web page for our repository on GitHub, though, nothing will have changed. That is because we have only committed the changes to our local repository, not the remote one hosted by GitHub. To do that, we need to use the git push command. Our local repository is automatically set up to sync with the remote repository hosted by GitHub. Of course, you can also set it up to sync with other remote repositories as well.

```
davids-air:chapter15 dave$ git push
Counting objects: 7, done.
Delta compression using up to 4 threads.
Compressing objects: 100% (4/4), done.
Writing objects: 100% (6/6), 552 bytes | 0 bytes/s, done.
Total 6 (delta 1), reused 0 (delta 0)
To https://github.com/davecom/chapter15.git
   04a7624..bdd5607  master -> master
```

Great, now if you visit the web page for the repository on GitHub, you will see the new chapter15test folder, and then you can browse to the files within it. GitHub will also show the most recent commit message (see Figure 15-4).

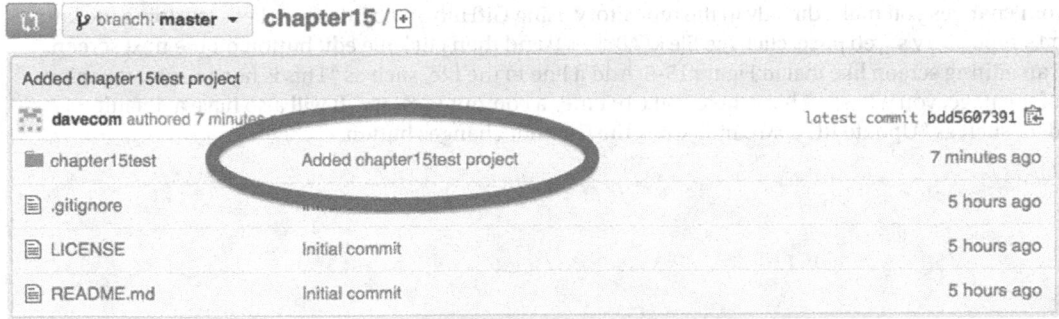

Figure 15-4. Commit message shown on GitHub

Let's try one more thing before moving on to syncing changes in the other direction. In Dart Editor, modify chapter15test.dart to print "Hello, Git!" instead of "Hello, World!". Save your changes. Then repeat the git add, git commit, and git push commands.

```
davids-air:chapter15 dave$ git status
# On branch master
# Changes not staged for commit:
#   (use "git add <file>..." to update what will be committed)
#   (use "git checkout -- <file>..." to discard changes in working directory)
#
#       modified:   chapter15test/bin/chapter15test.dart
#
no changes added to commit (use "git add" and/or "git commit -a")
davids-air:chapter15 dave$ git add *
davids-air:chapter15 dave$ git commit -m "Changed greeting"
[master e26c660] Changed greeting
 1 file changed, 1 insertion(+), 1 deletion(-)
davids-air:chapter15 dave$ git push
Counting objects: 9, done.
Delta compression using up to 4 threads.
Compressing objects: 100% (3/3), done.
Writing objects: 100% (5/5), 432 bytes | 0 bytes/s, done.
Total 5 (delta 1), reused 0 (delta 0)
To https://github.com/davecom/chapter15.git
   bdd5607..e26c660  master -> master
```

If you double check on GitHub.com, you will see that the change to "Hello, Git!" is reflected in the remote repository.

Pulling Changes

Changes that happen to your remote repository will not be automatically reflected in your local repository. Changes to the remote repository might occur when other contributors push changes, when you push changes from another computer, or from changes you make directly to the repository using GitHub's web interface. Let's try doing the latter. On the chapter15 repository's web page, click the file README.md[4] and then click the edit button on the next screen. You should see an editing screen like that in Figure 15-5. Add a line to the file, such as "This is not a useful repository." At the bottom of the page, you will see a box where you can enter a commit message. It will also have a default message provided, such as "Update README.md." Click the Commit changes button.

---

[4]The .md extension indicates that the README.md file is composed with Markdown. Markdown is a language for defining HTML formatting with a less verbose, more human readable syntax. To learn more, check out the Wikipedia article on Markdown at https://en.wikipedia.org/wiki/Markdown.

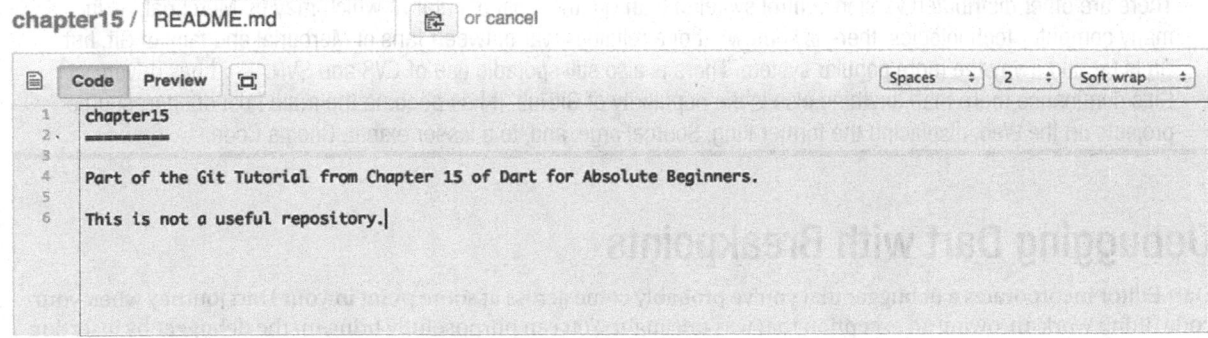

Figure 15-5. GitHub.com file-editing interface

In the terminal, run the command `git pull`. This reaches into the remote repository (in this case, it is automatically set up to look to GitHub), looks for changes, and pulls those changes down into the local repository. After you run the command, your README.md file will have the additional line you added on GitHub.com.

```
davids-air:chapter15 dave$ git pull
remote: Counting objects: 5, done.
remote: Compressing objects: 100% (3/3), done.
remote: Total 3 (delta 2), reused 0 (delta 0)
Unpacking objects: 100% (3/3), done.
From https://github.com/davecom/chapter15
   e26c660..3b16612  master      -> origin/master
Updating e26c660..3b16612
Fast-forward
 README.md | 2 ++
 1 file changed, 2 insertions(+)
```

Hopefully, you've gotten a solid taste of Git and are well on the way to incorporate it into your work flow. In this brief Git tutorial, I've left out the two most complicated things of all—merging conflicts and branching. If you're the lone developer of a simple repository, you may never encounter these complicated topics, but as part of a multi-person team, you certainly will. We've already strayed quite a bit from Dart, so before this turns into a book on Git, let's stop.

OTHER VERSION CONTROL SYSTEMS

Version control is not a new concept by any means. In the dark days, it might have just meant keeping separately named folders containing different versions of some program's source code as it evolved to mark each major milestone. However, freely available version control systems have been around since at least the 1970s.

A decade ago, two open-source projects had come to dominate the version control space: CVS (Concurrent Versions System) and its spiritual successor Subversion (known as SVN). Unlike Git, CVS and SVN are not distributed. They rely on a single centralized server keeping the most up-to-date version of a project. Distributed version control systems like Git allow for multiple copies and branches of a project to live on many computers that can each act as a clone for new repositories of the project. With distributed version control systems, there is not necessarily *one* central repository.

There are other distributed version control systems than Git, the most popular of which may be Mercurial. As in many computer technologies, there is somewhat of a religious war between fans of Mercurial and fans of Git, but Git is far and away the more popular system. There is also still sporadic use of CVS and SVN. What has driven Git's dominance more than anything else is the popularity of GitHub. It has become the main host of open-source projects on the Web, displacing the former king, SourceForge, and, to a lesser extent, Google Code.

Debugging Dart with Breakpoints

Dart Editor incorporates a debugger that you've probably come across at some point in your Dart journey when your code didn't work, throwing an exception that was uncaught. You can purposefully bring up the debugger by inserting breakpoints alongside your code, with Dart Editor. When your program is running and a breakpoint is encountered, the program will stop, and Dart Editor will allow you to inspect the state of all of the variables.

In the Chapter 5 section on recursive functions, there was a table, Table 5-1, that showed the values of a set of variables during each recursive call of a function addOn() with a call of addOn("Hello", "!", 2). Here's that table, reproduced for your benefit as Table 15-1.

Table 15-1. *The Iterations of addOn("Hello", "!", 2)*

Iteration	original	additional	times	times <= 0
1	"Hello"	"!"	2	false
2	"Hello! "	"!"	1	false
3	"Hello!! "	"!"	0	true

Using the breakpoints and the debugger, we will be able to verify that indeed these are the values of these variables during each iteration of the recursive function call. Create a new command-line program in Dart Editor called "addon." Fill addon.dart with Listing 15-1.

Listing 15-1. addon.dart

```
String addOn(String original, String additional, int times) {
  if (times <= 0) {  // exit condition to end "recursive loop"
    return original;
  }
  return addOn(original + additional, additional, times - 1);  // recursive call
}

void main() {
  print(addOn("Hello", "!", 2));
}
```

Our goal is to inspect the values of original, additional, and times at the beginning of each call of addOn(). Therefore, the break point should be inserted at the very beginning of the function. In Dart Editor, double-click inside the gray bar that appears to the left of your source code, at the line of the function declaration or the if-statement. A dot should appear in the gray bar similar to that in Figure 15-6. That's the breakpoint.

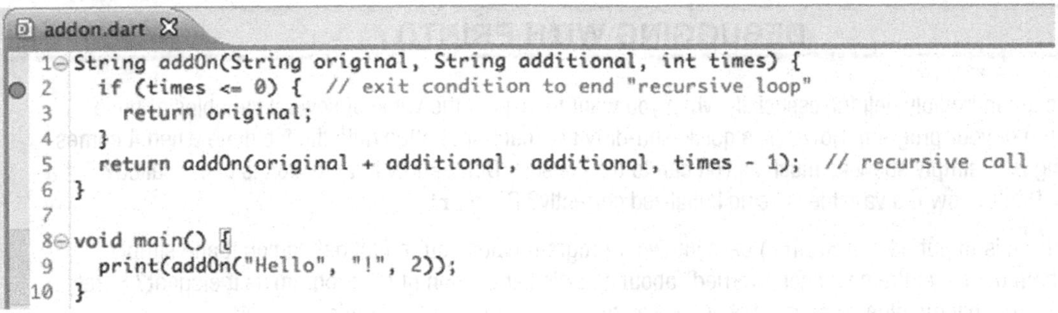

```
1⊖ String addOn(String original, String additional, int times) {
 2    if (times <= 0) {  // exit condition to end "recursive loop"
 3      return original;
 4    }
 5    return addOn(original + additional, additional, times - 1);  // recursive call
 6  }
 7
 8⊖ void main() {
 9    print(addOn("Hello", "!", 2));
10  }
```

Figure 15-6. *A breakpoint in Dart Editor*

During debug runs of your program launched from within Dart Editor, the program will always stop when it encounters the line that a breakpoint is next to. Try it now; run addon.dart. The program should stop virtually immediately as the breakpoint is reached. You will see a debugger in the right pane of Dart Editor. It will appear similar to Figure 15-7.

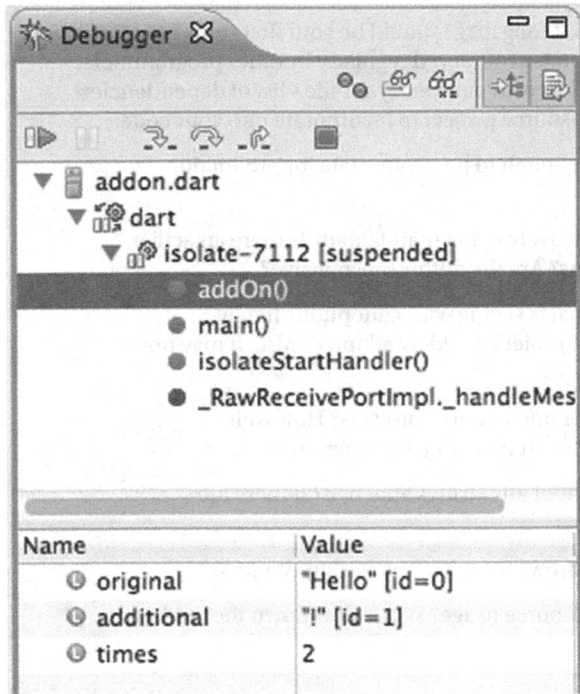

Figure 15-7. *Debugger as addOn( ) breakpoint is reached*

You will notice that in the debugger, the values of all of the local variables at that breakpoint are displayed. Using them, you can verify that Table 15-1 is accurate. If you click the resume button (it looks like a lowercase *l* with a right-facing triangle next to it), the program will continue until it hits the breakpoint again, when the addOn( ) function is called recursively. The program will stop again, and you should see the new values for all of the variables.

DEBUGGING WITH PRINT()

Breakpoints are incredibly helpful, especially when you want to inspect the value of several variables at once during the run of your program. However, a quick-and-dirty approach that often gets the job done when it comes to debugging is to simply spew as much as you can to the console. Don't know if a function is being called? Put a print() in. Don't know if a variable is being initialized correctly? Put a print() in.

A useful pattern is to put a lot of print() calls into your program when you're first debugging it and simply comment them out as you're no longer "worried" about a particular section of the program. Is it elegant? Surely, it is not. Is it probably the oldest and most obvious way to debug a program? Yes, it is.

Incorporating Open-Source Packages

There's no reason to reinvent the wheel. The standard library[5] included with the Dart SDK is great and very much follows a *batteries-included* philosophy,[6] in that it provides most of what you will need for your average web app. However, it may not be enough. Before you go and write a complex library yourself, it's best to check if someone hasn't already done the work for you.

GitHub (github.com) and Dart's pub package site (pub.dartlang.org) should be your first stops on your search. If you're working on something that you think must be a problem encountered regularly by other programmers, chances are there's already a pub package you can drop right in to your pubspec.yaml file's list of dependencies. Following are a few points to consider when choosing an open-source project to incorporate into your code:

- *Maturity*: How far along is the project? Is it robust enough to be appropriate for production software?

- *Support*: When was the project last updated? Is it actively being maintained? Is there an active user community that you can turn to with questions? Are the authors responsive?

- *Competition*: Is there another competing project that is seeing wider adoption? It may therefore be easier to find tutorials and support if a project is widely adopted. Also, it may not bode well for the future of the less popular project.

- *Dependencies*: Does the project rely on a lot of other open-source projects? How well maintained are they? Will you need to include all of that bloat in your program?

- *License*: Can you freely incorporate the project without any strings attached? If there are strings, are they acceptable to you?

- *Compatibility*: Does the project work with all web browsers and/or operating systems?

- *Size*: How big is the project in terms of code size/resource usage? Will it slow down the loading and/or execution of your program?

---

[5]When we're talking about a standard library, we're talking about the libraries (yes, plural, since the standard library is really composed of multiple component libraries) that are shipped with a language. In Dart, that would be anything that you don't need to add to your pubspec.yaml file as a dependency. dart:html and dart:math are part of Dart's standard library.
[6]Not every language includes as extensive a standard library as Dart. JavaScript and C, for example, two very popular languages, have quite Spartan standard libraries by modern standards. On the other hand, Python and Java arguably invented the so-called batteries-included standard library approach.

Considering all of these qualities may become somewhat overwhelming. Perhaps you only have one choice, though. Then, it's an easy decision. In most cases, go ahead and use the open-source option as opposed to rewriting something yourself. You can always contribute improvements back to the project if it's not yet perfect.

Any package that is listed on pub.dartlang.org can be included in your project by name as a dependency in pubspec.yaml. If you find a project that has not yet made it into pub but is listed on GitHub, you can still easily incorporate it into your project by using its Git clone URL. You can directly include this URL (the same one we were copying earlier in the chapter to clone Git repositories) in your pubspec.yaml file. When you add a dependency in the GUI interface for pubspec.yaml in Dart Editor, there is a drop-down box on the right that is labeled *Source*. The default option for source is hosted, but you can change it to git. Then you can enter the Git URL for the repository in the text box labeled *Path*. Please note that any repository you link to in this way should have its pubspec.yaml file in the root of the repository. Figure 15-8 shows a sample in which the GitHub repository for the project constraineD is added as a dependency.

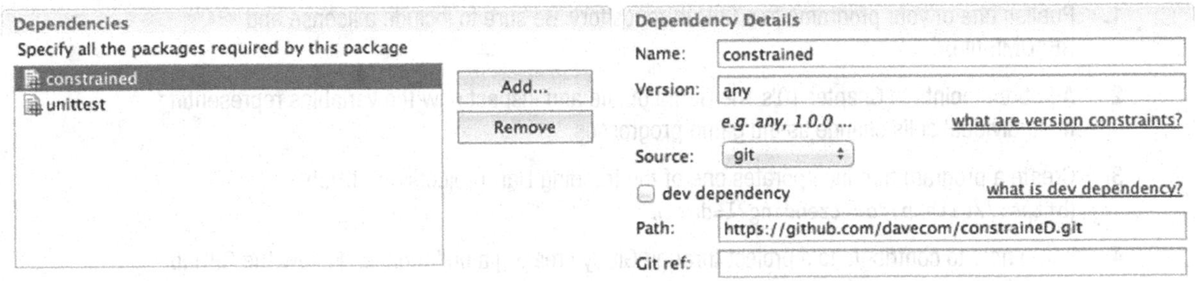

Figure 15-8. Adding a GitHub repository as a dependency to pubspec.yaml

API Documentation

In Chapter 1, we touched on several web resources that are helpful when you get stuck. In a sense, they're all tools, but none is more valuable than Dart's online API documentation. This is the site that it is most important to learn to use, and learn to use well. Throughout this book, we've referred to various parts of the standard library's API documentation. The main site is api.dartlang.org.

From the main site, you can drill down into any of the packages included in Dart's standard library. For example, maybe you want to explore dart:math further. After clicking dart:math in the left column, the main page of dart:math's online documentation comes up. You can further drill down to any of the classes or functions that are a part of the package.

The Dart API web site is essentially your Dart bible. It includes everything you need to know to use Dart's standard library effectively. It doesn't just describe what classes and methods are available to you, it also explains how to use them.

Commentators have said that programming is 20% learning to use a language and 80% learning to use its standard library. If that's the case, then the Dart API documentation is the most important tool at your disposal. Most of Dart's API documentation is also available to you from within Dart Editor, but some people find it easier to leave the Dart API documentation web site open in a web browser side by side with Dart Editor. You know you're a programmer when api.dartlang.org becomes your favorite bookmark.

Summary

Git is a distributed version control system that ensures catastrophe never befalls your projects. GitHub is an easy-to-use web site where you can set up a remote Git repository. GitHub has become the home of open-source software on the Web and has driven the adoption of Git. Breakpoints allow you to stop your program for inspection midway through a run. During the stop, you can inspect individual variables from within Dart Editor to see what their exact values are at that point in your program. It's silly to implement something from scratch when an open-source library already exists that can do the same thing. Check out GitHub and Dart's pub package web site before reinventing the wheel.

EXERCISES

1. Publish one of your programs to a GitHub repository. Be sure to include a license and README file.

2. Add breakpoints to Chapter 10's The Game of Life and inspect how the variables representing the individual cells change as the game progresses.

3. Create a program that incorporates one of the trending Dart projects on GitHub (https://github.com/trending?l=dart).

4. Learn how to contribute to a project through Git by creating a pull request. Follow the GitHub tutorial at https://help.github.com/articles/using-pull-requests.

5. Use Git to download the source code of the Dart language by cloning the bleeding-edge repository on GitHub (https://github.com/dart-lang/bleeding_edge). Poke around it a bit, maybe you'll find something interesting.

CHAPTER 16

■■■

Putting It All Together

This chapter could have been called "One Last Project," but that wouldn't sound like chapter titles at the end of other beginners' programming books, so instead, the title implicitly refers to the personal development journey that you have been on since we started learning Dart. For our last project of the book, we'll be building an app that creates printable word searches. Other than presenting a fairly interesting project, it's also the goal of this chapter to give you a taste of one class of problems that computers can generally solve more efficiently than humans (constraint satisfaction problems).

You've learned how to program, but what use is that if you don't know how to solve interesting problems with your code? Hopefully, this introduction will be a good segue into Chapter 17, where, once again worrying about your personal development journey, we work together to figure out if you want to learn things like computer science more deeply, now that you know some programming. The app we create in this chapter will put together much of the knowledge of the past 15 chapters into one medium-sized program. In doing so, you will create a program that

- Does something substantial
- Works with Dart's built-in data structures
- Utilizes an open source library
- Is an example of computer science in action
- Reuses modified components of past projects
- Has a smart object-oriented design

Constraint Satisfaction Problems

Constraint satisfaction problems are problems that can be defined by *variables* with finite, nonempty *domains* (possible values of those variables) and the relationships between those variables.[1] Hopefully, that didn't sound completely like Greek to you, but if it did, don't worry, because we'll go over those terms in depth. It happens to be quite a broad set of problems that can be defined as constraint satisfaction problems. For example, using a gift card to buy a new shirt at a clothing store could be a constraint satisfaction problem. The problem may have one variable called *shirt*. shirt's domain could be all of the available shirts in the store. shirt may have two *constraints*. One could be that its price is less than the value of the gift card. Another could be that shirt fits its intended recipient.

Constraint satisfaction problems get more interesting when they encompass multiple variables and constraints that intertwine those variables. Let's think about the example of Matt and Veronica carpooling to work. One variable is which car they take. Its domain is made up of two possibilities (Matt's car or Veronica's car). Another variable is which

---

[1]For more on constraint satisfaction problems, check out Chapter 6 of *Artificial Intelligence: A Modern Approach*, Third Edition, by Stuart Russell and Peter Norvig (Prentice Hall, 2009).

route they take. Its domain is made up of several routes that differ both by how long they are in distance and what points of interest they pass by. One constraint is the cost of the trip. It has to be less than their company will reimburse them for gas. It is figured out by combining the distance of a possible trip with the fuel economy of a possible car and the tolls along that route. Another constraint is how long it takes them to get to work (they are not willing to accept a commute that is longer than a specified amount of time). It is evaluated by combining the speed of the driver (only Matt drives Matt's car, and Veronica drives Veronica's car) with the length of the route. A final constraint is the availability of a drive-through restaurant along the route. It only concerns the route variable.

If we were to more formally define this carpooling problem, we may just list the variables, domains of each variable, and the constraints. The combination of these would be a constraint satisfaction problem.

- Variables:
  - Car
  - Route
- Domains:
  - Domain(Car): Matt's Car, Veronica's Car
  - Domain(Route): Highway, Main St., Side Streets, Scenic Route
- Constraints:
  - Cost of Trip Constraint(Car, Route): Trip must cost less than $10.
  - Length of Commute Constraint(Car, Route): The trip must take less than 30 minutes.
  - Drive-Through Constraint(Route): The route must pass by a drive-through restaurant.

If a constraint involves only one variable, it is known as a unary constraint. Drive-Through Constraint is a unary constraint. If a trip involves two variables, it is known as a binary constraint. Cost of Trip Constraint is a binary constraint. Later in the chapter, we will also work with constraints that involve more than two variables. Another problem that concerns binary constraints is the Australian Map Coloring Problem.

Australian Map Coloring Problem

The Australian Map Coloring Problem is an example of a classic set of constraint satisfaction problems known as map-coloring problems.[2] In these problems, a limited number of colors is available to fill in a geographic map. The map needs to be filled in such that no two regions that border one another are filled in with the same color. In the Australian variation of the problem, the goal is to color seven of the major states/territories of Australia with three different colors. The problem can be defined with seven variables (one for each state) and nine binary constraints. Tasmania is an island, so it has no constraints (no borders). In other words, it doesn't matter what color Tasmania is filled in with.

- Variables:
  - Western Australia
  - Northern Territory
  - South Australia
  - Queensland
  - New South Wales

---

[2]For more on map-coloring problems, see Russell and Norvig, page 203.

- Victoria
- Tasmania
- Domains:
  - Domain(Western Australia): Red, Green Blue
  - Domain(Northern Territory): Red, Green, Blue
  - Domain(South Australia): Red, Green, Blue
  - Domain(Queensland): Red, Green, Blue
  - Domain(New South Wales): Red, Green, Blue
  - Domain(Victoria): Red, Green, Blue
  - Domain(Tasmania): Red, Green, Blue
- Constraints:
  - Not the Same Color Constraint(Western Australia, Northern Territory)
  - Not the Same Color Constraint(Western Australia, South Australia)
  - Not the Same Color Constraint(South Australia, Northern Territory)
  - Not the Same Color Constraint(Queensland, Northern Territory)
  - Not the Same Color Constraint(Queensland, South Australia)
  - Not the Same Color Constraint(Queensland, New South Wales)
  - Not the Same Color Constraint(New South Wales, South Australia)
  - Not the Same Color Constraint(Victoria, South Australia)
  - Not the Same Color Constraint(Victoria, New South Wales)

A possible solution of the problem is shown in Figure 16-1.

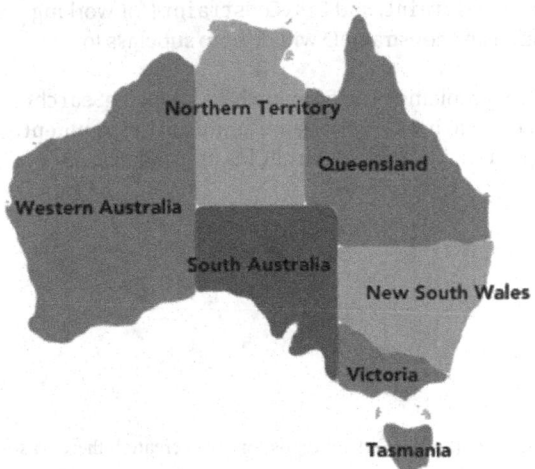

Figure 16-1. *A solution to the Australian Map Coloring Problem*

How Is a Constraint Satisfaction Problem Solved?

It's hard to explain how a human being solves a constraint satisfaction problem. Humans have something a computer doesn't—intuition. At their heart, constraint satisfaction problems are made up of logic. That's something that both humans and computers can understand, but the combination of intuition and understanding with logic allows a human to solve a range of constraint satisfaction problems right out of the box—without needing to be programmed. We can do it ad-hoc. A human would probably try to solve the Australian Map Coloring Problem incrementally. She could start by coloring Western Australia, see what colors she still has available, and then color Northern Territory and South Australia, etc. Without thinking too much, she would not necessarily be employing a system but more using common sense.

On the other hand, computers primarily solve constraint satisfaction problems with systematic search algorithms. The Australian Map Coloring Problem is small enough that a computer could use a *brute force* search (searching every possible combination of colors) and still solve the problem instantaneously. Ken Thompson, one of the most well-known computer scientists of the 20th century said, "When in doubt, use brute force."

However, there are better search algorithms than brute force for solving constraint satisfaction problems. *Backtracking* algorithms are one such better class of search algorithms. Backtracking algorithms dismiss possible solutions that won't work when they are only partially composed. For example, a backtracking algorithm for the Australian Map Coloring Problem would abandon a solution that began with Western Australia and the Northern Territory both being red, since it would not satisfy one of the constraints. The backtracking algorithms would, therefore, not waste time finding colors for the other variables and would ultimately find the solution much more quickly than a brute force search.

The constraineD Library

The open source library we'll be working with for the rest of the chapter is a rather primitive, still in alpha, constraint satisfaction problem solver called constraineD.[3] Why are we using a primitive, still in alpha, library? Because the author of this book wrote it specifically for use with this chapter, due to the fact that there is no other constraint satisfaction problem–solving library for Dart that was available at the time of writing.

There are two main classes in constraineD. CSP defines a constraint satisfaction problem. It has variables, domains, and constraints associated with it. The abstract class Constraint defines a constraint. It has one method that its subclasses need to implement called isSatisfied(). isSatisfied() returns a bool that signals whether a given assignment (possible domain selections for each variable in the constraint) satisfies a constraint. A Not the Same Color Constraint's isSatisfied() method would return true if both variables were assigned different colors. Constraint has three abstract subclasses: UnaryConstraint, BinaryConstraint, and ListConstraint (for working with more than two variables). These are the classes that a program using constraineD will need to subclass to solve a problem.

constraineD uses a simple recursive backtracking search to solve problems.[4] The function backtrackingSearch() is passed a CSP (with constraints, variables, and domains already added to it) and a Map representing the assignment of domain values to variables. The assignment is typically blank when backtrackingSearch() is first called.

---

[3]The capital *D* at the end of the name is for "Dart." Maybe it's a silly name, but after the GitHub repository was created, there was no going back.

[4]For a discussion of backtracking, see page 52 of *Artificial Intelligence in the 21st Century* by Stephen Lucci and Danny Kopec (Mercury, 2012). For a treatment specific to CSPs, see page 214 of Russell and Norvig.

Solving the Australian Map Coloring Problem Using constraineD

If you visit the GitHub repository for constraineD (https://github.com/davecom/constraineD), you will find four sample problems in the test directory. One of them is the Australian Map Coloring Problem, which is defined in mapcoloring.dart. Take a look at its code.

A subclass of BinaryConstraint, MapColoringConstraint, is defined. It ensures that two adjacent places cannot have the same color. The problem itself is defined almost as clearly as we did above using bullet points.

```
List variables = ["Western Australia", "Northern Territory",
    "South Australia", "Queensland", "New South Wales", "Victoria", "Tasmania"];
Map domains = {};
for (var variable in variables) {
  domains[variable] = ["r", "g", "b"];
}

CSP mapCSP = new CSP(variables, domains);

mapCSP.addBinaryConstraint(new MapColoringConstraint("Western Australia",
    "Northern Territory"));
mapCSP.addBinaryConstraint(new MapColoringConstraint("Western Australia",
    "South Australia"));
mapCSP.addBinaryConstraint(new MapColoringConstraint("South Australia",
    "Northern Territory"));
mapCSP.addBinaryConstraint(new MapColoringConstraint("Queensland",
    "Northern Territory"));
mapCSP.addBinaryConstraint(new MapColoringConstraint("Queensland",
    "South Australia"));
mapCSP.addBinaryConstraint(new MapColoringConstraint("Queensland",
    "New South Wales"));
mapCSP.addBinaryConstraint(new MapColoringConstraint("New South Wales",
    "South Australia"));
mapCSP.addBinaryConstraint(new MapColoringConstraint("Victoria",
    "South Australia"));
mapCSP.addBinaryConstraint(new MapColoringConstraint("Victoria",
    "New South Wales"));
```

The variables are defined just using String objects representing the names of the respective places. The colors that make up the domains are just individual letters, also represented by String objects. The CSP is created, and then the nine binary constraints are added. It almost reads like a natural language. Download constraineD and try running mapcoloring.dart. You should see a solution to the Australian Map Coloring Problem printed out to your console.

Word Search

A word search is a puzzle composed of a grid of letters containing hidden words. The player is provided with the list of hidden words. Her task is to find all of the hidden words within the grid, typically by circling them. The word search we will be creating will have no overlapping words. In other words, no two words will share the same cell on the grid, even if both words contain the same letter. This reduces the complexity of the solution significantly.

Getting Started

Create a new project in Dart Editor of type "Web Application." Call it "WordSearch." Edit pubspec.yaml to add the dependency constrained (browser, which you will see listed as a dependency, is added as a dependency to all projects of type "Web Application" created with Dart Editor). Specify the version of constrained as 0.0.3, as that is what this chapter is written to. Edit wordsearch.css to look like Listing 16-1.

Listing 16-1. wordsearch.css

```css
body {
  background-color: #F8F8F8;
  font-family: 'Open Sans', sans-serif;
  font-size: 14px;
  font-weight: normal;
  line-height: 1.2em;
  margin: 15px;
}

h1, p {
  color: #333;
}

.container {
  width: 80%;
  position: relative;
  border: 1px solid #ccc;
  background-color: #fff;
  padding: 20px;
  margin: 20px;
}
```

A CSS element that begins with a period, such as .container, defines a CSS *class*. A class is a set of attributes that can be applied to any HTML element. We will be applying .container to HTML <div> elements that divide our program into sections. Speaking of HTML, let's take a look at that. Listing 16-2 shows the HTML that you should put into wordsearch.html.

Listing 16-2. wordsearch.html

```html
<!DOCTYPE html>

<html>
  <head>
    <meta charset="utf-8">
    <title>Word Search</title>
    <link rel="stylesheet" href="wordsearch.css">
  </head>
  <body>
    <div class="container">
      <h1>Word Search</h1>
      <button id="hide">Toggle Controls View</button>
      <button id="print">Print</button>
    </div>
```

```html
    <div id="input_section" class="container">
      <p>Grid Width</p>
      <input id="grid_width" type="number" value="10">
      <p>Grid Height</p>
      <input id="grid_height" type="number" value="10">
      <p>Word List (comma separated)</p>
      <textarea id="word_list"></textarea>
      <br>
      <button id="create">Create</button>
    </div>

    <div id="output_section" class="container">
    </div>

    <script type="application/dart" src="wordsearch.dart"></script>
    <script src="packages/browser/dart.js"></script>
  </body>
</html>
```

We have three sections. The first holds the page's headline as well as two buttons. The first button is used for showing or hiding the next container, and the second button is for printing the page (yes, to actual, physical paper). The reason we may want to hide the second container is that it will look better when we print out the page on paper, without that section. As was just mentioned, the second section holds the controls for setting up the word search. The last section is currently blank but will be filled in with the word search and the words nicely printed after our program creates the grid.

Search Words

It's pretty obvious what the variables need to be in our word search constraint satisfaction problem—the words themselves. But, how should they be represented? It could make sense for them to just be String objects, but another option is to create a custom object. In this example, a custom class, SearchWord, was defined that held the actual word as a String instance variable. It has a single method, getDomain(), which returns the possible locations within the grid that the word can appear. If String objects were used instead of a custom class, getDomain() would be a stand-alone function instead of a method. Listing 16-3 shows the code for SearchWord, which should go into a new file you create with Dart Editor in the web folder labeled search_word.dart.

Listing 16-3. search_word.dart

```dart
part of wordsearch;

class SearchWord {
  String word;
  SearchWord(this.word);

  /// Returns all possible positioning of [word] within
  /// a [width] x [height] grid
  List<List<Point>>getDomain(int width, int height) {
    List<List<Point>>domain = [];
```

```
// go through every place in the grid
for (int x = 0; x < width; x++) {
  for (int y = 0; y < height; y++) {
    // forward
    if (x + word.length <= width) {
      List newPlacement = [];
      for (int i = 0; i < word.length; i++) {
        newPlacement.add(new Point(x + i, y));
      }
      domain.add(newPlacement);
    }
    // backwards
    if (x - word.length >= -1) { // 0 counts as a place
      List newPlacement = [];
      for (int i = 0; i < word.length; i++) {
        newPlacement.add(new Point(x - i, y));
      }
      domain.add(newPlacement);
    }
    // down
    if (y + word.length <= height) {
      List newPlacement = [];
      for (int i = 0; i < word.length; i++) {
        newPlacement.add(new Point(x, y + i));
      }
      domain.add(newPlacement);
    }
    // up
    if (y - word.length >= -1) { // 0 counts as a place
      List newPlacement = [];
      for (int i = 0; i < word.length; i++) {
        newPlacement.add(new Point(x, y - i));
      }
      domain.add(newPlacement);
    }
    // forward up diagonal
    if ((x + word.length <= width) && (y + word.length <= height)) {
      List newPlacement = [];
      for (int i = 0; i < word.length; i++) {
        newPlacement.add(new Point(x + i, y + i));
      }
      domain.add(newPlacement);
    }
    // backwards down diagonal
    if ((x - word.length >= -1) && (y - word.length >= -1)) {
      List newPlacement = [];
      for (int i = 0; i < word.length; i++) {
        newPlacement.add(new Point(x - i, y - i));
      }
      domain.add(newPlacement);
    }
```

```
    // forward down diagonal
    if ((x + word.length <= width) && (y - word.length >= -1)) {
      List newPlacement = [];
      for (int i = 0; i < word.length; i++) {
        newPlacement.add(new Point(x + i, y - i));
      }
      domain.add(newPlacement);
    }
    // backwards up diagonal
    if ((x - word.length >= -1) && (y + word.length <= height)) {
      List newPlacement = [];
      for (int i = 0; i < word.length; i++) {
        newPlacement.add(new Point(x - i, y + i));
      }
      domain.add(newPlacement);
    }
  }
}

  return domain;
 }
}
```

Why does getDomain() return a List<List<Point>>? Well, the domain of a variable is a list of all of the possible values of that variable. What are the possible values of a search word within a word search (say that six times fast)? They are all of the locations within the grid that the word can be placed, and each of those locations needs to also specify where the rest of its letters go.

For instance, if I have a two-by-two grid, and I want to place the word "GO" in it, I have all of the following possibilities:

```
GO  OG  GX  OX  XG  XO  GX  OX  XX  XX  XO  XG
XX  XX  OX  GX  XO  XG  XO  XG  GO  OG  GX  OX
```

Search words in a word search can go in eight directions: forward, backward, down, up, forward down diagonal, backward up diagonal, forward up diagonal, and backward down diagonal. getDomain() has to calculate all of these possibilities for every word in every possible location on the grid. For the first example, in our two-by-two grid, with "GO" written forward along the top of the grid, the List representing this may look like (note: this is not actual code, just a representation of its internal representation as a list) [(0,0), (1,0)]. The next position could be seen as [(1,0), (0,0)]. Then all of these possibilities get put together in the big List that is returned by the function as [[(0,0), (1,0)], [(1,0), (0,0)], etc.].

Why is this a List and not a Set? Because in this instance, order matters. When the word is rewritten in the grid, and the grid is drawn, it can't be jumbled. Actually, jumbling it would be an interesting game too. Can you imagine doing a word search, looking for the word "APPLE," and it actually being written in a backward diagonal as "PLAEP"? That might take you a while to find.

Facing Constraints

What constraints need to be imposed on our constraint satisfaction problem for Word Search? We could use many binary constraints, one between every two possible combinations of words, but that would be a bit cumbersome. Instead, we will use a single subclass of ListConstraint, WordSearchConstraint, which is satisfied when no two words are occupying the same space on the grid. Create a new file in Dart Editor in the web folder called word_search_constraint.dart and fill it with Listing 16-4.

Listing 16-4. `word_search_constraint.dart`

```
part of wordsearch;

class WordSearchConstraint extends ListConstraint {
  WordSearchConstraint(List words): super(words);

  /// This constraint is satisfied when no words overlap in the grid
  @override
  bool isSatisfied(Map assignment) {
    List allPointsUsed = [];
    for (List<Point> wordPlaces in assignment.values) {
      allPointsUsed.addAll(wordPlaces);
    }
    Set allPointsUsedSet = allPointsUsed.toSet();
    if (allPointsUsedSet.length < allPointsUsed.length) {  // duplicates check
      return false;  // must be an overlap of words
    } else {
      return true;
    }
  }
}
```

The `isSatisfied()` method combines all of the `List` objects representing all of the possible placements of every word in `assignment` and converts the combined `List` into a `Set`. It then checks if the combined `Set` has a shorter `length` than the combined `List`. `Set` objects do not allow duplicates (they are automatically removed), so if it has a shorter `length`, then we know some of the words were occupying the same space, because they had the same points within their respective `List`s. This is very similar to the revised `containsDuplicates()` function at the end of Chapter 6.

Defining a Grid

You've worked on a grid before. Chapter 10's The Game of Life used a grid to draw cells in a microbiology simulation. The grid for a word search is actually quite structurally similar. It also is rectangular and has cells, each representing a letter in the grid. The `Grid` and `Cell` classes presented here are highly modified, pared-down versions of the same classes from The Game of Life. Instead of redefining them, as we did here, you could also subclass the originals and override some of their methods (software reuse/inheritance for the win). Create a file called `grid.dart` and put it in the web folder. Fill it in with Listing 16-5.

Listing 16-5. `grid.dart`

```
part of wordsearch;

class Grid {
  final int numCellsWide;
  final int numCellsTall;
  CanvasElement wordSearchCanvas;
  Map<Point, Cell> cells = new Map();

  Grid(this.wordSearchCanvas, this.numCellsWide, this.numCellsTall) {
    Random r = new Random();
    const String ALPHABET = "ABCDEFGHIJKLMNOPQRSTUVWXYZ";
```

```
  // initialize all the cells
  for (int x = 0; x < numCellsWide; x++) {
    for (int y = 0; y < numCellsTall; y++) {
      Point location = new Point(x, y);
      // fill initially with random letters
      int randLoc = r.nextInt(ALPHABET.length);
      cells[location] = new Cell(location, ALPHABET[randLoc]);
    }
  }
}

/// draw the whole grid once
void drawOnce() {
  CanvasRenderingContext2D c2d = wordSearchCanvas.context2D;
  c2d.clearRect(0, 0, numCellsWide * Cell.WIDTH, numCellsTall * Cell.HEIGHT);
  for (Cell cell in cells.values) {
    cell.draw(c2d);
  }
}
}
```

Grid has an instance variable, cells, which maps Point objects to individual Cell objects on the grid. Grid's constructor creates all of the Cell objects for the grid, filling each one with a random letter at first. The letters of individual Cells are switched out later to their final forms. drawOnce() clears the canvas associated with the grid, goes through every Cell in cells, and tells it to draw itself. Create a file called cell.dart in the web directory and fill it with Listing 16-6.

Listing 16-6. cell.dart

```
part of wordsearch;

class Cell {
  String letter = "";
  Point location;

  static const int WIDTH = 20;
  static const int HEIGHT = 20;

  Cell(this.location, this.letter);

  /// Each Cell can draws itself
  void draw(CanvasRenderingContext2D c2d) {
    //have a black outline
    c2d.setStrokeColorRgb(0, 0, 0);  // black
    c2d.strokeRect(location.x * WIDTH, location.y * HEIGHT, WIDTH, HEIGHT);
    //draw letter
    c2d.textAlign = "center";  // text is drawn from the middle horizontally
    c2d.textBaseline = "middle";  // text is drawn from the middle vertically
    c2d.strokeText(letter.toUpperCase(), location.x * WIDTH + WIDTH / 2,
        location.y * HEIGHT + HEIGHT / 2, WIDTH);
    //print("X: ${location.x * WIDTH} Y: ${location.y * HEIGHT}");
  }
}
```

A Cell is just a way of maintaining the state of a letter and a point in the grid and being able to draw said items to the screen. Drawing the letter in the center of the cell takes a bit of finagling. The text drawing APIs that come with the HTML5 Canvas API are rather primitive. Figure 16-2 shows the classes related to Word Search that we've spoken about thus far. It includes the details of WordSearchConstraint's inheritance hierarchy vis-à-vis constraineD.

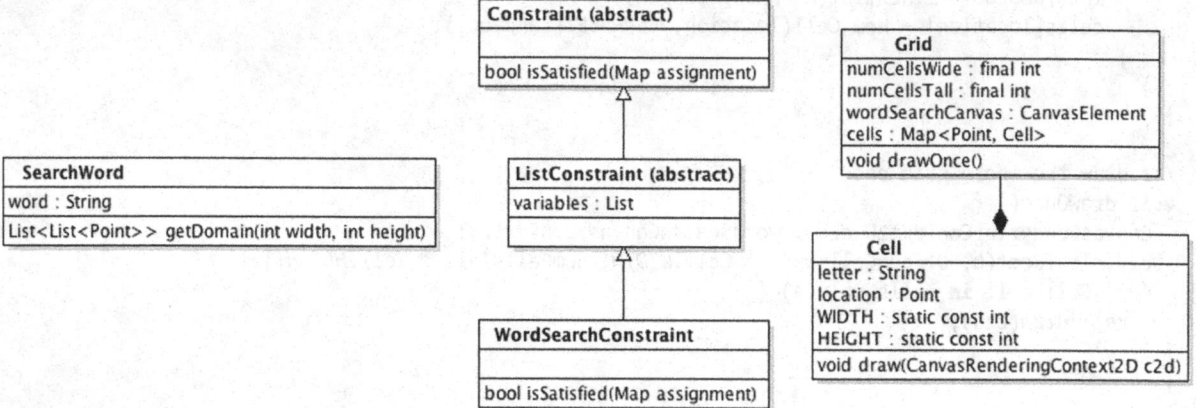

Figure 16-2. Classes for Word Search

The Glue

The glue that holds all of these classes together and actually utilizes constraineD to do a word search is in wordsearch.dart. It features a fairly linear design of four functions that are organized in the file from top to bottom. The first function calls the second, which calls the third, etc. The code is only broken up into functions for readability purposes. The functions are being explicitly used for code organization. wordsearch.dart is in Listing 16-7.

Listing 16-7. wordsearch.dart

```dart
library wordsearch;

import "dart:html";
import "dart:math";  // for Random, Point
import "package:constrained/constrained.dart";

part "search_word.dart";
part "word_search_constraint.dart";
part "cell.dart";
part "grid.dart";

void main() {  // setup event handlers for buttons
  querySelector("#create").onClick.listen(createWordSearch);
  querySelector("#print").onClick.listen((MouseEvent me) => window.print());
  querySelector("#hide").onClick.listen((MouseEvent me) {
    DivElement controlSection = (querySelector("#input_section") as DivElement);
    controlSection.hidden = !controlSection.hidden;  // just flip it
  });
}
```

```
/// Get parameters for grid from user and create Grid
void createWordSearch(MouseEvent event) {
  String widthText = (querySelector("#grid_width") as InputElement).value;
  String heightText = (querySelector("#grid_height") as InputElement).value;

  int gridWidth, gridHeight;
  try {
    gridWidth = int.parse(widthText);
    gridHeight = int.parse(heightText);
  } on FormatException {
    window.alert("Grid's dimensions must be defined with integers.");
    return;
  }

  if (gridWidth < 1 || gridHeight < 1) {
    window.alert("The grid must be at least 1 cell long in each dimension.");
    return;
  }

  String inputWordList = (querySelector("#word_list") as TextAreaElement).value;
  if (inputWordList.trim() == "") {
    window.alert("Word List can't be blank.");
    return;
  }

  List<String> words = inputWordList.split(",");

  populateGrid(words, gridWidth, gridHeight);  // try to fill in a grid with the words
}

/// Perform a bakcktracking search using constraineD to determine
/// how all of the words can fit in the grid.
void populateGrid(List<String> words, int width, int height) {
  // prepare words for search
  List<SearchWord> searchWords = [];
  Map<SearchWord, List<List<Point>>>domains = {};
  int sumOfWordLengths = 0;
  for (String word in words) {
    SearchWord sw = new SearchWord(word.trim());
    searchWords.add(sw);
    List<List<Point>>tempDomain = sw.getDomain(width, height);
    if (tempDomain.isEmpty) {
      window.alert("The word $word could not fit on the grid.");
      return;
    }

    sumOfWordLengths += sw.word.length;
    tempDomain.shuffle(); // dont' want boring solutions first
    domains[sw] = tempDomain;
  }
```

```
  if (sumOfWordLengths > width * height) {
    window.alert("There's not enough room on the grid for those words.");
    return;
  }

  // perform the search
  CSP wordSearchCSP = new CSP(searchWords, domains);
  wordSearchCSP.addListConstraint(new WordSearchConstraint(searchWords));
  backtrackingSearch(wordSearchCSP, {}).then((solution) {

    if (solution == null) {
      window.alert("Could not fit words on grid.");
    } else {
      // create display for grid
      CanvasElement wordSearchCanvas = new CanvasElement();
      wordSearchCanvas.width = width * Cell.WIDTH;
      wordSearchCanvas.height = height * Cell.HEIGHT;
      Grid wordSearchGrid = new Grid(wordSearchCanvas, width, height);

      // get search results and fill in grid
      for (SearchWord sw in solution.keys) {
        for (int i = 0; i < sw.word.length; i++) {
          wordSearchGrid.cells[solution[sw][i]].letter = sw.word[i];
        }
      }

      showGrid(wordSearchCanvas, wordSearchGrid, words);
    }
  });
}

/// Show a window containing the grid, the word list, and a print button
void showGrid(CanvasElement wordSearchCanvas, Grid wordSearchGrid, List<String> words) {
  // clear the output container draw main grid
  DivElement gridContainer = querySelector("#output_section");
  gridContainer.innerHtml = "";
  gridContainer.append(wordSearchCanvas);
  wordSearchGrid.drawOnce();

  // add word list
  UListElement listElement = new UListElement();
  gridContainer.append(listElement);
  for (String word in words) {
    LIElement itemElement = new LIElement();
    listElement.append(itemElement);
    itemElement.text = word.trim().toUpperCase();
  }
}
```

We're going to go over these four interconnected functions one by one. `main()` sets up listeners for the three buttons on the page. The `create` button starts the process of creating a new word search by calling `createWordSearch()`. The `print` button calls `window.print()`, which is shorthand for the user going to the File menu in her web browser and selecting "Print." The hide button uses the HTML/CSS element property hidden (a boolean) to make the <div> containing the main word search controls disappear and reappear. The purpose is not to pollute printed copies of the word search with the controls.

createWordSearch() reads the parameters of the word search from the HTML form controls. If any of the parameters are out of whack (such as if a word couldn't fit on the proposed grid size), then it balks and shows an error message to the user. If everything is okay, it calls populateGrid() to do the dirty work of actually using constraineD.

populateGrid() does further sanity checks on the parameters, but its main job is to create a CSP, along with accompanying SearchWord variables, domains, and a WordSearchConstraint. backTrackingSearch() is called on the CSP. It returns a Future. In the then() block of the Future, if a solution is found, it is drawn to the screen by creating a Grid attached to a Canvas, filling in its cells, and calling showGrid().

Finally, showGrid() adds HTML elements to the previously blank bottom <div> of the page called output_section (which is cleared first, in case there was a prior word search produced by calling gridContainer.innerHtml = ""). The added HTML elements are the canvas as well as a nicely formatted list of all of the words in the word search. Creating HTML elements on the fly like this is an alternative way of utilizing dart:html vs. defining all of your elements in the HTML file and calling querySelector() to pull each one. The disadvantage is that the structure of your document gets combined with its implementation. Separating implementation from design structure is generally considered good practice.

Your finished product should look something like Figure 16-3 (after clicking "Toggle Controls View" to hide the controls—showing them made the figure too large).

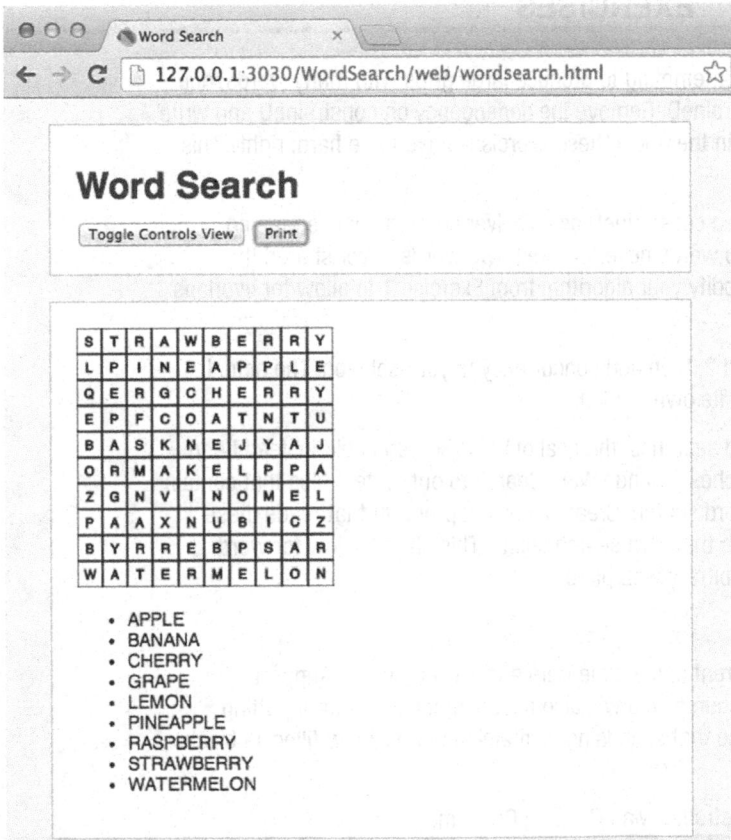

Figure 16-3. Word Search

You're Not Done Yet

Sometimes, you get to the end of a movie, and there's a terrible twist. This chapter is just like that. We're giving you a lot more work—and it's in the exercises. The problem is that the primitive backtracking search used by constraineD quickly gets overwhelmed by large grids that feature many words. If you try to create such a word search, it will seem like Word Search has locked up—but it hasn't really, it's just searching through such a large number of possibilities that it's taking forever. It's up to you, in the exercises, to overcome that challenge. If this is the type of challenge that interests you, you may want to pursue learning more about computer science, which is touched on in the next chapter.

Summary

Constraint satisfaction problems are all problems that can be defined with variables, finite domains, and constraints. They are well-suited for computational solutions using search algorithms. In a backtracking search, solutions that will not work are discarded before they are fully explored, based on early indicators of their failure. In a brute force search, every possibility is looked at. A map-coloring problem is a constraint satisfaction problem that involves using a limited number of colors to color a map in such a way that no two adjacent regions are filled with the same color. Word Search can be defined as a constraint satisfaction problem.

EXERCISES

1. Word Search really struggles when attempting to produce large grids with many words, due to the underlying algorithm in constraineD. Remove the dependency on constraineD and write your own set of functions for filling in the grid. (These exercises have to be hard, right? This is the final project!)

2. The version of Word Search that used constraineD as its solver created nonoverlapping word searches. This means that two words never crossed (two words never shared the same position/letter on the grid). Modify your algorithm from Exercise 1 to allow for overlaps between words.

3. If you accomplished Exercises 1 and 2, then add concurrency to your solution. The actual search for solutions should occur in its own Isolate.

4. Instead of generating printable word searches, the goal of Word Search could instead be to generate playable online word searches. Change Word Search to output text files that contain the specifications of a generated word search. Create a second program that reads these files and allows the user to complete the word search online. This should allow for word searches to be integrated into an arbitrary web page.

5. Add unit tests to Word Search.

6. A crossword puzzle is not very different in principle from a word search that supports overlapping words (Exercise 2). Of course, you will also need a mechanism for inputting clues. The grid should be modified so that spaces not containing words show filled-in black boxes instead of letters.

7. Create a graphical version of the Australian Map Coloring Problem.

■ ■ ■

# CHAPTER 17

Where to Go from Here

Can you still remember Hello World? It seems like ages ago that you were a complete novice trying to wrap your head around the concept of a variable. If you made it this far, you're probably proficient at Dart. You can create your own web apps that do something useful. That's great, but it can just be the beginning of your journey ordering around computers. You've learned enough to know how much you don't know!

Advance Your Core Dart Skills

What's the most frustrating topic that's been covered in this book? For many people, it's probably concurrency. However, for you, it may be something else. Just like this entire book has been about "learning by doing," you're not going to improve on that frustration unless you take it head on. If, for example, your Achilles' heel is concurrency, then write a program of your own design that depends on the dart:isolate package.

There are also advanced Dart topics that didn't make it into this book, by virtue of its target demographic (absolute beginners). The foremost may be Stream objects. A Stream object, like a Future, is used for representing data that has not yet been produced. However, unlike a Future, a Stream is used for a continuous set of data, instead of just a single object. You have actually used a Stream before. The onClick property of the Element class, used for responding to events in dart:html, is a Stream. To learn more about Stream objects, check out the article "Use Streams for Data" by Chris Buckett at www.dartlang.org/docs/tutorials/streams.

In Chapter 6, Dart's built-in data structures were talked about, but defining your own data structures was not. One of the most useful aspects of Dart data structures is that they can be iterated through with a for-in-loop. Any class that implements the Iterable interface (defined in dart:core, no imports necessary for classes in dart:core) can be iterated through with a for-in-loop.

Another topic of interest to asynchronous programming is *zones*. Zones enable errors in asynchronous code that are not fatal to be isolated. The article "Zones" by Florian Loitsch and Kathy Walrath is a good overview (www.dartlang.org/articles/zones).

The problem with online programming tutorials (for any language, not just Dart) is that the person writing one has no concept of where an individual reader's knowledge base lies previous to reading the tutorial. Presumably, that's one of the reasons readers still buy full-length books like *Dart for Absolute Beginners*. In every chapter, the author knows exactly what the reader understands up to that point. Now that you have read this book and have a generalized knowledge of Dart, you should be equipped to understand almost any online Dart tutorial you come across, even the ones on fairly esoteric topics. You now have a *base of knowledge* from which to work with as you explore more advanced Dart topics.

Project Ideas

You don't need to learn anything more to start on some exciting projects today, though. Here are ideas for several Dart projects that you can take on with just what you've learned in this book. Each could've easily been the project included in Chapter 16, but instead is left up to you.

- Create a Dart chess program that can play a competent game. It will be similar in principal to the Tic-Tac-Toe AI you developed in the Chapter 13 exercises. You can use the pub package chess for generating legal moves. Even with the library, this will be a difficult project.

- Create a version of the classic video game *Pong*. A simpler version will be two-player, while a more difficult assignment is to create a computer AI.

- Create a version of the classic video game *Breakout*.

- Create a web app that allows the user to enter her monthly budget and print out graphs showing how the budget is allocated.

- Create a calculator of inflation over time using official statistics from the government of your country. The calculator should be able to tell you $100 in 1973 is worth $X today. Store the inflation data in a text file.

- Create a portfolio web site that uses Dart to smartly present all of your most proud web app creations.

Learn Polymer.dart and/or Angular.dart

Chapter 8 covered dart:html in some depth. dart:html is a great library and includes much of the functionality of the popular JavaScript library *jQuery*. You can build a large client-side web app with dart:html. However, there are other options with more extensive capabilities out of the box.

Polymer.dart is a library for building web components. Web components are drop-in HTML elements that add new functionality to the HTML stack. When you define a web component with Polymer.dart you are essentially defining a new HTML tag that can then be flexibly placed wherever it's needed. The custom HTML tag can also feature custom HTML attributes and some primitive logic using the templating language built into Polymer.dart. More excitingly, a Polymer.dart element can feature two-way data binding between the web component and your Dart code. This enables the display of a variable to be automatically updated as the actual variable changes with your code. Polymer.dart is being promoted by the Dart language team as one of the main avenues for web development with Dart, so it is likely to be well-supported going forward. You can find out more about Polymer.dart on its official website at www.dartlang.org/polymer-dart.

Angular.dart is a port of Angular, a JavaScript framework supported by Google, to the Dart language. It is a large, client-side web development framework, built on mature technology. Angular.dart is also built upon the foundation of web components and enables two-way data binding. Angular.dart can be thought of as a higher-level framework than Polymer.dart. Angular.dart gives your web app structure with *models*, which hold data, and *controllers*, which coordinate the display of models in your HTML *views*. You can find Angular.dart online at https://angulardart.org. Like its JavaScript sister, Angular.dart is directly supported by Google, and several of its core developers are Google employees.

There are other frameworks for client-side Dart web development that are emerging. Polymer.dart and Angular.dart were simply the most mature at the time of this book's writing, so they got mentioned here. They both have solid backing from the Dart language project, so they shouldn't be going anywhere. However, you should check out all of the available options before picking a framework. The web framework space is one that tends to rapidly evolve, and that has nothing to do with Dart itself; it's just the nature of web development. Feel free to stick with dart:html, too, if it serves your needs.

Server-Side Dart

This book has been about teaching client-side web development with Dart—developing programs that run within a web browser, rather than those that execute on a remote server. That's the role that the language JavaScript has traditionally served. However, Dart is also emerging as a server-side language, which is the territory of not only JavaScript but also languages such as PHP and Java. To rehash the differences between server-side and client-side languages, check out Chapter 7. JavaScript moved into the realm of a serious server-side language competitor with the release of *node.js* a few years ago. It is now seen as an end-to-end language solution for both client-side and server-side web development. Dart aims also to be such a solution. You can program your entire complex web application, both the part that runs in the browser and the part that runs on the server, in Dart.

The `dart:io` package includes built-in support for setting up a simple web server. The key class for this is called `HttpServer`. Although it's possible to write your entire server-side app with just `dart:io`, it's certainly not ideal. It's too primitive a set of classes to provide the functionality that a modern server-side app requires. On the server-side, you need to worry about things like authentication, templating, database access, sessions, routing, etc. The paradigms necessary to understand for writing a server-side app are quite different from those for writing a client-side app.

In light of these requirements, it's best to build your server-side app with a web framework. Yes, just like there are client-side web frameworks, there are also server-side web frameworks. Have you heard of *Ruby on Rails*? That's actually a server-side web framework, not a language. *Ruby* is the name of the language, and *Ruby on Rails* is the name of the framework. In the Python world, *Python* is the language, while *Django* and *Flask* are the two most popular web frameworks.

Unfortunately, at the time of writing, there was no mature server-side web framework for Dart. Server-side Dart is still immature, in the sense that there is no de facto standard framework, most of the frameworks that do exist are still in beta, and none of the frameworks is well-tested in production. The two frameworks with the most traction are *start* and *Rikulo stream*. Will either of them have significant mindshare a year from now? Who knows? Will Google release its own server-side web framework? Maybe.

The other side of the equation, which is also still very immature in regard to Dart, is hosting. Although you can run server-side Dart apps on your local machine (and you should, for testing purposes, while developing them), your ultimate goal is probably to put your program on the public-facing World Wide Web. The best way to do this is with a managed Platform as a Service (PaaS) like Heroku, Google App Engine, or RedHat OpenShift. At the time of writing, none of these three services had official Dart support, although community-developed projects for all three can get Dart running on them. Google has announced future official support for Dart on App Engine, and it will likely be available by the time you read this book. If that's the case, App Engine is likely the go-to platform for your server-side Dart apps.

Working with Databases

If you end up writing server-side apps, whether in Dart or another language, you will need to understand databases, if you want to store any significant amount of data. Modern popular databases can broadly be categorized as *relational*, *SQL*-based databases, and *NoSQL* databases. There are good pub packages for working with both kinds from Dart.

Databases are used for storing records of data and retrieving them. You may ask why this just can't be done with basic file I/O. It can, but database programs are just a more efficient, industrial-strength method of storing and retrieving data. They also provide sophisticated query languages that allow for data to be retrieved intelligently. Imagine storing a school's student records in plain text files. To determine the valedictorian, you would need to write a custom function that opens all of the files, calculates every student's GPA, and finds the maximum. In a database query language like SQL, that would be a one-line statement. The most popular commercial database vendors are Oracle, Microsoft, and IBM. Databases are big business, and their commercial variants are big money.

Relational databases store data in tables and may have relationships between one table and another. The most popular open source (and free to use) relational SQL-based databases are *SQLite*, *MySQL*, and *PostgreSQL*. SQL stands for "Structured Query Language." It's a database query language that was originally developed by IBM in the 1970s. Whether by luck, happenstance, or merit, SQL has stood the test of time and is a useful skill to learn in and of itself. SQL is, in fact, a simple programming language.

SQLite (sqlite.org) is meant for smaller projects. While MySQL and PostgreSQL run as separate server processes (either locally or remote), SQLite runs locally and embeds within a program. It's actually one of the core storage technologies on the original iPhone. It's powerful enough to run small web sites. There are some early stage open source projects to connect SQLite with Dart. SQLite databases are simply stored in local files.

MySQL (mysql.com) claims to be the most popular open source database on the Web. It powers innumerable web sites and is the go-to product for most startups and new small business web sites. MySQL is so popular that most web hosting companies will provide you with an already set up MySQL installation as part of their most basic plan. The company behind MySQL was recently acquired by Oracle, which led to a fork of MySQL, called *MariaDB*. MariaDB (mariadb.org) can serve as a drop-in replacement of MySQL for most purposes. Either MySQL or MariaDB is a fine choice to start learning SQL with. The most mature, although still beta, MySQL connector for Dart is *SQLJocky* (http://pub.dartlang.org/packages/sqljocky).

PostgreSQL (postgresql.org) has a reputation for being the most scalable, feature-rich, and performant of the free, open source relational database solutions. Although not as popular as MySQL, PostgreSQL is still widely deployed, and there is a plethora of good tutorials and books written about using it. A community-derived PostgreSQL wrapper for Dart has been developed, creatively called *postgresql* (http://pub.dartlang.org/packages/postgresql). It is in beta.

NoSQL is a very broad category of databases that are defined by what they are not, rather than what they are. They are not SQL-based, relational databases. The most popular NoSQL variants are so-called *document-based* databases. Instead of storing records in tables, they store every record as an individual document. This leads to differing performance characteristics from SQL-based databases.

Although there are several NoSQL databases with Dart interfaces, the most notable is *MongoDB* (mongodb.org). MongoDB is an open source, free, document-based database that is a relatively new entrant to the database space (arriving in the late '00s, whereas all of the relational databases we spoke about are at least two decades old). MongoDB natively stores data in a *JSON* (JavaScript Object Notation)-like format. Dart's standard library has built-in support for JSON. Its Dart wrapper may be the most mature of any of the database wrappers currently out for Dart. *mongo_dart* is available from pub at http://pub.dartlang.org/packages/mongo_dart.

You don't need a server to get started learning these databases. All of them can be installed locally on your personal computer. You will find installation instructions on their respective web sites. Database administration is a field in and of itself. Running web sites has become complicated enough that there are several specialized personnel that run web sites at most big companies. One of them is usually a "database architect." That's a different job from that of the person who's responsible for keeping the database running, which is yet a different job from that of the guy who actually develops the app that utilizes the database. Typically, database administrators are trained in information technology (IT) rather than computer science. Unfortunately, the general public doesn't tend to know the difference between information technology and computer science, to the disservice of those in both fields. It's like the difference between being a person who builds an observatory and being the astronomer who uses the observatory to conduct research. One is an almost wholly applied field, while the other is more of a science.

Learn Computer Science

Contrary to popular belief, learning to program a computer is not learning computer science. At least, not in the broad sense. Certainly, nearly all computer scientists utilize programming on a daily basis, but programming is a tool for solving computer science problems, not the end of computer science in and of itself. Computer science is concerned with the study of how problems can be solved computationally. This often leads to an investigation of computers, but computer science is not necessarily just about computers as we think about them in our daily lives.

What Is Computer Science?

Computer science emerged as a discipline out of mathematics. In the early days of computer technology, most university courses on the subject would be taught out of math departments. However, computer science is not just math. It involves a hodgepodge of seemingly far-flung subdisciplines that are all united by their use of computational tools to solve problems.

Computer science is also certainly not about using computers any more than astronomy is about using telescopes. It just so happens that most computer scientists use computers so much that they're pretty good at it, but the academic discipline concerned with the use of computers, as opposed to the study of them, is information technology. As stated before, the confusion between the two is often irksome for members of both disciplines. Don't call your local university's computer science department to fix your computer! Call IT.

Artificial intelligence, programming languages, robotics, machine learning, computer vision, complex systems, computational theory, algorithms, and computer graphics are just some of the topics that fall under the umbrella of computer science. They're all incredibly interesting disciplines, depending on your temperament. Some are quite mathematically intense, while others require little more than a high school math education. Most of the mathematics involved with computer science can be learned outside of a formal education setting. (Well, any knowledge can be learned outside of a formal education setting, right?)

Computer science is generally more concerned with the development of software, rather than the development of hardware, although both are relevant. Electrical engineering is more concerned with computer hardware. Computer architecture is the subdiscipline of computer science that specifically addresses hardware concerns. It deals with things like the *instruction set* of the microprocessor and the *bus* that delivers information from memory to the microprocessor.

Some educational institutions offer applied degrees that are tangentially related to computer science but not as abstract. *Computer engineering* is an applied degree that cuts across both computer science and electrical engineering. *Software engineering* is a field concerned specifically with creating software and, therefore, programming. It goes beyond programming to also discuss the importance of various software development methodologies and how to manage team-based environments.

If you want to learn computer science on your own, outside of a formal education, you should start with some building blocks that will be applicable to almost all of the subdisciplines. This book was a good start. You should probably learn more about data structures, simple well-known algorithms, and a little bit about how computer hardware works at a lower level. From then on, it's really up to you. You can dig into artificial intelligence or robotics without knowing anything about computer vision. But when you want to build a robot that can detect human faces, you'll know which book to pick up next.

The best computer science schools in the United States (MIT,[1] Carnegie Mellon, Stanford, and Berkeley) offer some of their courses online for free to the public (course material of course—you won't get a grade!). You would do well to start a journey in computer science by taking one of their intro courses on your own time. It will likely repeat some of the material you learned in this book. Usually, computer science curriculums include another, second-level course that is still foundational in nature. That would also be a solid place to start. Don't worry about whether it's taught in another programming language. The more programming languages you know, the better.

Speaking specifically to people reading this book who may be thinking about computer science in a formal education setting (regardless of your age), computer science gives you powerful tools that will be useful in many interdisciplinary fields. For example, computational biology is the use of computer science techniques to do things like develop new pharmaceutical drugs and study protein folding. There is a growing need around the world for more highly trained computer scientists. Computer-based systems are continuing to transform fields as far-flung as entertainment and medicine, and the global community needs not just people who know how to use computers (information technologists) but also people who know how to solve the problems that underlie computational technology.

However, computer science is not for everyone. It can also be a frustrating and, frankly, boring subject. You may find programming interesting but the nitty-gritty of how an algorithm works completely uninspiring. It's important to emphasize that programming is just a part of a computer science education; it's a means to an end. Many students take introductory classes and are pumped about programming but then get frustrated by the material outside of programming.

---

[1]MIT's Open Courseware (http://ocw.mit.edu) is a free platform providing course materials from a variety of subjects from one of the world's leading engineering/scientific institutions. Its Computer Science and Electrical Engineering department offers the full videos of lectures, assignments, and quizzes that a student taking the course would see. The course *Introduction to Computer Science and Programming*, taught in Python, is a good fit for someone thinking about learning computer science. Further information is available at http://ocw.mit.edu/courses/electrical-engineering-and-computer-science/6-00sc-introduction-to-computer-science-and-programming-spring-2011/.

There is a growing number of professional programmers who don't have a formal computer science education. This may be especially prevalent in Silicon Valley's startup culture. There's no doubt that a self-taught programmer can be absolutely superb at his job as a software developer. The larger question is, does a self-taught programmer know everything that's going on beneath his code and why, for example, one search algorithm may be a better choice than another for a particular application? And does it really matter if he does? That's an ongoing debate in software companies of all sizes. At a minimum, a formal education is supposed to ensure that all degree recipients have some basic set of knowledge. Those without a degree may or may not have that basic set of knowledge but may also be better programmers than those that do...

In short, if you're interested in programming, you should continue to explore it, whether or not you're also interested in computer science. You can find out the latter pretty quickly, without having to complete a whole degree in it. Your programming skills will be useful to you, whether or not you ultimately become a computer scientist. Today, more than ever, programming is a useful tool in almost every discipline, from accounting to botany. Computer science is just one direction to go with it.

Examples of Computer Science Problems in This Book

Despite not being a book about computer science, *Dart for Absolute Beginners* actually contains a fair number of sample problems that you'd find in an introductory computer science course. These include (but are not limited to)

- The Monty Hall Problem (Chapter 4)—typically taught in a discrete math course

- Fibonacci Sequence (Chapter 5)—taught as an example of recursion in an introductory programming course

- The Game of Life (Chapter 10)—seen in introductory programming courses

- Tic-Tac-Toe (Chapter 13, especially exercises)—the MiniMax AI algorithm is often part of an introductory artificial intelligence course

- The Dining Philosophers (Chapter 14)—a more complicated version of this problem is a classic concurrency example that will appear in a second-level programming course

- The Australian Map Coloring Problem (Chapter 16)—solving constraint satisfaction problems like map-coloring problems is the purview (among many other topics) of an introductory artificial intelligence course

If these problems appealed to you, then maybe you should give computer science a shot. There are also a lot of computer sciency topics in Chapter 18's interview with Dart's creators. Check that out and see if any of the discussion catches your fancy.

Learn Another Language

There's something to be said for knowing one or two programming languages inside out, but it's also a good idea to have a broad exposure to many of them. They do things in different ways and have differing performance characteristics (which has more to do with their implementations than anything else). They're also broadly applicable for different types of applications. For example, you can't use C (as you can JavaScript and Dart) to write a client-side web app (at least not without jumping through many, many hoops). At the same time, you wouldn't want to write an operating system in Python, due to performance constraints. By learning how a computational problem is solved in another language, you may come to appreciate alternative approaches that are valuable in your "home" language.

The following languages have each been included because they represent a broad cross section of syntax, programming style/paradigm, and application niches. They are all widely available with mature cross-platform implementations. Many more languages could've been included that fit that criteria. These are just a sampling.

Each language is presented with a short description, an example is Chapter 5's Fibonacci function—fib(), and resources from which to learn more. All four of these are excellent second languages to learn, and with the Dart you've learned in this book, you're ready to jump headfirst into any of them.

Python

Python is a general-purpose object-oriented programming language that is widely used across many industries from video game studios to Google. Python is popular as a scripting language (language for doing quick automated tasks), server-side web language, and is increasingly used by scientists. Python is a practical language for server-side web programming today, unlike Dart, which is still maturing in the server space.

Python features an elegant, minimalist syntax that utilizes white space (tabs, spaces) for structuring code. Python is often seen as one of the most human-readable languages around. It has a large, batteries-included standard library. For these reasons, Python has become popular in academia as an introductory programming language.

Unfortunately, Python is rather slow. In practice, computer hardware is so fast that Python's performance is not a factor for most of the programs that are written with it. There are several implementations of it available, but by far the most common is the one available at python.org, maintained by the Python Software Foundation and the language's original creator, Guido van Rossum. Python comes preinstalled on OS X and most Linux distributions. You can run it by just typing python in a terminal window. Listing 17-1 shows the Fibonacci function defined with Python. You'll notice no squiggly brackets and no semicolons.

Listing 17-1. fib.py

```python
def fib(n):
    if (n < 2):
        return n
    return fib(n - 2) + fib(n - 1)
```

Python's official documentation is available at python.org. There are good online tutorials available there. The title *Beginning Python*, Second Edition, by Magnus Lie Hetland (Apress, 2008) would be an appropriate follow-on to this book, in terms of its content level, although it's a bit dated. *Learn Python the Hard Way*, Third Edition, by Zed Shaw (Addison-Wesley, 2013), is a good book that has the same learning-by-doing philosophy as *Dart for Absolute Beginners*. You can purchase a print copy or get it for free at http://learnpythonthehardway.org.

JavaScript

JavaScript, standardized as ECMAScript, has been available in every mainstream web browser since 1996. That's one massive platform. Invented by Brendan Eich at Netscape in 1995, JavaScript was intended as a lightweight scripting language to make web pages more interactive. It has evolved into the lingua franca of modern programming, although it sometimes pushes against the edges of its original design limitations (hence the reason for Dart). JavaScript has also become a server-side language, popularized by *node.js*.

JavaScript is object-oriented and somewhat functional in style, but it's not class-based like Dart (although the next version of it, ECMAScript 6, will be). It's prototype-based, which means that objects are created, strangely enough, by adding functionality to cloned primitive objects. It also means that objects can be modified on the fly (new instance variables and methods can be added to instantiated objects). Functions are first-class citizens in JavaScript, as they are in Dart. Subjectively, Dart code doesn't really look that different from JavaScript on a line-by-line basis. JavaScript should be fairly easy to pick up for a Dart programmer; it's just missing a lot of Dart's nice features.

Of course, JavaScript fills the same niche as Dart, and the two are competitors for developer mindshare. That doesn't mean you need to fall into the Dart camp or the JavaScript camp. Knowing both is useful, especially since the majority of legacy web code is written in JavaScript. When running in browsers that don't have a Dart VM (which is almost all browsers today), your Dart code is actually running as converted JavaScript code. JavaScript is not a particularly big language, so it shouldn't take you long to feel comfortable with it. Listing 17-2 shows the Fibonacci function in JavaScript. It's pretty much identical to the Dart version, except for the keyword function.

Listing 17-2. fib.js

```javascript
function fib(n) {
    if (n < 2) {
        return n;
    }
    return fib(n - 2) + fib(n - 1);
}
```

There are countless JavaScript tutorials online, some of them very good. Codecademy (codecademy.com) takes a particularly interactive approach. An appropriate book, in terms of content level, to follow *Dart for Absolute Beginners*, is the Apress title *Beginning JavaScript with DOM Scripting and Ajax*, Second Edition, by Russ Ferguson and Christian Heilmann (2013).

C

C is *the* systems programming language of the past three decades. Every popular operating system on the planet is implemented largely in C. C is fast. It's so fast that most other languages are measured in performance relative to C. C is as close as you can get to machine code outside of assembly language.[2] C's syntax became the template for C++, Java, C#, Dart, JavaScript, and more.

C is also probably the most difficult language listed here for a beginner to grasp. It is not object-oriented or functional (it's a classic, procedural language), and memory must be managed manually by the programmer. Many a new programmer struggles with C *pointers*, which are variables that point directly to an address in memory. Yes, with C, you manually manage memory addresses, in a sense. For the same reason, C is incredibly powerful. If you need to write something that takes advantage of every feature of a hardware platform, C is your go-to language. Because it's relatively low-level (compared to other languages discussed here), a C program will generally be more lines of code than its equivalent in one of these other languages.

C was created by Dennis Ritchie and Brian Kernighan at AT&T in the early 1970s. It was the primary language used to develop Unix, a highly influential operating system, which Linux and OS X are descendants of. C has a small standard library, which is supplemented by each operating system with platform-specific libraries. Listing 17-3 shows the Fibonacci function in C. It's identical to its Dart counterpart.

Listing 17-3. fib.c

```c
int fib(int n) {
    if (n < 2) {
        return n;
    }
    return fib(n - 2) + fib(n - 1);
}
```

The classic text on the C programming language is *The C Programming Language*, Second Edition, by Kernighan and Ritchie (Prentice Hall, 1988). Although a great book, it's unfortunately no longer up to date, since the language has evolved and *The C Programming Language* was not updated for the last two revisions of the C standard. Most of what you learn in that text is still relevant, but it's probably not the best teaching text. The latest edition of the Apress title *Beginning C*, Fifth Edition, by Ivor Horton (2013), is likely a better choice.

---

[2]The lowest level human readable language for a particular hardware platform. Assembly language mirrors machine language but uses familiar English-like words. Assembly language for one microprocessor architecture will differ significantly from assembly language for another microprocessor architecture. For example, the assembly of your phone, running an ARM microprocessor, will be different from the assembly language of your desktop computer, running an x86-64 microprocessor.

Scheme

Scheme is included here because it's a functional language with a quite different syntax. In earlier chapters, there was discussion of the difference between a procedural, object-oriented, and functional style of programming. In this book, you were exposed to the first two, but not the latter. Scheme is a functional language with many implementations. There are so many implementations of Scheme, in fact, that it's hard to know which one to choose. For experimentation, it doesn't really matter too much. Gambit Scheme is one implementation that's mature, cross-platform, easy to install, and well-documented (http://gambitscheme.org). Racket (racket-lang.org) is a language that evolved from Scheme and features an easy-to-use IDE.

Scheme's syntax is incredibly parentheses-heavy. It helps to use an editor that recognizes the start and stop of parentheses. Scheme is a very minimalist language. You can learn all of the keywords and syntax in a matter of hours. It may look foreign (operators come before operands for example), but there's not much to memorize. Its standard library is also quite Spartan.

Scheme evolved at MIT in the 1970s from one of the oldest programming languages around—Lisp. It was created by Guy L. Steele and Gerald Jay Sussman. It features just as many parentheses as Lisp, with a more minimalist mindset. Listing 17-4 shows the Fibonacci function in Scheme. There are all of those parentheses! Once again, the operator comes before the operands, so adding 1 and 1 in Scheme would be (+ 1 1). The best way to read the Fibonacci function written in Scheme below might be by comparing each of its lines to the equivalent line in Dart.

Listing 17-4. fib.scm

```
(define (fib n)
    (if (<n 2)
        n
        (+ (fib (- n 1)) (fib (- n 2)))))
```

The classic text on Scheme is *Structure and Interpretation of Computer Programs*, Second Edition, by Harold Abelson and Gerald Jay Sussman, with Julie Sussman (MIT Press, 1996). It is available for free online at http://mitpress.mit.edu/sicp/. You can, of course, also buy a print edition. The text has been in continuous use in introductory programming courses at the university level for multiple decades.

Learn How to Set Up a Web Server

Whether you're doing client-side or server-side development, you need a web server on which to put your programs. There are countless companies ready to charge you a small fee and do this for you, but it might be smart to learn how to do it yourself. Setting up a web server doesn't involve any programming—just a lot of jargon, managing esoteric configuration files, and reading documentation.

You can rent space on a remote server with which to set up your web server through something like Amazon EC2, or you can just use your personal computer. The latter is a good choice when you're just playing around. Your operating system may very well come with a built-in web server that you can turn on, as most PC operating systems do. It may not be especially configurable, but it will work for testing client-side Dart pages. If you want to learn something a bit more heavyweight, the most popular web server available, Apache, is easy to acquire for free from http://httpd.apache.org.

Whether you work with Apache, nginx (nginx.org), Microsoft IIS, or any of the other myriad of web servers, you will likely find its configuration archaic. It's not especially hard to get these pieces of software serving simple sites. However, doing anything sophisticated with them requires obscure know-how. There are tutorials and books, but serving web pages two decades post–web inception shouldn't be this hard, right? That's why so many people are willing to pay others to do it for them.

That's really the point. Web servers are hard to configure for sophisticated tasks, which is why learning how to manipulate them is a valuable skill that may aid you with some of your programming projects. In larger companies, people are hired to do this sort of work; it's called system administration. A new field, called DevOps, is at the intersection of software development and system administration.

DevOps engineers work to make developing and deploying software a seamless process for a company's programmers. You might be able to figure out how to get your app deployed on a web server running on your PC, but how do you make it scalable, so that it can handle millions of users? DevOps is an evolving field.

Learn Web Design

As was painfully obvious from the appearance of some of the examples in this book, it is not a book on web design. You know how to program, but that doesn't mean you know how to make your programs look pretty/professional/ intuitive. But, design is not just about how something looks; it's also about how it works. How do you design a user interface that's easy to use and natural?

There was once a time when the Web was young that web designers were charging as much money as software developers. A person whose occupation is "web designer" is not necessarily responsible for doing any actual programming. The general public doesn't usually understand that HTML and CSS are not actually programming languages.

Nevertheless, good web design is critical if you want to create a successful web app. You can be the best programmer in the world, but if your interface seems like it was designed by an amateur, nobody will use it. You can get a long way with templates. If what you're designing doesn't need to be original, then templates might be all that you require.

Whether you use templates or code yourself, you'll need an intimate knowledge of HTML and CSS to really do professional-level web design. The resources in Appendix D can help, but really more than anything else, it's time and dedication that will help you learn—just like with learning programming. Unfortunately, HTML and CSS, as you may have noticed, are a bit less structured and more finicky than they really should be, considering how much of the world's document display they power. Which is why you should consider using a CSS framework or design tool, as we will discuss soon.

A good book on design principles, especially relevant to the Web, is *Don't Make Me Think, Revisited: A Common Sense Approach to Web Usability*, Third Edition, by Steve Krug (New Riders, 2014). There is a certain je ne sais quoi that great designers possess, and not everyone can be a great web designer. Perhaps it's taste. Again, there are always templates...

Learn a WYSIWYG Web Design Tool

You're going to need to know some HTML and CSS, even if you go this route, but a WYSIWYG tool can really help those with limited HTML skills be productive in web design. The 800-pound gorilla among WYSIWYG web design tools is Adobe Dreamweaver. It's expensive. As part of the Adobe Creative Cloud, it can easily cost hundreds of dollars annually to get access to. There are educational and other discounts available. There are other tools, too, but no other single package that has gained as much traction as Dreamweaver.

Learn a Graphics Package

As you may have noticed, building web apps often involves working with a lot of little graphics. Becoming good with an illustration/image manipulation program is a great 21st century skill, even apart from web design. Adobe Photoshop is the de facto industry standard. Like Adobe Dreamweaver, it's expensive and can easily run to hundreds of dollars a year, at the regular subscription price. Another category of graphics programs is vector illustration editors.

These programs deal with geometric primitives for creating scalable pictures that look great at any resolution. Once again, Adobe dominates the space with Adobe Illustrator. Here are a few alternatives for various platforms that are less expensive (and, unfortunately, a bit less capable) than Adobe's offerings and still highly recommendable:

- *Paint.net* (Windows, free): A general purpose image editor. Not to be confused with the program *Paint* that used to come bundled with Windows. `www.getpaint.net`

- *Pixelmator* (OS X, commercial): An inexpensive but elegant general-purpose editor. `www.pixelmator.com`

- *GIMP* (Linux & cross-platform, free): The Swiss army knife image editor of the open source world. `www.gimp.org`

- *Inkscape* (Cross-platform, free): Arguably the best open source vector graphics illustration program. `http://inkscape.org`

- *iDraw* (OS X, commercial): An inexpensive but feature-rich vector graphics program for OS X and iPad. `www.indeeo.com/idraw/`

Learn a CSS Framework

Of all the things you can learn to make your Dart web projects look better, perhaps none will pay off more than learning a CSS framework. A CSS framework is a library of predefined CSS styles that attempts to make improving the layout and look of your web pages easier. A good CSS framework will make standard HTML tags look modern and congruent with one another by default. Just dropping a CSS framework into your web app can have some instantaneous benefits.

Do you need your web app to look as good on mobile devices as it does on personal computers out of the box? That's known as *responsive* design. Designs that respond and adjust to being executed on a different device are responsive. A CSS framework will take a lot of the guesswork out of making your design responsive. Most CSS frameworks are responsive out of the box.

Many CSS frameworks have emerged, but the only one that's become a bit of a meme on the Internet is *Bootstrap*. Bootstrap was originally created by the folks at Twitter. It's easy to use, easy to deploy, and very full-featured. Without even learning Bootstrap, your app will look better if you just *use* Bootstrap.

Bootstrap will not only help you with how the individual HTML elements in your app look, it will also help you with layout. Bootstrap sees web pages as being on a grid. You define where the rows of the grid begin and end and which column of the grid each HTML element goes into.

In the early days of the Web, HTML was laid out using tables. Then layout became a matter of a lot of custom <div> elements. Today, a good CSS framework handles this for you. Bootstrap and other CSS frameworks are available freely through commercial content delivery networks (CDNs). A CDN puts the resource you're requesting on a server geographically close to your users. This improves the speed of delivery and also relieves your server of the bandwidth of transferring the CSS framework.

To learn more about using Bootstrap and responsive HTML/CSS in general, you can check out the Apress title *Beginning Responsive Web Design with HTML5 and CSS,* by Jonathan Fielding (2014). You can also learn much of Bootstrap through its very good documentation at `http://getbootstrap.com`.

Get Involved with the Dart Community

Dart has a vibrant online community filled with helpful people. The two places this is most evident are on the official Dart mailing list *Dart Misc,* available in Google Groups at `https://groups.google.com/a/dartlang.org/forum/?fromgroups#!forum/misc` and on the Google+ community Dartisans. Both are open groups in which a mixture of beginners, advanced developers, and Google employees discuss Dart and help each other out with issues.

Dartisans is on the Web at `https://plus.google.com/communities/114566943291919232850`. Here are some other ways that you can get involved with Dart online (some of which you've already encountered in this book):

- Contribute to an open source Dart project on GitHub (or start one)

- Answer or ask Dart questions on Stack Overflow

- Subscribe to blogs about Dart (or write one)

- Contribute Dart programs you're proud of to `builtwithdart.com`

- Experiment with some of the alternative Dart IDEs like Spark and the JetBrains IDE WebStorm, which has a Dart plug-in (`www.dartlang.org/tools/webstorm/`) available for it. Then provide your feedback to the developers.

- Report Dart and Dart Editor bugs you come across at `https://code.google.com/p/dart/issues/entry`.

- Follow Google's Dart Team on Twitter at `@dart_Lang`.

Get in Touch with the Author

Do you have comments or questions regarding *Dart for Absolute Beginners*? You can reach the author via Twitter @davekopec or by e-mail at dartbook@oaksnow.com. Please submit any errors you may have found through the Errata section of the *Dart for Absolute Beginners* product page on Apress's web site at `www.apress.com/9781430264811`.

Summary

Your next steps are up to you. You're ready to strike out on your own and build upon the foundation that *Dart for Absolute Beginners* has laid. Good luck and best wishes!

CHAPTER 18

∎∎∎

Interview with Dart's Creators

Lars Bak and Kasper Lund, two world-renowned Danish computer scientists, created the Dart programming language in 2011 while employed by Google. Before starting the Dart project, they created Google's V8 JavaScript engine. In late February 2014, they sat down for an interview to discuss the creation of Dart, its intent, and their perspective on its use as a first programming language. They were affable, entertaining, and possessed the ability to break down complex topics in a way that all readers will be able to appreciate. Of course, it goes without saying that a project as large as Dart is a team effort. Although Lars and Kasper started the project and continue to lead it, there are many pivotal players on the Google team.

Lars Bak has been working on cutting-edge virtual machines for nearly three decades. He was the technical lead of the HotSpot Java virtual machine while at Sun Microsystems in the 1990s. In the 2000s, while at Google, he worked on the Chrome web browser project and led the development of V8, its high-performance JavaScript engine. He holds 18 US software patents. Bak received an M.S. in computer science from Aarhus University in 1988.

Kasper Lund began his career at Sun Microsystems, where he worked on a Java virtual machine for cell phones (CLDC HI). He cofounded OOVM A/S, a virtual machine company, before moving on to Google, where he was a key player on the V8 team. Lund received an M.S. in computer science from Aarhus University in 2003.

Interview with Lars Bak and Kasper Lund

February 26, 2014

Part 1. Dart's Formulation and Intent

David Kopec: *I think the readers would be interested to learn a little bit about your backgrounds. What led up to Dart? So, please tell us about your careers right before Dart and how it all got started for the two of you.*

Lars Bak: I've been creating virtual machines for dynamic languages since '86, and I started working with Kasper in the year 2000, after we met at Aarhus University. I had just returned to Denmark after nine years in the US, and I was interested in designing a fast Java virtual machine for mobile phones. So, our first project together was for Sun Microsystems, initially just as a two-person team. When that product launched, we left and founded a startup company that built a Smalltalk platform for embedded devices. Two years later, we sold the company, and in 2006, we joined Google. The first task at Google was to design and implement V8 [Chrome's JavaScript engine]. We simply wanted to make web applications faster, in order to boost application innovation. V8 had a positive impact on the browser industry. To my mind, it enticed the industry to invest in faster JavaScript systems. I think we're all benefiting from that now.

JavaScript is not very structured, so it was a challenge to make it run fast. While building V8, we had to come up with several interesting implementation tricks to make it run fast. On the other hand, it was also frustrating to see that web-application developers were struggling with the lack of structure in JavaScript.

Kasper Lund: We saw people get a lot of power out of V8 and having faster JavaScript engines, in general, and we saw them building pretty amazing things on top of them. And you still see that today—people are building some pretty amazing things for the Web. But it's really, really hard to do it. And people are investing lots of time and talent in trying to build something great on top of these engines, because they're really hard to control. So even though the foundation is a lot faster than it was, it's still really hard to make use of it. So, we decided to change the game a little bit.

Lars Bak: We also saw that large applications written in JavaScript were very hard to maintain. Everything in JavaScript is dynamic, so it is hard to see a program's structure. Just setting up the application involves executing JavaScript code. Because of that, several companies came up with tools on top of JavaScript to make applications more maintainable. At Google, we developed the Closure Compiler, where type annotations can be placed in comments.

David Kopec: *Great, thank you. Let's go back to 2011 a little bit. What was going on at Google at the time that led to the creation of Dart? What was the impetus at the company for creating Dart?*

Lars Bak: Both Kasper and I were basically partied out on JavaScript. We took one quarter off and basically hacked out a new language, a library, and a virtual machine in three months. The programming language was called Spot, and that was basically an attempt to make a small, consistent, but structured programming language. The result was very appealing, in that it looked great, and it had the properties we were looking for—class-based model, Smalltalk-based object model—and it seemed right for maintainability of large applications. Is that right, Kasper?

Kasper Lund: Yeah, so it was very simple and in many ways, a boiled-down attempt at something that would really make programming for the Web a lot simpler and a lot more structured. We prototyped that and built something in a quarter. It turned out to be good enough that we could sell the idea of trying out something a little more radical in the web space. Google lives off the Web in a sense. So making the Web more attractive for developers fits right in.

Lars Bak: It was a blast, by the way. It was so refreshing to start from scratch and do something new. The outcome of that was basically the proposal for the Dart project. We had the benefit of sitting in Denmark, fairly far away from the Google headquarters. The starting point was Spot, but the idea was to make sure we made a system that was compatible with the existing Web. We could not take Spot as-is, because it was not translatable to JavaScript. We did not have a complete language design, but we had sort of an idea of what we wanted. We didn't really know if we wanted parameterized types or not. And we were unsure how we could proceed and ensure it was efficient on top of JavaScript. So it was a very interesting process to refine the language and make sure we could translate it to JavaScript and at the same time ensure the virtual machine was fast.

David Kopec: *And how did what the two of you learned from V8 inform the design of Dart? What lessons did you take out of V8?*

Kasper Lund: So, there were a bunch of different lessons. In many ways, you could say that the positive lessons include that you can make a fairly dynamic system run very efficiently, as long as people write in a structured way. Dart demonstrates that you can go even further than you can go with JavaScript. But at the core of it, it's two dynamic systems. One is a little more structured than the other, and you can make them run pretty fast. That's the positive takeaway.

Lars Bak: Another great thing about JavaScript and the Web is that you have instant gratification. You can experiment with code and then run it without having a compile step in between. That allows programmers to do rapid prototyping. And this is also the main reason why we have gradual typing in Dart. You can start programming without using types and then add them later as your code matures.

Kasper Lund: And there's something very powerful about being able to write code in a text editor and just refresh your browser and it just runs. And we wanted to preserve that, definitely. I think one of the negative lessons is that complexity at the core of a VM is very, very painful, not just for the developers of the VM, but also for people trying to build apps on top of it. Even a sophisticated system like V8 has lots and lots of corner cases where things behave differently or perform differently from how people expect. So, we really wanted to make sure that the design of Dart allowed us to not have these weird pitfalls and hidden trapdoors that lock people in a corner and don't allow them to escape from it.

Lars Bak: I think by design JavaScript has been created so that the application will continue, despite how [poorly] the code is written. For example, if you access a property, and it's not there, you just get *undefined* back. If you set a property, and the property is not there, you'll create a new property. In certain cases, that's good; on the other hand, if you have spelling errors in property names, the code will still run without exposing the error. We prefer programming errors to be [matched] at runtime by exceptions. Another interesting and powerful feature in JavaScript is eval(), where you can take any string and turn it into code and run it. As you can imagine, this turns out to be a security problem. This also prevents you from performing code tree shaking, since all the code can potentially be used. In Dart, we don't allow eval() and on-the-fly code patching. This gives us the option to do whole program analysis and perform tree shaking.

David Kopec: *Denmark has a great tradition of computer science. I know both of you are graduates of Aarhus University, as is Bjarne Stroustrup, the creator of C++. Is there anything in that tradition that made its way into Dart?*

Lars Bak: Only the constructors in Dart have partially been inspired by C++. You're right, though. Aarhus University has a background of language design. We both had the same professor at Aarhus University, Ole Lehrmann Madsen, who has been doing language design for many years—notably for the BETA programming language—and certainly, some of the type parts of Dart have been inspired by that. BETA is a successor to Simula 67, so [it is] also a very classic object-oriented language.

Kasper Lund: I think Lars's comment about the type system is spot on. The object-oriented nature of Dart and the way we deal with covariance and contravariance in the type system—those things are certainly inspired and somewhat based on ideas that come from BETA, which is a language mostly developed at Aarhus.

David Kopec: *A lot of readers will have heard of languages like Ruby and Python and other dynamic languages. You chose this interesting [paradigm of] optional typing [for Dart]. I'm wondering how the lessons of the popular dynamic languages of the past decade or so have informed the decision to go with optional typing?*

Kasper Lund: One thing that's interesting is that when you look at the documentation for the core APIs of those languages, it's actually not trivial to follow. What are you supposed to do with these methods? What are you supposed to pass in? There's a lot of text that goes with these methods to describe what you're supposed to do with them. In many ways, that's text that a tool cannot really use to help you understand the APIs and deal with them. So, I think having optional types is one of the really big strengths of Dart—it gives you the ability to document your interfaces and your APIs in a much better way than you could without them.

Lars Bak: Types help state the intent of a library by annotating the interfaces. If you have several teams working on the same project, static types really help catch errors on the library boundaries. In the mid-'90s, I worked on a language called Strongtalk, a Smalltalk system with optional static typing. It is great to have untyped code when you do prototyping and then switch to typed code when you harden the application structure. I cannot comment on Ruby and Python, since we do not have much experience using those languages.

Kasper Lund: What you see with those languages is that it's fairly common for people to start having some sort of notion of typing anyway; they try to give their methods or parameters certain names to indicate what you're supposed to pass in there. So, they're trying to sort of include some typing in there to make it easier to understand what's supposed to be going on. And in a sense, having a real type system that's optional, so you can use it the way you want to and in a way that makes sense to you, is just an improvement over that.

Lars Bak: One thing I would like to say is that we tried very hard to not make Dart an advanced programming language. Hopefully, when you look at Dart code, you know exactly what you're getting. I believe this kind of immediacy is great for learning a new programming language. I've always had a problem with programming languages, like Java, where some constructs are syntactic sugar. This makes it hard for the programmer to understand what is executed and even harder to debug the code. We're taking the other approach with Dart. It's sort of like C, where if you see a line in Dart, you know how it will be executed on the machine. That will help give the knowledgeable programmer control over the system much faster, because they know what's going on.

David Kopec: *Is there anything we've missed regarding influences on Dart?*

Lars Bak: Both Kasper and I have spent a lot of time optimizing virtual machines. In designing this language, we've been very careful in making sure all the language constructs can be implemented efficiently. Usually, the standard way of designing a programming language is to design it first and then implement it afterward. But we decided early on to do the implementation along with the programming language design. I think that has helped us already with the first release of Dart. We could show fairly decent performance numbers running on top of the Dart VM.

Kasper Lund: I think one thing that many people may not realize is that the way we do objects in Dart is heavily inspired by Smalltalk—a language that most people probably don't know today. But if you go back and look at a simple, nice object-oriented language like Smalltalk, you will find some of our inspiration for how to create an object system that's easy to reason about.

David Kopec: *Lars, why don't you think Strongtalk succeeded [commercially] as a language (Lars worked on Strongtalk)?*

Lars Bak: There are two parts to it. One is that when you take a programming system like Strongtalk and also previous Smalltalk systems, they were designed as an all-inclusive system—the programming environment along with the runtime. So, when you start it up, you have the programming environment and the code of your application in the same space. That is very complicated for most programmers to understand. I think it works well for universities and people who really like to understand the entire system. But it's really complex to understand what an application is and how you extract it from such an environment and then run it afterward. So, that's one part. The other part is, like it or not, the syntax of Smalltalk is just not for most people. You don't have a class syntax, you have a method syntax, and the rest is in the graphical environment. We knew when we started Dart that without curly brace syntax, we'd go nowhere. So, we had to be very conservative. I think the Smalltalk environment around the program was a problem, and also its syntax. But the object model and simplicity were actually great.

Part 2. Dart As a First Programming Language

David Kopec: *What makes Dart a great first language?*

Kasper Lund: I think a big part of what makes Dart a great first language is that it has plain and simple semantics. If you look at the code, you have a very good idea of what's going on. There are few surprises in there. And the other thing is that it's relatively ceremony-free. The first program you write can literally be a one-liner that will do something for you. You don't have to throw weird incantations at the compiler to make it run. In that way, it's very simple. I think the tool chain supports it well too: you don't have to compile to anything; you can actually just run it straight away. So, those things combined give you a very gentle way of getting started and getting something up and running. And I think that's truly important when you're talking about absolute beginners of any kind of language.

Lars Bak: Certainly, writing small programs and getting them to work is important. But you can do that in many languages. I think that at least, when you contrast it to JavaScript, that it's very easy to reason about and see what's going on. We should not forget that it's really object-oriented with classes, whereas JavaScript is not. So, when you try to model stuff in JavaScript, you often get confused, because you have to set up the inheritance structure by manipulating prototypes. I've been in the object-oriented world since '84. I think that class-based modeling is easy to understand for people. Classes create descriptions, and at runtime, you can make instances of them. I find this very intuitive. One feature we have added to Dart to make it a great first programming language is factory constructors. So, for instance, if you want to create a `List`, you say `new List`, and you'll get one. `List` is an interface, but the factory [constructor] will return an instance of the default `List` implementation. You only have to understand an abstract interface. If you take Java, you need to specify the concrete class you want to instantiate. This means you only have to know a few basics before you are up and running.

Kasper Lund: When it comes to the core libraries, Dart is more lightweight and flexible than something like Java, where you have to be very explicit about everything, and you have to mention the concrete class you want to instantiate everywhere. But at the same time, Dart is more complete and feature-rich than something like JavaScript, which basically has no core library. In JavaScript, you're sort of on your own. There's very little built-in functionality. So, that means that whenever you look at someone else's JavaScript code, they'll probably be using things in a very different way. There's little or no consensus on how to do things. In Dart, we do have a set of core libraries that's well-structured and well-defined. It's not huge, but it's there, and it gives a good common ground for all libraries. It's easy to see what a library is doing just by looking at the types and understanding how Lists, Maps, etc. work together. So, I think that makes it a lot easier to understand than something like JavaScript, where you basically have arrays and objects that are sort of the same thing but not really. It's very confusing—in particular, to new programmers.

Lars Bak: Another tiny example: we don't do the same kind of implicit conversion as in JavaScript. Dart does not implicitly convert a string into an integer and an integer into a boolean. All this simplicity will help a novice programmer understand what's going on.

David Kopec: *What elements of Dart do you think a new programmer will struggle with? Maybe there's an element that's actually more difficult than in another language. Is there anything that you can think of? And, how should programmers work on getting over their struggle with that part of the language?*

Lars Bak: The constructor syntax might, at first, seem complicated. We decided to split a constructor into an initialization part and a body part. There are good reasons for this. You get clean semantics and a guarantee that no instance method is called until all fields have been initialized. In Dart, often the body part is not used.

Kasper Lund: I think one area a lot of people will struggle with if they're absolute beginners will be closures and async programming based on closures. It's not a Dart-only problem. It's a problem for any language that has an asynchronous programming model built into it, where closures are the way you model these things. It's a little bit hard to wrap your head around. For simple cases like a simple event listener, it's not that bad, but it can get fairly complicated to build even simple things in an asynchronous way. I think that's an area where lots of people will struggle a little bit with how that all fits together. It's built on simple building blocks, but it's still hard to reason about.

Lars Bak: That's true, Kasper, but you have to say that Dart closures are well-defined, right? They actually capture the right context.

Kasper Lund: Yes, closures are way better defined in Dart than they are in, say, JavaScript. How they're bound and how references to "this" inside a closure always resolves to the right thing will make it much easier to get by, and it will let you focus on the closure-based control-flow issues, instead of the nitty-gritty details of how they fight for variables. I think we have taken care of that part for you. It's very sane and simple. The beginner can focus on the truly hard part, which is understanding the asynchronous programming model.

Lars Bak: We're forced to do that in Dart [the asynchronous programming model], because we have to translate to JavaScript, and we have to run inside the browser. (There's nothing we can do about that.) Real parallelism is just not possible.

One thing I'd like to mention about the simplicity of the language is that you should look at what we didn't put into Dart [laughs]. People were initially complaining that we didn't have advanced language constructs. But that was on purpose! We didn't want to make a complicated language. Some wanted tail calls in the language; others wanted non-local returns. We simply decided that such features would just make it harder for novice programmers to understand. We've been really conservative and tried not to invent new things. We went for the rule that inexperienced programmers should be relatively productive in Dart within an hour or two.

David Kopec: *Do you have any advice for someone who's learning Dart as a first programming language? Maybe going back to when you were first learning how to program. Obviously, you guys eventually became master programmers. What kind of nontechnical strategies should somebody be using, in terms of their study, to become a great programmer?*

Kasper Lund: Run your stuff often!

Lars Bak: I'll try to comment on what Kasper said. The best way to become a good programmer is to understand what's going on when you execute the program. When I started programming, debugging was absolutely impossible for the platforms I was using. You had to rely on print statements. I think with the systems we have today, that have immediacy, you can [better] understand what's going on. That makes it much easier to become a good programmer than in the old days. You become a great programmer when you understand how programs execute on the underlying platform. Understanding the basic complexity is important, but so is understanding performance. We tried with Dart to make performance predictable, so the programmer is comfortable using the platform.

Kasper Lund: It's sort of a technical piece of advice, but learn to love your debugger. Use it even when your code works—step through your code and figure out what it does. I think that's actually very good advice. Lots of people don't really do that. They would rather run their program through to completion and see what it printed and then scratch their heads while they try to reason about what actually happened. Stepping into the debugger to see what's happening when your code runs is actually very powerful.

Lars Bak: Again, system tools are very important. An example is an execution time profiler. Most people think they know where time is spent in a program. However, I have yet to meet someone who can predict it. So, unless you run a profiler on your program and see where the time goes, you most likely have no clue. I think the exercise of profiling a program, tuning it, making it fast, and so on, is one of the things that will also make you a better programmer. In the process of making the virtual machines that we've done over the years, profiling is pretty much what we do all day long.

Kasper Lund: It's good fun.

David Kopec: *What was your first programming language?*

Kasper Lund: I started with BASIC.

Lars Bak: Yeah, I also tried a bit of BASIC. But it was first at university that I really started to program. My first real programming language was a homebred programming language from Aarhus University that was called AKA, a static programming language with recursive types. I sometimes get asked whether I would have become a better programmer if I had started early. I think that really depends on the person. For me, it worked out OK.

Kasper Lund: One thing I think is a strength of the education in Aarhus, when it comes to computer science, is that you're exposed to many different languages. I don't know any programmer on our team who's afraid of diving into different languages. So people feel free to change and pick the right tool for a given task. I think that using many different languages gives you a good feel for what a language actually is and how it works. You're not tied down to just being able to use one language and one library. I think that's very helpful. Some people are very married to their technologies. Over time, that might not be the best career move.

Lars Bak: I think in both Kasper and my case, we've been doing many different projects. Starting new projects is great, and it introduces you to many programming languages and platforms.

David Kopec: *But don't walk away from Dart too soon [laughs]. Now, after readers have gone through* Dart for Absolute Beginners *and they've become proficient with Dart, what should they do next? What's an advanced concept with Dart that they should take on, now that they're proficient in the basics, that will help them the most either with their career or with their hobby as a programmer?*

Lars Bak: In order to become very efficient, the programmer should start participating in the community and pick up Dart pub packages that have been written, experiment with them, and write new apps. If they can improve the existing packages, [they should] make contributions back to the community. We haven't talked about these packages, but in essence, they are libraries that can be shared by the community and improved over time. When this book is out, you will see that we have pushed Dart both on the client-side and the server-side. Ideally, people should try to write end-to-end applications in Dart where it makes sense. I hope this will create a very good end-to-end experience.

Kasper Lund: I recommend finding someone to hack with. It's relatively easy today to find people to collaborate with, over the Internet. Usually, people learn things on their own; they buy a book and try to get better at it. Once they know the basics, it's a good time to try to build something with someone else—through contributing to pub packages, submitting pull requests, through Github, whatever. But getting that experience with building something that others are participating in as well is very good. Realizing that someone else has to work with your code makes you a better programmer. For me, that's the logical step, after learning the basics, on the path from being a nonprogrammer to being a programmer.

Lars Bak: One thing—this might be a little bit out of context—is we didn't talk about why we're doing this, why we're doing Dart at Google.

David Kopec: Yeah, I was trying to get at that at the beginning, but I feel like there really hasn't been enough said about it.

Lars Bak: I just want to say there's been a lot of speculation about why we're doing Dart. Our only goal at Google is to make programmers more efficient, so we can innovate on the Web. And that's very simple, and it's a cool, cool goal to work toward, that is, to make sure programmers are more efficient when programming in Dart compared to other systems. And we hope we can succeed.

Kasper Lund: Yeah, we definitely want to bring more programmers to the Web and have them be productive writing apps for the Web. That's a big part of our goal.

Lars Bak: At the same time, if we don't innovate, we will fail. When people are talking about [how] you can only use one language or one platform, that's rubbish. What you actually want is a toolbox of technologies, so you can pick the tool from the toolbox that is most efficient for the task. You shouldn't be afraid of using different technologies. So, we hope that Dart is one of those tools that will make programming more productive. Already now, we get positive feedback on the productivity [that comes with] using Dart. So, we're halfway there.

David Kopec: *If Dart is a great first language, what's a great second language?*

Kasper Lund: I think it depends on what you're doing. In the web space, Dart is a great first and second language. On the server-side, that's probably true too. There are other, more exotic languages—perhaps purely functional ones—that may change how you see things a little bit, that might be fun to try out. A lot of the more exotic languages are not necessarily languages that a lot of people will be comfortable writing huge apps in, but they might change your perception a little bit. Like logic programming. Things that are more out there, let's say, in many ways.

Lars Bak: Selecting a programming language is hard, and it is often based on several factors: the task at hand, ease of use, set of available libraries, and whether the programmer likes the language or not. For me, experimenting with a simple scalable parallel programming language will be next on the list.[1]

David Kopec: *Kasper and Lars, I want to thank you so much for taking this time out of your busy schedules. Are there any last words you have for our beginning programmers who are just starting out with Dart?*

Kasper Lund: Have fun.

Lars Bak: We hope that the programmers reading your book and trying out the samples will feel empowered by using Dart.

---

[1]For the interested reader, two such programming languages are Erlang and Google's own Go.

■ ■ ■

Dart Cheat Sheet

This appendix is by no means meant to be a comprehensive Dart reference. Nor is it an exhaustive review of every language feature covered in the book. Instead, it is meant to be a quick-reference guide to the core language and some of the most commonly used classes in the standard library. If you've read the whole book, you will have seen all of this material before. If the material of a particular section is covered wholly in a chapter or two, then those chapters are listed in parentheses after the topic. The purpose of this appendix is to quickly give you an example of how something may appear syntactically. It is not meant to explain "why." For that, you'll have to read the book! There is no new material in this appendix. All of the content has been covered in the main text in far greater depth.

The Basics

Dart's basic syntax is straightforward, consistent, and similar to that of other popular languages, such as C, JavaScript, Java, and C#.

Declaring and Initializing Variables (Chapter 3)

Variables are declared in Dart optionally using types.

```
var m;   // no type specified
int n;   // n is specified as an int
```

When they are declared, variables can also be initialized.

```
var m = 4;
int n = 5;
```

Multiple variables of the same type can be declared at once.

```
int n = 5, o = 88, p;  // p is not initialized with a value
```

The new operator is used for initializing a new instance of a class. After a class is initialized, its constructor is immediately called. Parameters to the constructor are passed at initialization time.

```
Point p = new Point(24, 36);
```

Literals (Chapter 3, Chapter 6)

Literals are used for creating objects, based on specific predetermined values. Literal syntax exists for Dart's core built-in types (see Table A-1).

Table A-1. *Fundamental Dart Types That Can Be Created with Literals*

Type	Description	Example Literals
int	Integers	5, -20, 0
double	Floating-Point Numbers	3.14159, -3.2, 0.00
String	Strings	"hello", "g", "To be or not to be?"
bool	Booleans	true, false
List	Lists (Chapter 6)	[1,2,3], ["hi", "bye"]
Map	Maps (Chapter 6)	{"x": 5, "y":2}

Common Operators

Dart's built-in operators provide the backbone of the language (see Tables A-2, A-3, and A-4). There are more operators than those covered here, but these are the ones that were examined in this book. Dart also allows operator overloading, in which operator behavior for a particular class is specified (see Chapter 12).

Table A-2. *Arithmetic Operators*

Operator	Description	Example
++	Increment integer by 1	x++; ++x;
--	Decrement integer by 1	x--; --x;
+=	Increment integer by arbitrary amount	x += 34; // increment x by 34
*	Multiplication	x = y * 5;
/	Division	x = 6 / 3;
~/	Integer Division	x = 6 ~/ 4; // x is 1
+	Addition	x = y + 2;
-	Subtraction	x = 20 - 4;
%	Remainder (modulo)	x = 6 % 4; // x is 2

Table A-3. *Operators That Return Boolean Values*

Operator	Description	Example
==	Equal to	if (x == y) {...}
!=	Not equal to	if (x != y) {...}
>	Greater than	if (x > y) {...}
<	Less than	if (x < y) {...}
>=	Greater than or equal to	if (x >=y) {...}
<=	Less than or equal to	if (x <= y) {...}
!	Not	if (!x) {...}
||	Logical Or	if (x || y) {...}
&&	Logical And	if (x && y) {...}
is	Check the type of an object	if (x is Element) {...}

Table A-4. *Other Operators*

Operator	Description	Example
.	Access variables/properties and call methods on objects	y = x.children; x.executeTimely();
..	Cascade operator –lets you make multiple calls on the same object	x = new Car() ..resetOdometer() ..paintRed() ..oilLife = 100.0;
+	String concatenation (when used between two String objects)	x = "Hello" + "there!"; // x is "Hello there!"

[]	Index into List objects or Map objects	x[2] = 34; // sets element 2 of a List, x, to 34
		y["gallons"] = 34; // sets the value associated
		with the key "gallons" in a Map, y, to 34.

()	Call function	myFunction();
=	Assignment operator	x = 5;
as	Cast an object from one type to another	(x as ImageElement).src = "...";
?	Conditional operator—if the statement is true then returns first alternative; otherwise, second	hot = (temp > 75) ? true : false;

Control Structures (Chapter 3)

`if`-statements are used for branching, based on the validity of a particular condition.

```
if (j > 5) { // execute following lines if statement in () is true
...
} else if (j < 2) {  // if first statement was false and this statement is true then:
...
} else {  // executed only if all other statements were false
...
}
```

`switch`-statements are convenient when branching correctly would require many `else-if`-statements.

```
switch (x) {
  case 5:
    ...
    break;
  case 6:
    ...
    break;
  default:
    ...
    break;
}
```

The `?` operator is similar in concept to a very short `if`-statement. If the statement before the `?` evaluates to `true`, then the first statement after it is evaluated. Otherwise, the second statement after it (the two statements are divided by a `:`) is evaluated.

```
String casualPants = (temp > 75) ? "shorts" : "jeans";
```

Loops (Chapter 3, Chapter 6)

`for`-loops are probably the most commonly used loops. They are declared with a setup step; conditional step; and step to be completed on each loop iteration (`for (setup step; conditional step; iteration step)`). The setup step is run before the loop's first iteration. The conditional step is executed once at the beginning of each iteration. The last step is executed after each loop iteration. The loop continues to iterate until the conditional step is false.

```
for (int i = 0; i < 10; i++) {...}
for (Cell cell = new Cell(); cell.color != blue; cell.blink()) {...}
```

`while`-loops keep executing until a condition is no longer true. A `do-while`-loop is like a `while`-loop, except its condition is evaluated after each iteration, instead of before.

```
while (x < 5) {...}
do {...} while (x < 5);
```

for-in-loops are used for going through the contents of an Iterable. All of the collection classes that come with the Dart SDK implement Iterable.

```
List j = [1, 5, 9];
for (int x in j) {
  print(x);  // will print 1 then 5 then 9
}
```

Numbers

int is the class of integers, and double is the class for floating-point numbers. Both int and double are subclasses of num. Both int and double provide static parse() methods for intepreting String objects as their respective type of numbers. They usually should be wrapped with exception handling code, in case something goes wrong, such as a FormatException.

```
String inTemp;
double userAnswer;
inTemp = stdin.readLineSync();
try {
  userAnswer = double.parse(inTemp);
} on FormatException {  // uh oh, could not be turned into double
  print("Could not interpret input.");
  return;
}
```

A literal number is determined as an int or double, based on the presence of a decimal point.

Strings

Strings are used for representing text. In Dart, strings can contain any character specified in the Unicode specification, which includes non-Latin characters, such as those found in Mandarin or Arabic. Strings are instances of the String class, which has several useful methods for manipulating them. Both double quotes (") and single quotes (') can be used for specifying String literals. Pick one or the other style and stick with it.

"hello" is equivalent to 'hello'.

Variable values can be interpolated within String literals, using $ for single variables and ${} for the result of an expression.

```
String weather = "It's $temperature degrees and cloudy.";
String countdown = "It's ${2069 - year} years from the big anniversary.";
```

The String method split() divides a String by some character and returns a List.

```
List fruits = "apple,cherry,orange".split(",");  // fruits is ["apple", "cherry", "orange"]
```

The trim() method removes whitespace on the edges of a String, and the toLowerCase() and toUpperCase() methods are often useful when comparing one String to another. The + operator can be used for concatenating one String to the end of another String.

```
String fullName = "John" + " " + "Smith";  // fullName will be "John Smith"
```

Constants and Final Variables

The keyword const is used to specify that a variable's value will not be changed after its initial declaration/initialization. In other words, the value is wholly known at compile time, as opposed to runtime.

```
const WHEELS_ON_CAR = 4;
const List MY_FAVORITE_FLAVORS = const ["Apple", "Orange", "Grape"];
```

It is illegal to modify a constant after it has been declared. Constants can be optimized by the compiler. Final variables are immutable. They cannot be changed after they are initialized, although unlike constants, they can be initialized at runtime.

```
final int d = 5;  // d can now not be changed again
```

Giving Programs Structure

In Dart, functions are first-class citizens. Dart has several superb built-in data structures. Dart is fully object-based and has advanced object-oriented constructs. Dart provides ample facilities for giving programs structure.

Functions (Chapter 5)

Functions are defined with a title, parameters (if any), and a body. They can also specify their return type. Dart has special syntactic sugar for short, one-line functions.

```
add(var x, var y) {
  return x + y;  // control ends, value returned as return value
}
int add(int x, int y) {...}  // specifies return type and parameter types
void doSomething() {...}  // no return expected
int z = add(1, 2);  // add() called with arguments 1, 2 for parameters x, y
int luckyNumber() => 7;  // short syntax for single line functions, return is implied
```

Functions can appear within other functions. Anonymous functions are functions without a name.

```
void main() {
  String exclaimIt(String s) => s + "!";  // function within function
  print(exclaimIt("Hey"));
}
```

Optional parameters are parameters that do not need to be provided when a function is called. They are left up to the discretion of the caller. Dart supports both positional and named optional parameters. Optional parameters can have default values.

```
void repeat(String word, [int repetitions = 1, String exclamation = ""]) {
  for (int i = 0; i < repetitions; i++) {
    print(word + exclamation);  // the + operator can concatenate strings
  }
}  // could be called with repeat("Dog", 2, "!");
```

```
void repeat(String word, {int repetitions: 1, String exclamation: ""}) {
  for (int i = 0; i < repetitions; i++) {
    print(word + exclamation);  // the + operator can concatenate strings
  }
}  // could be called with repeat("Dog", repetitions: 2, exclamation: "!");
```

Lists (Chapter 6)

List objects hold ordered, sequential data.

```
List l1 = [];  // a blank List
List l2 = new List();  // also a blank List
List m = [1, 3, 5];  // List created using literal
```

You can index into a List to grab a specific element by its index. List objects are zero-indexed.

```
int v = m[1];  // v is 3
```

The add() method adds an element to the end of a List, while remove() can be used to remove a specific element. Finally, removeLast() gets rid of the last element in a List. List objects can also be declared to contain a specific type with <> syntax.

```
List<String> sList = ["hello", "goodbye"];  // specifying that sList will contain Strings.
sList.add("heya");  // sList is now ["hello", "goodbye", "heya"]
sList.remove("goodbye");
sList.removeLast();  // sList is ["hello"]
```

Maps (Chapter 6)

Map objects associate data (values) with identifiers (keys).

```
Map a = {}; // empty Map
Map c = new Map(); // also an empty Map
Map nameAge = {"Matt": 27, "John": 18, "Sarah": 17, "Larry": 80};
Map employees = {345: {"name": "Donald Smith", "Department": "Accounting", "Salary": 1000},
                 220: {"name": "Mark Anderson", "Department": "Sales", "Salary": 950},
                 572: {"name": "Elizabeth Brahmen", "Department": "Marketing", "Salary": 975}};
```

Values can be looked up or set via their keys, with similar syntax to indexing into a List.

```
Map productPrice = {"Gum": 0.95, "Soda": 1.05, "Chips": 1.99};
double gumPrice = productPrice["Gum"];  //gumPrice is now 0.95
productPrice["Cookie"] = 0.50;  //a new key/value pair added to productPrice
productPrice["Soda"] = gumPrice;  //the value for the key "Soda" is now 0.95
```

As with List objects, Map objects can have their contained types specified at declaration.

```
Map<String, double> productPrice = {"Gum": 0.95, "Soda": 1.05, "Chips": 1.99};
```

Sets (Chapter 6)

Set objects are for storing unique, unordered data. A set cannot contain two identical elements.

```
Set blankSet = new Set();  // empty set
```

As with List objects, Set objects can have their contained types specified at instantiation time.

```
Set<String> jerryColors = new Set.from(["blue", "red", "green"]);
```

Set objects are a convenient way to check for duplicates in a List.

```
bool containsDuplicates(List l) {
  Set s = new Set.from(l);  //create a new Set by converting the List
  if (s.length < l.length) {
    return true;
  }
  return false;
}
```

Defining Classes (Chapter 10, Chapter 11)

Classes are the fundamental building blocks of objects. They describe the methods, instance variables, and properties that a class contains. Class definitions additionally specify the relationship between one class and another. The constructor of a class is a special method that is used for initializing it (see Chapter 10 for some nuance on constructors). A variable or method specified with an underscore (_) is "private" to the library in which the class is defined.

```
class Dice {
  /// Instance Variables
  int _sides = 6;
  int _numberOfDice = 2;
  List<int> _values = [];

  /// Properties
  int get maximumValue => sides * numberOfDice;
  int get numberOfDice => _numberOfDice;
  int get sides => _sides;
  /// total is the sum of [_values]
  int get total => _values.fold(0, (first, second) => first + second);

  /// Constructor
  /// constructs a new Dice object, setting _sides and _numberOfDice
  Dice(this._sides, this._numberOfDice);

  /// Methods
  /// generate random values for [_values]
  void roll() {
    List newValues = [];
    Random rand = new Random();
```

```
  for (int i = 0; i < numberOfDice; i++) {
    newValues.add(rand.nextInt(sides) + 1);  // number from 1 to sides
  }
    _values = newValues;
}

  /// print the values of the dice
  void printDice() => print(_values);
}
```

The abstract keyword is used for defining an abstract class (a class that can't be instantiated and only serves as a superclass of other classes). The extends keyword is used for defining a class as the subclass of another class. Only one class can appear after extends.

```
abstract class Shape {
  double get perimeter;
  double get area;
  String get description;
}

class Circle extends Shape {
  double radius;
  Circle(this.radius);

  double get perimeter => radius * 2 * PI;
  double get area => PI * (radius * radius);
  String get description => "I am a circle with radius $radius";
}
```

Subclasses can refer to their superclass with the keyword super. this refers to the instance of the class currently being worked from within. Classes implicitly define their own interfaces. One class can implement another class's interface, by using the implements keyword. A class can implement multiple interfaces.

```
class A {
  void silly() {
    print("A's Silly");
  }
}

class B {
  void awesome() {
    print("B's Awesome");
  }
}

class C implements A, B {
  void silly() {
    print("C's Silly");
  }
```

```
  void awesome() {
    print("C's Awesome");
  }
}
```

A class can be cast from one class to another, using the as operator.

```
A c = new C();
(c as C).awesome();
```

Classes that have no constructors, are subclasses of Object, and make no calls to super can be used as mixins. Mixins are functionality that is appended to another class. The with keyword is used to declare that a class uses a mixin.

```
class TimeStamp {
  DateTime creationTime = new DateTime.now();
  void printTimeStamp() {
    print(creationTime);
  }
}

class NewBorn extends Patient with TimeStamp {
  NewBorn(String name) : super(name);
}
```

NewBorn now has the printTimeStamp() method.

Libraries (Chapter 10)

Libraries are useful for packaging reusable Dart code. Defining a library compiles all of the files of the library into one package. All of the import statements for the files included in the library are specified in the library declaration. Each file includes part of library_name at its top.

```
library pig;

import "dart:math";  // for Random
import "dart:io";  // for stdin

part "dice.dart";
part "player.dart";
```

In dice.dart, you'll see:

```
part of pig;
```

Key Packages in the Standard Library

Dart comes with an extensive standard library, divided into logical bundled packages.

dart:html (Chapter 8)

dart:html is the library used for manipulating the Document Object Module (DOM). Element is a key class. It is the base class for all of the classes in dart:html that are used to represent elements of an HTML document. querySelector() is a function used for grabbing DOM elements by their CSS class, id attribute, or tag type, based on their CSS selector. For example, a <div> tag with id fish could be grabbed with querySelector("#fish").

There are Element subclasses, such as ImageElement, CanvasElement, ButtonElement, etc., that represent specific HTML tags. Each of these classes has properties that correspond to the specific attributes of the HTML tag in question. In addition, all Element objects also have the methods getAttribute() and setAttribute() to manipulate them.

```
ImageElement ie = (querySelector("#fish_image") as ImageElement);
ie.src = "pike.png";
```

All Element objects have the generic properties text and innerHtml, which represent the string for display contained in an Element and the HTML that represents the tags within it, respectively.

```
DivElement myDiv = new DivElement();
ButtonElement myButton = new ButtonElement();
myDiv.innerHtml = "<strong>My Strong Text</strong>";
myButton.text = "Click Me!";
```

One Element gets added as a child of another, using the append() method.

```
myDiv.append(myButton);
```

Events that occur within the browser to an Element can be captured by adding listeners to various named ElementStream properties of an Element, such as onClick and onKeyDown, that process the events. Listeners are functions that have an object representing the event in question as a parameter.

```
myButton.onClick.listen((MouseEvent me) => ...);
```

Changes to the DOM that are made from a Dart program are implemented in real time by the browser. dart:html also includes extensive support for working with the HTML Canvas element. CanvasElement has a property, context2D, that has numerous methods for drawing graphical primitives to the screen.

```
CanvasRenderingContext2D myCanvasContext = myCanvas.context2D;
myCanvasContext.setFillColorRgb(255,0,0);   // RGB is Red, Green, Blue levels from 0-255 each
myCanvasContext.fillRect(myCanvas.width/2, myCanvas.height/2, 100, 200);   // x, y width, height
```

Quick error messages can be displayed to the screen as dialog boxes, with window.alert().

```
window.alert("Error: invalid input.");
```

Table A-5 shows some common HTML tags/elements and their respective classes in dart:html.

Table A-5. *Common HTML Tags and Their dart:html Element Subclasses*

Tag	Description	dart:html Element
<a>	Anchor (link)	AnchorElement
<div>	Div	DivElement
<span>	Span	SpanElement
<p>	Paragraph	ParagraphElement
<img>	Image	ImageElement
<canvas>	HTML Canvas	CanvasElement
<input>	Input form	InputElement
<ul>	Unordered List	UListElement
<ol>	Ordered List	OListElement
<li>	List Item	LIElement
<button>	Button	ButtonElement

dart:io (Chapter 4, Chapter 14)

Reading input from the command line is easy using stdin.readLineSync().

```
String temp = stdin.readLineSync();  // read in from the keyboard
```

Remember to check that the input is really formatted as you want it, before using it. The File class can be used for reading files in a command-line application.

```
File file = new File("pandp.txt");
file.readAsString().then((String fileContent) => print(fileContent));
```

dart:math

The Random class is useful for generating random numbers, using its methods nextInt() and nextDouble().

```
Random rand = new Random();
int choice = rand.nextInt(3);        // creates random integer between 0 and 2
double choice2 = rand.nextDouble();  // between 0.0 (inclusive) and 1.0 (exclusive)
```

The built-in constant PI represents the special number pi.

```
print(PI);
```

The class Point represents a point on a two-dimensional plane. Every Point object has an x and a y coordinate expressed as properties. The Point class has its +, -, * and == operators overloaded.

```
Point a = new Point(2, 2);
Point b = new Point(4, 4);
b = b - a;
print(b);  // prints Point(2, 2)
```

```
a = a * 2;
print(a);  // prints Point(4, 4)
a = b + a;
print(a);  // prints Point(6, 6);
if ((b + b) == (a - b)) {  // this is true
  print("Both sides of the equation hold equivalent values.");
}
```

Rectangle is a class for representing geometric rectangles. A Rectangle is initialized, based on its top-left corner, width, and height. It has the very useful methods containsPoint() and intersects() to check its relationship with points and other rectangles in the two-dimensional plane.

For comparing numbers, dart:math provides the convenience functions max() and min(), which operate on any two num objects.

unittest (Chapter 13)

unittest does not come prepackaged with the Dart SDK. You need to add it to your pubspec.yaml before using it and import it as import 'package:unittest/unittest.dart';.

The test() function is the core of unittest. It takes a String name for a test and a function defining a test. Calls of expect() within a test define what it means to pass a test.

```
test("exclaim() test", (){
  String original = "I'm testing";
  expect(exclaim(original), equals("I'm testing!"));
});
```

expect() has several matchers like equals(), which is seen above. The first parameter of expect() is the object being tested and the second is the matcher. Table A-6 shows several common matchers.

Table A-6. *Selected Common Matchers in the unittest Library*

Matcher	Parameter Type
isTrue	None
isFalse	None
isNull	None
isNotNull	None
isEmpty	None
equals()	Object
greaterThan()	num
lessThan()	num
closeTo()	num, num (the latter is the delta allowed)
equalsIgnoringCase()	String

(continued)

Table A-6. (*continued*)

Matcher	Parameter Type
equalsIgnoringWhitespace()	String
matches()	RegExp
orderedEquals()	Iterable
unorderedEquals()	Iterable
containsValue() (used with a Map)	Object

Multiple tests can be put together within a single group. Groups are defined using calls of the group() function.

```dart
group("exclaim tests", () {
  List testCases = [["Dog", "Dog!"], ["", "!"], ["H e l l o ", "H e l l o !"]];
  for (List testCase in testCases) {
    test(testCase[0], (){
      expect(exclaim(testCase[0]), equals(testCase[1]));
    });
  }
});
```

group() takes the name of the group as its first parameter and a function where tests are defined as its second parameter. Groups are helpful for organization purposes. When tests are run, the tests within the same group will be nicely outputted together.

dart:async (Chapter 8, Chapter 14)

The Timer class of dart:async is useful for scheduling things that need to occur periodically, or things that need to occur just one time in the future.

```dart
Timer t = new Timer(const Duration(seconds: 2), () {
  clickedCard.src = CARD_BACK;
  tempClicked.src = CARD_BACK;
});  // one time
```

This Timer attempts to execute update() every 17 milliseconds. The actual accuracy of that time period depends on whether other code running is easily interrupted.

```dart
Timer t = new Timer.periodic(const Duration(milliseconds:17), update);
```

dart:async is also the home of Future, a key class used throughout the Dart standard library. It is used for getting the result of a computation after an asynchronous task has completed. The then() method of Future is called with a function that will execute, once the Future completes, including its result as a parameter.

```dart
Future<String> f = HttpRequest.getString("pandp.txt");
f.then((String s) => print(s));
```

Future objects have built-in mechanisms for catching errors.

```dart
f.then((String s) => print(s)).catchError((Error e) => print(e.toString()));
```

Finally, Future objects can be strung together.

```
File file = new File("pandp.txt");
file.readAsString().then((String fileContent) {
  print(fileContent);
  return new File("pandp.txt").readAsString();
}).then((String fileContent) => print(fileContent));
```

dart:isolate (Chapter 14)

An isolate is an independent, concurrent process, with its own separate memory space. Isolates are spawned at the point of a function call. They use ReceivePort and SendPort objects for intra-process communication. The SendPort method send() is used for sending data across the wire. The ReceivePort method listen() asynchronously receives data coming across the wire.

```
void calcPi(SendPort sp) {
  ...
  sp.send(pi);  // send the result back
}

void main() {
  ReceivePort rp = new ReceivePort();
  rp.listen((data) {  // data is what we receive from sp.send()
    print("Pi is $data");
    rp.close();  // we're done, close up shop
  });
  Isolate.spawn(calcPi, rp.sendPort);  // start the Isolate
}
```

General Style Conventions

While style is not enforced, it's good practice to follow style conventions when they make sense. This book broke from general Dart style recommendations by declaring local variables with their type, instead of with the generic var. This was done to ease the beginner's type understanding and, subjectively, to improve code clarity. However, there were many style conventions that were rigorously followed—and you should follow them too.

- Class names should be written in uppercase CamelCase.

- Class instance variables, properties, and method names should be written with lowercase camelCase.

- Constants should be written in ALL_UPPERCASE_WITH_UNDERSCORES_FOR_SPACES.

- Variable names should be descriptive.

- Code should be well-commented.

- There should be spacing around operators.

- Indentations should be two spaces.

- When in doubt, use Dart Editor's "Format" command, available in the contextual menu, brought up by right-clicking in an editor window.

For more Dart style recommendations, check out the article "Dart Style Guide" by Bob Nystrom at www.dartlang.org/articles/style-guide.

History of Web Programming

To fully appreciate Dart's place in the Web development ecosystem and its purpose, it's necessary to understand a little bit about where that ecosystem has come from. This appendix is not about Dart; it's about what led up to Dart. It's about the languages that have been used for programming the Web throughout its history.

■ **Note**   This appendix is not meant to provide reference-quality material. It contains speculation, suppositions, and opinion. The technologies/programming languages mentioned were built by incredibly smart and dedicated people who did not have the foresight of twenty-five years of the Web that we have today. Any slights pointed toward them must be read with that context in mind.

Client Side

In the beginning, the Web was static. A page was downloaded, and it didn't change. When Tim Berners-Lee released the first web browser in 1990, web pages consisted of text with a little styling and links to other web pages. It was a web of information—not of interactivity. One has to remember the technology of the time. A cutting-edge microprocessor in 1990 operated at 50 megahertz, and the average personal computer had a few megabytes of RAM. The speed of computers has improved exponentially since then.

Over time, the technologies available in web browsers for content presentation became more impressive. Images were added. The ability to play sounds was added. Browsers included the ability to extend themselves with plug-ins. CSS was introduced to improve styling. New HTML tags were introduced to improve layout.

Even as web pages became prettier, they still lacked the capabilities of native applications. Web browsers were in essence just HTML document viewers. They lacked the ability to respond to users in any kind of dynamic way. In order for the Web to become a platform that could compete as a venue for interactive applications, client-side browser programming languages were developed.

Java Applets

Java 1.0 was released in 1995 by Sun Microsystems,[1] and it made a big splash. It promised to be a new, memory-safe, secure, object-oriented, platform-independent programming language/software runtime with familiar syntax. A cool aspect of the new language/platform were so-called applets. Java applets are Java programs that run with a graphical user interface in a predefined rectangle on a web page.

---

[1]Oracle, "The History of Java Technology," www.oracle.com/technetwork/java/javase/overview/javahistory-index-198355.html.

The promise of Java applets was that programs could be written once and run on any platform that had a Java runtime environment and a web browser. This write once, run anywhere philosophy aimed to make the distinction between running a program on a Mac versus on Windows (or on a Unix workstation) irrelevant. Netscape Navigator was the first web browser to support Java applets.

The reality in the late 1990s was that Java applets were slow to load, had inconsistent user interfaces, and suffered from incompatibilities after Microsoft bundled its own Java runtime environment with Internet Explorer (a lawsuit was brought over this), which had subtle differences from the runtime deployed by Sun. Java applets can still be run today on any web browser with a Java plug-in, but they're becoming increasingly rare. The lack of support for Java applets on mobile platforms like iOS has sped along their demise.

JavaScript

The introduction of JavaScript happened practically in parallel with that of Java applets. JavaScript also launched in 1995, and Netscape Navigator was the first web browser to ship with it. Indeed, JavaScript was the creation of Brendan Eich, a Netscape employee, and the story goes that he designed the whole language in ten days. JavaScript was not originally meant to be used for the same kind of applications as Java applets. It was supposed to be a lightweight scripting language. There had been previous attempts at providing scripting languages in a web browser, but none of them had the backing of a major player like Netscape or Microsoft until JavaScript. The name *JavaScript* was a marketing ploy to take advantage of the hype around Java. JavaScript is not based on Java in any meaningful way.

JavaScript was standardized as ECMAScript by Ecma International. JavaScript was popular enough that Microsoft incorporated a slightly modified version of it in Internet Explorer the following year. The incompatibilities between Microsoft's version of JavaScript and Netscape's version, despite the ECMAScript standard, plagues web developers to this day when they need to maintain compatibility with older versions of Internet Explorer (newer versions are much more standards compliant).

While JavaScript quickly gained popularity, for the first decade of its life it was utilized almost exclusively for what we would consider today to be quite small use cases. A major reason for this was its speed (or lack thereof). The original JavaScript engines were interpreted. It wasn't until the 2000s that JavaScript engines commonly included a just-in-time (JIT) compiler.

Over the past decade, as the speed of JavaScript engines increased, its features expanded, and its compatibility across browsers improved; it began to be used for increasingly significant applications. Browser apps increased in complexity to the point where they rivaled native software. JavaScript also increasingly became popular on the server (see the "Server-Side" section later in this appendix).

Today, JavaScript is the lingua franca of the Web. There are very few, if any, of the most popular web sites in the world that are not powered largely by JavaScript on the client side. By any measure, JavaScript is one of the most popular programming languages in existence. For a little more on JavaScript from a technical standpoint, check out Chapter 17's section on it.

VBScript

Microsoft once had a tendency to leverage its near monopoly status in the industry to push proprietary technologies that would encourage platform lock-in. VBScript was arguably one such proprietary technology. VBScript was added to Internet Explorer in 1996 as a kind of Microsoft ecosystem alternative to JavaScript. VBScript leveraged the Visual Basic name in a similar fashion to JavaScript leveraging Java's brand (in name only).

VBScript attempted to fill a niche similar to that JavaScript had—a lightweight scripting language for making web pages more interactive. Due to its proprietary nature, however, web sites with VBScript could not function properly in non-Microsoft web browsers. This was okay for a while, when Internet Explorer had about 90% market share in the early 2000s; however, proprietary technologies are considered antithetical to the ideals of the open Web.

VBScript lost out to JavaScript but found its way into some other Microsoft products. As of Internet Explorer 11, it has been deprecated as a scripting language for the web browser.[2] It hasn't been a real player on the Web for more than a decade.

Flash

Flash is a platform for interactive content that is most commonly used for games and streaming video. It actually extends beyond the Web, but we'll keep our discussion limited to the Flash web browser plug-in. Flash was originally developed in the 1990s by several different companies before coming under the guise of Adobe, after its 2005 acquisition of Macromedia. Flash is programmed with the ActionScript language. Interestingly, ActionScript is derived from ECMAScript, the same standard as JavaScript.

In a world where Java applets were too slow-loading, and JavaScript was too unsophisticated, Flash came to dominate the niche of web-delivered richly interactive experiences. The Flash browser plug-in was at one point installed on more than 90% of web browsers and commonly came bundled with new computers. Flash was everywhere.

Flash's big challenger came in the form of improved JavaScript engines and APIs. The smartphone revolution rendered another blow to Flash, as mobile web browsers didn't include plug-in support, most famously the original iPhone. Steve Jobs wrote an open letter in 2010 criticizing Flash as a proprietary, legacy technology whose time had passed.[3] The letter was controversial, but it ultimately signaled a shift in the industry away from Flash and toward HTML5 and JavaScript technologies.

However, Flash is still the main language used for web games and streaming video on laptop and desktop web browsers. There are JavaScript and HTML5 technologies that are making inroads, but the Flash plug-in will likely still be with us for years to come. With that said, it's probably not a good idea to develop new web applications in Flash.

Silverlight

Silverlight is another Microsoft technology that was seemingly developed as an answer to an industry de-facto standard. As VBScript was an answer to JavaScript, Silverlight was an answer to Flash. Microsoft Silverlight is based on the technologies of the .NET Framework, Microsoft's sophisticated software stack that underlies most of its modern platforms. Silverlight is delivered chiefly in the form of a web browser plug-in.

Silverlight applications can be programmed from several different programming languages, but the browser plug-in never saw widespread adoption outside of the Microsoft ecosystem. The notable exception has been Netflix, which plans to move away from Silverlight in a future version.[4] First released in 2007, Silverlight may have simply come too late to market to garner widespread adoption.

The official Silverlight browser plug-in is only available on Windows and OS X. Although a free software version of Silverlight is available that runs on Linux and other operating systems, as with Flash, you will be leaving iOS and Android users in the lurch, if you develop your site with Silverlight. Further, Microsoft's support for Silverlight appears to be waning. Stick with Dart and JavaScript.

Recent Developments

It seems a rule in web technology (if not all technology) that any platform that comes to dominate a space will quickly have newcomers attempting to displace it. When it comes to JavaScript, the strategy seems to be more one of acceptance of it as a standard, while attempting to work around it. *Embrace and extend* if you will.

---

[2]Microsoft, "VBScript is no longer supported in IE11 edge mode for the Internet zone," http://msdn.microsoft.com/en-us/library/ie/dn384057(v=vs.85).aspx.

[3]Steve Jobs, "Thoughts on Flash," www.apple.com/hotnews/thoughts-on-flash, 2010.

[4]Anthony Park and Mark Watson, "HTML5 Video at Netflix," http://techblog.netflix.com/2013/04/html5-video-at-netflix.html, 2013.

The chief JavaScript alternatives all compile to JavaScript. You obviously already know about **Dart**, Google's effort that launched in 2011. Dart is an entire alternative platform. **CoffeeScript** is a less ambitious effort. It's basically a set of syntactic sugar that makes JavaScript more readable and adds a few more advanced language constructs that reduce the size of an equivalent program (in terms of lines of code). Of course, the benefits of a syntax change are up to the whims of an individual. Some people will prefer CoffeeScript's syntax (which borrows from Ruby and Python), while others will prefer traditional JavaScript.

CoffeeScript has gained some traction. It is a popular language on GitHub and was even included in the 3.1 release of the popular web development framework Ruby on Rails.[5] CoffeeScript does not represent a paradigm shift. It represents an influential direction for client-side languages, as far as programmatic syntax is concerned.

Microsoft had an answer to JavaScript and an answer to Flash. Surely, it must have an answer to Dart... Of course it does! **TypeScript**, first appearing in 2012, is Microsoft's player in this space. Unlike Dart, TypeScript does not represent a completely separate platform but instead is a superset of JavaScript. In fact, many of TypeScript's features are expected to appear in the forthcoming JavaScript standard ECMAScript 6.

Like Dart, TypeScript aims to relieve the difficulty of cleanly building modern, significantly sized applications that live in the browser. Also like Dart, it includes support for classes and optional types. That's where the similarities end. TypeScript does not represent a new platform. It represents an improved environment for building JavaScript applications. There is no TypeScript VM. If Dart didn't exist, TypeScript would be a more compelling pure JavaScript alternative. But, as it stands, most of the features inherent in TypeScript will be included in the near future in JavaScript anyway. As a superset of JavaScript, TypeScript also inherits JavaScript's faults.

Although seldom mentioned in the tech media, **Haxe** is a rather remarkable language. It not only compiles to JavaScript but also to Flash, PHP, C++, Java, and more. It's truly a platform-independent language, if there ever was one. At the same time, its syntax is close to ECMAScript, so it looks familiar to JavaScript and Flash developers. Haxe first appeared in 2005. RedHat's experimental language, **Ceylon**, also compiles to JavaScript.

Server Side

The difference between server-side and client-side programming is delineated in Chapter 7. The diversity of solutions for server-side development far outstrips that of the client side. The alleviating factor that enables so many more possibilities for the server side is the lack of necessity to run in the browser. There are web frameworks available for just about every programming language in mainstream use. The job of a server-side web framework basically boils down to receiving a request, processing it (and any user-supplied parameters), and outputting HTML back to the web server, ready to be served to the user. The story of server-side web development has been a story of making this process (and everything that goes with the process step, such as database access) easier.

CGI

CGI stands for *Common Gateway Interface*. It's an interface, first developed in 1993, that allows a request sent to a web server to result in the execution of a program on the server. The content generated by the program can then be sent back to the client via the web server. A CGI program can essentially be written in any language. The interface was developed as a standard that all web servers could implement.

Although uncommon today, it wasn't unusual to see large CGI programs built in C or C++ in the 1990s. They were ubiquitous languages that offered tremendous speed at a time when computer hardware, even on the server side, struggled to keep up with the demands that were placed on it. The problem with C and C++ is that they're memory unsafe and don't have tremendous built-in facilities for text processing, which is the purview of much web work. These points make writing CGI programs in C or C++ arguably more difficult than in other languages. That didn't stop Amazon from building a large part of its original 1995 site in C.[6]

---

[5]Peter Cooper, "Rails 3.1 Adopts CoffeeScript, jQuery, Sass and... Controversy," www.rubyinside.com/rails-3-1-adopts-coffeescript-jquery-sass-and-controversy-4669.html, 2011.
[6]Brad Stone, *The Everything Store: Jeff Bezos and the Age of Amazon* (Boston, MA: Little, Brown, 2013), p. 36.

C and C++ were so widely used (outside the Web) that their syntax became the template for most of the languages used on both the client side and the server side of the Web in the 1990s, including JavaScript, Java, Perl, and PHP. Today, it's rare for a server-side web application to be developed in C or C++. However, a program built in another language may call a C/C++ library for performance reasons. An example would be a Python-based genetics research web app that calls C code for doing numerical analysis. The logic of building the app may be all Python, but the computationally intense bit will be C. For a little more information about C, see Chapter 17.

Many of the languages that became popular on the Web began by being utilized through CGI. Most of them later gained their own web server extensions that bypass CGI for performance reasons. CGI continues to be an option on modern web servers.

Perl

For many years, Perl was the glue that held together the Internet, operating through the Common Gateway Interface to power many early web sites, both large and small. It was the first higher-level language to be widely deployed for server-side web programming. Perl, created by Larry Wall in the late 1980s as a scripting language, actually predates the Web. Perl has extensive capabilities for processing text—a task critical in web development (HTML is just text, after all).

So, why didn't Perl maintain its popularity? One of Perl's slogans is "There's more than one way to do it." That's not always a good thing. Perl gained a reputation for being the language most likely to be used for writing cryptic, unreadable code. If everyone does things their own way, and individual style trumps common conventions, then that's a recipe for a lot of mutually difficult-to-read code.

Perl has been stuck in a versioning nightmare since a new redesigned version, Perl 6, was announced in 2000. Fourteen years later, Perl 6 continues to be in development, while Perl 5 has diminished in popularity. Larry Wall continues to lead Perl as its Benevolent Dictator for Life (BDFL). Several popular web sites continue to be developed in Perl, including Craigslist, which hired Larry Wall in late 2013.[7]

PHP

PHP began as a set of C CGI scripts that Ramsus Lerdorf used on his personal home page in 1994. It evolved into a templating language, and over time, a distinct programming language that somewhat resembles Perl. PHP lives side by side with HTML. It has the ability to be embedded in tags within an HTML document, which makes deployment as simple as uploading a PHP file to a web server. This simplicity of deployment is likely what rocketed PHP to become the most popular server-side web language among small-to-medium-size web sites. It's practically unheard of to sign up for a small business web host and not have the web server come with built-in PHP support.

PHP even powers the most popular content-management system in the world, WordPress. In fact, PHP is so popular, even today, that it gets mocked by developers from other language communities for the poor quality of the code developed with it. As a popular, easy-to-deploy, ubiquitous language, PHP attracts a wide swath of developers, including many just starting out. Naturally, if inexperienced developers make up a large set of your user base, code quality will suffer. It's in a similar situation on the server side as JavaScript on the client side, which is also sometimes mocked by other language communities.

Are these criticisms fair? The answer is largely no. High-performance, beautifully engineered code is written by top-tier talent in PHP every day. Facebook was largely written in PHP.[8] PHP is relatively high-performance compared to some of the other popular modern server-side offerings. PHP may have been the accident of one man's tinkering, and largely unplanned as a language, but it's clearly been successful for a reason: it's easy to get started with and relatively high-performance.

---

[7]Jim Buckmaster, "Artist. Formerly known," http://blog.craigslist.org/2013/10/15/artist-formerly-known.
[8]Brian Shire, "PHP and Facebook," www.facebook.com/notes/facebook/php-and-facebook/2356432130, 2007.

ASP

ASP was Microsoft's original entry into the server-side web technology war. ASP, which stands for *Active Server Pages*, could, in its original 1996 incarnation, most readily be compared to PHP. It had an emphasis on embedding logic in tags alongside HTML. With an emphasis on Windows Server operating systems, ASP never had a fighting chance of reaching PHP's level of ubiquity, given that the majority of web servers run Linux or other Unix-like operating systems. ASP was replaced by ASP.NET, a version tailored for Microsoft's multi-language .NET platform. Microsoft released a paper in 2003 titled "Migrating from PHP to ASP.NET," comparing PHP and ASP.NET, that may be interesting from a historical perspective.[9]

Java

The big excitement when Java launched surrounded using it for building write-once-run-anywhere desktop applications and Java applets. Over the years, Java did achieve dominance across a wide array of devices from mobile phones and credit cards to DVD players, but it never achieved prominence on the desktop outside of the corporate world. It did, however, find a surprising niche as the power behind many industrial-strength web infrastructures. J2EE (Java 2 Enterprise Edition), released in 1999, was the first major version of Java that explicitly targeted large-scale web infrastructure developers.

Sun Microsystems, the creator of Java, envisioned Java as an open specification that other corporations could implement. IBM, RedHat, and others created J2EE implementations that could run the same server-side programs that ran on Sun's J2EE application server. This created an ecosystem of industrial-strength enterprise-grade Java application servers backed by the world's biggest enterprise tech companies. Java flourished and became the preferred enterprise server-side technology.

JSP, or Java Server Pages, a part of J2EE, allows Java to be embedded with HTML similarly to PHP. Java continues to be widely deployed in the enterprise world for server-side stacks, due to its high performance, maturity, large pool of developers, and advanced libraries. Newer languages that run on the Java Virtual Machine (JVM—similar in principal to the Dart VM), such as Scala, Clojure, and Groovy, have their own popular web frameworks (Play is one, for example) that have the added benefit of being able to interact with legacy Java libraries. Further, versions of Ruby and Python (JRuby and Jython), two popular languages to be mentioned shortly, also run on the JVM.

For all of the reasons expounded in the last paragraph, the Java platform continues to be compelling. It probably has lost web developer mindshare, not so much because of its faults, but, instead, because what's come after it is so compelling. A concentration during the last decade on rapid application development frameworks with batteries included, such as Ruby on Rails and Python with Django, has captured the imagination of the industry, because these frameworks allow developers to build more quickly than with traditional solutions like Java.

Python

Python, like Perl, was originally created by a single developer as a scripting language for Unix-like systems. In this case, the year was 1991 (just four years after Perl), and the creator was Guido van Rossum. While Perl was successful on the server side of the Web almost from the beginning, it took until the 2000s for Python to become a mainstream server-side web language. For more about Python, the language, see Chapter 17.

Python's clean, easy-to-follow syntax and batteries-included philosophy makes it a great language for getting things done quickly. However, that didn't make it a great language for building web apps until web frameworks that matched the elegance of the core language became available. The most prominent Python web framework is by far Django. Django began life in 2003 for internal use at a newspaper and was released to the public initially in 2005. Django follows a classic and powerful software development paradigm known as MVC (Model View Controller), which emphasizes the separation of data from display.

---

[9]Microsoft, "Migrating from PHP to ASP.NET," http://msdn.microsoft.com/en-us/library/aa479002.aspx, 2003.

Django is not the only game in town. Python is somewhat notorious for the proliferation of so-called microframeworks. These are small web frameworks that don't necessarily include all of the features of a full-service framework like Django but make it very easy to get smaller web apps built quickly, due to their logical defaults and concise setup. The most popular microframework is probably Flask. Hello World in Flask (showing a web page that displays "Hello World") is just a few lines of Python.

If Python's syntax is so praised and it has such great frameworks available, then why isn't everyone using it for server-side web app development? Python's popular implementation has relatively poor performance compared to some of the other options available, which makes it unsuitable for some applications. Further, Python deployment is trickier for beginners than something like PHP, where a file with embedded HTML just gets dropped on a server. However, Python is still very popular today and probably doesn't compete as much with PHP developers as it does with Ruby developers. Also, similarly to Perl, Python has suffered from a botched version transition from Python 2 to Python 3 (no letters please!), although Python 3 has been gaining traction as of late, five years after its debut. Like Larry Wall with Perl, Guido van Rossum continues working as Python's BDFL.

Ruby

Ruby is a language first released by Yukihiro Matsumoto in 1995. Like Python, it features clean syntax and a thoroughly object-oriented design. Outside of Japan, Ruby failed to gain significant popularity until the release of the web framework Ruby on Rails (also known just as Rails). Ruby on Rails led to an explosion of interest in Ruby (mostly to use Rails), due to high developer productivity in the framework.

Ruby is coupled with a popular packaging system called RubyGems that is analogous to Dart's pub. The combination of a vibrant gems ecosystem with Ruby on Rails has allowed for the rapid development of many web apps. It is a pretty commonly held belief that an equivalent web application can be built with fewer lines of code with Ruby on Rails than with comparable web frameworks for other languages.

There's a lot of "magic" that goes on behind the scenes of a Ruby on Rails web application that allows just a few lines of code to provide an impressive array of functionality. This magic has been criticized, because it is thought that it leads to a situation in which novice developers build complex web applications without understanding fully what's going on behind the scenes. It is so easy with RubyGems to include an open source project that adds significant functionality to a Rails application that it is trivial. This notoriously leads to many poorly supported gems underlying the architecture of Rails applications.

Also like Python, Ruby's most popular implementation suffers from performance problems (indeed, even worse ones than Python's). Twitter was originally developed largely in Ruby on Rails but, due to performance and scaling considerations, had to move several pieces of its stack to JVM-based languages (Scala and Java) as it grew.[10] Ruby on Rails development offers many similar advantages and pitfalls to Python with Django. Choosing between the two has more to do with personal preference (with regard to language syntax and how the frameworks work) than any inherent advantage of one over the other. When you don't need to worry about large scale, as most beginning developers don't, both are excellent options for modern server-side web app development.

JavaScript

JavaScript has only become a popular server-side option since the advent of high-performance JavaScript VMs during the last decade. Netscape actually shipped a server-side JavaScript framework as early as the mid-'90s, but it was not really until the release of Node.js in 2009 that server-side JavaScript began to flourish. Node.js is a platform for building asynchronous web apps using JavaScript. One of the most popular frameworks for Node.js is Express.js.

---

[10]Alex Williams, "Once Again, Twitter Drops Ruby for Java," http://readwrite.com/2011/04/11/twitter-drops-ruby-for-java#awesm=~oCSaqvGb5QSBsn, April 11, 2011.

Why is JavaScript on the server side a good idea? The key benefit is the ability to use one language for both the client side and the server side. This familiarity arguably enables an environment in which code reuse is optimized and developer skillsets can more easily span both domains.

Node.js provides not just an application server but also a packaging environment. npm is a package manager, analogous to pub. Plain vanilla JavaScript does not provide a clear path for package management.

JavaScript on the server-side, and specifically Node.js, is seeing adoption in the corporate world. Microsoft helped port Node.js to Windows.[11] Walmart is utilizing Node.js to back its online store.[12] These are recent developments within the last three years. Clearly, server-side JavaScript has momentum.

Trends

The biggest trend in server-side web development of the past ten years has actually come from the client side. The advent of fast client-side JavaScript and the popularity of AJAX has allowed logic that was once exclusively the realm of the server side to be pushed into the browser. This has caused the focus of server-side development to be less on building full MVC applications and more on supplying data to be displayed by complex JavaScript front ends. It is not uncommon for a single server-side application, serving JSON, to deliver data for a web client built in JavaScript, an iOS client built in Objective-C, and an Android client built in Java. In fact, this may be the epitome of what's viewed as a "modern" architecture.

Another clear trend is use of the same programming language on the client and server. This is most obvious with JavaScript's Node.js, but there are other examples. Dart is one. There are several projects that put Python in the browser via compilation of Python to JavaScript (pyjs, Skulpt, PyPy.js). There are similar JavaScript compilers for Haskell, Clojure, and many other languages that are also used on the server side. The best known other-language-to-JavaScript compiler may be another Google-sponsored project, called Google Web Toolkit (GWT). Google Web Toolkit compiles Java to JavaScript.

Finally, one more trend has been language experimentation. The number of languages with viable server-side web frameworks seems to be ever-expanding. There are languages that are beautiful in their functional purity, like Haskell, and languages bent on simplicity, like Go. There are languages that thrive when put to the test of concurrency, like Erlang, and languages that are hyper-modern in their feature set, like F#. All of them are being used to build industrial-strength web applications that would've been built with PHP or Java a decade ago.

The overall focus of all of these trends is on simplifying the toolset and letting developers work in the environment they are most comfortable with. There's an incredible diversity of options available for server-side web programming today. With a lot of choice also comes a lot of fragmentation and little fiefdoms. Do you have a big server-side web app coded in Haskell? It's going to be a very specialized (and probably expensive) set of developers that can service it.

How do you pick a server-side language/framework in such a fast-moving landscape? Take advantage of these trends. If your application can move much of its logic to the client side, do so. Then you can code it largely in Dart. If you can simplify your life by using Dart on both the client and server, go for it! If the specialization of one of the many languages that have robust server-side frameworks available is good for your application, then take advantage of it, as long as its ecosystem looks viable going forward.

---

[11]Ryan Dahl, "Porting Node to Windows with Microsoft's Help," http://blog.nodejs.org/2011/06/23/porting-node-to-windows-with-microsoft%25e2%2580%2599s-help, June 23, 2011.

[12]Eran Hammer (Interview), "Node Black Friday at Walmart with Eran Hammer," http://thechangelog.com/116, January 11, 2014.

Where Does Dart Fit In?

Dart emerged at the end of these time lines, both on the client side and the server side. It incorporates a lot of great thinking from its predecessors. It's a balanced language. It's not necessarily overtly focused on a single niche in the same way that a Haskell or PHP might be. It's most comparable to JavaScript in that it runs both in the browser and on the server. However, syntactically it shares a great resemblance with Java.

Dart is meant to be an accessible language suitable for developing both small and large web apps. It contains facilities for rapid prototyping. Yet, it also has features that make building large applications easier than with JavaScript. At the same time, it's compatible with today's client-side infrastructure, because it compiles to JavaScript. Dart tries to take a Goldilocks position.

Dart has many of the modern features present in languages that have emerged over the past few years, yet its syntax is reminiscent of older languages. Dart is not the fastest language available, but it's faster than JavaScript (when run on its own VM) and the most popular implementations of Ruby and Python. Is a lack of specialization a problem for Dart when JavaScript is seen as good enough by many? Only time will tell.

Evolution of the Web Browser

Alongside the ever-changing landscape of client-side and server-side web programming languages has been a parallel history of browser development and enhancements to HTML/CSS. In the beginning (i.e., 1990), there was Tim Berners-Lee's original Web Browser for NeXTSTEP called WorldWideWeb. The HTML spec and that original browser didn't even support images, let alone CSS. Mosaic was the first widely used multiplatform web browser, and it was released in 1993 by a team at the National Center for Supercomputing Applications (NCSA) at the University of Illinois at Urbana-Champaign.

Microsoft and Netscape Duke It Out[13]

Mosaic led to two spinoff browsers. Netscape Navigator was a commercial program released in 1994 and built by a team of ex-Mosaic engineers at the nascent Netscape Communications Corporation. As a commercial entity, the Netscape team had to purposely avoid using any of the old source code from Mosaic. Netscape quickly succeeded Mosaic as the browser of choice for early web users.

Microsoft, realizing the web platform was a threat to its dominance of desktop personal computing, licensed the technology behind Mosaic from an entity called Spyglass Inc., which in turn had licensed the source code to Mosaic from the NCSA. Microsoft released Internet Explorer 1.0 in 1995. Over several revisions during the next few years, Internet Explorer took significant market share from Netscape.

The period of Netscape and Internet Explorer competition (roughly 1995 to 2000) was one in which several client-side technologies previously mentioned were developed and popularized, including JavaScript, VBScript, Java, and Flash. Unfortunately, at least with regard to the former three, they led to significant incompatibilities between dueling feature sets in Netscape and Internet Explorer.

A JavaScript program written for Netscape would not necessarily run unmodified on Internet Explorer. Likewise, a Java program coded for Microsoft's Java Virtual Machine (JVM) would not necessarily run correctly in Netscape/Sun's JVM. A VBScript program wouldn't run in Netscape at all.

Even the HTML spec itself was up for dueling visions. There were tags that one browser supported and the other didn't. Even more common, a tag/style displayed in one browser could look very different on the other. Even today, it's important to check how a site looks in all of the popular browsers, but back then, it was also a matter of coding around the inconsistencies and building specialized versions of a program/site for each browser.

---

[13]For more on the early history of the Web, check out The Internet History Podcast at www.internethistorypodcast.com.

During this period, there were no major platforms that mattered other than personal computers, and they ran Microsoft Windows or Mac OS. Those were the main platforms that Netscape and Internet Explorer supported. There was no worry about supporting browsers popular on smartphones or tablets or game consoles (although early versions of browsers for all of these existed).

Microsoft's coupling of Internet Explorer with its dominant Windows operating system and proprietary version of the JVM led to lawsuits, but in the scheme of things, they didn't really matter too much for the average web developer. By the year 2000, Internet Explorer had won. Microsoft's browser attained more than 80% market share. Netscape was sold to AOL, and the source code to its browser was given to a not-for-profit foundation known as Mozilla.

Firefox Emerges from the Ashes of Netscape

Mozilla released an open source browser, based on the last version of Netscape, that made little headway in challenging Internet Explorer's hegemony. During the period of Internet Explorer's domination, it was not uncommon for sites to be coded for it to such a degree that they would not work in alternative web browsers. The first significant challenger to Internet Explorer came out of Mozilla in 2002. Firefox was a stripped down, more lightweight version of the open sourced Netscape components that gained a quick following in some international markets.

The interest in Firefox coincided with a reemphasis on open standards in the industry (including specifications like CSS and HTML 4). The goal was to avoid the fragmentation of the 1990s and ease the difficulty of web developers' day jobs. It didn't happen quickly. There was little incentive for Microsoft to move quickly to adopt standards to help erode its dominant position.

In 2003, Apple released its own web browser, Safari, only for Macintosh, and based on open source technology earlier used in the Linux world. The same year, Microsoft announced it would not release any new versions of Internet Explorer for Macintosh. Although Windows had more than 90% market share among personal computers, this did provide a further impetus for web developers to build sites based on open standards and cross-browser compatibility.

Mobile and a Revitalized Browser Ecosystem

There were versions of Safari for Windows that didn't make much of a dent in the market, but it was the version of Safari that came with the original iPhone in 2007 that really changed the game. Mobile web browsers had existed since the 1990s, but they were limited in functionality, due to the weak microprocessors and user-interface technologies that existed on mobile phones up to that point. The iPhone was the first smartphone to offer a full web browser experience that made web sites designed for desktop browsers easy to read on the go. And the iPhone's Safari depended on open standards.

Most important, the iPhone's Safari didn't support plug-ins. This meant no JVM (no Java applets) and no Flash. The iPhone was a sensation, and if web developers wanted to capitalize on its success, they would need to code to the open web standards (namely JavaScript, HTML, and CSS) that it supported. It was also the beginning of concern for making sites that worked well on many highly different screen sizes. While the iPhone could display sites written for big monitors that accompany desktop web browsers, sites looked better when their content was responsive to different screen sizes.

Google's Android followed in 2008 and largely reinforced the changes brought about by the iPhone. And these were yet further reinforced by the iPad and Android tablets. It's unusual today for a site not to be coded to look great on both mobile and desktop.

Google also released its own desktop web browser, Google Chrome, in 2008, based on the same open source project, WebKit, as Apple's Safari. Chrome's superfast JavaScript VM, V8, was a revelation. It enabled applications to be coded for the browser that were previously only done natively. It led to an arms race in JavaScript VMs between all of the major players—Mozilla, Apple, Microsoft, and Google—which ultimately pushed the state of the art on the Web forward.

Whole platforms emerged, based on browser technologies. Palm launched the ill-fated WebOS, which was ultimately scattered in pieces across HP and LG. Google launched an operating system called Chrome OS that has seen some success in low-end laptops. Mozilla launched Firefox OS, an operating system for smartphones targeted at emerging markets and low-end handsets.

By the mid-2010s, Microsoft was no longer dominant in the browser space. Web developers today care as much, if not more, about what Google, Apple, and Mozilla think about web standards as they do about Microsoft. On the other hand, there are still many older versions of Internet Explorer floating around corporate environments that need be coded to for major applications. Microsoft, whether as a result of a change in its corporate culture or a shifting competitive landscape, has embraced open standards in the past few years. The most recent versions of Internet Explorer are on the cutting-edge, standards wise.

HTML5, the current version of the HTML specification, embraces facilities for managing the changes that have occurred over the past decade with regard to the web development ecosystem. For instance, it includes facilities for displaying rich content like video, audio, and graphics that were once the purview of Java applets and Flash. It also has built-in support for displaying content in ways that is responsive to differing screen sizes.

Firefox and Chrome have adopted rapid release cycles that bring innovation to users as quickly as possible. At the same time, users are treated to constant upgrades with little discernable difference between sequential versions. Table B-1 summarizes the browser world today.

Table B-1. *Web Browsers Today*

	Internet Explorer	Firefox	Safari	Chrome
Developer	Microsoft	Mozilla	Apple	Google
First Appeared	1995	2002	2003	2008
Release Cycle	Traditional	Rapid	Traditional	Rapid
Rendering Engine	Trident	Gecko	WebKit	Blink (forked from WebKit in 2013)
JavaScript Engine	Chakra	SpiderMonkey	Nitro	V8
Open Source?	No	Yes	Engine Only	Based on open source Chromium project
Desktop Platforms	Windows	Cross-Platform	OS X	Cross-Platform
Mobile Platforms	Windows	Android, Firefox OS	iOS	Android, iOS
Other Platforms	Xbox			Chrome OS

There are other browsers too, such as Opera, which has mobile versions, desktop versions, and versions for specialty markets like the Nintendo Wii. Most alternatives to the big four use the same rendering engine as one of them and so can be expected to render things in a similar fashion. For example, Opera has adopted the Blink engine used by Google Chrome. Another example is the experimental browser included on some versions of Amazon's e-ink based Kindle e-readers, which runs an engine based on WebKit, the same engine used in Apple's Safari.

There are differences between the mobile and desktop versions of the big four. In other words, Internet Explorer for Windows Phone doesn't necessarily support all of the same technologies as Internet Explorer for desktop computers. More and more, the emphasis for new web sites has been on designing mobile first, as usership naturally moves to mobile devices.

Importance Today

Why does it matter how web apps were coded 20 years ago? It matters because there's been a clear progression, both on the server side and the client side, in web technology. Each technology exists today as a response to what came before it. PHP would likely never have existed if writing web apps in C wasn't cumbersome. Dart is a direct response to the difficulty of building large-scale applications in JavaScript.

The browser wars ultimately resulted in the adoption of open standards. That's arguably good for almost everybody (save the former dominance of Internet Explorer, perhaps). Web developers today largely don't need to worry about coding platform-specific hacks.

By understanding the history, it's possible to tease out trends that will continue to affect the industry. By understanding these trends, a developer can ensure that he's riding the wave of technology, instead of swimming against it. If you could see the direction the industry was going in ten years ago, you certainly would have been careful not to code a large application in VBScript. Today, that might be Flash.

There are right answers when choosing a web technology to build with. It's important to understand what your alternatives are. It's important to code with an eye toward the future and understand the mistakes that others have made in the past. The Web can be complicated, but it's generally getting less painful with each passing year.

■ ■ ■

Dart Timeline

Dart is a young language. This timeline aims to put the advent of Dart in chronological context.

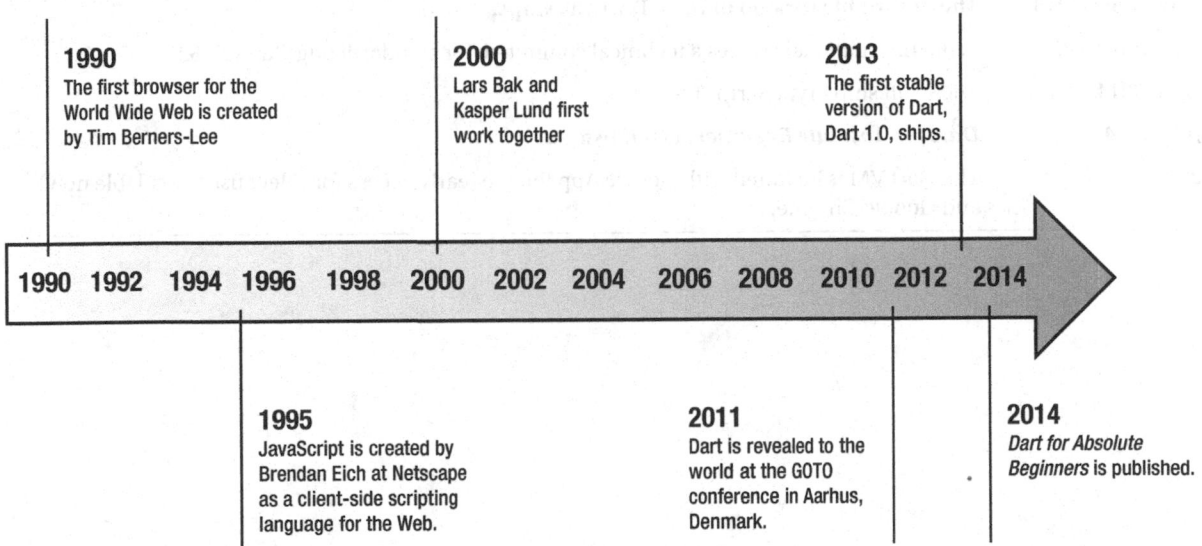

1990
The first browser for the World Wide Web is created by Tim Berners-Lee

2000
Lars Bak and Kasper Lund first work together

2013
The first stable version of Dart, Dart 1.0, ships.

1990 1992 1994 1996 1998 2000 2002 2004 2006 2008 2010 2012 2014

1995
JavaScript is created by Brendan Eich at Netscape as a client-side scripting language for the Web.

2011
Dart is revealed to the world at the GOTO conference in Aarhus, Denmark.

2014
Dart for Absolute Beginners is published.

Date	Event
1990	**The first browser for the World Wide Web is created by Tim Berners-Lee.**
1995	**JavaScript is created by Brendan Eich at Netscape as a client-side scripting language for the Web.**
1997	JavaScript is standardized as ECMAScript by Ecma International. The two most popular web browsers of the period (Netscape Navigator and Microsoft Internet Explorer) both support slightly different versions of JavaScript.
2000	**Lars Bak and Kasper Lund, creators of Dart, first work together.**
February 2005	Jesse James Garrett coins the term *Ajax,* which refers to the use of JavaScript for creating advanced asynchronous web applications. A renaissance in JavaScript use for advanced web applications arguably originates in this period.

(continued)

Date	Event
2006	Bak and Lund join Google and lead the development of V8, a JavaScript engine with superior performance vs. its predecessors.
2010	Bak and Lund create an experimental language called Spot over a three-month time period.
November 2010	A memo circulates within Google titled "Future of JavaScript." It states that JavaScript has fundamental flaws that cannot be easily overcome. It further states that while Google will continue to work on evolving JavaScript, it will also hedge its bets by developing a new language called Dash.
October 2011	**Dart is revealed to the world at the GOTO conference in Aarhus, Denmark.**
June 2012	The first book-length work on Dart, *Dart for Hipsters* by Chris Strom, is published.
October 2012	Microsoft announces its answer to Dart, TypeScript, which is a superset of JavaScript.
November 2013	**The first stable version of Dart, Dart 1.0, ships.**
December 2013	Ecma International creates a technical committee for standardizing Dart (TC52).
April 2014	Microsoft ships TypeScript 1.0.
July 2014	***Dart for Absolute Beginners* is published.**
2014?	The Dart VM is included with Google App Engine (early access for select users available now) and Google Chrome.

APPENDIX D

Great Resources

In this appendix, some fantastic resources with which to learn more about a particular subject are listed. Some have been mentioned, scattered throughout the book in the text and the footnotes, while others are new to this appendix.

■ **Author's Note**   I have only included resources that I have explored myself and can recommend. This doesn't mean excluded resources are not recommendable, just that I haven't read them myself.

Dart

Books

Dart: Up and Running

Kathy Walrath, Seth Ladd (O'Reilly, Sebastopol, CA: 2012).

This title is useful as both a reference source and an everyday companion to Dart programming. It complements *Dart for Absolute Beginners* nicely.

`http://shop.oreilly.com/product/0636920025719.do`

Free online updated edition: `www.dartlang.org/docs/dart-up-and-running`

Learning Dart

Dzenan Ridjanovic, Ivo Balbaert (Packt Publishing, Birmingham, UK: 2012)

Learning Dart is an appropriate follow-up to *Dart for Absolute Beginners,* since it covers more complex projects. One of its best features is its fantastic web site, `http://learningdart.org`, which has live examples of all of the projects from the book.

`www.packtpub.com/learning-dart/book`

Web Sites

The Main Dart Web Site

`www.dartlang.org`

This is the main home page of Dart on the Web, which you are doubtless already familiar with. The site features ample tutorials and is the place to find the latest version of Dart Editor and the SDK.

Dart API Documentation

```
http://api.dartlang.org
```

This is your bible when programming Dart. The API documentation for Dart is generally pretty good. Even though the descriptive sections of the more esoteric APIs leave something to be desired, it's still the best and most authoritative resource we've got.

Dartisans

```
https://plus.google.com/communities/114566943291919232850
```

The official Google+ community for the Dart language is full of helpful folks and lively discussion. Come here for a more conversational atmosphere than that offered by Stack Overflow.

Stack Overflow

```
www.stackoverflow.com
```

If you have a question that you can't find an answer to with a search engine, then Stack Overflow should probably be your first stop. Be forewarned: the community does not like answering questions that were already answered. Be sure to tag your questions with "Dart."

The Dartosphere

```
http://dartosphere.org
```

A compendium of some of the most active Dart blogs. Reading these posts regularly will keep you abreast of the latest happenings on the platform.

Dart Mailing Lists

```
https://groups.google.com/a/dartlang.org/forum/#!forumsearch
```

The Dart mailing lists are active. Most discussion belongs in *Dart Misc*. This is a good place for discussion that is too long-form for Stack Overflow or Dartisans.

Articles

"Dart Style Guide"

Bob Nystrom

```
www.dartlang.org/articles/style-guide
```

You can't go wrong sticking to the style guidelines that Bob outlines, as they're the same ones almost everybody else in the Dart community will be using. Consistency with regard to style is a blessing.

"Idiomatic Dart"

Bob Nystrom

www.dartlang.org/articles/idiomatic-dart

More than just style, this article goes into the preferred ways of utilizing Dart constructs. This is an article about programming patterns.

"Mixins in Dart"

Gilad Bracha

www.dartlang.org/articles/mixins

A good introduction to one of the more advanced object-oriented topics covered in this book. This article is concise and readable.

"The Event Loop and Dart"

Kathy Walrath

www.dartlang.org/articles/event-loop

This article is a bit more technical in scope than the others listed here, but it will give you an insight into how asynchronous programming in Dart really works. This is probably the best guide on the topic out there.

"Zones"

Florian Loitsch, Kathy Walrath

www.dartlang.org/articles/zones

Zones are a topic that didn't make the cut for *Dart for Absolute Beginners*. They are useful to know about when writing complex asynchronous applications.

"Using JavaScript from Dart"

Shailen Tuli

www.dartlang.org/articles/js-dart-interop

This article covers what you need to know to get started using the dart:js library. With that knowledge in hand, you'll be able to take advantage of the large universe of JavaScript libraries available on the Net.

"Unit Testing with Dart"

Graham Wheeler

www.dartlang.org/articles/dart-unit-tests

A more detailed treatment of unit testing than that covered in Chapter 13, this article really digs in, in-depth. You won't need another guide after reading this extensive article.

HTML & CSS
Books

The Truth About HTML5

Luke Stevens, RJ Owen (Apress, New York: 2013)

A somewhat advanced, but helpful, guide to the pitfalls and benefits of various elements of the HTML5 specification. This is not a reference text but, rather, a lot of practical advice on how to utilize HTML effectively.

www.apress.com/9781430264156

Beginning Responsive Web Design with HTML5 and CSS3

Jonathan Fielding (Apress, New York: 2014)

This guidebook is focused on making web apps that work well on any kind of device. Importantly, it includes discussion of the very popular Bootstrap CSS framework, which most readers will find very helpful.

www.apress.com/9781430266945

HTML and CSS: Design and Build Websites

Jon Duckett (John Wiley & Sons, Hoboken, NJ: 2011)

This is a hold-your-hand guide to HTML for the novice. Readers of *Dart for Absolute Beginners* will already know a lot of the information covered in the first few chapters, but if you want a beautifully laid out, comprehensive yet gradually introduced guide to the basics of HTML and CSS, you could do a lot worse.

www.wiley.com/WileyCDA/WileyTitle/productCd-1118008189.html

HTML5 Canvas

Steve Fulton, Jeff Fulton (O'Reilly, Sebastopol, CA: 2013)

An in-depth look at the HTML5 canvas element. While geared toward JavaScript, this book will still be valuable if programming, say, a game with the canvas in Dart, since the canvas APIs of dart:html are very similar to those of JavaScript.

http://shop.oreilly.com/product/0636920026266.do

Free online edition: http://chimera.labs.oreilly.com/books/1234000001654/index.html

Web Sites

Mozilla Developer Network

https://developer.mozilla.org/

The nonprofit behind the Firefox web browser offers a superb resource containing up-to-date reference material on all HTML tags and CSS attributes.

W3Schools

www.w3schools.com

It's not the prettiest web site on the Net, but W3Schools offers comprehensive reference material for web standards as well as pretty good beginners' tutorials. It's generally a very reliable source. Their color picker is useful for figuring out HTML color values.

A Second Programming Language
Books
Python

Learn Python the Hard Way

Zed Shaw (Addison-Wesley, Boston: 2013)

Zed is a well-known developer, and his book is highly regarded. It takes a fairly radical learning approach that some may find jarring but many will appreciate for its quick onboarding process.Available free online: http://learnpythonthehardway.org

Beginning Python

Magnus Lie Hetland (Apress, New York: 2008)

A little dated but still a good follow-on to this book, in terms of its content level.

www.apress.com/9781590599822

JavaScript

Beginning JavaScript with DOM Scripting and Ajax

Russ Ferguson, Christian Heilmann (Apress, New York: 2013)

If online tutorials don't suffice, then this is a nice follow-on to *Dart for Absolute Beginners*. It covers JavaScript from a practical point of view.

www.apress.com/9781430250920

C

The C Programming Language, 2nd Edition

Brian W. Kernighan, Dennis M. Ritchie (Prentice Hall, Englewood Cliffs, NJ: 1988)

This is the classic book on C. It's quite dated but still useful as an overview and a way to gain insight into the language designer's mind. It's not an easy book, but it is a good one. Make sure to get the second edition.

Beginning C

Ivor Horton (Apress, New York: 2013)

Teaches C programming from the very beginning. There are a lot of C guidebooks out there, and this is viewed as one of the better ones, and unlike many of the others, it's up to date!

www.apress.com/9781430248811

Scheme

Structure and Interpretation of Computer Programs

Harold Abelson, Gerald Jay Sussman, with Julie Sussman (MIT Press, Cambridge, MA: 1996)

This is a classic first-year programming textbook that happens to teach using the Scheme programming language. It has been in active use in introductory programming courses for decades. It will make you think differently about how a computer program is structured and provide new insights into design patterns. You'll need a Scheme interpreter to use with it. You can try out Gambit Scheme at gambitscheme.org.

Free online edition: http://mitpress.mit.edu/sicp

Other

Books

Artificial Intelligence: A Modern Approach

Stuart Russell, Peter Norvig (Prentice Hall, Englewood Cliffs, NJ: 2009)

If you enjoyed the constraint satisfaction problems of Chapter 16, then Chapter 6 of this book is for you. This textbook is the de-facto reference work for the artificial intelligence community.

Artificial Intelligence in the 21st Century

Stephen Lucci, Danny Kopec (Mercury Learning and Information, Boston: 2012)

A more gentle introduction to artificial intelligence than Russell and Norvig, this textbook is appropriate for readers of all levels, although designed as an accompaniment to a first undergraduate artificial intelligence course. There's a lot of interesting material, even for those without a CS background.

Don't Make Me Think, Revisited: A Common Sense Approach to Web Usability, 3rd Edition

Steve Krug (New Riders Press, San Francisco: 2013)

This is one of the best books on web design out there, and it has recently been updated for the modern Web. When you talk about web design with somebody in the know, chances are they've read this book.

Index

Get the eBook for only $10!

> Now you can take the weightless companion with you anywhere, anytime. Your purchase of this book entitles you to 3 electronic versions for only $10.

This Apress title will prove so indispensible that you'll want to carry it with you everywhere, which is why we are offering the eBook in **3 formats** for only $10 if you have already purchased the print book.

Convenient and fully searchable, the PDF version enables you to easily find and copy code—or perform examples by quickly toggling between instructions and applications. The MOBI format is ideal for your Kindle, while the ePUB can be utilized on a variety of mobile devices.

Go to www.apress.com/promo/tendollars to purchase your companion eBook.

Apress®
THE EXPERT'S VOICE™